# THE BATTLE FOR CONSCIOUSNESS THEORY

'Rajiv Malhotra is a well-known name whose writings combine the ancient wisdom of India with the rigorous scholarship that the modern age demands. Consistent with the Yuga dharma, his writings are a beautiful synthesis of faith and reason, antiquity and modernity, thereby placing him in a unique position to look at present-day events and movements in light of Sanātana Dharma, the Eternal Truths revealed in man's greatest of all adventures, the adventure of Consciousness. His recent work takes up this most important frontier of Consciousness studies that is going to revolutionize the future.

Consciousness has traditionally been the domain of the mystic but we now see a growing interest among scientists in this most important yet least understood field of human studies. But the question is whether we can study Consciousness as a 'phenomenon' by applying the cannons of the rational mind, given that Consciousness surpasses reason and antedates creation itself.

The answer given by the Indian mystics is quite clear. One must first learn to step back and withdraw from form, name, and identity with pure Consciousness before one can have even the right to speak about it. And among the mystics who have explored the heights and depths of Consciousness, none has written so much about it and with such clarity as Sri Aurobindo.

However, there have been attempts to usurp his original discoveries and present them not only as someone else's own — which would not be so damaging — but to twist them, remove the most important elements from them, distort them so that they are no longer recognizable, and then present them to the world neatly packaged for consumption. This is the subject of the present work and Rajiv Malhotra does it with a rare finesse of which he alone is perhaps capable.

Having made a thorough study of Sri Aurobindo and been acquainted with the writings of Ken Wilber and others, I fully endorse the thesis and findings of the authors. This work is deeply appreciated, and its courage and clarity are laudable. I wish and hope that this book is widely read and circulated and finds its rightful place not only in every library that claims to be complete but in the home of every reader who is serious and committed to understanding this most important subject.'

**Dr Alok Pandey,**
Sri Aurobindo Ashram, Pondicherry

'This book is an eye-opener, not only in helping the world recognize the magnitude of Sri Aurobindo's unique contribution towards the evolution of self and consciousness, but also a deep look at how various Western thinkers and spiritualists have fed on and hijacked Indian thought and dominated the discourse by their power of universal outreach and opinion making. This book calls upon us urgently to introspect and confront our wisdom'.

**Dr Shruti Nada Poddar,**
Heritage Conservationist, Indologist, Educationist,
Founder of Shruti Foundation, Member of INTACH Governing Council

'Practitioners of Indian spiritual disciplines worldwide would be happy to know that an invaluable instrument like Rajiv Malhotra is doing for them what they themselves are unable to do. This undertaking deserves all the support and encouragement it can get. You have mine. All strength to your arms'.

**Devan Nair,**
(late) former President of the Republic of Singapore

'Rather than guiding us towards spiritual awakening and understanding, Ken Wilber's ideas often lead us astray, obscuring the richness and significance of the original teachings. Drawing from Sri Aurobindo and the ancient Indian traditions, this book meticulously deconstructs Wilber's system and guides us back to the wellspring of these ideas. By reclaiming their original context, it facilitates a deeper understanding of Wilber's borrowed ideas and points us to the more authentic path for our spiritual journeys. The book's significance cannot be overstated in today's era of growing interest in the spiritual evolution of humanity worldwide'.

**Dr Vladimir Yatsenko,**
Director of Research, Sri Aurobindo Integral Life Center, South Carolina

'*The Battle for Consciousness Theory* is an essential read for anyone invested in preserving the integrity of consciousness studies. The esteemed authors of this book meticulously expose the appropriation and distortion of Sri Aurobindo's profound insights by Ken Wilber. Their extensive research reveals how Wilber's rise involved the marginalization of core Indian sources and redefining the landscape of Integral Theory at the expense of Vedic traditions. This book not only restores the rightful place of Sri Aurobindo's contributions but also critically examines the pervasive influence of Western Universalism and stands as a definitive defense against the annexation of Indian philosophical heritage. This book is a must-read for scholars, practitioners, and anyone committed to preserving the sanctity of spiritual knowledge'.

**Prof. (Dr) Sampadananda Mishra,**
Director, Centre for Human Sciences, Rishihood University

'I appreciate your efforts in making Sri Aurobindo and The Mother – and the traditions behind them – better known worldwide'.

**Georges van Vrekhem,**
(late) prominent Flemish writer on Sri Aurobindo

# THE BATTLE FOR CONSCIOUSNESS THEORY

## A Response to Ken Wilber's Appropriation of Sri Aurobindo's Work and Other Indian Thought

RAJIV MALHOTRA

MANOGNA SASTRY • KUNDAN SINGH

ink | OCCAM

ISBN: 978-81-972231-6-7

First published in India 2024
This edition published 2024

BluOne Ink Pvt. Ltd
A-76, 2nd Floor, Sector 136, Noida
Uttar Pradesh 201301
www.bluone.ink
publisher@bluone.ink

Printed at Nutech Print Services - India



ink | OCCAM

*This book is dedicated to the memory of K.D. Sethna, Kireet Joshi, and Devan Nair, who were amongst a few of the true representatives of Sri Aurobindo's legacy and who wanted me to write this book since the 1990s.*

# Contents

# Preface

by Rajiv Malhotra

## The Story Behind the Book

As a student of physics, I learned the importance of combining both theory and experiment to investigate the physical world. A theoretical model's credibility depends on its ability to explain empirical data. Conversely, novel experiments are used as case studies to test the models. Both aspects must be mutually supportive. Science advances when new theories are propounded and tested successfully with empirical data; this loop of new theories challenging and replacing the old continues indefinitely. There is no 'finality' of knowledge. In other words, fundamental theories are never closed to questioning, challenging, and being superseded.

I took early retirement from my career as a technocrat and entrepreneur to pursue a similar approach in the field of civilization studies. My focus has been on developing *new theoretical models and frameworks* and testing them using concrete examples, and then using real-world feedback to refine the theories. I have a passion for theorizing and applying my models to specific case studies, and hence constantly advancing my understanding. Only then can I address the root of a problem and not merely engage in firefighting the symptoms. I use live encounters with the toughest of opponents as a means to strengthen my arguments and make my models more robust.

My *svadharma* (duty of an individual) is to ignite a Vedic renaissance for the benefit of all humanity in this epoch. I am especially interested in developing theories that *challenge Western philosophical, religious, and social theories* that have dominated for the past few centuries. This Western discourse and its trendy theories are deeply installed in intellectual milieus everywhere, and the Indian elite is amongst its most loyal consumers.

Taking control of the discourse on our own terms is at the heart of intellectual decolonization. This requires using *our way of thinking*, which is far deeper than merely producing *our content*. My entire body of work emanates from the underlying paradigms, frameworks, and theoretical models I enjoy building.

Following are some of the theories I have developed:

- *Western Universalism* as the West's interpretative lens that has become globalized
- *Integral Unity* as distinct from *Synthetic Unity* – divergent models of reality
- *History-Centrism* as distinct from *Adhyātma-Vidyā* – different spiritual pathways
- *The Myth of Sameness*
- The Indian Grand Narrative
- The U-Turn Theory
- The Theory of Digestion
- The Theory of Sanskrit Non-Translatables
- Moron Smriti
- Hinduphobia
- Breaking India Forces
- Vedic Social Sciences
- Indian Mind Sciences
- Vedic School of Thought

Several other theories are currently being developed.

These theories are not isolated from each other. They are not one-off or stand-alone models. Instead, they are comprehensive, interrelated, and intercoupled, comprising an overarching worldview. My books, articles, talks, and other interactions focus on explaining the worldview comprising these theories.

Each of these original frameworks calls for a paradigm shift, provoking people to re-examine the 'normal' premises being taken for granted, either consciously or unconsciously. I have endeavored to excavate and bring to the surface issues that are often invisible because they are built into the ubiquitous and universal lens of the West.

Such breakthroughs require stepping back from the prevailing paradigm and problematizing it. This demands creativity and audacity. It is a risky business in which one typically finds oneself a lone fighter with a pioneering spirit. I have used my experience in arguing and debating with opponents to build and test robust models and teach others to incorporate them in their lives.

While some of my theories offer completely new and original ideas, in many cases they confirm what various people instinctively felt but were unable to conceptualize with clarity and/or were unsure and lacked the confidence to express. Hindus have often conveyed to me, 'I had a similar inkling but did not crystallize it so clearly'; or 'you have given me the confidence by supplying the evidence and now I can project my views openly'. A clear and assertive articulation can make people self-conscious of their compromised lives and guide them to decolonize themselves internally. Gradually, they become more comfortable and confident to take controversial positions publicly on grounds of principles.

In this process, numerous other concepts have emerged that are related to these novel theories. For instance, *poison pill* is a device to protect our civilizational assets from getting digested into Western Universalism. The *Hindu Good News* is an effective and easy way to argue in defense of our Vedic system. The concept of *pūrva pakṣa* is the revival of an ancient system of studying one's opponent thoroughly and with respect, and then responding with an *uttara pakṣa*. I am mentoring young scholars to become *intellectual kṣatriya-s* and join our *home team*. They will be our warriors in the global *kurukṣetra*, in which we must engage. Also, *sepoys* are those Indians who have sold out and are serving the opponents. We must stop *feeding the crocodiles*, implying we should not pamper enemies in the false hope that they will reciprocate and become our allies.

As part of our celebration to commemorate the thirtieth anniversary of Infinity Foundation, my team is preparing books to curate and teach my most important original frameworks along with the special vocabulary I have generated to disseminate these ideas.

I refer to this body of knowledge as our *Vedic School of Thought*.

Infinity Foundation is developing a curriculum to teach this widely as an alternative to Western Universalism.

A project such as this faces major challenges, both from intellectual hegemons that are the incumbents defending their positions, as well as from the Indians who are either sold out and serving the global machinery or are defending the 'comfort zones' of their personal lives.

By their very nature, such theoretical models are meant to be disruptive and controversial, and to undermine the prevailing consensus among most elites. Therefore, each of my theories has invited attacks from powerful individuals and institutions including the academia, media, policy think tanks, government agencies, and so forth. Consequently, I have turned these attacks into opportunities to test and refine my frameworks over the past three decades. This is the reason I constantly seek fresh problem areas that I can use as case studies to apply my theories.

My quest, as described above, provides the background to the present volume. While developing the theories of U-Turn, Digestion, Integral and Synthetic Unity, and Western Universalism, I discovered the American theorist Ken Wilber as a major case study worthy of investigation. I found that he had systematically digested Sri Aurobindo's seminal ideas and reformulated them into his own 'Integral Theory'. This is a classic U-Turn leading to the Digestion of Vedic frameworks. I discovered the following:

- Wilber had subordinated the entire Vedic intellectual tradition and substituted in its place his own theories that are ensconced within Western philosophy, social sciences, and history.
- In effect, he was feeding Western Universalism at the expense of Vedic tradition.
- The violence being perpetrated was that the Integral Unity inherent in the Vedic system was being taken apart and turned into a Synthetic Unity.

When I discovered this in the mid-1990s, I first tried to engage Wilber and/or his vast entourage of Western followers. However, they were simply not interested in an honest conversation concerning his sweeping appropriations and distortions. He was considered too big to be challenged and held accountable.

Perhaps they assumed that nobody competent in Vedic thought would stick his/her neck out and defy Wilber's hold over the emerging field of Integral Consciousness Studies.

This is why, I decided a quarter century ago, to turn Wilber into an important case study for applying my theories. I developed the metanarrative on his digestion of Indian thought. I started curating detailed information on his large body of work and its relationship with Sri Aurobindo.

As my project gathered momentum, I delivered dozens of talks in India and across the USA, held numerous private discussions with key stakeholders to solicit their involvement, and engaged in online debates in several forums. That was back in the 1990s.

Sadly, I failed to generate serious interest even among those professing to be Sri Aurobindo's followers, or others championing the Vedic traditions. They tended to be dismissive of the significance of my project. Many considered it too controversial. It was more rewarding to align themselves with Western intellectual forces appropriating our tradition and formulating some kind of 'new' theoretical framework as part of Western Universalism. At best, they were willing to help me superficially. However, I needed scholars with serious commitment because Wilber's corpus of work is too big for one individual to deconstruct.

To drill into Wilber's work, Infinity Foundation gave several grants to subject-matter experts on Sri Aurobindo asking them to help gather examples, sources and evidence that could be used in writing my book. Some of these third-party engagements are mentioned in Part 1 of this book.

During these twenty-five years, many individuals have contributed information for my analysis and scrutiny. I have accepted some of their raw data and rejected some. I cherry-picked what fit my thesis and style of argumentation, summarized it as appropriate, and decided where and how to use it. This book is a product of numerous collaborations over the past quarter century.

More recently, I decided to build a home team of young scholars. Some of my book projects offer an opportunity to mentor young scholars as co-authors for my writings. The intention here is to train as many scholars as possible to use our school of thought and apply it to different phenomena.

In this regard, I am pleased to introduce Manogna Sastry and Kundan Singh as co-authors for this book and as important members of our home team. As ardent followers and serious scholars of Sri Aurobindo, they are also committed to Infinity Foundation as part of their svadharma and will take my work into the future. Manogna is a scholar at Infinity Foundation India and has helped me as a research assistant on a few of my projects and is now a published author. Kundan's importance to our movement stems from his love for his guru-s, which has been the driving force for his commitment to this project. I see both as role models who will inspire others to join this *yajña*.

Finally, I wish to dedicate this book to three stalwarts of Sri Aurobindo's movement, each of whom I had the privilege of knowing during the early years of my work on this book.

I met K.D. Sethna (named 'Amal Kiran' by Sri Aurobindo) in the 1990s in the Ashram Nursing Home. Though in his late years, he was vibrant and enthusiastic to hear my interest in critiquing Ken Wilber's appropriation of Sri Aurobindo's work. He encouraged me to pursue my U-Turn Theory and my Theory of Digestion of Indian culture into the West. He referred me to many of his writings as source materials for my project. K.D. Sethna, with a wide-ranging intellect and interest in numerous subjects, was one of the close disciples of the sage. A prolific writer of more than fifty books on poetry, literature, philosophy, psychology and issues of nationhood, he was appointed editor of *Mother India*, a monthly review of culture published by the Sri Aurobindo Ashram.

Many of his provocative arguments were years ahead of their time. For instance, he wrote that *Bande Mataram* was a better National Anthem than Rabindranath Tagore's *Jana Gana Mana*. He argued that Gandhi's view of India's independence was limited, writing: '*We were overawed by the material prowess and pomp of our foreign rulers and our efforts to find our true selves were spoiled by either an unthinking imitation of the West or else a defensive anti-Western conservatism*'. He felt that most Indians including Gandhi misunderstood the concept of *ahimsa* (non-violence) and he referred to this mistake as '*an unconscious collaboration with anti-civilisation forces and, far from being a merit, a pernicious mistake*'. He also vigorously debunked the Aryan Invasion Theory.

K.D. Sethna was glad to learn of my various projects as part of my Digestion series. In particular, he supported my analysis of Teilhard de Chardin in comparison to Sri Aurobindo – a topic on which he had written a book. He appreciated that I was also studying Bede Griffiths, the Anglican theologian, for bringing seminal ideas from Hinduism into Christianity, and gave me his book of correspondence with Bede Griffith. He reviewed my evaluation of Carl Jung in light of Indian thought and provided his critique of Jung's views on the collective unconscious. K.D. Sethna was one of the early intellectuals who inspired my work. He encouraged me to write this book.

Another seminal figure who inspired and encouraged me was Kireet Joshi. As a senior scholar on Sri Aurobindo, he authored numerous books that made the writings easily accessible to the public. He served as special secretary, education and was a trusted advisor in late prime minister, Indira Gandhi's government and later became educational advisor to the Gujarat government when Shri Narendra Modi was chief minister. I was introduced to him by S.P. Hinduja when the latter approached me to advise him on his **Dharam Hinduja Indic Research Center at Columbia University. He had established this foundation in memory of his late son, Dharam Hinduja. Kireet bhai (as I referred to him) was also an advisor to the Hindujas and we shared a lot in common on Indic civilization.**

**About a quarter century ago, Infinity Foundation sponsored annual meetings in the USA for Sri Aurobindo's followers and Kireet bhai was among the important speakers we invited.** He was also chairman of Auroville Foundation. Infinity Foundation was at that time a major funding source for the Auroville Village Action Group. Kireet bhai and I met several times in his Delhi office, and he introduced my research work to his numerous contacts in the government. He appointed me to the International Advisory Council of Auroville in 2004; but when the National Democratic Alliance government of Atal Bihari Vajpayee lost the election, he and all his appointees were removed and replaced by those aligned with Ken Wilber's camp.

The third Aurobindonian I wish to express my debt to is Devan Nair, late president of the Republic of Singapore. He, too, was one of the invitees to the USA meetings sponsored by Infinity Foundation. As explained in Part 1 of this book, I faced reluctance on part of the leaders of the Aurobindonian movement to critique Ken Wilber. They wanted our funding but did not want to include any discussion concerning Wilber. In fact, most of them gave mitigating arguments to absolve Wilber of any issues and controversies. It was Devan Nair who stood up for me and publicly defended my work in this regard. He openly criticized this attitude, calling them 'navel-gazing Aurobindonians'. This term stuck and I used it frequently. He became an active participant in my Indic Traditions Yahoo e-group where I discussed my various projects starting in the year 2000. Devan Nair routinely reprimanded the 'navel-gazing Aurobindonians' in physical meetings in the USA as well as online. He encouraged me to continue the fight even though most of those being hoisted as leaders of the Aurobindonian movement declined to offer any help to defend their guru against Wilber's distortions.

July 2024
Princeton, New Jersey, USA

# Preface

## by the Co-Authors

We are delighted to be part of this historic book, one that is destined to provoke a much-needed debate and inform our generation of scholars. The landscape of Indian civilizational studies has been shaped by many players and forces over the past several centuries, especially in post-colonial times. There have been towering figures and intellectual giants who championed the Indian voice even during intensely adversarial periods. It is on the shoulders of such giants that we feel grateful to stand and take our discourse further.

Rajiv Malhotra is among the prominent scholars and writers who is conspicuous for his pioneering work in engaging and countering various challenges in the intellectual kurukṣetra. Through his Infinity Foundation, a unique legacy of thirty years has seen the creation of path-breaking paradigms and various assets wielded effectively in the intellectual debate. He has not only continuously recognized the morphology of Indological discourse over the past three decades, but also actively created newer impactful frameworks for engagement. He has mentored intellectual kṣatriya-s to use their work effectively in responding to existing challenges and to critically think about what lies ahead. We are proud to be part of Infinity Foundation's home team.

The Rajiv Malhotra school of thought is thus a unique endeavor that has been consistently and systematically built over decades and been applied and robustly tested in the intellectual battlefields.

This book is an embodiment of this fine mentorship: Rajiv Malhotra recognized the deep consequences of the appropriation and distortion of the works of one of India's greatest sages, Sri Aurobindo. As co-authors of this book, we owe our tremendous learning curves and the chiseling of our *dṛṣṭi* to the foundation's guidance. We hope this book can trigger vital discussions and find the vast readership that it duly deserves.

Manogna Sastry and Kundan Singh
July 2024
Senior Research Fellows, Infinity Foundation

# Introduction

India (Bhārata) has always held a powerful influence in many fields of human endeavor all the way up to modern times, even as the ancient Egyptians, Chinese, Persians, and Greeks began their own civilizational journeys. Many philosophical systems being taught as Western discoveries, in reality, have their origins in India. These systems have traveled long and convoluted paths not always organically, through various intermediaries to eventually become reformulated as Western. A number of 'new' Western paradigms over the past two centuries owe a debt to Indian traditions. India's influence has impacted modern views on life, evolution, philosophy, psychology, linguistics, and innumerable other fields. The depth of India's profound impact is even more apparent in recent times.

In the mid-1990s, Infinity Foundation (IF) pioneered the funding of research in the USA on Indian civilization. As a result of its intense engagements with these investigations, the foundation discovered the following:

- At the popular level, the concepts of yoga, karma, dharma, *prāṇāyāma*, *āsana,* and so forth, are becoming part of the global lexicon, introducing new ways of looking at the world and at oneself.
- However, the deeper levels of Indian influence that are far more profound tend to remain unknown to people at large. The reason is those Western experts who digest them into their own formulations are, at best, uninterested in acknowledging their Indian sources. It is unfortunate when this influence becomes truncated due to deliberate actions for selfish reasons.

A common refrain is that Indian traditions are redundant at best, abusive at worst, and hence in dire need of being placed under Western tutelage and replacement. To add insult to injury, we found that Western scholars were also fond of denigrating the very Indian traditions from which they were busy appropriating gems of wisdom. It is ironic that such 'Western thought' is oftentimes the intellectual platform used to denigrate Indian sources. This is a form of re-colonialism, updated for the postmodern age.

The myth of Western superiority has, in some instances, been built on de-legitimizing others' knowledge systems. Often, only when knowledge is classified as Western is it deemed legitimate. Until it gets appropriated and receives a stamp of approval from the West, knowledge is classified as exotic, mystical, artistic, and so forth. But it cannot be deemed 'scientific', 'rational', and so on.

This Western indulgence to appropriate with the one hand while denigrating with the other is a form of intellectual arson: the arsonist robs a bank and then burns it down to hide evidence.

A good example of the above syndrome is the digestion of the works of Sri Aurobindo (born Aurobindo Ghose in Calcutta, 1872-1950), who has been an exemplary embodiment of Indian genius, spiritual perfection, and ethos. Arguably, none can parallel the sheer profundity and comprehensiveness of his work on the evolution of human consciousness. His commentaries on the *Veda*-s, the *Upaniṣad*-s, the *Bhagavad Gīta,* and writings on philosophy and culture showcase the deep Indian roots of his spirituality.

Sri Aurobindo was also a freedom fighter whose writings laid the foundation for nationalism (including his writings as editor of the English weekly newspaper *Bande Mataram*) and built the case for a modern Indian civilizational state based on the millennia-old cultural heritage of the country. Much has been written about Sri Aurobindo's work as a yogi and philosopher: two of his books, *The Life Divine* and *The Synthesis of Yoga,* have been analyzed and studied not only in India but across the world. His poetic works evolved in harmony with his *sādhana* as a yogi and culminated in *Savitri: A Legend and A Symbol,* the twenty-four-thousand-line māntric poem.

Sri Aurobindo and his spiritual collaborator, The Mother (born Mirra Alfassa in Paris, France; 1878-1973), spent decades in Pondicherry (now Puducherry), on the southern coast of India, making it home to the global Aurobindonian movement. Seekers and scholars of consciousness studies from all over the world have been drawn to the ashram to learn and imbibe the yogi's profound insights and unique and comprehensive philosophy of Integral Yoga. The transformative potential of Integral Yoga has spread the Aurobindonian movement worldwide through individuals, communities, and organizations.

Sri Aurobindo Ashram in Pondicherry is a key player responsible for preserving the integrity of his teachings and transmitting them appropriately. In this book, we will evaluate the ashram's performance. Founded in 1926, though informally coming into existence after Sri Aurobindo moved to Pondicherry in 1910, the ashram has served as the center where individuals from various nationalities have converged to live a life dedicated to his work while also conducting various activities such as publishing his writings.

Auroville (largely in the southern state of Tamil Nadu), an international township near Pondicherry, is another important center of the Aurobindonian movement. Envisaged and formulated by The Mother and founded in 1968, she describes it as follows: 'Auroville wants to be a universal town where men and women of all countries are able to live in peace and progressive harmony, above all creeds, all politics and all nationalities. The purpose of Auroville is to "realize human unity"'.[1]

Besides these two major hubs in India, there are a number of study and yoga centers as well as educational institutions worldwide dedicated to disseminating Sri Aurobindo's teachings. The California Institute of Integral Studies (CIIS) founded in 1968 in San Francisco is an important academic institution that was created specifically for bringing his teachings to the United States of America. This book evaluates its performance in this regard.

The present volume provides deep insights into the developments that shaped (and distorted) the Aurobindonian discourse at the end of the twentieth century. As an Aurobindonian himself, Rajiv Malhotra worked with key individuals and organizations during the period 1997-2003, rallying support to challenge the co-opting and digestion of Sri Aurobindo's work that had been taking place.

This book is written in two parts. Part 1 summarizes Malhotra's extensive engagement with leaders of the Sri Aurobindo movement in India and the USA, during which he brought to their attention the distortions and appropriations of the teachings of their guru by the American thinker Ken Wilber. In parallel, Infinity Foundation was also funding numerous projects in Pondicherry and Auroville to support the movement. At both places, Malhotra discovered a lack of concern and response from the Aurobindonians to address the issues facing their movement outside the perimeters of their comfortable cocoons. Most were uninterested and/or incapable of defending their guru's work from being misrepresented and appropriated. This account draws heavily from Malhotra's correspondence as well as archival material and publications of Infinity Foundation. The title 'Navel-Gazing Aurobindonians' for Part 1 was suggested by Devan Nair, former president of the Republic of Singapore and a lifelong Aurobindonian himself.

Part 2 is a systematic analysis of the digestion of Sri Aurobindo's work by Ken Wilber and exposes its numerous flaws. Taken together, they form the first, and only, comprehensive analysis of the hijacking of Sri Aurobindo's work that has been a global phenomenon.

Since the mid-1990s, Rajiv Malhotra has been actively raising serious concerns about the treatment of Indian spiritual traditions by Westerners and Westernized Indians. He was engaged in the pūrva pakṣa of the state of India/dharma studies in academics and amongst the public at large; of special interest to him was the way Sri Aurobindo's works were being treated.

Malhotra wanted to understand the mechanisms with which the Western-centric academic system has appropriated India's contributions without proper attribution. With his vast lived experience in the USA and strong roots in India, he wanted to build a dialogue among different civilizations based on sincere acknowledgment and a level playing field. He wanted to raise the following kinds of questions: Who studies India as a career, what topics do they select, and what lenses and methods do they use? Who funds all this, and with what motives? What major theories and conclusions have they reached, and how valid are they? What is the impact of this new discourse on the legacies of India's foremost spiritual guru-s?

Malhotra became a prolific interrogator and critic of Western academia and embarked on a long-term journey to investigate, debate, argue, and when forced upon him, fight the established scholars at the foremost institutions.

Ken Wilber became an important case study for Malhotra to apply certain fundamental frameworks he had been developing as part of his lens to interpret the world. Some of the most relevant frameworks for the present volume are:

- **Sameness and Digestion**: Discusses the sweeping claim that cultures and thought systems are basically what lead to the digestion of one culture into a subordinate part of another.
- **Integral Unity vs. Synthetic Unity**: Explains one of the most fundamental differences between Indian and Western worldviews in their respective ideas of the nature of unity of things.
- **The Theory of Digestion**: This is at the heart of the syndrome being discussed in this book. It is a theory of *how* and *why* an entire system can become digested into another and the destruction it causes.
- **U-Turn Theory**: While Digestion occurs at the level of an entire civilization or a school of thought, the U-Turn Theory explains how Western individuals undertake a journey of appropriation, distortion, and repackaging. The U-Turns by individuals result in the Digestion of entire civilizational systems.

These frameworks are summarized below as they are applied throughout the analysis in this book.

## Sameness and Digestion

One of the systemic problems Malhotra discovered was the widespread mapping of Indian concepts onto Western categories. This was considered normal and natural using the colonial lens of Western Universalism. It led him to conclude that Indian Mind Sciences and Indian Psychology had been digested by Western scholars into Western frameworks that were repurposed for this use. Valuable Indian theories and practices, which constituted Bhāratīya civilizational assets, had been appropriated by Western scholars and repackaged as their original contributions. If this had happened apropos to Western sources of knowledge, it would have been attacked and prosecuted as plagiarism or theft of Intellectual Property. Malhotra found himself a lone crusader in exposing this arrogance of mighty Western institutions.

Thus began his systematic model-building of the difference between Integral Unity and Synthetic Unity, as well as his signature U-Turn Theory and the Theory of Digestion.

He began researching into the Indian influences on leading Western figures such as Immanuel Kant, Georg Friedrich Hegel, William James, Carl Jung, Alfred North Whitehead, and many others. He used his Infinity Foundation to investigate the Western appropriations. He discovered the clever use of language by many Westerners to claim originality of ideas that were, in fact, quintessentially Indian.

Popular American culture has had a long-standing love affair with many Indian spiritual traditions, thanks to the guru-s who had arrived from India and established movements on American soil. However, these systems have been digested into Western frameworks and Western history. Malhotra discovered that religious studies in American academia did not include topics like yoga and meditation as part of Hinduism as they were being rapidly appropriated by American scientists in other departments like psychology, cognitive sciences, neuroscience, and so on.

Various Western luminaries have integrated Indian ideas of the nature of consciousness into their own systems and spread them as liberal Christianity, New Age, and 'Western science'.

Meanwhile, the focus of Hinduism studies was on the anthropology of Indian people's suffering and poverty. The lens used in religious studies was primarily from the social sciences.

## Integral Unity vs. Synthetic Unity

One of the most fundamental frameworks to differentiate Indian and Western thought concerns the distinction and incompatibility between Integral Unity and Synthetic Unity. This distinction is explained in detail in the book *Being Different: An Indian Challenge to Western Universalism* by Malhotra.

When one examines a plant, one sees a unity that runs through every cell and part. In beholding it, one sees the existence of the seed that held it in its kernel, the soil and water that nurtured it, the sunlight that helped it grow, and the plant itself that produces the seed that ensures it can be sown again. At the end of its life, it returns to the earth once again, becoming compost for a new seed. There is an inherent wholeness represented in the existence and factors of the plant's life cycle that is unified and complete in each of its constituent parts, functionality, and the final creation. The very impetus towards creation, the organizing structure, and the mechanism of creation are all internal and inherent to the plant itself, even though the factors that help catalyze the creation may be external.

Consider, in comparison, an object such as a car. Each part is assembled and forged by bringing together distinct elements externally, with the explicit purpose of creating an instrument that serves a purpose.

The intrinsic unity seen in the first case i.e. the plant, best represents the paradigm of Integral Unity while the manufacturing of a car is representative of the contrasting idea of Synthetic Unity.

The defining principle of Integral Unity is that the whole alone exists – even the parts that make up the whole are correlative to it and do not have a separate, and independent existence. In the first example, the leaf of a plant cannot exist independently; its dependence is unidirectional with respect to the plant (whole). At the same time, the principle of organization and the structure of creation are inherent to the entire system represented by the plant.

In the case of Synthetic Unity, the fundamental principle is that of independent and separate existence of parts that make up the whole at the essential level. The organizing principle of assembly and its mechanism and structure are external to the product itself, i.e. it is superimposed on the parts to make the whole from outside the system that constitutes it. Synthetic Unity is thus, at its highest conception, a force of convenience and pragmatism. Co-operatives and political systems are examples of such unity purely for pragmatic reasons.

Western science has had tremendous success in creating technological progress using the principles of Synthetic Unity, yet faces challenges when considering the 'emergence' of consciousness from something made of matter, such as the brain. The approach of reductionism is a signature of Synthetic Unity, where phenomena and processes are studied by breaking them down into fundamental parts and studying the interactions between them. Integral Unity, on the other hand, begins with the premise of the Ultimate, from which phenomena emerge. *While Western neuroscience studies the 'emergence' of consciousness, the dhārmic schools of thought believe in consciousness being the source of all manifestations.* Thus, the focus of inquiry centers around the various forms of manifestations of consciousness, with each form unified with the whole.

The two major schools of thought – dhārmic and Western – are characterized by these two forms of unity; the former is Integral in nature, while the latter is characterized by Synthetic Unity. The specific characteristics of Integral Unity observed in dhārmic ways of life include:

1. All entities (physical, mental, emotional, linguistic, spiritual, or anything else), while apparently separate, do not have an actual existence or selfhood independent of the unity. Philosophers refer to this as the absence of separate 'essences' or 'substances'. Buddhists call this emptiness *śūnyata*, though not in the nihilistic sense.
2. The whole is independent and indivisible. Nothing other than itself exists. It is not part of a bigger unity or some other higher reality.
3. This unity includes within it the potential that generates all phenomena. Diversity is not imported from without, but unity is itself pregnant with it.

Furthermore, in the dhārmic traditions, the integrally unified entities are not static but exist in flux. Everything – all matter, spirit, humanity, every individual element down to the tiniest particle, every moment in time, and every unit of space – is ever-changing.[2]

The Ultimate whole is manifested in each part, and each part has a relative existence via the whole. Science, spirituality, philosophy, music, dance, arts, architecture, economics, literature, politics, and society of dhārmic systems are all embedded with this signature framework of Integral Unity. Each form has its own structure but reflects a larger unity. Among the various concepts within a domain of knowledge and even among multiple disciplines, the same unifying principles are found. (The same four *puruṣārtha*-s for instance, of dhārmic life, find expositions by different disciplines, thus retaining a cogency that is characteristic of Integral Unity.)

The book *Being Different* explains the concept of *bandhu* as the 'correspondence principle' and link that holds together various parts of the larger whole:

> All aspects of the world stem from a common ineffable source, and what we perceive as nature is but a pointer to a higher reality. There is interlinking among various faces of this reality such as sounds, numbers, colours and ideas and this interlinking is bandhu. The subtle and transcendental worlds on one side correspond with the perceptible world on the other. The term describes the relationship of the microcosm to the macrocosm wherein the former is the map of the latter and paradoxically, one mirrors the other.[3]

The Vedic principle of bandhu is analogous to quantum entanglement in quantum mechanics. An entangled pair of particles is inseparable at the level of existence, i.e. any change in parameters, for instance, the spin of one particle, instantaneously affects the other particle of the pair, immaterial of the distance of separation between the two particles. Dhārmic metaphysics is built on such unified principles.

One of the greatest exponents of Integral Unity in dhārmic systems has been Sri Aurobindo. Through his mammoth work spanning studies of the *Veda*-s, the *Upaniṣad*-s, the *Śāstra*-s, Yoga, Sāṃkhyā, the *Bhagavad Gītā* and more importantly, through his own experiences as a yogi, he considered the conditions for unifying different approaches to the same ultimate reality. Firmly rooted in dhārmic metaphysics, Sri Aurobindo considers the thesis and arguments of each – the materialist, the ascetic, the nihilist, the Vedāntic differences, while being faithful to the individual lenses and not trying to force-fit one with the other in order to create a larger framework. The most fundamental and unique dhārmic concept of *saccidānanda*, which finds itself to be the summum bonum of adhyātmic vidyā, is the ultimate reality of Sri Aurobindo's model of Integral (*pūrṇa*) Yoga.

*The use of a synthetic lens to dissect a system with Integral Unity will produce a distorted view.* Even worse, when one combines concepts from different systems with no in-built unity, s/he produces disharmony even though on the surface it could be made to appear unified. Ken Wilber's problem in synthesizing disparate systems will become clear as we give examples throughout this book.

## The Theory of Digestion

The U-Turn Theory and the Theory of Digestion emerged as a result of Malhotra's numerous debates with opponents, during which he discovered the Western tendency to appropriate Indian knowledge and claim it as their own.

Digestion shares certain similarities with the process of inculturation which has been Christianity's strategy for conquest and conversion for centuries across the globe.[4] The digestion of one culture by another is typically carried out under the guise of a desire to integrate, reduce differences, and gradually dilute and sideline the less dominant culture. At the level of popular culture, India and the West may meet as equals, but at deeper levels, where the core assumptions of a civilization reside, the playing field is tilted, as there has been an inherent power asymmetry between the West and non-West due to political and economic causes over the past couple of centuries.

Cultural appropriation gives a false impression of equalization. The less powerful culture is assimilated into the dominant one in such a way that:

1. the dominant civilization dismembers the weaker one into parts from which it picks and chooses the pieces it wants to appropriate;
2. these appropriated elements get mapped onto the language and social structures of the dominant civilization's history and paradigms, leaving little, if any, traces of the links to the source tradition;
3. the civilization that was digested gets depleted of its cultural and social capital because the appropriated elements are modified to fit the host's history; these elements are shown to be disconnected from, and even in conflict with, the source civilization; and
4. the depleted civilization enters the proverbial museum as yet another dead culture, ceasing to pose a threat to the dominant one.

After being digested, what is left of a civilization is waste to be excreted and destroyed. The erasure of differences is what makes a culture vulnerable to becoming digested and recast in the image of the host's frameworks and structures. The dominant side superimposes its concepts, aesthetics, language, paradigms, historical template, and philosophy, positioning them as the universal worldview. Concurrently, the images, symbols, histories, and languages of the weaker culture get absorbed, with inevitable distortion, into the dominant one.

One justification has been that the West itself mutates and evolves as a result of digesting and that is good for humanity. Also, some historians believe that the enhancement of the predator civilization and corresponding depletion of the civilization being preyed upon are a desirable march of world civilization – with the West positioned as the engine driving humanity forward.

In this view, the non-Western civilizations are considered relevant only as sources of Western civilization (as in 'our past'), as theatres in which the West operates ('our civilizing mission'), or as threats to Western interest ('our frontiers'). The interests and identities of the cultures that get digested are of little consequence.

Besides the obvious racism inherent in such arguments, there is the collective loss of human diversity and shared accomplishments. In harvesting the fruits of other civilizations, the West has destroyed their roots, thereby eliminating their ability to produce more bountiful harvests. The elements appropriated are terminal, as the residual skeletons of the digested civilizations are incapable of further creative contributions. Just as the non-West bequeathed gifts have enriched the world (even though, in most cases, these are reclassified as Western history and progress), undeniably, much more would have been produced from those sources had they not been digested.

The following figure illustrates the various processes at work. The digestion is analogous to the food consumed by a host in that what is useful gets assimilated, while that which does not fit the host's structure gets eliminated as waste. Consequently, the source tradition, similar to the food, ceases to exist, and the host (i.e. the West) gets strengthened. The overall diversity of cultures suffers because there is greater homogeneity due to the loss of the source tradition.

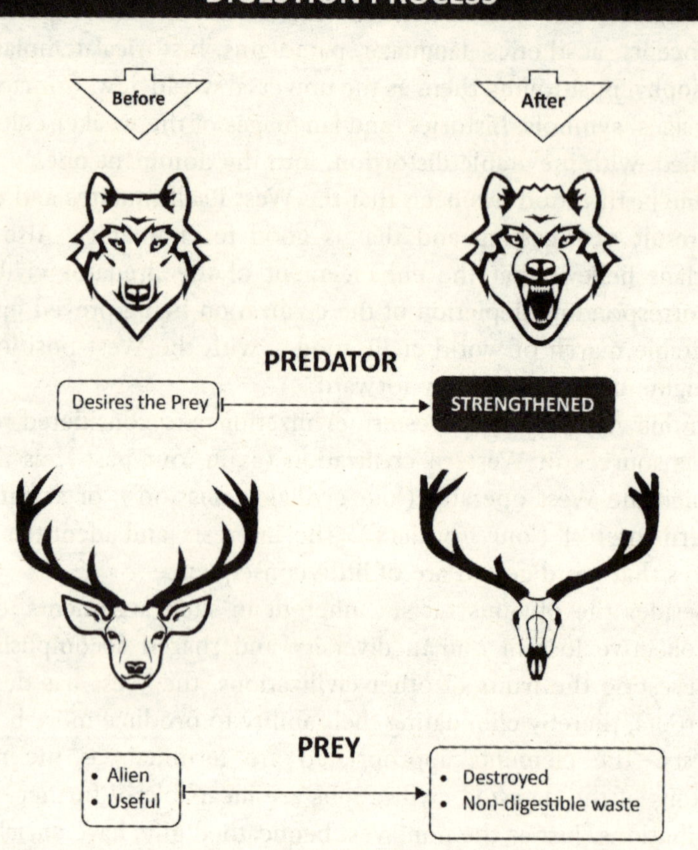


**Figure 1: The Digestion Process**

## The U-Turn Theory

Another crucial theory formulated by Malhotra is the U-Turn Theory. It focuses on the appropriation by individuals rather than by a school of thought or an institution. It explains the trajectory of Westerners using a conceptual model of patterns that describe their typical journeys into Indian traditions. Malhotra's starting point was to understand the ways in which the dominant Western culture has been rapidly appropriating Indian Mind Sciences and then erasing the origins. The version presented here is a *subset* of a bigger, and more comprehensive, model.

The U-Turn Theory provides a structural framework for the types of actors and their postures and describes the stages of their journeys using a prototype roadmap. It examines both the demand and supply sides of this knowledge transfer.

It is a framework in which one may analyze interactions between cultures and even sub-cultures. It addresses issues concerning how elements are transferred between cultures, especially when there is an asymmetry of power involved.

The theory posits five distinct stages in which the Western attitude toward the dhārmic traditions shifts and changes. These are:

1. **Stage 1 (Discipleship)**: Deep immersion into Indian sources.

In the initial stage, the Western scholar is a very objective student of the Indian traditions, and/or a disciple of a guru or lineage. S/he writes with the deepest respect for these traditions. The scholars at this stage may belong to several categories:

- Many scholars at this stage may genuinely aspire to give up their Western religious affiliations, and adopt Hinduism/Buddhism, since India has helped such a person undergo a personal transformation.
- Scholars sometimes remain in this stage for the long haul, while others move on to subsequent stages, not necessarily in the exact sequence of this model.
- Some scholars wish to retain their public Judeo-Christian or Western secular identities and are forthright that they are engaged only in an intellectual fact-finding exercise with no desire to adopt the Indian practices or identities.

  Others may have a premeditated game plan to disguise their Western allegiance, and to later return to their original Western cultural identity. They use this stage as an *anthropological technique* to open the channels of communication from the Indian side, by getting Indians to drop their guard and welcome them as genuine seekers.

2. **Stage 2 (Decontextualization)**: The knowledge and practices are reworked as part of the generic universal heritage erasing their Indian specificity and cultural roots.

In this stage, Indian traditions are repackaged as 'original' discoveries by the Western scholar, or are relocated by interpolating within obscure Greek, Christian or other 'Western' texts, or are assumed to be generic thoughts found in all cultures.

In many instances, this is done to further the author's academic career, or to expand the market for the author's books, tapes and seminars, by distancing himself from the negative stereotype of the 'caste, cows, curry' traditions.

Essentially, it is the personal ego hijacking what has been learnt, to serve its own selfish purposes. Many lofty arguments are put forth to justify this as being in the public interest.

3. **Stage 3 (Recontextualization)**: The re-tooled Indian heritage is presented as rooted in Western history or as the modern innovation of Western heroes.

If a given scholar's ego is strongly rooted in Western religion, because of strong *saṃskāra*-s, s/he returns to Judaism or Christianity, with bounties of freshly appropriated knowledge to enrich it. Alternatively, the scholar repackages the material in secular vernacular, such as 'Western psychology' or 'phenomenology' or some other 'scientific' jargon. This leads to mushrooming sales of books, tapes and invitations to seminars, as the Western audiences congratulate themselves for their own culture's sophistication.

Such Western scholars then become icons and symbols of the West, eliminating the need for subsequent students and practitioners to read or learn from the source Indian culture or to even give back. In the process, the Indian traditions may now be relocated as museum pieces with mere historical significance, sometimes accorded great respect, but their roots are no longer nurtured as *living* traditions.

Joseph Campbell, the American scholar of comparative mythology and religion, described this as the 'Hero's return' home. This celebration may be compared to how Napoleon was welcomed by the French nation as he marched through the streets of Paris displaying his captured loot from North Africa – slaves, ivory, gold, and other items of value. The Western archetype of a hero depends heavily upon the conquest of others.

Sometimes, the Western scholar who brings back the adhyātmika bounty from India does not hesitate to acknowledge his debt to Indian traditions. However, it is his Western readers, students and followers who find it problematic to base their worldview and practice on an Indian tradition, and insist on Western origins to feel pride in their own collective ego. The scholar often merely gives in to this social pressure, or becomes complicit over time, as has happened in the cases of both T.S. Eliot and Carl Jung.

This U-Turn essentially rewards the hero to take a culture apart into its components, and pluck out some key parts here and there, while denigrating the rest, in an act of violence. What happens when a dominant culture appropriates the prized elements of a colonized culture, selectively implants these into the dominant culture's own meme-plex, and simultaneously denigrates the residue as 'waste'?

- They compromise the integrity of the colonized culture, just as a predator selectively digests what it wants from the prey to become healthier and leaves the rest to rot. While the dominant culture strengthens its own cultural capital, this is done at the expense of the colonized culture that loses cohesiveness and gets devalued.
- Conquerors often display their plundered property as a mark of pride. The term 'Ornamental-ism' has been used to describe the appropriation of cultural assets from the colonized, and their display as the pride of the colonizers.
- Too often, these appropriations are justified by the appropriators as a favor to the colonized people. King George V, when asked why he wore India's Kohinoor diamond on his crown, is known to have said words to the effect: '*The people of India should feel proud that the King of England has selected their diamond as the one he wears*'. This is how 'Christian Yoga' and various New Age appropriations from Indian culture are sometimes presented, as being a great compliment to Indians.
- Malhotra also came across the logic by some pro-India people that civilizations must progress under Darwinian evolution of the strong conquering and digesting the weak, in order that the best of the prey becomes a part of the predator.

Too many Indians are ignorant about this cultural game theory and feel proud that the dominant civilization has turned their culture and symbols into its own property – as active practices, or as passive ornaments to wear, or as museum pieces. In the long run, this reduces the colonized into pets or children or patients, under the care of the dominant culture, and not acknowledged as equals. Their contribution to the future of humanity gets truncated.

4. **Stage 4 (Arson)**: The residue of the Indian sources is denigrated as misguided and flawed, at best, dangerous and toxic, at worst.

Only some scholars proceed intentionally to the next stage, in which they – or their followers – trash the Indian traditions as being 'primitive', 'irrational', 'socially backward', or 'abusive'. This furthers the West's claims of originality, because it tries to absolve them from links to the baggage of the denigrated traditions. One may think of this as a form of *academic arson*: U-Turns have often had the effect, perhaps unintentionally, of plunder with the one hand, and denigration of the victim, with the other.

To understand this Western tendency, one must understand the discontinuities in many Western traditions, and how they differ from the lineages and continuity in the Indian knowledge traditions:

- Sampradāya-s are Indian lineages and traditions that change over time, and yet also retain *continuity with the past.*
- The West's approach to progress is often discontinuous, and emphasis is placed on explicitly discarding the past.
- To an Indian, there would be no need to claim originality by denigrating the guru or traditional source; but to the Western ego, it is sometimes important to show one's heroism by trying to prove the inferiority of the past sources.
- Note how books were burnt and leaders who refused to accept new ideas were persecuted, whereas in India progress did not try to eradicate the past.

It is relatively easy for the Westerner to acknowledge the past that is located *within* Western thought, because that is part of his/her reconstructed collective ego. However, it is very difficult to accept that his/her past also lies in non-Western origins in positive ways.

Hence, U-Turns also serve to bring about these historical discontinuities.

It might be surmised that Stage 4 is a sort of cultural Oedipus complex at work, though this angle has not been pursued vigorously. The Oedipus complex can lead to murdering one's father to possess the mother to perceive oneself as an adult. One could postulate that the Indian source tradition is the father to be murdered. The mother is the spiritual and intellectual knowledge of India that is to be captured, minus the identity and context of Indian culture. This fuels the West's growth and enhances its ego.

In some instances, Stages 3 and 4 occur in reverse sequence.

5. **Stage 5 (Re-exported to India)**: The bodies of knowledge are repackaged and exported back to India in Western terminologies. It is also at this stage when elitist Indians become proxies for Western culture, i.e. *sepoys*. By joining the Western Grand Narrative, even as second-class citizens who live below the glass ceiling, they get an ego boost, and feel superior to 'other' Indians.

The seriousness of this stage is exacerbated by the fact that elitist Indians are seen as role models of success by the masses of India, and hence their sepoy mindset tends to percolate downwards into the middle strata of society. They are also powerfully positioned in institutions such as those concerning higher education in the humanities, media, public policy making, influential Non-Governmental Organizations (NGOs), and global human rights movements. Their 'superior' (i.e. Westernized) communication skills make them appear credible spokespersons for Indian culture in the eyes of Western media, academia and opinion leaders. Their sophisticated networking amongst one another gives them a force multiplier.

Intellectual decolonizing would necessitate a successful encounter with the sepoys, and intervention in their well-funded programs to reproduce themselves into the next generation.

The following diagram shows these stages.

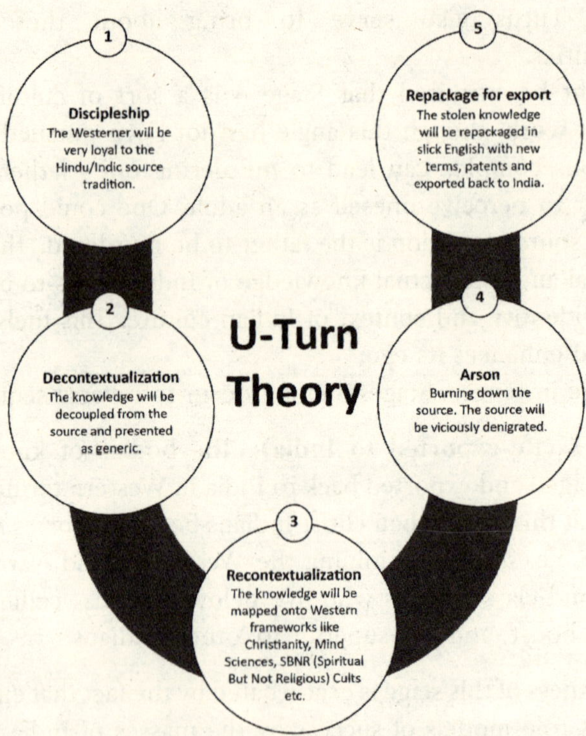


**Figure 2: U-Turn Theory**

Not all U-Turn stages mentioned previously take place in every case, and these stages might not occur in this exact sequence each time. Often, one scholar ends his/her career at a certain stage of this U-Turn process, and the Western successors of that line of inquiry continue further along this process.[5]

Another way to understand U-Turns is by examining the way contexts are manipulated at each stage and how Indian knowledge gets re-characterized:

In Stage 1, the knowledge and experience are understood in their native context.

In Stage 2, the Indian context is removed and replaced by as much 'generic' or 'universal' context as possible – i.e. it gets *decontextualized.* However, this is seldom a stable long-term representation of knowledge, as the dominant culture is well organized to push it further along the U-Turn process.

In Stage 3, the knowledge is later *recontextualized* into Judeo-Christianity and/or 'Western' science, often with patents, trademarks, and other claims to ownership.

In Stage 4, the source Indian traditions are *miscontextualized* and *demonized* to make them seem inferior and not worthy of such positive cultural assets.

For example, 'Christian Yoga' and 'Christian Centering Prayer' are presently in Stage 3. Already, many churches have entered Stage 4 by denigrating Hinduism/Buddhism while promoting these 'Christian' practices.

Too often, Indians evaluate Stage 2 as if it were the final stage. They fail to see the history of Stage 2 as an intermediate stage that leads to these other eventual stages. Also, they fail to demand as quid pro quo that Christianity must also turn itself into a Stage 2 'generic' spirituality by dropping claims of exclusivity that form the basis of aggressive proselytization. If Hinduism-Buddhism is to become generic for the betterment of humanity, then why not also (i) genericize Abrahamic religions by turning their historical Grand Narratives into ahistorical messages; (ii) recontextualize Jesus as one of many avatāra-s; and (iii) help people become better *within* their native spiritual paths as opposed to requiring a conversion.

Another consequence of the U-Turn process is *backward projection.* This refers to the tendency to use one's current context to reinterpret the prior stages of one's experiences in hindsight. For instance, it is common for scholars in Stages 2, 3, or 4 to claim that their learning in Stage 1 was misguided, or the work of the Devil, or because of being duped by an Indian guru, or the result of naïveté – even though it may have lasted fruitfully for several decades.

Usually, backward projection entails erasing or downplaying the prior stages, which are acknowledged with embarrassment, and only when explicitly asked to do so. The most recent stage is given overriding prominence, to the extent of superseding the prior stages, and not just augmenting them.

The U-Turners oftentimes use volumes of Indian knowledge and practices to fill the gaping holes in their own traditions and believe that this is merely a restoration of old lost knowledge. Indian traditions serve as a 'filler' to connect the dots of their own tradition in a way that makes the West seem to own everything that it learned from India. The Indian traditions then get reduced to what is called 'shareware' in the software industry – an assortment of free-standing items available in the public domain to cut and paste into the dominant culture's *proprietary* Grand Narratives.

It is also important to note that Eurocentrism is most often unintentional and unconscious because the person is deeply immersed in the myths of Western identity. Unconscious Eurocentrism is simply an archetype that shapes the 'truth'.

Today, 'South Asianized *desis*' (as they call themselves) are often in Stage 5 and tripping over each other to prove their accomplishments as sepoys working for the dominant culture. Their knowledge of Indian culture is largely through stereotypes imbibed from persons in Stages 2 through 4. They have blindly accepted these stereotypes due to their own ignorance, identity shame, and the superior *brand value* of Western theories and have re-engineered their own identities to fit into the dominant culture's Grand Narrative.

## Stereotyping Indian Traditions

As a result of his encounters with Westerners as well as Indians in various ideological camps, Malhotra uncovered several mental blocks and falsehoods in the way India and its traditions were being characterized. Some of these are summarized below.

### *Allegations of world-negation and absence of empiricism*

Malhotra discovered that Indian philosophy was not being taught in university philosophy departments except in a few like the Universities of Hawai'i and Texas, where certain individual professors were based. As a result, there were serious misunderstandings concerning Indian spiritual systems because these cannot be divorced from philosophy.

A common misunderstanding was that Indian thought (like Advaita Vedānta) is world-negating. This view holds that the world is considered to be ultimately *mithya* or *māyā*, and hence false. These interpretations were being fed by Indian translations, according to which Hindus are other-worldly, escapist, devoid of positive psychology and individualism. Indian philosophy seemed to encourage extreme introversion and antimaterialism, thereby hindering progress in the *laukika* (materialistic, pragmatic) realm. India's great thinkers were aloof from practical problems, and hence there has always been poverty, superstition, irrationality, and so on. This was mapped onto Western depictions of primitive societies they had encountered on other continents. According to this view, India depended on Western interventions to save its people from darkness. This Western bias was often supported by some Hindu leaders promoting renunciation of the material world.

Western scholarship described this problem as India's lack of 'positive psychology', in which the goal is to strengthen the ego into a healthy and positive one. The criticism was that Indian psychology was negative because guru-s taught withdrawal and abandoning the ego without first making it whole and strong using positive methods.

Western scholars appropriated adhyātma-vidyā as first-person empiricism and claimed that empiricism was absent in Indian traditions. Therefore, they argued, they were the original discoverers of these practices.

It was further claimed that Indian systems lacked second-person methods (I-You relationships), which is a serious deficiency because love, interpersonal engagements, and social harmony reflect second-person qualities.

Furthermore, the West was believed to have used scientific instrumentation as its unique achievement to study inner phenomena, i.e. third-person empiricism. Indian traditions have been accused of lacking this, and therefore, had been unscientific prior to their Western discovery.

### *Buddhism better positioned*

Malhotra discovered the immense contrast between the status of Buddhism and Hinduism in contemporary Western academic discourse. One factor was that there were large numbers of loyal practicing White Buddhists in the academia who were citing Buddhist sources while explaining Buddhist concepts in scientific frameworks. Hindu sources, however, were not being similarly acknowledged because there were almost no practicing Hindu scholars involved in such research publications. This insight led Infinity Foundation to sponsor conferences and nurture scholars across India who would write academic papers, books, and course materials explaining Indian

Mind Sciences and theories of consciousness in contemporary terms.

### *Social injustice allegations*

Indian culture, especially Hinduism, was heavily stereotyped, disparaged, dismissed, and even openly accused of being primitive and abusive of women, lower castes, Muslims, Christians, etc. This provoked Malhotra to initiate his rebuttals and fight what he called Hinduphobia.

### *Colonization*

Malhotra discovered that scholars in India were mostly following Western research methods, theories, and vocabulary because they craved acceptance in Western conferences, journals, and faculty. They depended on Western funding and institutions for their careers while failing to understand their core subject matter to formulate original rebuttals.

Postcolonial scholarship in India has failed because it is not competent to use native and indigenous categories to reverse the gaze and critique the West in Indian frameworks, nor is it able to recognize the threats of appropriation, digestion, and distortion of the Indian contributions being done by Western scholars.

This amounted to a blatant colonization of Indian civilization and heritage by its own people. Indian scholars were either ignorant of the problem and unable or unwilling to respond to it, or in some cases, becoming a part of the Western 'sepoy army' actively undermining Indian traditions.

During this mammoth initiative, Malhotra met many important voices in the fields of mind sciences encompassing psychology, cognitive sciences, consciousness studies, and related fields.

After his intense research into both Indian and Western systems, as well as frequent encounters and debates with various opponents, Malhotra's insights took many years to take shape and crystallize. These were important breakthroughs that allowed Infinity Foundation to take a strong stand and refute Western misunderstandings of Indian thought. This helped shape the foundation's vision and action plan for decolonizing the Indian Mind Sciences and practices that were not even academically taught or researched in India's own curricula. Indian university curricula and research were teaching almost exclusively Western psychology and looking at Indian practices from a Western lens.

PART ONE

# The 'Navel-Gazing Aurobindonians'

# Chapter 1

# The Importance of Challenging Wilberism

## CHAPTER SUMMARY

- In this chapter, Rajiv Malhotra gives his personal account of how the works of Sri Aurobindo were appropriated by the American thinker Ken Wilber. After a detailed study of Wilber's works, Malhotra exposed the fundamental misunderstandings in his writings and mapped the way Wilber had hijacked Sri Aurobindo's core teachings. The chapter summarily considers Ken Wilber's U-Turn journey through the five stages of his work.

- Recognizing the imminent danger of Sri Aurobindo's work being fundamentally co-opted, Infinity Foundation funded research and efforts to reclaim the Integral worldview from Wilber and his followers.

- Malhotra had been debating against the Wilberization of Sri Aurobindo studies but had run into mental blocks even from many of those who regarded themselves as hardcore followers of Sri Aurobindo.

- The chapter introduces Malhotra's multi-year attempts in numerous forums to bring the Aurobindonians into this conversation to defend their guru and his legacy and ensure that his teachings are transmitted with integrity.

## Ken Wilber's U-Turn

Rajiv Malhotra has engaged with the problems of Digestion and U-Turn by studying specific Western thinkers and schools of thought and discovering their unacknowledged Indian sources. While studying the works of Sri Aurobindo, he encountered many Aurobindonians who were following and supporting the counterfeit systems developed by prominent Westerners. Ken Wilber came up frequently as the biggest name taking advantage of the neglect of Sri Aurobindo studies.

Malhotra used his theories of Digestion and U-Turn to model how Wilber had transitioned in his work: from being respectful of Sri Aurobindo and other Indian sources in his initial writings, to downgrading their importance over time, and eventually completely dropping them from his writings. Alongside, he positioned himself as a genius and his followers enthroned him 'the Einstein of consciousness'.

The choice to focus on Wilber was driven by a sense of alarm as to how the lifetime work of one of the greatest sages was being appropriated and wholly distorted. Malhotra targeted Wilber as a prime case study of Digestion and U-Turn.

Ken Wilber is currently positioned as a leader in psychology, human evolution, self-help and life-coaching, leadership development, and multiple spiritual movements. He is considered the pioneer of Integral Psychology and is described as follows:

> Wilber is now the most translated writer on consciousness studies in the United States. He is seen as an important representative of transpersonal psychology, which emerged in the sixties from humanistic psychology, and which concerns itself explicitly with spirituality. For the fundamental and pioneering nature of his insights, he has been called "the Einstein of consciousness" research. —*Yoga Journal.*[1]

> The twenty-first century literally has three choices: Aristotle, Nietzsche, or Ken Wilber. —Jack Crittenden Ph.D.[2]

> Ken Wilber is one of the most important philosophers in the world today. Often referred to as "the Einstein of consciousness," Ken is the originator of the first truly comprehensive or integrative

> philosophy, aptly named Integral Theory—"one of the first believable world philosophies," as Ken himself puts it. Incorporating cultural studies, anthropology, systems theory, developmental psychology, biology, and spirituality, it has been applied in fields as diverse as sustainability, psychotherapy, spirituality, education, business, medicine, politics, sports, and art.[3]

Ken Wilber was appointed inaugural chancellor at Ubiquity University in California, which was heavily funded by some ultra-wealthy Americans. He is referred to as the developer of the Integral Theory, 'the most seminal concept for humanity'.[4] Ubiquity offers graduate degree programs, including doctoral degrees, in various areas of 'Wisdom Studies' under its School of Science and Consciousness. It also offers courses such as *The Dance of Shiva: A Pilgrimage to South India* taught by the British scholar Andrew Harvey, who teaches Christian elements, especially of his Christian Benedictine mystic teacher Father Bede Griffiths, as part of the course, the content of which is completely Hindu.[5]

Wilber's version of Integral Theory is the basis of Ubiquity's entire curriculum, and he is described as the 'foundational figure for the university'.

Wilber has been a prolific author since the 1970s, and in his earliest material, he comes across as one trying to bring the profound realizations of the Eastern knowledge systems, primarily from the work of Sri Aurobindo, to the Western world of materialism, and synthesize the two. Over the following decades, Wilber's work comprised quintessential Indian terms brought into the Westerner's vocabulary, but increasingly in a manner that diluted the ideas or sidelined some of its greatest proponents over the ages.

Part 2 of this book traces how the concepts of involution (first coined in the twentieth century by Swami Vivekananda) and evolution, central to Sri Aurobindo's model of the evolution of human consciousness, get co-opted into Wilber's core thesis. Several other key concepts have been lifted from Sri Aurobindo's work without attribution, except in passing.

Wilber's work over the decades is categorized into different stages using his own schema; he uses the same organizing principle to classify the world's leading thinkers and systems from every culture. He gives himself a unique spot at the top of the pyramid; his Indian sources are placed lower than many Westerners in his hierarchy.

His early writings relied heavily on Sri Aurobindo's work, especially *The Life Divine* and *The Synthesis of Yoga,* as explained in the West by followers such as Haridas Chaudhuri who founded the California Institute of Asian Studies, renamed the California Institute of Integral Studies (CIIS) after the latter passed away. Wilber initially used Advaita Vedānta to refute prior Western thinkers and hence create a special place for himself among Westerners. This was Stage 1 of the U-Turn, wherein he was hospitable to dharma.

Concurrently, he positioned himself as a compiler of broad knowledge while sacrificing depth. He adopted the framework of perennialism popularized by previous Western scholars like Aldous Huxley and Huston Smith, who had in turn, been influenced by Sri Ramakrishna Paramahansa and Swami Vivekananda. Perennialism became the frame into which he could fit the vast diversity of Indian spiritual traditions. He replaced deep ideas with generic substitutes and made flawed equivalences. For instance, he equated all non-dualistic traditions across the broad spectrum of mystic traditions and ignored their subtle nuances. At this stage, he was at least candid about his appropriations, citing examples from Indian and other Eastern traditions and acknowledging the potential for further exploration. Many years later, when he formulated his intellectual journey as a chronology of stages, he referred to this as Wilber-I.

During Wilber-II, he began to appropriate the elaborate explanations of involution-evolution originally expounded by Swami Vivekananda and Sri Aurobindo. The *Atman Project: A Transpersonal View of Human Development* falsely presents involution-evolution as a generic idea common to all spiritual traditions. Wilber makes only sparse, inconsequential references to Indian thought in explaining this, almost as if he wants his readers to ignore the Indian sources. In fact, he attributes the notion of involution to the philosopher Arthur Lovejoy and scholar of religious studies Huston Smith, who in turn, had adopted the concept from Swami Vivekananda.

When faced with complex situations where he lacks credibility and personal experience, Wilber resorts to quoting Sri Aurobindo to legitimize his explanations. In other words, he is not yet sufficiently established with his own credibility and pontificates standing on the shoulders of Sri Aurobindo. But where he expects to get away with his own statements, Wilber claims ownership of the Indian ideas. He uses involution-evolution as the foundation to formulate his own version of developmental and dynamic transpersonal psychology. A major source of inaccuracies is that he did not have, or claim to have, direct spiritual experiences and relied on the testimony of secondary accounts by various Western intermediaries.

In the preface of *The Atman Project*, Wilber states that his ideas of involution-evolution 'coincide' with those of Sri Aurobindo, implying that he developed them independently. He goes on to cleverly marginalize Sri Aurobindo, often citing his words with a generic attribution like, 'according to many sages...'.[6] Sri Aurobindo's elucidations of involution-evolution are buried in a table in the appendix among a long list of theorists from several other traditions. In contrast, Wilber meticulously cites and references every Western source.

In this second stage of U-Turn, Wilber co-opts Sri Aurobindo's core concept of 'Ascend and Integrate'. In *The Life Divine*, Sri Aurobindo explains 'Ascend and Integrate' as a pattern of evolution whereby the prior level of consciousness is transcended but not left behind; rather, it is included and moved forward as a subset integrated into the higher level.[7] For example, upon achieving a state higher than ordinary rationality, one does not stop being rational, but one's rationality is no longer a limiting factor. It is analogous to saying that upon learning to run, one does not forget walking. Wilber replaces 'Ascend and Integrate' with his own phrase 'Transcend and Include',[8] claiming this as his huge original discovery.

In addition, Wilber claims to have resolved the 'Pre-Trans fallacy', once again co-opting from Sri Aurobindo. This was an important confusion among many Westerners whose framework of the human mind was limited only to pre-rational and rational states and did not include a third dimension — one that is even higher than the rational adult state. This may be called the 'trans-rational' state, which we often refer to as the '*ṛṣi*' state of consciousness. In this state, the individual *has all rational faculties but is not limited by them.* He is fully capable of logic, intellect, etc., but goes beyond what ordinary people can cognize. Here the *buddhi*/intellect is awakened more fully. The trans-state is a superset of the rational state and is not divorced from rationality. A hallmark of all dharma systems is their emphasis on the evolution of consciousness towards this higher state.

The pre-trans fallacy is as follows: Westerners who are unfamiliar with higher states of consciousness assume that the pre- and the trans-states are the same since each is different from the rational state, and they show superficial similarities. Since both are different from the rational state, it gives the false impression of the two being the same. Hence, claims of mystics are often denigrated as a regression to the child's pre-rational state. Western researchers observing a mystic's lifestyle can falsely conclude that his mental state is the same as that of a child and, therefore in need of developing into adulthood. Sri Ramakrishna exhibited child-like behavior but was not a child.

Indeed, this is precisely the point that Carl Jung incorrectly concluded about the Indian sage Ramana Maharshi (1879-1950). Jung traveled by train to the town where Ramana Maharshi lived but refused at the last minute to alight from the train and visit the famous ṛṣi. Basing his views entirely on third-party accounts, Jung described Ramana Maharshi as pre-rational, an escapist, and other-worldly, and therefore unfit for an intelligent engagement. He conflated the trans-rational state of the ṛṣi with the pre-rational state of the child.

Wilber rightly criticizes the confusion between pre-rational and post-rational in the minds of Europe's Romantics: They had assumed that any post-rational state would be non-rational and hence like a child's pre-rational state, i.e. it would be regressive. However, in later stages of his writings, he superimposes this position of Europe's Romantics onto Sri Aurobindo. This mapping of Europe's experiences onto others presumes that European history is universal history and European thought is universal truth. A universalizing of the White gaze is made possible because Whiteness itself has not been gazed at and relativized in the same manner as non-White cultures have been studied by White anthropologists. It also demonstrates either Wilber's lack of understanding of Sri Aurobindo's work or his wilful distortion of it.

Many Westerners who appropriate Indian spiritual ideas later accuse the very same Indian tradition of being 'like a child' compared with the rational West. Hence, they argue that Indians must first evolve to be rational like Westerners before they can truly advance further to the supra-rational state. In other words, India's journey forward must go through a phase of Westernization.

Having grasped this error, Wilber claims to have discovered an original resolution to the theories of the mind. He writes, 'perhaps no other idea of mine has caused such turmoil'.[9] While he devised his pre-trans fallacy theory from Sri Aurobindo's ideas, he went on to add insult to injury by accusing Sri Aurobindo of not being fully evolved to the supra-rational state that Wilber claimed to have discovered as his *own* state.

As he moves further in his writings, Wilber falsely alleges a 'fatal deficiency' of 'other-worldliness' in Indian knowledge systems and rejects them as irrelevant to progress in this world. By finding a flaw in the Western notion of perennialism, he claims he can ignore all the systems he had lumped together as 'perennial', including all Indian thought. While appropriating Sri Aurobindo's extensive elaborations on the lower states of consciousness, Wilber claims that Indian systems lack insight into such lower states[10] and suggests that Western psychology could remedy the 'defect' of other-worldliness.[11]

A recurring pattern of Wilber's career is that each time his fallacious thinking and artificial synthesis put him in a corner, he attributes his error to flaws in Eastern ideas. And, each time he resolves his own blindness with the help of an Indian idea, he claims that he has now superseded the Indian sources.

Wilber-IV onwards, he explains that he can supersede Sri Aurobindo's theories because of advances in Western science and postmodernism theories which had occurred after Sri Aurobindo's time.

In each of the phases that mark his career, one notices an increasing overturning of the balance in favor of crediting and acknowledging Westerners, while appropriating native Indian concepts.

Our overriding issue with Wilber is that his entire model is synthetic and not integral. He copies ideas, disassembles them into his own jargon, and then reassembles them with synthetic unity and not integral unity. The book *Being Different: An Indian Challenge to Western Universalism* explains the fundamental differences between integral unity and synthetic unity. In Part 2 of this volume, we analyze Wilber's core thesis from this lens.

Indian traditions place a significant emphasis on pūrṇa – a concept that can be loosely translated as integrality. However, Wilber uses integrality as a synthetic amalgamation of disconnected ideas from separate thinkers that lack causal connections and may even be mutually incompatible. Wilber's use of integral is merely an organizing principle to bring together unrelated Western systems, some of which may oppose one another and be in mutual contradiction. The result is an assorted collection of disparate concepts with internal incoherence and conflicts.

While various schools of Indian thought may differ on many issues, most acknowledge *sat-cit-ānanda/saccidānanda* as the primary reality – a singular, all-encompassing, all-constituting unity consciousness, existence, and bliss that gives form and individualizes. From this perspective, physical matter and the human mind are considered intermediary forms of the conscious evolutionary process. While Western transpersonal and phenomenological approaches depict meditation as a technique for specific experiences or personal growth, the Indian traditions view it as a process aimed at realizing saccidānanda as the primary reality.

Western scientific methodology, rooted in the primacy of observable phenomena and following a reductionist approach, contrasts with the broader epistemic scope of Indian knowledge. Even scholars who dedicate their lives to studying and explaining Indian thought often carry embedded conceptions influenced by Western scientific paradigms. Western scientific traditions have a narrower bandwidth than Indian knowledge systems. Any attempt to digest Indian systems into Western ones ends up distorting and trivializing the rich depth of Indian thought.

While a detailed study of each of Wilber's major ideas and appropriations is found in Part 2 of this book, the following table is a handy summary:

| Key Idea | Sri Aurobindo | Ken Wilber |
|---|---|---|
| Perennialism | Writes against perennialism; respects the unique contributions of each culture. | Falsely calls Sri Aurobindo a perennialist; fails to correctly attribute key unique ideas to the sage. |
| Involution-Evolution | Takes Swami Vivekananda's ideas further; clearly writes about the ascent of Matter-Life-Mind and descent of the Divine Consciousness. | Claims it to be an original contribution. |
| Pre-Trans fallacy | Describes in detail various levels and layers of consciousness, while also explaining how at times there could be superficial similarities between levels of consciousness but they are qualitatively different. | Appropriates these ideas from Sri Aurobindo and formulates his pre-trans fallacy theory without any acknowledgment to Sri Aurobindo. |
| Levels of Mind | Writes in detail about the various ascending planes of the Mind. | Appropriates the same and calls it *The Great Chain of Being*, while crediting other Westerners for it. |
| Stages of Evolution | Considers in detail the stages and features of evolution; manifests consciousness in increasing planes of complexity. | Introduces twenty tenets of holarchical evolution by appropriating without acknowledgment from Sri Aurobindo's ideas. |
| Integral Transformation | Each plane when transcended becomes purified to bring down the Spirit – Ascend and Integrate. | Appropriates the same idea and calls it Transcend and Include. |

| Key Idea | Sri Aurobindo | Ken Wilber |
|---|---|---|
| The Vectors of Transformation | Integral Yoga not only speaks of upward ascent but also the emergence of the psychic to take over horizontally the actions of life. | Claims to uniquely establish the same while accusing Sri Aurobindo of being linear. |
| Other-worldliness vs. Integral Life | Integrates from many schools of ancient wisdom and takes further his ideas of Integral Yoga; says this very world is the realm of action for Yoga, 'All Life is Yoga' and that the world is real. | Falsely accuses Sri Aurobindo of having no worldly impact while claiming to give an Integral theory that reconciles the spiritual and the corporeal. |

## Rajiv Malhotra's Attempts to Collaborate with Aurobindonians

In many leading circles of academic scholars and New-Age intellectuals, Ken Wilber is an icon with a stature comparable to Carl Jung. A number of funding sources in the West support his large-scale global movement. His huge Western following, however, has failed to recognize that his earlier books explicitly followed the description of consciousness states as per Sri Aurobindo's experiences.

Infinity Foundation wanted to reach out to the largely liberal Western supporters of these movements to convince them of the importance of preserving the continuity of Indian traditions. The tree of Indian wisdom has not borne its final fruits, and many more harvests remain that would benefit humanity. In many cases, the repackaged ideas that were being bootlegged by Westerners had failed to be authentic. The source traditions had to be nurtured on their native soil and not allowed to atrophy.

We also argued that U-Turns and digestions empower expansionist and predatory civilizations by making them stronger and more hegemonic while depleting and eventually killing their prey. The histories of pagans, Native Americans, and even Indians under colonialism show that *the digestion of conquered peoples' civilizational assets did not change the predator into a benign creature.* Rather, it produced an even fiercer predator that had brought into its service the elite among the conquered people. In other words, the short-term positive consequences of appropriation should not intoxicate us into ignoring the opposite long-term implications of feeding and fattening fundamentally malignant civilizations that depend upon expansion for their survival.

Finally, we tried to argue that ethics demands that those Westerners who had drunk from the well of Indian traditions and thereby evolved themselves personally and/or developed their careers, businesses, or social stature should pay their debts to the mother tradition by publicly acknowledging these sources.

Unfortunately, most Western liberals were disappointing in their subtle chauvinism and unwillingness to behave the way true liberals should. In fact, some lashed out at Malhotra for pointing out that many of their most cherished thought leaders had lavishly appropriated critical ideas from India.

Worse still, almost all Indian intellectuals and spiritualists seemed uninformed of the issues. Malhotra intensified his debates against the Wilberization of Sri Aurobindo studies and tried to get Aurobindonians to help. Putting our resources to work in the 1990s, Infinity Foundation's central interest was researching integral thought that would explain and apply Sri Aurobindo's teachings while contrasting and critiquing Ken Wilber's appropriations, distortions, and agendas. So, the foundation widely announced the availability of grants for such projects.

However, Malhotra ran into mental blocks from even the prominent leaders of the Sri Aurobindo movement. It became important for him to counter these Aurobindonians. The following chapters detail the attempts to mobilize Aurobindonians and the intense arguments that precipitated.

Chapter 2

# Lobbying the Aurobindonians

## CHAPTER SUMMARY

- Rajiv Malhotra traveled to Pondicherry and Auroville to discuss the process of Wilberization described in the previous chapter and to explore ways to counter it.
- These interactions shaped Infinity Foundation's positions on the digestion of Indian spirituality and solidified its resolve to respond.
- Malhotra was shocked by the reactions and responses of many Indian scholars and found them ignorant and defeatist: Most of them were unaware of the serious appropriations taking place; when informed, they were dismissive of the implications; some had bought into the world-negating image that the West had associated with Indian spirituality; and many refused to put their careers in jeopardy to defend the work of their guru.
- Malhotra held several public and private talks. He gave two important interviews in Auroville in the year 2000 regarding Infinity Foundation's efforts to address the situation. This led to wider discussions among Aurobindonians worldwide, both in person in Auroville and online.
- He encountered a wide array of questions regarding not only Sri Aurobindo studies but also the teaching and fair representation of Hinduism in Western academia. These exchanges highlighted Infinity Foundation's role, and many Aurobindonians wrote back to Malhotra with newer awareness and understanding.

## Attempts to Mobilize Aurobindonians

Rajiv Malhotra spent the summer of 2000 in Auroville and Pondicherry for two main reasons: (i) to review the IF-sponsored Auroville Village Development Project; and (ii) to evaluate Auroville as a possible location for students from Princeton Day School in the USA as part of a program being launched by Infinity Foundation.

He expanded the scope of the trip to establish contact with Sri Aurobindo's followers as intellectual resources. He had almost single-handedly been debating Wilber's appropriations of Sri Aurobindo and needed help. Just prior to his visit, he wrote to Julian Lines of Matagiri (an organization dedicated to Sri Aurobindo and The Mother in New York, USA):

> I am in the process of launching a new organization called EDUCATIONAL COUNCIL ON INDIC TRADITIONS, whose focus shall be the relationship of Indic wisdom (both ancient and modern), on the world's civilization. ... Sri Aurobindo is someone to focus on in particular. ... we would like to offer grants for work that could be essays, monograph(s) or even a full-scale book on the subject.[1]

Julian Lines forwarded Malhotra's emails to various Sri Aurobindo followers and recommended them as potential grant recipients. Some of them showed interest. Malhotra explained the following reasons for fighting the appropriation of Sri Aurobindo's ideas:

1. Since the repackaging is bootlegged and not authentic, its benefits are not real. It could even be counter-productive because it could result in a loss of credibility for genuine knowledge.
2. If the genuine sources of knowledge are not nurtured, further insights will not emerge, and the knowledge system will become frozen.
3. Western writers publishing all sorts of theories have insufficient personal spiritual experience to make the claims. Hence, their work is largely unreliable and ego-driven.
4. It is unethical to not honor one's teachers from whom one has learned.

Infinity Foundation's stated objective was to create several projects in the academia that would formally recognize Sri Aurobindo in the same league as Sigmund Freud and Carl Jung without middlemen creating their own distortions. The intense engagements in the USA and India were crystallizing the challenge: Eurocentric biases, lack of Indian sources of funding to champion authentic investigations, and a lack of vision and awareness among leaders on how the distortions were eating away at the roots of Indian knowledge systems.

Infinity Foundation's stance on the matter stood in stark contrast with many Indians at the time. This is summarized in the table below.

| Issue | Positions of many Indians | Infinity Foundation's position |
|---|---|---|
| U-Turns in general | • Not seen as a problem.<br>• Often seen as a favor to us.<br>• 'All rivers lead to the ocean' – truth will prevail in the end.<br>• 'Let's not be too mental'<br>• It may be an issue but not my battle to fight. | • Serious long-term consequences.<br>• Developed systematic model with many case studies.<br>• Challenged the U-Turners publicly. |
| Wilberization | • Unaware of the phenomena.<br>• Same outlook for U-Turns in general. | • Launched major critique of Wilber's appropriation of Sri Aurobindo studies.<br>• Triggered major arguments with many Aurobindonians. |
| Indian thought considered life-negating | • Many agreed that Indian thought was life-negating, citing selective interpretations of Advaita Vedānta. | • Cited counterarguments that Indian civilization has been life-affirming. |

| | | |
|---|---|---|
| Lack of deconstruction of the West | • Intellectual leaders inexperienced and even disinterested.<br>• Lack of clear understanding of Sri Aurobindo's own work despite being prominent Aurobindonians. | • Took on many important issues persistently.<br>• Rigorous pūrva pakṣa of Western works and study from Indian lens.<br>• Cited Sri Aurobindo's works (e.g. *The Foundations of Indian Culture*) and those by his contemporaries like K.D. Sethna. |
| Funding role is critical | • Dependent on unreliable funding by the Indian government and subversive funding by Templeton Foundation. | • Entrepreneurial and rapid response approach to make grants and project management for optimal results.<br>• The foundation became the only major and consistent source of private funding. |

## Sellout by Aurobindonians

The year 2000, in which Malhotra was trying to provoke Aurobindonians into action, was also the time Wilber's Integral Institute in Colorado, USA was taking off. Wilber was looking to rapidly hijack the integral movement, and this institute was his vehicle to bring together theorists not only from psychology, academia, and spirituality but also from domains where integral principles could be applied such as education, politics, business, and medicine. The institute aimed to set itself up as the biggest umbrella for everything Integral.[2]

Wilber's ambition had gone completely unnoticed by Sri Aurobindo scholars. Malhotra was the only person tracking these developments. He raised the alarm on Wilber's maneuver that would completely sideline Sri Aurobindo from the integral movement. It was shocking that Wilber required those joining his new Integral Institute to surrender all their

Intellectual Property to it and to let the institute decide what knowledge would be licensed to whom, for what purpose, and under what terms. This was blatant intellectual imperialism!

Malhotra sent the following email to a wide list of Aurobindonians to draw their attention to these developments:

> Friends, attached is an outline of the **recently announced INTEGRAL INSTITUTE by Ken Wilber**. All his early books, in which he developed his thesis, were so full of reverence for Sri Aurobindo, and even in his recent books he at least gives reference to Sri Aurobindo. Therefore, does it appear strange to you that suddenly there is this large collection of individuals and institutes coming together to supposedly co-create this new higher consciousness, ...**YET there is no link, relationship or reference whatsoever to Sri Aurobindo's organizations in India, Europe or the US who have been doing this for decades, or to anything linked to him**?
>
> **Are these people trying to fade away Sri Aurobindo, and for what purpose?** Jung had studied Indian philosophy for decades, lectured about it, incorporated it to create most of his 'breakthrough' claims. But in the final stage of his life, he could not avoid the European temptation to reject Indian thought as 'world negating', without giving a clear justification. Most Jungians I come across today know nothing of this appropriation, and some even try to 'export' these ideas back to the East as yet another Western scientific advancement. In the case of Wilber appropriating Sri Aurobindo, **the appropriators are still active, and their record of appropriation is very fresh and clear. Should this new institute be discussed** (a) during my trip to Auroville/Pondicherry and (b) at the July 5th to 9th annual A.U.M. (All USA Meet of followers of Sri Aurobindo and Mother's teachings) event in Connecticut?[3]

Malhotra expected a response from the Aurobindonians on how they would push back against Wilber. Instead, he was alarmed by the situation at Auroville: Residents there wanted to join Wilber's scheme even though that would put Sri Aurobindo's work and legacy below the framework and institution controlled by Wilber. For instance, Bhavana, an American Christian living in Auroville and involved in the Village

Development Project funded by Infinity Foundation, supported the idea that Auroville should join this initiative in a junior position. She wrote:

> I wonder if it might not be a good strategy to have Auroville's "World Centre for Human Unity" send a proposal to Integral Institute (I-I) for inclusion in the Institute. (I hope Deepti has been telling you about this major project in Auroville to create – or re-create ourselves as an institution for higher learning focused on research into all aspects of human unity.) That way Auroville itself could be a faculty of the I-I. US based Aurobindonians can actively pursue the application and represent us there.[4]

Malhotra fiercely opposed this proposed sellout. Most Aurobindonians seemed to miss the fundamental issue of their guru's work being appropriated, distorted, digested into someone else's framework, and located under an outsider's corporate umbrella. Many of the disciples at Sri Aurobindo Ashram in Pondicherry and the followers in Auroville were unconcerned with Wilber's subversions. They cited excuses to avoid getting involved in this cause. The following factors seemed to be at play:

1. **Ignorance**: Most scholars and followers of Sri Aurobindo studies in India, both in Auroville and at Sri Aurobindo Ashram, were not even aware of the extent to which Wilber was distorting Sri Aurobindo's work.
2. **Escapism**: Many of them dismissed the issues and were apathetic about Wilber taking over global consciousness studies and positioning himself as the preeminent thinker of the time.
3. **Foolishness**: Many followers of Sri Aurobindo were foolish enough to think that it may be a better idea to join Wilber's movement, surrender all Intellectual Property, and be taken over instead of defending their guru's work.
4. **Selfishness**: There were many Aurobindonians who were not willing to stand up to the Wilber tsunami out of fear that it might damage their academic careers and positions.

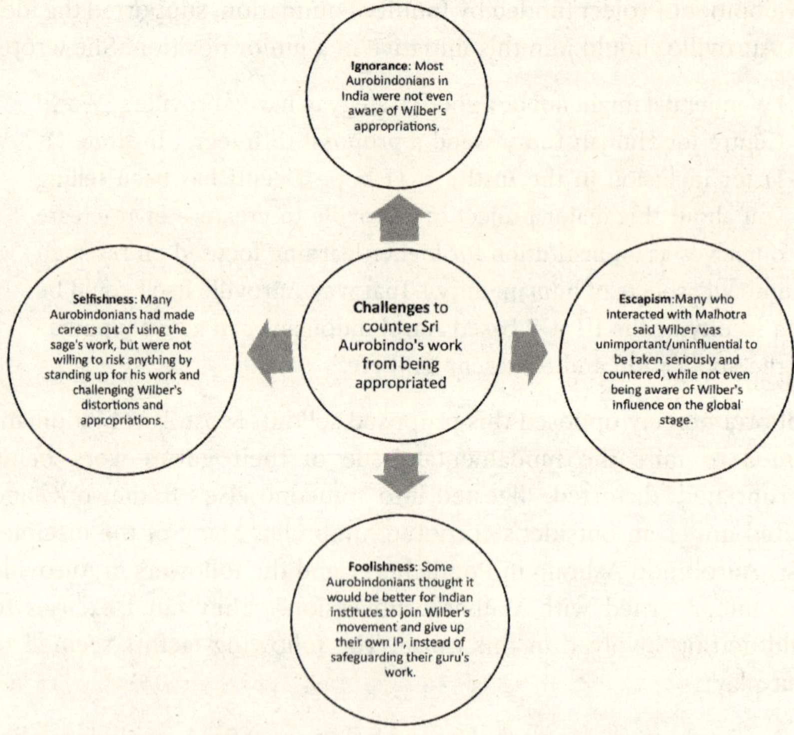


**Figure 3: Challenges to Defending Sri Aurobindo's Work**

## Auroville Talks on the Academic Crisis of Hinduism Studies

Apart from engaging with the Aurobindonian scholars online, Malhotra also began to reach out to the larger public. One of the first public engagements came during his trip to Pondicherry and Auroville in the summer of 2000. Two of his interviews appeared in local newspapers in which he criticized Western academia for sidelining Indian thought. This took the Aurobindonians by storm and led to a substantial provocation of their complacency about U-Turns and appropriations and what was then their blind adoration of Westerners like Wilber. Excerpts from Malhotra's talk and interviews are discussed.

The first is an interaction between Malhotra and an Auroville leader, Deepti. This was part of the Sri Aurobindo World Centre Talk Series.[5] Some of the key points he highlighted were the Wilberization of Sri Aurobindo studies, its implications for the movement, and the misappropriation of India's spiritual riches and heritage.

The second public engagement was a follow up Q&A and discussion in Auroville. This saw a lively exchange among Malhotra, Tapas, Bindu, Anu, Bruno, Jean Yves, Olivier, Serge, Claude, David and Bhaga. Many common explanations given on the inaction by Aurobindonians on countering Wilber and others emerged during this important exchange.

The key points of these public engagements serve as a statement of Infinity Foundation's analysis of the situation at that time. Based on Malhotra's extensive engagements and reflections, he had uncovered, crystallized and articulated all this in the year 2000. There are many novel insights herein and most are still valid today.

## Disconnect Between Philosophy, Religion, Psychology, and Social Sciences

Malhotra spoke about his discovery that Western academia has three different departments relevant to Indian thought: philosophy, religion, psychology, and maybe even medicine. This separation in the West is not merely a political turf battle but is deeply ingrained in the histories of these disciplines and their respective frameworks of knowledge. It is well known that the West has had a long history of conflict between science and religion.

Indians do not understand this important insight because there was no such split between science and religion in India. The serious implication is that Indian traditions do not fit entirely in any one of these departments and cannot be chopped up into such boundaries because they are integrated seamlessly.

The philosophy departments in the West are the most chauvinistic and place themselves on a higher pedestal than religious studies. They assert that they only allow knowledge that is about 'truth', and are dismissive of religious studies as a field that has vague standards and includes all kinds of 'beliefs' of people. They look down on religious studies as a cluster of myths, cults, esoteric practices, and odd people of all kinds. Philosophy, on the other hand, is serious work by rational minds.

To his surprise, Malhotra found that Indian philosophy was not being taught in philosophy departments at most American universities. A core reason for rejecting Indian philosophy as legitimate was (and still is to a large extent) that Western philosophers cannot accept claims of spiritual or higher states of consciousness.

Malhotra tried hard to convince philosophy departments that students should learn to think in myriad ways, not just what the Greeks and the Europeans had to say, but what Confucius, the Buddha, Vedānta *ācārya*-s, and Sri Aurobindo had to say. This would make the graduates intellectually richer. Philosophy departments, however, are like fortresses that protect their sense of superiority. According to most Western philosophers, other cultures can do art, cook food, make music, and have history, but philosophy is the cream of intellectual output and the exclusive preserve of the West.

Apart from the University of Texas in Austin and the University of Hawai'i (that houses the East-West Center, which incidentally was inaugurated by S. Radhakrishnan, the second president of India {1962-7}), no major institutions in the USA offered advanced degrees in Indian philosophy at the time. The separation between philosophy and religion in Western academics has been a serious problem for us.

Another systemic problem was that most Indian universities did not produce high-quality Ph.Ds. in Indian philosophy. It was fashionable to teach Western philosophy, and not Indian, even in mainstream Indian universities. Therefore, even though a university in the USA agreed to start a department of Indian philosophy, it was difficult to find qualified scholars with the required Western credentials yet rooted in traditional Hindu/Vedic knowledge. Judaism, Christianity, Islam and Buddhism—each had several faculty members that were both unapologetically staunch practitioners of their respective faiths and also highly qualified with Western academic credentials. The situation with Hinduism was just the opposite.

Malhotra succeeded in setting up a collaboration with the philosophy department at Rutgers University in New Jersey to hold a conference on *Quantum Physics and Eastern Philosophy*, for which Infinity Foundation gave a grant. Unfortunately, the conference mostly focused on Western philosophical frameworks, and the participants openly expressed negative attitudes towards Indian philosophy.

A more successful entry into a philosophy department was at the University of Hawai'i thanks to Arindam Chakrabarti, who at the time was a young academician combining his training under a Hindu guru with his Oxford Ph.D. that entailed a thorough grounding in Western philosophy. Infinity Foundation started a program at the University of Hawai'i that continued uninterrupted for almost eight years. It was a large and comprehensive funding for teaching courses, visiting professors and speakers, multiple annual fellowships to Ph.D. students, and specific conferences. They produced over a dozen influential lectures by some of the most prominent philosophers in the world.

There was a lot of drama at the New York City-based Columbia University when Infinity Foundation entered into a signed agreement and gave a major grant to fund a course on various philosophies of non-dualism. The scope defined was not limited to Vedic non-dualism as there are Buddhist and other non-dualisms too; the foundation also wanted to bring in Quantum Mechanics as a non-dual philosophical system. Malhotra learned a great deal from the hostile reaction coming in from Akeel Bilgrami, the chair of philosophy at Columbia and a sophisticated Muslim apologist but officially an atheist. He did not at all want the philosophy department to get involved in such a program.

The project was passed to the religion department at Columbia, where it sat for a year before Robert (Bob) Thurman, the academic and prolific author of books on Tibetan Buddhism, took responsibility for implementing a grant that had already been paid for. The course on non-duality at the undergraduate and graduate levels was extremely successful, and Malhotra participated heavily. The enthusiasm of students was mainly due to the support from White American Buddhists.

After facing stiff resistance from several such philosophy departments, Malhotra simultaneously began knocking on both doors: religious studies and philosophy departments. The religion departments were happy to receive grants to teach Hinduism and Buddhism, which is where Infinity Foundation began entering most universities. The problem, however, was that these departments are usually not qualified to teach philosophy in any depth, and Hindu-Buddhist traditions cannot be divided into separate religion and philosophy buckets.

An important area of intervention for the foundation concerned the scientific tradition built into dharma and the resulting scientific achievements in India's past. Malhotra had become a vocal critic of Western appropriators of Indian scientific knowledge, the foremost one being the John Templeton Foundation, headquartered in Pennsylvania. He wanted to bring into the academic world the notion that dharma bridges the topics included in Western notions of science as well as religion. At that time, the Templeton Foundation was starting 'science and religion' academic programs in many universities, but their approach focused on privileging Judeo-Christian frameworks. In fact, Malhotra was criticizing them for digesting Indian spiritual systems into their pseudo-Biblical frameworks.

In this context, an opportunity opened up for Infinity Foundation to introduce 'science and religion' as a course with an emphasis on dharma rather than Judeo-Christianity. This was at the University of California, Santa Barbara (UCSB), where the Buddhist physicist B. Alan Wallace was on the faculty. He had been introduced to IF by Bob Thurman. Wallace and Malhotra convinced the chair of Religious Studies at UCSB that a dharma framework would be novel and popular and differentiate UCSB from all the other places run by Templeton.

This is how Infinity Foundation funded a multi-year program for B. Alan Wallace to teach a very successful course in the UCSB Religion Department, titled *Science and Religion*. The curriculum comprised mainly Quantum Physics, Mādhyamaka Buddhism, and Vedānta. It showed Indian philosophies and dharma metaphysics related to the modern discoveries in science. The course became one of the university's most successful and popular ones.

Malhotra wanted to dig deeper and figure out why neither philosophy nor religion departments included the positive aspects of Hinduism that Westerners were busy adopting like yoga, meditation, vegetarianism, feminine spirituality, spiritual ecology, and so forth. He discovered that these had become key topics in various other departments but were not classified as having anything to do with Hinduism. For instance, psychology departments were researching yoga and meditation, but only in a secularized form. At times, they would acknowledge that the origins were in 'the East' or 'in Asia' or at best, in India. In many instances, they would digest these contributions of Hinduism into some generic framework like 'all traditions worldwide have found similar ideas and practices', and so on.

He discovered that many cutting-edge topics in psychology departments were being identified as transpersonal psychology, science of consciousness, spiritual evolution theory, human evolution potential, etc. However, he found that such ideas had been borrowed from Patañjali, Buddhism, Sri Aurobindo, Vedānta or Kāśmīrī Śaivism, and so forth. Upon confronting the Westerners teaching these established traditions as something original, privately they would often agree with him and even confess that they had learned these in India from a guru or by reading about Indian traditions.

The typical excuse extended went roughly as follows: 'We are helping the tradition by not naming it as a source because it looks more legitimate and scientific to claim that we have discovered it ourselves in the West. Westerners are accepted to be scientific and rational people. But if these ideas were presented as coming from some mystical, poor, old civilization, not many people would want to believe them. So, we are doing a favor to the tradition by repackaging its ideas and calling them our own'. Ironically, many Indians find this acceptable, and even consider it a matter of great pride to say that what they practice is of Western origin.

Malhotra found this to be unpalatable and racist and provoked him into numerous debates, both online and in person. Ironically, many Indians supported the Western view and preferred to avoid mentioning the Hindu origins of their practices. This was a serious case of an inferiority complex.

Another problem he observed in the West was the emphasis on originality: One must publish material that can be claimed as 'original'. So, it is not good enough to say that one is simply explaining Sri Aurobindo or some tradition. Many who learned under Indian teachers for decades have later distanced themselves or even started to trash their sources just to prove and claim originality.

Even when Western scholars acknowledge an Indian source, it is not established as 'knowledge' in the Western sense until one of them legitimizes it using scientific methods. For instance, the claims of an advanced meditator are not scientific, but measuring brain scans to show an empirical correlation makes it into something acceptable by a scientific journal. In essence, being able to take old traditional ideas and 'prove' them using modern empirical tests and logic is sufficient enough to claim original discovery. This is the reason why a whole lot of academic jargon is created: to allow scholars to claim they have started new thinking.

As a result, self-proclaimed intellectuals and experts such as Wilber then use such scientific 'discoveries' as the basis to once again reinforce Western frameworks and contain works of Indian guru-s such as Sri Aurobindo's as being outdated and hence superseded. Malhotra found it quite amusing that a Westerner who cannot meditate is called the discoverer because he has measured the empirical effects of meditation in a laboratory. The entire Western academic system works this way, constantly reinforcing its hegemony. Indian scholars are so inbred and living in cocoons that they are blithely unaware of all this.

Meanwhile, the advanced meditator who demonstrates this higher state of consciousness remains an unknown subject of an experiment – like a sort of rat in an experiment. In social sciences, the non-White person being studied is called the 'native informant', and the scholar using the Western methodologies to study him/her is called the social 'scientist'.

Many such instances and years of conceptual development led Malhotra to formulate his U-Turn Theory on the processes at work when Indian knowledge gets digested into the West and turned into Western Intellectual Property.

Psychology departments in the West or in India were not teaching anything that could be called Indian approaches to psychology. This led Malhotra to launch major interventions to champion the discipline of 'Indian Psychology' – a way to acknowledge Indian contributions.

He started confronting scholars of Hinduism, questioning why they did not mention or include within Hinduism topics such as yoga, Āyurveda, meditation, contributions to mathematics, science, or Sri Aurobindo's Theory of Consciousness. A common excuse put forth was that such topics are outside the scope of 'religion' per se. Malhotra understood that because such positive aspects were being removed from the branding of Hinduism and repackaged in various Western ways Hinduism was being reduced to a portrayal of meaningless rituals, social ills, and exotica. He coined the term 'caste, cows, curry' as the focus of Hinduism studies in academia.

In fact, by delving into the career backgrounds of the professors of Hinduism in Western universities, he found that the trend was those with backgrounds in anthropology and social sciences rather than philosophy. They did not emphasize the ideas or philosophy behind the religion to highlight the sensibility in the practices. The focus was mainly on social structure, the role of women, caste, the various gods and goddesses, and rituals. A student was not encouraged to understand if there was any sense in any of it. Malhotra believed that such a student would graduate with the mindset of Hinduism being very exotic, theatrical, emotional, and devoid of any sense, especially in a modern context. He discovered that Buddhism was taught with a deeper respect for its profound ideas because most teachers of Buddhism are practicing Buddhists. In the case of Hinduism, most teachers are not practicing Hindus.

He uncovered a serious double standard in teaching religion: Judeo-Christianity is taught as absolute with unique historical facts concerning what God said and the human responses. Indian traditions, however, were not premised on history-centrism. The ṛṣi-s explained the traditions as discoveries made in higher states of consciousness, discoveries that are available to every human because we are all saccidānanda. Rather than pursuing this approach to teaching Hinduism, the academics adopted social sciences lenses like anthropology, human rights, and so forth. It became trendy to use Freudian psychoanalysis with Hindu deities, guru-s, and practices as patients to be diagnosed. The professor became like a doctor detecting problems with the entire system of Hinduism.

Malhotra laments that in India there are no academic departments for religious studies. Hence, religion has been studied mainly by Leftists using their social science lenses to prove that it is abusive. This has fed the global portrayal of Hinduism. In the USA, Hindus are rarely in control of Hinduism studies, and most teachers are non-Hindu Westerners. Even when Indians with Hindu names are teaching it, they are almost always trained through the Marxist lens. The traditional guru-s are unaware of this entire deeply insidious situation and are unable to respond despite their enormous stature, credibility with the public, and unlimited resources at their disposal.

On the other hand, Buddhism is taught mostly by Whites who practice Buddhism. Buddhism is appreciated because the people who teach it have faith and pride and elucidate it from personal experience. The teaching of Hinduism, however, is by people who do not want to be known to have anything to do with it, except from a distance, like a taboo.

To study these issues, Malhotra explained that Infinity Foundation had started a new non-profit foundation, the Educational Council on Indic Traditions (ECIT). One of its goals was to challenge false stereotypes and biases against Hinduism through research, curating a massive library of evidence, and developing powerful responses. The other goal was to publish a series of books on the history of ideas that birthed from India but were not properly attributed to it.

## Disappointment: Aurobindonians' Apathy

A majority of Aurobindonians in the discussions, like most other Indians elsewhere, did not take these issues seriously. They underestimated the power of the Western academia to shape the discourse, and trivialized its impact on policies, media portrayals, school education, and eventually, personal and family lives.

During the discussions, some Aurobindonians felt that Malhotra was evangelical in trying to represent the Hindu faith aggressively, which they felt uncomfortable supporting. A typical voice said that religion was a private affair of the individual: 'I think religion is a matter of experience; it's not something academic that is codified. If you try to codify, then you will end up with fundamentalists'. Malhotra countered by clarifying that nobody including him, wanted fundamentalists to take over, and therefore, it is imperative that a fair portrayal of Hinduism is presented by actual practitioners of the religion. He made it clear that he was not asking for Sri Aurobindo to be treated without criticism but that his work must be fairly represented and discussed.

Another participant, Bruno, pointed out that since proselytization and propaganda are not native to India, it is tough for the Indic side to respond to the challenges. Malhotra agreed that this was an important point and the manner in which Hinduism was taught in India was different from the USA. He believed that in America, formal school and college education was a very powerful force in shaping values, beliefs, attitudes, and the informal, non-institutional methods of those who practice yoga, meditation, or turn vegetarian, form only about ten percent. For this minority ten percent, it doesn't matter what is taught at Harvard, but the majority of Americans get their values, beliefs, and what they consider to be the truth from the academic setting or the powerful media, which is shaped by what journalists learned in college. Therefore, tackling the issue of how Hinduism was taught at universities was paramount.

Jean Yves then offered another common explanation of the appropriation of Sri Aurobindo's works. He said that those Westerners using Sri Aurobindo's work without acknowledgment 'are not pillaging' but developing them independently. Malhotra responded that his exchanges with the Western appropriators showed they were well informed about Sri Aurobindo, and only upon probing deeply, the extent of their understanding gets exposed. And therefore, the co-opting is not unconscious.

Serge and Olivier said the situation in France was similar regarding studying Indian philosophy. The French people were open to India, but the institutions and scholars were insular – they believed that philosophy had to be Greek by definition.

Some Aurobindonians asked how they could help Infinity Foundation. Malhotra informed them of the availability of grants to show how various Western thinkers had reformulated Indian ideas as their own. He was also open to conferences and starting a chair on Sri Aurobindo studies.

Malhotra's public discussions generated interest from many voices, such as Brant Cortright (then director of the Integral Counseling Program at CIIS), who sent the following email to Malhotra:

> ... have come to a greater appreciation of what you are doing as a result of your interview in Pondicherry, ... It gave me a broader context to see what the Infinity Foundation is doing, and, since I am living in a somewhat rarified atmosphere here in San Francisco and at CIIS, a cold splash of reality about most of America and academia... I also have a revision of the chapter in my book on Ken Wilber's spectrum theory coming out in 3 or 4 months. This revision updates his positions and my critique of his model, particularly in regard to his (mis)appropriation and (mis)understanding of Sri Aurobindo... I think you might find it amusing.[6]

Malhotra's efforts gradually began to resonate with a larger audience. At least he was creating awareness on crucial issues. He was becoming non-ignorable by senior Aurobindonians and therefore, controversial.

Chapter 3

# An Initial Home Team Emerges

## CHAPTER SUMMARY

- Among the first few scholars to show interest in helping Rajiv Malhotra were Brant Cortright and Kundan Singh (CIIS), along with Matthijs Cornelissen (Pondicherry). Each of these individuals developed a distinct relationship with Infinity Foundation, and emerged as the foundation's initial home team to move forward with its agenda. Their brief backgrounds are as follows:
- **Brant Cortright** was initially interested in and supportive of engaging on the issues. He applied and received a grant from IF to attend the *International Conference on Integral Psychology* in Pondicherry in January 2001, where he delivered the *Infinity Lecture on Integral Psychology*. He referred his CIIS colleague, Stuart Sovatsky, to enter the scene and join IF's intellectual team. However, upon closer scrutiny, Malhotra and Cortright had disagreements about the place of Sri Aurobindo in the global context and he deactivated himself from this work.
- **Stuart Sovatsky** turned out to be one of the most effective and consistent scholars in helping Infinity Foundation shape its inner sciences projects over the next several years. He was sponsored by the foundation to represent it in seven conferences and seminars, both in India and the USA, where he seeded many ideas among Indian scholars very courageously.
- **Matthijs Cornelissen** proved to be a major resource to bring opportunities to Infinity Foundation for sponsoring activities and

scholars within India in Indian approaches to psychology. This helped to bring IF's five years of USA-based activities into India. In the very first email exchange he requested funding for his *International Conference on Integral Psychology* in Pondicherry in January 2001. Thereafter, IF funded him routinely for several years.

- **Kundan Singh**, a devout follower of the teachings of both Sri Aurobindo and The Mother, was a Ph.D. student at CIIS when he met Malhotra. He became an active supporter of the foundation's activities and received travel grants to three international conferences.

This chapter explains their respective roles.

During the 1990s, Rajiv Malhotra observed a pattern in the way many borrowings from India were being misappropriated and distorted by scholars from the West. He had been following their work and had attended several seminars and conferences, which helped crystallize his thoughts regarding these misappropriations. He found that many established people such as the French philosopher Pierre Teilhard de Chardin and cultural historian Thomas Berry, seemed to have borrowed ideas from Sri Aurobindo but did not attribute them to him. Malhotra wanted concrete evidence of these borrowings. It is in the backdrop of this quest that Infinity Foundation issued a call for grant proposals to write about Sri Aurobindo's contribution to the twentieth century.

## Matthijs Cornelissen

One of the Aurobindonians who responded to Infinity Foundation's call and started a lasting and fruitful relationship was Matthijs Cornelissen, a long-time resident of Sri Aurobindo Ashram, Pondicherry. He helped introduce the foundation to other Aurobindonians, brought information about events in India with funding recommendations for IF, and served as an advisor to bridge the USA-based knowledge and team of scholars that had been developed by Infinity Foundation for use in India.

Cornelissen's own position on Wilberism at the time was somewhat ambiguous, despite being director of Archives and Research Projects at the ashram and organizer of the Integral Psychology Conference of January 2001. On the one hand, he criticized Wilber's arrogant appropriation of Sri Aurobindo and wrote, '*...funny how Wilber places himself in the center of his great wheel! It is true that Wilber doesn't acknowledge anymore how much of his ideas he owes to Sri Aurobindo*' but, on the other hand, he also downplayed, and even supported, the benefits of Wilberism by suggesting, '*...to me, it doesn't matter too much, as long as the ideas are spreading. Sooner or later, those who are serious about it will find out the value of the original sources*'. Unfortunately, this 'faith' about spreading the truth is falsely placed, as is evident from the history of Western civilization's appropriations from others while subverting them in parallel.

Similarly, Cornelissen's agreement on Jung's appropriations was hedged and diplomatically managed. He charged Jung for daring to '*take credit for "discovering" the "collective unconscious" which is simply a misnomer and a rather poor conceptualization of inner worlds known since millennia in India and even in the mystical traditions of Europe*'. But he also quickly protected Jungians by adding, '*Whatever their faults may be, the Jungians are still moving in the right direction, even if not fast enough for our taste*'.[1]

Malhotra's rejoinder to this defense of Jungians was unambiguous:

> The shame is that after appropriating from Indic traditions, Jung was overcome by his cultural membership so he found himself denouncing Indic traditions. Since there was no logical complaint, he resorted to the classical 'world negating' label as the method of last resort to discourage his students from directly studying Indian material, lest they discover his appropriation. This practice is widespread today, and the new Council is meant to address that. These ... need to be rectified so that these wisdom traditions enjoy the respect they deserve, and so that persons such as you, me, Kundan [a Ph.D. student at CIIS] thousands of others no longer have to disguise their spiritual practice out of fear of ridicule.[2]

Cornelissen gave examples of U-Turns from his own experience. He cited Max Velmans, emeritus professor of psychology at Goldsmith College, University of London, who had written about a scientifically sound methodology for spiritual approaches but who '*hardly ever refers to any but Western scientists in his writings*'. Cornelissen was surprised to discover that Velmans had extensive knowledge about Sri Aurobindo's works and '*still more surprised when he explained that he fully agreed with what Sri Aurobindo says*'. However, Cornelissen defended Velmans for not acknowledging the Indian sources because this would help make these ideas scientifically credible by building them one brick at a time. Cornelissen considered this a good instance of '*those quietly spiritual people who do good work from within the system without making too much fuss about it*'.[3]

Cornelissen's position was not in agreement with Infinity Foundation's core philosophy, which was formed through its various engagements with American academia on this subject. Malhotra wrote back, '*This is also a typical explanation I hear as to why people appropriate without acknowledgment*'. To counter this, he sent the following quotes from top-level academicians in very prestigious institutions, who have no such fear of saying that 'science' includes this first-person inner science and that the Western academia was biased against teaching anything non-Western.[4] Two among these are B. Alan Wallace (expert on physics and Tibetan Buddhism) and Piet Hut (Dutch-American astrophysicist), whose views are worth sharing:

> **Modern Western academia defines science, philosophy, and religion by its own uniquely Western criteria: Anything deemed "science" must fit the modern Western criteria of third person empiricism; anything deemed "philosophy" must be similar in spirit and content to Plato, Aristotle, and the subsequent schools of Western philosophical speculation; and anything deemed a "religion" is so designated insofar as it bears characteristics similar to Christianity and Judaism.** With this ethnocentric bias, academic departments of the sciences regularly exclude any non-Western disciplines for exploring the natural world, as if the West had a monopoly on such knowledge. Specifically, psychology departments rarely include any non-Western approaches to studying the mind, despite the fact that this has been a far more central concern of rational and experiential inquiry in various non-Western cultures, especially India, than ... in Western civilization. **Academic philosophy departments regularly exclude all non-Western philosophies based on the irrational assumption that other civilizations have nothing to offer this field.** Finally, non-

> Western religions are still profoundly under-represented in many religious studies departments. In the global village that the world has become, it is absurdly parochial to continue on this ethnocentric course. The sciences, philosophies, and religions of non-Western cultures have a great deal of wisdom and knowledge to offer to modern understanding. (**B. Alan Wallace**, professor of Religion, University of California, Santa Barbara.)[5]
>
> **For the last five hundred years, Western scholarship has de-emphasized the subject pole of experience.** The almost exclusive focus on objectivity allowed science to prosper. ...the time has come to shift to a more balanced way of looking at experience. Within the Western mindset, it is difficult to address the current imbalance. Most of our received alternatives don't allow enough playing room. We are used to thinking in terms of science vs. church, ... but both the reformation and the counter-reformation shared attempts to move towards more objectivity, leaving little room for the rich contemplative traditions. Other dichotomies, such as materialism vs. idealism, tend to provide caricatures for the subject pole of experience, either as the functioning of a machine or as a solipsistic mastermind. ... science will have to come to grips with the study of the subject in the near future, using a suitable methodology. ... **Rather than trying to reinvent the wheel, it would be very useful for Westerners to pay attention to what has been achieved elsewhere - not just out of respect for others, but actually for its own interest.** (**Piet Hut**, Institute of Advanced Studies, Princeton, NJ.)[6]

Malhotra suggested that rather than Cornelissen encouraging Velmans' negation of Indian sources, one should encourage and provoke him to 'come out'. This would also be a spiritual step forward for him in terms of removing the inner contradiction and becoming free. '*The public mask is very oppressive. Getting relief from it is a big help*', he wrote.

The above exchange between Malhotra and Cornelissen demonstrated one of the classic excuses proffered by Western academics when asked to apply the same standards of attribution to ideas they accord their Western peers and ancestors versus those outside their system. There are two issues Malhotra points out above: Firstly, Western 'science' was coming to grips and opening itself to the understanding that objective, third-person empiricism alone fails to explain and account for the various phenomena of the human mind and first-person experiences, which form the bedrock of Indian yogic methods and lead the understanding of mind sciences in a far different and better manner. Acknowledging this and borrowing concepts and ideas from Eastern systems can be a wonderful experience for humanity at large when acknowledgment of the Eastern sources is made fairly as well.

Instead, the unfair practice of not crediting Indian sources was being justified by Aurobindonians under the cover of doing science and even Indic systems a favor by providing credibility to the latter. This second part is truly revealing: Indic yogic systems have existed independently as credible, and verifiable pursuits for millennia; to suggest that they need the Western stamp of approval, while in reality they are acting as sources for Western progress, is a farcical defense.

In fact, Sri Aurobindo and The Mother had themselves written about the differences between the yogic approach and the Western scientific approach, though in a manner befitting them and devoid of any insidiousness that modern Aurobindonians were condoning. The Mother has written:

**Knowledge of the Scientist and the Yogi**

> The climax of the ordinary consciousness is Science. **For Science, what is upon the earth is true, simply because it is there. What it calls Nature is for it the final reality, and its aim is to build up a theory to explain the workings of it.** So it climbs as high as the physical mind can go and tries to find out the causes of what it assumes to be the true, the real world. But in fact it adapts "causes" to "effects", for it has already taken that which is for the true, the real, and seeks only to explain it mentally. **For the yogic consciousness, however, this world is not the final reality.** Rising above the mind into the Overmind and then into the Supermind, it enters the divine world of first truths, and looking down from there sees what has happened to those truths here. How distorted they have become, how completely falsified! So the so-called world of fact is for the Yogi a falsehood and not at all the only true reality.

It is not what it ought to be, it is almost the very opposite; whereas for the scientist it is absolutely fundamental.

Our aim is to change things. **The scientist says that whatever is, is natural and cannot be changed at heart. But, really speaking, the laws of which he usually speaks are of his own mental making; and because he accepts Nature as it is as the very basis, things do not and cannot change for him in any complete sense. ... all this can be changed, because we know that there is something above, a divine truth seeking manifestation. There are no fixed laws here; even Science in its undogmatic moments recognises that the laws are mere mental constructions.** There are only cases, and if the mind could apply itself to all the circumstances it would find that no two cases are similar. Laws are for the mind's convenience, but the process of supramental manifestation is different, we may even say it is the reverse of the mind. In the supramental realisation, each thing will carry in itself a truth which will manifest at each instant without being bound by what has been or what will follow. That elaborate linking of the past with the present, which gives things in Nature such an air of unchangeable determinism is altogether the mind's way of conceiving and is no proof that all that exists is inevitable and cannot be otherwise.

The knowledge possessed by the Yogi is also an answer to the terrible theory that all that takes place is God's direct working. For once you rise to the Supermind you immediately perceive that the world is false and distorted. The supramental truth has not at all found manifestation. How then can the world be a genuine expression of the Divine? Only when the Supermind is established and rules here, then alone the Supreme Will may be said to have authentically manifested. ...**we must steer clear of the dangerous exaggeration of the sense of the falsehood of the world, which comes to those who have risen to the higher consciousness.**[7]

## Brant Cortright

As mentioned earlier, another Aurobindonian who responded to Infinity Foundation's provocations and grant offers was Brant Cortright, director of the Integral Counseling Psychology Program at CIIS. Matthijs Cornelissen introduced him to Infinity Foundation.

Malhotra wrote to Cortright in May 2000, introducing himself and IF and, in particular, his work on Wilber's appropriations and distortions of Sri Aurobindo's oeuvre. Cortright responded that he was aware of how Wilber was demonstrating poor scholarship in his work:

> I can understand your suspicion around how Sri Aurobindo's teachings will be used. I myself feel very critical of Wilber's works and how Aurobindo's ideas have been incorporated into them without proper referencing. ... A careful reading of Wilber shows, ... that he oftentimes references more to obscure and conceal than to reveal his sources. He is not the only writer I know of who does this, but that does not make it any more acceptable. **Ripping off Aurobindo and giving merely a nod or tip of the hat rather than disclosing the deep influence he has had is shoddy scholarship.** ...This is not my intention. ...**I personally think that Wilber does not really "get" Aurobindo or the profundity of his teachings.** I can say more about this at some other time.
>
> I do not want to get off track by going too far into Wilber, ... In my previous book I criticized Wilber's central ideas. Wilber's book after that changed the key area I critiqued but tried to cover his tracks by claiming he had really thought this for some time. No one I have talked to who is knowledgeable about Wilber actually believed this ruse, but for most of the public it worked. For this and for other reasons that I need not detail here, I am not interested in a project which involves a collaboration with Wilber. I simply do not trust his personal or professional integrity.

Malhotra raised another important issue: the connections between the work of Sri Aurobindo and his contemporary, Teilhard de Chardin. While Cortright could not offer any particular references on the matter, he acknowledged the huge amount of work on Malhotra's plate in countering Wilber. Cortright also found Malhotra's U-Turn Theory interesting.

> Your question about the psychological motivations for why writers and scholars disavow the sources of their intellectual and spiritual

> inspiration ... why they then turn on these sources and attack them, is a profound question. I have often thought of this question in terms of movements, less so in terms of individuals.
>
> You have a considerable challenge on your hands. The powers that be in straight academia have a considerable narcissistic investment in their current knowledge base. Anything as powerful and profound as Vedantic wisdom is bound to be a significant threat, unless it is, as you say, pigeonholed and circumscribed and made peripheral. ...what you are doing is extremely important and essential.[8]

However, Cortright's defense of Thomas Berry, a prominent Christian theologian, deserves closer examination. He remarked, '*Thomas Berry not only is aware of Aurobindo but holds him in high esteem. In a book he wrote called* ***The Religions of India****, he hails Aurobindo as one of the most outstanding of India's thinkers who produced some of the most significant theological writings in Indian history*'.[9]

This was an unacceptable defense of Thomas Berry, or anyone else for that matter, if the basis was that he praised some Indian thinker, especially if the praise of greatness is relative *to* other Indians. It is deceptive and condescending for Westerners to praise an Indian's greatness among other Indians. Wilber, too, has praised Sri Aurobindo as one of India's greatest minds, and most Aurobindonians have failed to see this sleight of hand in protecting the West's claim of universalism while relativizing others' greatness. In the case of Berry's work, he has also been a digester, but that is discussed in a future work.

## Kundan Singh

Malhotra first corresponded with Kundan Singh in June 2000, when the latter was pursuing his Ph.D. in East-West Psychology at CIIS and had completed his first semester. This turned into a fruitful long-term collaboration.

Malhotra was looking for speakers that the Infinity Foundation could sponsor for the Integral Psychology conference in Pondicherry in 2001. Cornelissen referred to Kundan Singh as a potential candidate. Malhotra's main ask was that the selected candidate must possess the ability to contribute in an impactful way through serious scholarship. He was full of ideas on how Sri Aurobindo studies could be elevated and was looking for a candidate to join forces on it.

During the initial exchange, Kundan Singh sent across two of his papers: *Postmodernism and Beyond: The Meeting of East and West* and *Ramakrishna: The Initiator of Integral Yoga*. The first was written for CIIS as part of his application for admission. It outlined the basic ideas he intended to develop fully during his Ph.D. dissertation. The second paper was written more recently while fulfilling the requirement for a course on Integral Psychology he had taken at CIIS.

The exchange between Malhotra and Singh continued on a regular frequency. Singh became part of the Yahoo e-group, where Malhotra actively published articles on the state of Indic studies. Malhotra took a keen interest in nurturing Singh's work and encouraged him to understand the entire appropriation taking place of Sri Aurobindo's core oeuvre by Wilber. Singh started to actively engage on the matter with fellow scholars in the e-group.

### *Grants from Infinity Foundation*

In September 2000, Singh applied for a travel grant from Infinity Foundation in order to present the paper titled *Postmodernism and Beyond: The Meeting of East and West* – at the Integral Psychology conference. A grant of fifteen hundred dollars was given to CIIS for this explicit purpose. In fact, IF also wished to sponsor two candidates from CIIS for the conference and funded the travel of the second candidate as well.

After the conference, Singh wrote an enthusiastic mail to Malhotra in February 2001, thanking him for the travel grant. He mentioned that the conference had been a huge success and his paper had been very well received. He then sent across a short report of the conference to Infinity Foundation's archives.

During this period, Malhotra continued to engage with CIIS more deeply, meeting the then president of the institute, Joseph Subbiondo in San Francisco. Singh, meanwhile, attended the All-USA Meeting (AUM) 2001, an annual conference dedicated to discussing the work of Sri Aurobindo and The Mother in the USA and beyond.

In September 2001, Singh wrote to Malhotra, applying for a travel grant to attend the IIT Kharagpur conference to present a new paper. Infinity Foundation issued the grant to CIIS for use in this purpose.

### *Work on Wilber*

Throughout 2000-1, Singh continued sharing his work on psychology, and Malhotra encouraged him with feedback and conference travel grants.

Singh was also interacting with other Aurobindonians, including Suneet Varma of the University of Delhi and also those involved with The Gnostic Centre in Gurugram, Haryana, which was committed to introducing consciousness studies in Indian academia; Singh was helping formulate courses and syllabi. He successfully requested a travel grant from Infinity Foundation for another conference in Pondicherry on Indian Psychology. He also wanted to write a piece on Sri Aurobindo's Thoughts on Indian Culture to post on the Indic Traditions e-group and use it to counter the moronic responses Malhotra received from most Indians when he approached them regarding the need for defending it.

Meanwhile, Malhotra had been delving deeper into Wilber's appropriations and documenting the change in his work during each of his phases. As formulated in the stages of the U-Turn Theory, Wilber had now ceased referring to Sri Aurobindo with any acknowledgment and relegated him to a mere footnote in his works. Malhotra was keen on a systematic and extensive study of Wilber's works to compare and study the roots and shaping of his ideas. Singh wrote to Malhotra:

> I am getting some wonderful insights from reading Wilber with a fresh pair of lens. One of the things that struck me was his very linear, and consequently limited, understanding of the human evolution. ... Sri Aurobindo sees evolution happening in rhythms and cycles, and not in a linear fashion. Once we take the latter perspective into account, the western world does not remain the sole harbinger of civilization—many others have contributed powerfully, significantly and profoundly. Wilber is very Eurocentric, and perhaps that is the reason that he is finding so much favor with the West...
>
> ... Wilber can be totally demolished from Sri Aurobindo's perspective. His limited understanding of postmodernity makes

> my task even simpler—there too he adopts a very linear approach. Postmodernity will help in a vertical and a horizontal expansion of universal consciousness—according to Sri Aurobindo, this time it will not be limited to the East alone, which was conquered by the barbaric West as a result of the reversal of consciousness that the Nature decided to bring about.[10]

Indra Sen (1903-94; a devout follower of Sri Aurobindo and The Mother, psychologist, and author) had, in fact, coined the term *Integral Psychology* in the 1940s and subsequently authored a major book with that title much before Wilber patented the term under his name. Aster Patel had become a resident of Auroville at that point and was very supportive of the comparative work Infinity Foundation had undertaken between Sri Aurobindo and Wilber. She introduced Singh to Kireet Joshi, chairman of both the Rashtriya Ved Vidya Pratishthan and the Auroville Trust.

In 2003, Singh became the chief coordinator for the Third International Conference on Integral Psychology at CIIS.[11] The conference saw participation from important Aurobindonians including Brant Cortright, Matthijs Cornelissen, and Suneet Varma amongst others.

## Other Aurobindonians

One of the scholars who initially appeared promising was Dennis Hargiss, introduced to Malhotra by Julian Lines. Hargiss had many months of meetings and email exchanges with Malhotra which showed considerable resonance. Hargiss was a teaching assistant at Harvard, in tune with Sri Aurobindo's writings, and possessed an innate ability to quote extensively from his works. He entered into a prolonged engagement with IF on various proposed projects. He was invited by IF to attend the 2001 conference in Pondicherry and also participated in meetings of scholars at Columbia University to plan the Indic Colloquium organized jointly by Infinity Foundation and Columbia.

Hargiss had introduced Malhotra to John Carman of Harvard, one of the best-known scholars of Hinduism in academia. The two spent many hours together on a train journey from Boston to New Jersey as the retired professor was on his way to Washington, D.C. During the course of this conversation, he made two remarks that left a lasting impact on Malhotra's thinking:

1. Carman stated that post-retirement he wished to return to his family's third-generation Christian evangelical missionary in south India. It was a shocker coming from a scholar regarded as the preeminent expert on Hinduism studies, especially Śrī Rāmānujācārya, and the mentor and teacher of the American scholar, Vasudha Narayanan and many others in power. Malhotra had naïvely assumed that teaching and researching Hinduism was a labor of love and never presumed other dimensions and drivers behind one's lifelong pursuit of it.
2. Carman stated confidently that while Non-Resident Indians had bright kids that went to college, 'you lose them once they leave home'. He explained that he and other Westerners teaching our kids had greater impact on their minds because they were away from home for four years and had a chance to rethink and re-evaluate their ideas about Hinduism and their parents' traditions. He also stated with authority that he and others in similar positions understood our kids better than most parents did.

Malhotra explored the idea with Hargiss to use the latter's Harvard contacts and organize a conference on *Indic Contributions to Modern Psychology*. It would include the variety of topics Infinity Foundation had identified for its book projects. The intent was to invite established voices on various topics related to India's contributions to Western thought, including opponents like Wilber. Harvard was to be given a grant by Infinity Foundation for the conference. Malhotra wrote:

> Let's organize a conference at Harvard around Sept 2001 on 'Indic Contributions to Modern Psychology'. Included would be the variety of Topics listed in my earlier email for the book project. We would invite all the big names to this conference associated with these topics, including Wilber, Sheldrake, Carolyn Myss, Deepak Chopra, Paul Ortega-Muller (Kashmir Shaivism), someone from TM, Kirit (sic) Joshi, each of you; some Jungian historian; Transpersonal/Humanistic psychology historian scholar;

> Joe Liozzo (Columbia – Buddhism); Reiki scholar; Dream Yoga scholar Stephen Laberge; and many more. Those who don't want to show up, say Wilber, because they are not at the center of the show, would be substituted by someone else to position/critique their work in their absence. For the majors, there would also be a panel to discuss their work in light of prior Indic ideas, letting this forum reveal sources, similarities etc. Infinity Foundation could give a grant to sponsor this.[12]

The conference ran into roadblocks at Harvard and did not materialize. Also, Malhotra got a sense that Hargiss was going through a personal U-Turn back into liberal Christianity and that Hargiss and his female colleague were skilled at speaking both languages: the very Indian language seeped in *Savitri* and other thoughts of Sri Aurobindo, and his deep-rooted Christianity. Their approaches and trajectories fit a sort of U-Turn and appropriation from Indian traditions mapped onto Western thought. This was not obvious at first and surfaced only after months of in-depth discussions and provocations.

Another Aurobindonian with whom Malhotra collaborated was the American Aurobindonian, Alan Sasha Lithman. He came to India in 1969 motivated by the works of Sri Aurobindo to meet The Mother, from whom he received the name 'Savitra'. Lithman initially stayed at Sri Aurobindo Ashram, then moved to Auroville, where he lived for twenty years, starting in 1970, after which he relocated back to the USA. He authored the first book on Auroville in 1980, *Auroville: Sun-Word Rising (A Trust for the Earth)*. In 1971, The Mother encouraged him to begin a bridge-building process with the USA. His outreach activities helped jump-start Auroville's reforestation program.

After Lithman's return to the USA in 1990, he wrote *The Savitri Legend: A Transformational Tale* and was working on his new book, *An Evolutionary Agenda for the Third Millennium: A Primer for the Mutation of Consciousness*, when he met Malhotra. Malhotra corresponded via email with him for several months, culminating in Infinity Foundation giving him a grant to write his book, which was published in 2003. The book credits Sri Aurobindo to a large extent. It became an important influence on several American thinkers of consciousness studies, but his readers have fully digested it into something Western with no credit to

Sri Aurobindo or anything Indian. Lithman, being a devout follower of Sri Aurobindo and The Mother and having lived in Auroville for two decades, has not championed Infinity Foundation's campaign to push back against the misappropriations by Wilber.

An Aurobindonian who has always been aligned with Malhotra's battles to protect the integrity of Sri Aurobindo's teachings is Anand Reddy. He is director at the Sri Aurobindo Centre for Advanced Research (SACAR) in Pondicherry, and very loyal to the sage's vision. Malhotra had several fruitful interactions with him and Infinity Foundation provided SACAR a grant for holding the second meeting of the core-group for Indian Psychology in 2004.

Chapter 4

# Reclaiming Integral Psychology

## CHAPTER SUMMARY

- Infinity Foundation provided sponsorship and strategic advice for the *International Conference on Indian Psychology* held at Pondicherry in 2001 under the leadership of Matthijs Cornelissen.
- Brant Cortright delivered ***The Infinity Lecture on Integral Psychology*** at the conference. The phrase *Integral Psychology* was selected by Infinity Foundation specifically to challenge Wilber's claim of copyright of the term.
- Several Pondicherry/Auroville residents had become supporters, and/or fearful, of Ken Wilber and were *against* using the term *Integral Psychology* for the conference as Wilber had appropriated and copyrighted it. However, Infinity Foundation argued successfully that the term must be preserved and not conceded to Wilber.
- The conference was a huge success, with opportunities opening up for Cornelissen to take forward Integral Psychology from the environs of only the sādhaka-s to academia and university departments.
- During the conference, Malhotra observed that amidst all the discussions, there was barely any mention of the mechanisms already present in Indian traditions to build healthy egos and manage inner psychology positively. Despite Sri Aurobindo himself having written extensively on the matter, Aurobindonians were not drawing from his material and its relevance in contemporary times.

- Malhotra proposed a series of books that would counter the world-negating image gifted to India by Western academics and unfortunately, reinforced by Indian scholars. The proposed books and conferences centered around Indic influences on modern psychology, spiritual thought, and the emerging worldview. Stuart Sovatsky sent in his proposal based on similar themes as well.

## Fighting for the Term *Integral Psychology*

In May 2000, Cornelissen requested Infinity Foundation's financial and intellectual help for a conference scheduled for January 2001 in Pondicherry, which aimed at bridging Sri Aurobindo's work and the science of psychology. Infinity promptly offered funding along with strategic advice and publicized it widely among its contacts.

Having seen Indian psychology being discounted and discredited by the West as a whole, Malhotra suggested that Cornelissen should broaden the scope of the conference by making it an annual event including themes beyond psychology such as human evolution and spirituality, and publishing a journal or conference proceedings.[1] Cornelissen, however, explained that his focus at the time was limited to Sri Aurobindo and that he was disinterested in wider Indian psychology.[2] He appreciated the fact that the foundation was supporting scholars generously and requested extending the funding to Brant Cortright as well as the American psychologist Bahman A.K. Shirazi, dean of the School of Consciousness and Transformation at CIIS.

Cortright was delighted to be selected to deliver the ***Infinity Lecture on Integral Psychology***: 'I appreciate your positive response to the grant request. I am really excited at the prospect of going to India (where I have always wanted to go) and to Pondicherry (which is the part of India I most want to visit). To be able to do this as part of my work is a great gift, and I sincerely thank you for it'.[3]

A major victory for Indian psychology came about even before the events of the conference, i.e. the fight over the term ***Integral Psychology***. The term had been developed by Sri Aurobindo's devotees decades ago and was the title of at least one prominent book by Indra Sen, a sādhaka of the ashram.[4] Yet, Wilber had copyrighted it and announced his plan to centrally control *Integral Psychology.* Malhotra was the first to voice his dissent at that time. It was so important to him that he decided to visit Pondicherry and Auroville to spread awareness and generate support from Aurobindonians. He chose *Integral Psychology* as the title of the conference specifically to challenge Wilber's claim of copyrighting it.

Throughout the planning phase of the conference in 2000, Malhotra had intense online debates with Aurobindonians about the dangers of selling out to Wilber; a specific debate centered around ownership of this term. Several Pondicherry/Auroville residents had become supporters, and/or fearful, of Wilber and were *against* using the term *Integral Psychology* for the conference, wanting to concede it to him.

The fears among Aurobindonians that Wilber might have legal ownership of *Integral Psychology* proved to be unfounded. On the contrary, Malhotra's firm defiance of Wilber's misappropriation made many other Aurobindonians bolder in their assertiveness on behalf of Indic traditions. For instance Shirazi, while discussing the various methodological approaches at the conference, compared the works of Indra Sen, Ken Wilber, and Haridas Chaudhuri and criticized Wilber for juxtaposing many different philosophical and psychological systems. He described Wilberism as one grand map that was unnecessarily complex, as well as of limited use.

## International Conference on Integral Psychology in Pondicherry, 2001[5]

Infinity Foundation played a key role in shaping this pivotal event, providing intellectual and political support against Wilberism and nurturing key issues via its online forums. It also provided the largest amount of funding through the sponsorship of foreign scholars, including Kundan Singh and Brant Cortright amongst others.

Post the event, Cornelissen was euphoric and considered the conference a major turning point in bridging global scientific (academic) psychology and Sri Aurobindo's thought. He expressed his gratitude to Infinity Foundation for its funding and support.[6] The event also built his personal credibility, and he began championing Infinity Foundation's vision and offering advice in this area. His edited volume of papers from the conference titled *Consciousness and its Transformation* was funded by Infinity Foundation. In addition, the conference also led to two universities in India to introduce *Integral Psychology* as part of their curriculum:

> One of the immediate outcomes of the Integral Psychology conference has been a very encouraging interest from a few Indian Universities. Two psychology professors at universities in South India, who attended the conference, have invited me to give workshops for their students. They seem to be eager to **introduce a full Integral Psychology course at least in their own universities...**this could start **on a trial basis within a year... Even the Sri Aurobindo International Centre of Education (the Ashram school/college) has suddenly shown interest to start an Integral Psychology course**, so I may teach there next year and use that as another testing ground. This in itself might be **a sign of a major revolution, given the symbolic nature of much of what happens in the Ashram and Auroville.**[7]

This was a historic event to bring Indian psychology into Indian academia: from only 5 academic scholars in attendance, the movement which went onto include Indian Psychology, grew to 120 at the next conference held in 2002.

On the surface, Cortright's delivery of the ***Infinity Foundation Lecture*** on Sri Aurobindo's work described him as the greatest psychologist the world has ever known. Scratching beneath this compliment, however, one uncovers Cortright's tendency to contain Sri Aurobindo by making his system dependent upon Western thought. This, in effect, potentially legitimizes Wilber's claim of superseding Sri Aurobindo.

According to Cortright, Integral Psychology is born when we fuse Sri Aurobindo's teachings with the findings of depth psychology, the latter being the European ingredient necessary to make Sri Aurobindo's system work. His reasoning was that until a healthy ego has been formed, the chances of spiritual bypassing (a condition where one uses spiritual ideas to avoid confronting one's psychological issues) are very strong. Implicit in this statement is the assumption that Indian traditions lack the resources to develop a healthy ego. Malhotra had for long been refuting this Western bias.

To underscore the necessity of Western psychology, Cortright explained the limits inherent in Sri Aurobindo's thoughts: 'Psychotherapy is a type of vital discipline Sri Aurobindo and the (sic) Mother did not have access to, because it is only in the past 20 or 30 years that psychotherapy has come of age as a mature and effective discipline'. In support of Cortright's position, the psychiatrist Alok Pandey suggested that for practitioners of yoga, psychotherapy should become part of sādhana.

Michael Miovic, a Harvard-based psychiatrist, took a position aligned with that of Malhotra's saying that Sri Aurobindo emphasized the proper formation of the ego before a yogic discipline was undertaken to transcend the ego.

Kundan Singh stated that postmodernism deconstructs itself by turning its very arguments on itself. He asserted that postmodernism, which is feared by many as nihilistic in nature, is a very potent force that is leading us into the next stage of evolution, where the inquiry into the nature of reality will be made using a mystical mode. However, Malhotra has cautioned against this: While in theory such a deconstruction opens new creative possibilities, in practice these deconstructions are one-sided and heavily invested in targeting Indian civilization. Though the West is also being deconstructed, that is countered by powerful voices asserting Western frameworks. In the case of India, however, the counter voices speaking on its behalf are relatively feeble. In other words, postmodernism does not dismantle all the old structures equally; certain structures are protected while others are dismantled. Postmodernism is a weapon being used by those in power.

## Defending Positive Psychology in Indian Systems

Malhotra responded to Cortright's core thesis by explaining that Indian thought greatly emphasized processes to achieve the sāttvic life and thus produce a healthy ego. He believed that the scholars at the conference seemed to ignore the vast range of theories and practices embedded in Indian traditions intended to create healthy egos through empowerment and positive psychological management. In fact, Sri Aurobindo himself had written extensively on these topics in correspondence with individual sādhaka-s and in his essays.[8]

Wilber (like many other Western scholars before him) held a deep bias that India did not have frameworks for first-, second-, and third-person perspectives in studying consciousness. These scholars maintain that while India has tools for first-person analysis, i.e. meditation and theories of selfhood, it lacks frameworks for second- and third-person perspectives of the external world. The sheer repetition of this maxim by scholars had ignored the incisive structures India had built on second- and third-person approaches.

Given the fundamental unity of all existence, Indian systems have studied and pursued to perfection all aspects of humanity and the outer world. The first-, second-, and third-person perspectives are seen through the puruṣārtha system, as explained by Sri Aurobindo extensively in many of his works. He actively and explicitly denied the charge that India only had mechanisms for the first-person lens:

> **Equally is it a misrepresentation to say that Indian culture denies all value to life, detaches from terrestrial interests and insists on the unimportance of the life of the moment. To read these European comments one would imagine that in all Indian thought there was nothing but the nihilistic school** of Buddhism and the monistic illusionism of Shankara and that all Indian art, literature and social thinking were nothing but the statement of their recoil from the falsehood and vanity of things. It does not follow that because these things are what the average European has heard about India or what most interests or strikes the European scholar in her thought, therefore they are, however great may have been their influence, the whole of Indian thinking. **The ancient civilisation of India founded itself very expressly upon four human interests; first, desire and enjoyment, next, material, economic and other aims and needs of the mind and body, thirdly, ethical conduct and the right law of individual and social life, and, lastly spiritual liberation; kāma, artha, dharma, mokṣa. The business of culture and social organisation was to lead, to satisfy, to support these things in man and to build some harmony of their forms and motives. Except in very rare cases the satisfaction of the three mundane objects must run before the other; fullness of life must precede the surpassing of life.**

> The debt to the family, the community and the gods could not be scamped; earth must have her due and the relative its play, even if beyond it there was the glory of heaven or the peace of the Absolute. **There was no preaching of a general rush to the cave and the hermitage.**[9]

Most Western scholars like Wilber fail to recognize that yoga is not āsana and prāṇāyāma alone but a complex and holistic endeavor to create a powerful and healthy individual that can manifest good for himself/herself and society as a whole. Regimens encompassing healthy eating and choices such as a sāttvic lifestyle aim to bring the benefits of discipline and compassion for fellow beings while combining remarkable scientific knowledge and were explored to their fullest in Āyurveda.

Indian understanding of human psychology was so deeply penetrative that it designed comprehensive sub-structures to accommodate, refine, and elevate all pursuits. *Chanting of mantra*-s is a prime example of invoking higher states of consciousness under the training of the right guru, and manifesting physically specific intentions. The pursuits of rituals, dance, music, and art are all sacred ways of first-person inquiries and spiritual transformation in India and differ from the desacralized performing arts of the West.[10] Sri Aurobindo wrote on this in 1910, that while there can be several approaches to art across cultures of the world, for art to be a spiritual tool of sādhana, the Indian approach must prevail:

> ...Spirituality is a wider thing than formal religion and it is in the service of spirituality that Art reaches its highest self-expression. Spirituality is a single word expressive of three lines of human aspiration towards divine knowledge, divine love and joy, divine strength, and that will be the highest and most perfect Art, which, while satisfying the physical requirements of the aesthetic sense, the laws of formal beauty, the emotional demand of humanity, the portrayal of life and outward reality, as the best European Art satisfies these requirements, reaches beyond them and expresses inner spiritual truth, the deeper not obvious reality of things, the joy of God in the world and its beauty and desirability and the manifestation of divine force and energy in phenomenal creation. **This is what Indian Art alone attempted thoroughly and in the**

> **effort it often dispensed, either deliberately or from impatience, with the lower, yet not negligible perfections which the more material European demanded. Therefore Art has flowed in two separate streams in Europe and Asia, so diverse that it is only now that the European aesthetic sense has so far trained itself as to begin to appreciate the artistic convention, aims and traditions of Asia. Asia's future development will unite these two streams in one deep and grandiose flood of artistic self-expression perfecting the aesthetic evolution of humanity. But if Art is to reach towards the highest, the Indian tendency must dominate.**[11]

The Indian second-person processes are rich in one's engagement with other beings, not just humans but all living creatures. The system of Tantra is essentially a second-person approach to spiritual advancement through sensory engagements in a disciplined manner. Interpersonal relationships with family, guru-s, and even deities are examples of strong second-person frameworks. These are integral to Indian spirituality and even have specific saṃskāra-s associated with them such as the ones shown in the following figure.[12] This system is unique to India, based on native structures, and aims to elevate human interactions to their highest potential.

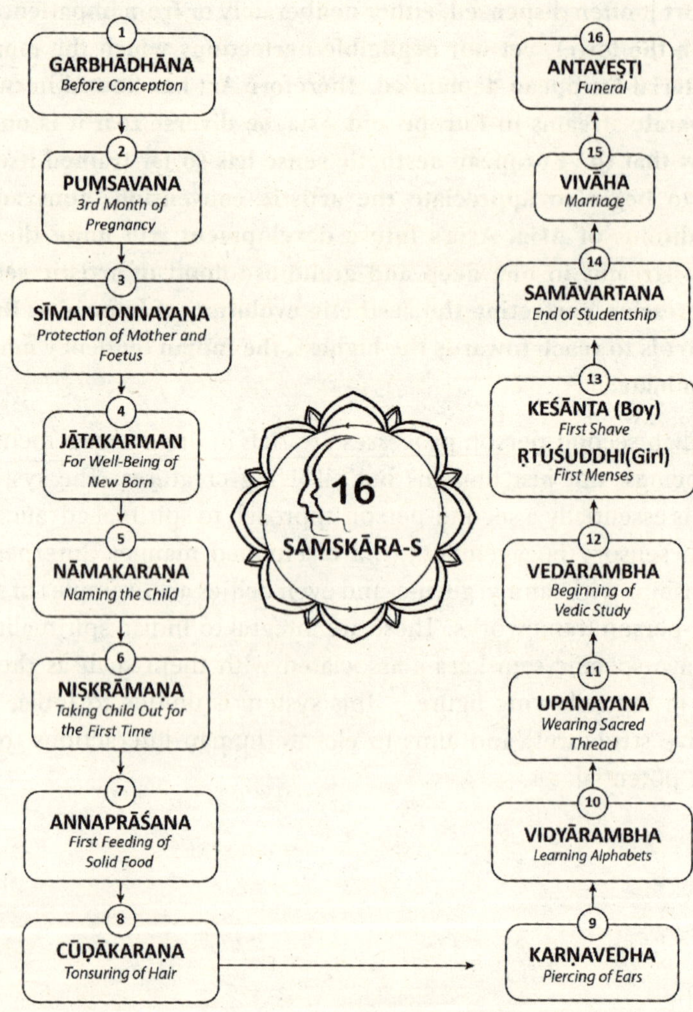


**Figure 4: Sixteen Saṃskāra-s**

Since all existence is a divine manifestation, all third-person concepts, objects, and knowledge are ultimately sacred. This includes all postures towards nature, the cosmos, other creatures, society, politics, and in fact, everything out there. All Indian knowledge systems are third-person domains and are integrally unified with first- and second-person approaches: literature, philosophies, ethics, law, politics, social justice, the sciences, the arts and crafts. Sri Aurobindo writes:

> **The symmetric character of ancient Indian life and the vivid variety of its literature were inconsistent with any exclusive other-worldly direction. The great mass of Sanskrit literature is a literature of human life**; certain philosophic and religious writings are devoted to the withdrawal from it, but even these are not as a rule contemptuous of its value. If the Indian mind gave the highest importance to a spiritual release, and whatever the positivist mood may say, a spiritual liberation of some kind is the highest possibility of the human spirit, it was not interested in that alone. **It looked equally at ethics, law, politics, society, the sciences, the arts and crafts, everything that appertains to human life. It thought on these things deeply and scrutinisingly and it wrote of them with power and knowledge.** What a fine monument of political and administrative genius is the Śukra-Nīti, to take one example only, and what a mirror of the practical organization of a great civilized people! ... **The documents which prove these things are now available to anyone who cares to study. It is time that this parrot talk about the unpractical, metaphysical, quietistic, anti-vital character of Indian civilisation should cease and give place to a true and understanding estimate.**[13]

Malhotra found that scholars seemed to have accepted Western limitations and distortions in interpreting Indian traditions. One could argue that Indian systems of psychology include a richer repertoire of first-, second-, and third-person resources, both (i) to recover healthy egos; and (ii) to positively develop these into higher states of consciousness. One must debate the very definition of what constitutes a healthy ego – the West's 'freedom-to' must be contrasted with India's balance between 'freedom-to' and 'freedom-from'.

The strategy to glorify the other-worldliness and world-negation of Indian thought has been achieved by focusing solely on the goal of mokṣa as the be-all and end-all of Indian traditions. This results from the projection of the 'one life only' theology of the Abrahamic religions and is based on ignorance of the real meaning of mokṣa over multiple rebirths. The limited 'one life only' notion of the West naturally has spawned solutions of desperation and greed to bring 'the good life' to a mundane level. Under this Hegelian (named after the German philosopher Georg

Hegel) scheme of 'progress', they portray that Indian civilization should be grateful for the opportunity to escape from its misery by accepting the solutions of the West. Infinity Foundation's twenty-volume series, the *History of Indian Science and Technology*, was inspired precisely by the need to counter the false historiographies of Indian civilization as being primitive and not pragmatic.

On understanding this point, the enormous harm done by anthropological and social studies of India using Western sponsorship, funding, models, etc., – i.e. the 'caste, cows, curry, dowry' theories of India – become clearer. These serve to block out the precious insights into what Indian civilization has to offer the world at large and protect the controlling status quo of vested interests.

## Patañjali's Positive Yoga Philosophy

Patañjali's yoga philosophy offers further examples. This philosophy is not based upon mere theoretical, speculative, or inferential knowledge. Instead, it is an empirical, pragmatic, and experiential approach to the whole human condition and not an escapist or other-worldly outlook. It is not content with philosophy that is disconnected from our human embodiment and worldly activity. Its purpose is the integration of one's being with action in this world. The word 'yoga' itself means making whole – wholeness of the practitioner and wholeness of his/her relationship with the world. It starts with a precise diagnosis of the various psychological afflictions (*kleśa*-s) and ignorance (*avidyā*) that give rise to malfunctioning or misalignment of the mind.

While yoga does involve a temporary cessation of the mind in order to cleanse it of false identifications, cravings, and selfishness, what actually 'dissolves' is the locus of misidentification, confusion, and dissatisfaction. The state of *kaivalya* (often translated as aloneness) in no way destroys or negates the personality of the yogin but leads to embodied freedom as *jīvanmukta* (liberated while still in the body).

Hence, it is misleading to conclude that it leads to an incapacitated, isolated, or mindless state of inactivity or amoral activity. Besides individual fulfillment, the 'eight-limbed' path (*aṣṭāṅga*-yoga) emphasizes organic continuity, balance, and integration with the world.

Ian Whicher, an academic scholar specializing in the study of yoga and a grant recipient from Infinity Foundation, explains that yoga, as taught by Patañjali and now practiced by tens of millions of Westerners, is indeed a world-affirming way of life. In his paper titled *Countering World-Negation: The World Affirming and Integrative Dimension of Classical Yoga*, he writes:

> Classical Yoga acknowledges the intrinsic value of "support" and "sustenance" and the interdependence of all living (embodied) entities, thus upholding organic continuity, balance, and integration within the natural and social world...The yogin perceives the natural order (ṛta) of cosmic existence, "unites" with, and embodies that order. To fail to see clearly is to fall into disorder, disharmony, and conflict with oneself and the world. To be ensconced in ignorance implies disunion with the natural order of life and inextricably results in a failure to embody that order. Through Yoga one gains proper access to the world and is therefore established in right relationship to the world. Far from being denied or renounced, the world, for the yogin, has become transformed, properly engaged.[14]

Being detached from the ego's fruits of action does not imply the inability to act effectively. Actions must also be ethically sound, reasonable, and justifiable. Yogic morality is not out of obedience to an externally policed code of conduct (as the Western systems have been from the Bible to the European Enlightenment movement), but as an intrinsic response from one's sāttvic nature. Whicher writes:

> The yogin's spiritual journey – far from being an "a-moral process" – is a highly moral process! The yogin's commitment to the sattvification of consciousness, including the cultivation of moral virtues such as compassion (karuṇā) and nonviolence (ahiṃsā), is not an "a-moral" enterprise, nor is it an expression of indifference, aloofness, or an uncaring attitude to others. Moral disciplines are engaged as a natural outgrowth of intelligent (sattvic) self-understanding, insight, and commitment to self-transcendence that takes consciousness out of its identification with the rigid structure of the monadic ego, thereby reversing the inveterate tendency of this ego to inflate itself at the expense of its responsibility in relation to others.[15]

Rather than turning the person into a zombie or imbecile incapable of acting positively, the person liberated from shortsightedness and narrow-mindedness becomes far more capable of engaging the world affirmatively and with confidence. Whicher continues:

> Yoga does not destroy or anesthetize our feelings and emotions thereby encouraging neglect and indifference toward others. On the contrary, the process of 'cessation' (nirodha) steadies one for a life of compassion, discernment, and service informed by a 'seeing' that is able to understand (literally meaning 'to stand among, hence observe') – and is in touch with – the needs of others. What seems especially relevant for our understanding of Yoga ethics is the enhanced capacity generated in Yoga for empathic identification with the object one seeks to understand. This is a far cry from the portrayal of the yogin as a disengaged figure, psychologically and physically removed from the human relational sphere, who in an obstinate and obtrusive fashion severs all ties with the world...In Yoga philosophy "seeing" is not only a cognitive term but implies purity of mind, that is, it has moral content and value. Nor is knowledge (jñāna, vidyā) in the Yoga tradition to be misconstrued as a 'bloodless' or 'heartless' gnosis.[16]

Whicher concludes his analysis of the philosophy of yoga as a gift to humanity precisely for engaging the world positively:

> The liberated yogin actualizes the potential to live a fully integrated life in the world. ...there is no reason why the liberated yogin cannot be portrayed as a vital, creative, thoughtful, empathetic, balanced, happy, and wise person. Having adopted an integrative orientation to life, the enlightened being can endeavor to transform, enrich, and ennoble the world...Yoga combines discerning knowledge with an emotional, affective, and moral sensibility allowing for a participatory epistemology that incorporates the moral amplitude for empathic identification with the world, that is, with the objects or persons one seeks to understand. The enhanced perception gained through Yoga must be interwoven with Yoga's rich affective and moral dimensions to form a spirituality that does not become entangled in a web of antinomianism, but which retains the integrity

and vitality to transform our lives and the lives of others in an effective manner.[17]

## Karma Yoga as Socially Engaged Hinduism

One persistent Western misconception is that the doctrine of karma makes Indians fatalistic and therefore, lack concern for poverty and suffering, even as they lack ambition and a sense of personal responsibility. The same critics fail to question why the Protestant doctrine of predestination did not doom Europeans to fatalistic idleness. Wilber and others have used this misunderstanding of India to justify that while Indic ideas brought us to a certain point, we must now evolve beyond them as India's material poverty indicates a lack of a positive holistic outlook and pragmatism.

Wilber seems to ignore India's pre-colonial history, her contributions to art, music, and science, and current energetic rush toward modernity. He also misses the fact that one of the main paths to liberation for a Hindu is *karma yoga* – the yoga of right action. One of its various meanings is the performance of selfless service as a way to relieve suffering, and as a spiritual practice.

While it has been a common claim since the times of the colonial missionaries that serving the poor is a Christian or secular Western idea per se and that it is necessary for people like Mother Teresa to provide selfless service in India, the tradition of social service is deeply rooted within India's culture. An Indian guru who was especially devoted to service in the name of Lord Hanuman was Neem Karoli Baba (1900-73). In the late 1960s, Baba was discovered by Western seekers, including Ram Dass (born Richard Alpert), who became famous for first bringing his teachings to the West. One of Baba's simplest teachings was: 'Feed everyone'. As their guru's life came to its end, his followers began to put that vision into action.

One of the first was Larry Brilliant, a young doctor who had lived with Baba in India for two years. In 1973, Baba told him to shed his ashram robes, don a suit, and join the World Health Organization's (WHO) campaign to eradicate smallpox as a 'gift from God'.[18] Brilliant joined a team of 1,50,000 people who made one billion house calls throughout India and Nepal. He was so transformed by his socially engaged practice inspired by Baba that he joined Ram Dass to start the Seva Foundation. 'Seva' means selfless service, and the organization's key statement is: 'To be fully human, we must translate our compassion and concern into useful service'.[19] In 2006, Brilliant was named chief executive officer of Google.org, a 'hybrid charity', i.e. in addition to grants, it seeks to leverage Google's wealth with investments for sustainable development. When his picture appeared in *The New York Times* upon joining Google, a photo of Neem Karoli Baba was visible in the background. Brilliant did not make a U-Turn away from the source that had shaped his worldview so profoundly.

The use of yoga and meditation in a prison setting was pioneered in India by Kiran Bedi. She was the first woman Indian Police Service officer, and her career included two years as inspector general of New Delhi's Tihar Jail, one of India's largest prison complexes. According to one description, '... The jail was a mad house ...The inmates were treated like animals... A fear psychosis prevailed. With no constructive or creative activity, poor hygiene and overcrowding, it's unfortunate inmates behaved the way criminals were "expected to"'.[20] Bedi brought yoga and Vipassanā meditation teachers into the prison, and soon a large number of inmates were practicing these under the direct guidance of S.N. Goenka, the renowned meditation teacher who also taught Ram Dass, Daniel Goleman, and other disciples of Neem Karoli Baba.

From India, the principle of prison as a space for respectful spiritual development using yoga and meditation has spread worldwide, and various studies in the West have established its benefits to reduce repeat crime by instilling a positive outlook to life in the inmates.[21]

Arguably what popularized these 'new' ideas from India like seva, working with the sick and those with terminal illnesses, was an essay written by Stephen Levine (proponent of Theravada Buddhism and well-known for writing on death and dying) and Ram Dass in 1977, titled *Dying: An Opportunity for Awakening.*

Although the new American openness to death has now been U-Turned, and its historical roots and context often come with a Christian emphasis, the Indic roots of the conscious dying movement are undeniable.[22]

## Debate: How Does Integral Yoga Relate to Social Action?

In order to promote a dialogue between Aurobindonians and other voices, Malhotra began cross-posting between IndicTraditions and an e-group, Auroconf, used by Aurobindonians. However, criticisms of Wilber suddenly triggered anger from an Aurobindonian, Chandresh Desai, who believed that forums like Auroconf should not be concerned with issues such as the misappropriation of Sri Aurobindo's works.

Yet Malhotra persisted in bringing to the Aurobindonians' attention the situation concerning Wilber and found it frustrating that on trying to get concrete and actionable responses, he would instead receive lofty words of idealism and contradictions. Desai's position typified those who accused Malhotra of being negative, and yet their denial was a form of escapism. The following exchange between 6-12 June 2002 is illustrative:

> **Chandresh**: Rather than a lifelong pursuit of confronting people who appropriate from spiritual research done in India, it is more beneficial focusing on using spiritual research whether done in India or anywhere else for one's spiritual growth. If any knowledge of the past, whether from India or from anywhere else, is lost because of attacks from some other conquering civilization, then an active soul open to intuitive channels and receiving guidance directly from the divine, can restate the lost knowledge of the past. The concept of India, America, Hindu, Muslim has to be replaced by the concept of human race, human aspirations, human problems and human solutions. And I don't think we need to worry that someone will take away something from us that we deserve. An increasing jnana, bhakti and karma yoga will ensure that we get all that we deserve.

> **Rajiv:** Chandresh, we are talking past each other. Every word you say is basic Vedanta. This has been repeated far too many times in forum after forum. But I am unable to get my points across about "social theory" – which is not easy when people are not open to anything new being possible. This "block" is, very unlike the real spirit of Aurobindo...My issue specifically pertained to social and not individual, and to the relationship between these. Your response misses the issue.

**Chandresh:** Social engagement is not something I do not believe in. But I do not trust social engagement to mean pulling up collars of westerners who misappropriate works of Indian origin...What I am mentioning is a social engagement that focuses on learning how to be of use to others. My social engagement is learning to wear different caps, speak different languages so that I can mix with different sets of people and can attempt to bring out the good qualities that exist in that specific group in a manner and form that is natural to that group. This point, which is of a different nature than what you make, is because from the yogi perspective, the latter social engagement is a better way of spending time and resources than the former one.

**Chandresh:** A purely intellectual cannot understand the nuances of yogic practice and experience, which is the focus of auroconf. Confronting misappropriations is not necessarily the most fruitful use of yogic energy. Yogic external action is vast and is socially engaged. It could deal with misappropriations at times, but that's not its focus, because it may perceive such a focus to be counterproductive, or find some other action to produce a result sought by such a focus.

**Chandresh:** Sri A has himself addressed some of the fallacies in the Western thought about Indic traditions in his book *Foundations of Indian Culture*. It was a very important thing when the Indians were under British dominance, which could have lead (sic) one to think the inferiority of Indian capabilities. Considering the times, the book would have created a very hard-hitting stimulation to those who did not bother to look up Indic research and a hard-hitting blow to those who were wrong or incomplete in their understanding of Indic research into reexamining the research. But in the present times, though I would want to address misappropriations and/or confront misappropriations at times, in general, though embezzling, I feel the mis-appropriators are assisting in preparing the audience they attract, towards something more powerful and comprehensive.

**Rajiv:** Chandresh, what motivates you into "purely intellectual discussions" such as these, given your view that such a mind cannot understand the nuances of yogic practice? I am curious as to how this differs from having an argument with Wilber.

In response to these discussions about the responsibility of a yogi in the face of 'external' challenges, Malhotra wrote and posted the following short essay:

**Yoga and 'Unpleasant' Actions:**
**Response by Rajiv Malhotra**

A recent debate, on whether Wilber's misappropriations deserved a response from practicing yogi-s, but were reluctant to 'engage', reminds me of several similar instances. The common thread of logic is: Even after getting convinced that something wrong is going on, the person recoils at the very thought of engaging the issue socially, especially when it comes to confronting the opponent. In justifying this 'world-negation' stance, in the face of social injustice, s/he uses various arguments, such as:

**INNER ONLY THEORY**: I am a yogi and do not believe in criticizing others, because mine is internal sādhana.

**ILLUSION THEORY**: Since it is all mithya anyway, why bother 'fixing' this external illusory reality. (By implication, Mother Teresa's sponsors are right in that Indic culture is inherently inferior on this count. Ronald B. Inden (University of Chicago) called this the 'patient-doctor' relationship, in which the colonized gets placed in an institution run by the colonizer.)

**SAMENESS THEORY**: Just as every drop of water that falls from the sky ultimately reaches the ocean, no matter what path it takes, so also every jiva ultimately reaches Brahman. Therefore, why should I criticize another's path?

**'KARMA = FATALISM' THEORY**: To the extent it could be called 'suffering' (while in reality it is only mithya), it is what is meant to be happening, based on *prarabdh* caused by one's past life karma.

Yet, on the other side, there are many arguments that oppose this world-negation:

**Historically, Indians were also very advanced in the Outer realm** as compared to, say, Europeans of that time. This is evidenced from Harappan times to pre-colonial times in materialistic, artistic and economic competence. Hence, Outer is not in opposition to Inner, based on historical evidence. (This makes it vital to set the historical textbooks right.) Hence, Jung's warning to Westerners to be wary against the practice of yoga for it would make them less scientific, rational, and progressive, was based on his false diagnosis of modern poverty in India.

**After attaining moksha/nirvana, great figures in Classical India engaged the world** – the Buddha, Shankara, Ramanuja, Abhinavagupta, Kabir, Ramakrishna, Sri Aurobindo, and many others. Inner heights did not make them neglect the Outer; on the contrary, they became more committed to Outer engagement.

**The whole moral of the *Bhagvad Gita* is on this very issue: Arjuna starts off as world-negating, using the arguments similar to #1 through #4 above. The entire scripture revolves around the importance of a yogi being also able to engage the Outer realm, including actions that appear 'unpleasant'. This has to be done with dispassion.** Any yogi who complains that responding to Wilber (for instance) is un-yogic should re-read the *Gita*.

**Brahmin and kshatriya dharmas are job descriptions for work pertaining to Inner and Outer realms, respectively. This separation and distinction are very deeply enshrined in Hindu thought.** It equates roughly to today's Western notion of separation of church and state, falsely considered a unique discovery of the Western mind. (Basing these jobs on birth is a corruption and abuse of the system, just as nepotism today in favoring one's children.) This doctrine also emphasizes that neither can be subverted or ignored by the other.

**It seems that conquerors emphasized this world-negating loftiness, because it enabled them to make Hindus into their servants, yet in a manner that the Hindus could feel was in their own best interest.** It started with Muslim conquerors agreeing to not slaughter the captured provided they became slaves, and in many cases also agreed to get castrated. This ethos of weakness, dependence, and servitude became the opposite of the dominant culture's own self-image as being in charge and destined to rule. The British continued this direction far deeper and in more sophisticated ways than the Muslims. Post-Independence India adopted this ethos in certain ways as well. This led to over-emphasis on certain selected aspects of Hindu texts, without looking at the complete picture provided therein.

Gandhi is falsely portrayed as 'tolerant', when he emphasized the importance to stand against injustice. He promoted non-violent resistance and engagement with the opponents, or else there would have been no movement against the British. His was a path of intense self-sacrifice to 'confront' the opponent so as to bring down the mechanisms that sustained it – largely economic boycotts and refusal to obey unjust laws. Too many so-called 'Gandhians' today are using a false interpretation of Gandhi as a way to legitimize being lazy, inactive, and armchair revolutionaries. Gandhi's first requirement, of starting with one's supreme self-sacrifice – 'be the change that you want to see in the world' – is not evident in their personal lives.

**All rivers do not end up in one big ocean.** Some also end up in the Dead Sea. Otherwise, there would be moral relativism, in which 'anything goes', including adharmic ways. '**Hinduism = way of life' has become a dangerous copout by those failing to properly explain what it means.** Even the drug culture, Al Qaeda lifestyle, corruption and so forth, is 'a way of life'. In fact, EVERY lifestyle is 'a way of life' of one kind or another. Hence, #3 above is a false idea.

**Karma is NOT fatalism**. On the contrary, by explaining the present circumstance using a comprehensive system, it compels the person to take full responsibility for his choices 'to be made' in the present moment, and to stop blaming the universe for the present moment.

Advaita Vedānta is the only worldview, out of many Hindu theologies, that could possibly be interpreted as being world-negating. **All other worldviews, include many Vedanta interpretations, Kashmir Shaivism, Sakta/Devi paths, and so forth, are explicitly world affirming.** Even Advaita Vedanta is not calling for becoming morons in the face of social responsibility;

that is just a copout by those often seeking to glamorize selfish laziness. (Consider, for instance, Swami Dayananda Saraswati of the Arsha Vidya Gurukulam in Pennsylvania. He is one of the foremost proponents of Advaita Vedānta today. Yet, he has tirelessly worked in social activism in all sorts of projects worldwide for many decades. Followers should learn from his life lived, as an example of Advaita Vedanta in action.)

**Sri Aurobindo inspired The Mother to build a whole city of Auroville in India, specifically as an experiment in the Outer realm to imbibe certain principles.** A visit there convinces one that this project is not founded on a world disengagement philosophy. With so many exemplars living their world-affirming lives as role models, why do so many Hindus continue to buy this nonsense about glorified moronism as the way to enlightenment?

I welcome feedback on this. It is not specifically with respect to Ken Wilber, as that is merely the latest instance to manifest this meme-plex (of world-negation) sitting within a vast number of Hindus, Buddhists, Jainas, and neo-Indic thinkers of various sorts.[23]

## Proposals to Counter India's World-negating Image

Countering this world-negating image associated with India became paramount to Malhotra. He proposed a series of books and conferences that would consider and counter specific aspects of this broad and generalized portrayal of India. The main goal was to document and discuss India's vast contributions to the global scientific, economic, and social community that elevated human lives. Considering that Sri Aurobindo himself had written so extensively and eloquently on India's contributions, Malhotra had hoped at least some Aurobindonians would respond. The proposals were as follows:

**Proposed Book/Conference: *Indic Influences on Modern Psychology*; *Spiritual Thought and the Emerging Worldview***

**INTRODUCTION**: India's History and its Role in World Civilization – Is the 'World-Negating' Image Valid? DE-NEGATING INDIC CIVILIZATION'S IMAGE.

Many Westerners have had a tough time believing that Asians could do original science, although they could produce literature, speculative metaphysics, mysticism, and art. The introduction will challenge the standard Western portrayal of India's civilization as irrational and 'world-negating'.

## 1. ANCIENT INDIA'S RATIONAL CONTRIBUTIONS TO THE WORLD

The list of ancient India's contributions to the world's civilizations, including mathematics, astronomy, philosophy, linguistics, and technology until 1000 C.E., is the topic for a separate series of books planned. Unfortunately, these have been ignored because they challenge the Western superiority narrative.

## 2. ECONOMIC HISTORY OF INDIA

India was extremely wealthy until the mid-1800s by every account of Europe's own visitors and historians.[24] But in 1900, India had gone down to under two percent whereas America and the West had eighty-four percent of the world's share, due to colonization.

## 3. HISTORY OF INDIA'S PLUNDER

The first phase discusses India's plundering, citing authors such as Will Durant.[25] The second section will be the colonial phase, showing how taxation of India's wealth funded Europe's Industrial Revolution, and how India provided much of the raw material and market for the finished goods.

## 4. INDIC INFLUENCE IN SHAPING MODERN WESTERN HISTORY

The most important aspects of modern European history that were largely shaped by India's influence include: trade with India driving exploration of the New World; the Rise of the Industrial Revolution; modern and postmodern literature in the West; European Indology's role in the 'Aryanization' of German national identity; modern psychology, cognitive sciences and the emerging worldview; development of European and Asian languages and linguistics.[26]

**5. INTERPRETATION OF 'WORLD-NEGATING' INDIAN PHILOSOPHY**

Textual interpretations by expert Indian philosophers will be used to debunk this world-negating image that has been popularized by a selective use of Indian texts, often out of context.

**6. SOCIO-PSYCHOLOGICAL ANALYSIS OF TODAY'S SCHOLARSHIP**

I shall present logical and methodological flaws in much of the West's scholarship, which places the blame for India's present social, ecological and human conditions upon its indigenous religions and civilization as opposed to the history of invasions and oppression. This portrayal has become a way to justify the case that globalization equals Westernization, since the indigenous cultures are shown as inherently inferior.

**7. SUCCESS OF CONTEMPORARY INDIANS IN THE WEST**

This item is very adequately documented and is hardly the sign of people from a world negating, 'mystical', irrational, unprogressive civilization as alleged.

**CONCLUSION**

The challenge to the 'world-negating' attitude is very consequential, because it compels scholars to revisit Jung's rejection of yoga; he felt that it was dangerous for Westerners because it would make them backward. But in defiance of Jung's instructions, there are now over ten million Americans practicing yoga very openly, and this has not resulted in them becoming world-negating, regressive, unproductive or irrational as of now. Others who made similar U-Turns that must be re-evaluated include Teilhard de Chardin, and the Austrian occultist Rudolf Steiner amongst many other contemporary Westerners.

In this phase, the counter to the Wilberization of Sri Aurobindo studies took two parts: firstly, an in-depth study of Wilber's core work and responding to it from a true Aurobindonian lens and secondly, challenging the incorrect portrayal of India as a world-negating civilization. Both led to separate, and independent themes of scholarship at Infinity Foundation and the development of original frameworks, vocabularies, and path-breaking contributions to modern Indology.

Chapter 5

# The Debate Becomes Global

## CHAPTER SUMMARY

- Rajiv Malhotra wanted forums such as the All-USA Meeting, the conference in the USA by Aurobindonians, to discuss the issue of Wilberization. The organizers wanted Infinity Foundation to provide funding but were hesitant to discuss Wilber's appropriation and misrepresentation.
- Interestingly, Devan Nair, the former president of the Republic of Singapore and an active Aurobindonian, emerged among the few voices supporting Malhotra's challenge to Wilber.
- Both Malhotra and Nair exchanged views on online e-groups with other Aurobindonians. They discussed the denigration of India in colonial scholarship, how it served as a roadmap for later appropriation of Indian wisdom, and the sad state of Sri Aurobindo studies in India at the time.
- Devan Nair also wrote a separate piece wholeheartedly supporting Malhotra's positions and calling upon Aurobindonians to rise to the intellectual challenge. He described many Aurobindonians as 'navel-gazing'.

## The Annual Meeting of Aurobindonians Seeks Funding

Infinity Foundation was approached to sponsor speakers for the annual All-USA Meeting of followers of Sri Aurobindo and The Mother's teachings in 2001.

Kalpana Patel, the main organizer of AUM 2001, wrote to Malhotra asking to fund the conference planned for July at Mount Alverno Conference Center in Redwood City, California. She wanted IF's help to cover travel and other costs of some speakers and supplied a tentative list: Kireet Joshi, Guy Ryckaert, David (Dave) Frawley, Devan Nair, Alok Pandey, Prema Nandakumar, Amit Goswami, and Tara Jauhar. The commitment was urgent in order to plan the speakers' travel. Upon receiving an encouraging response from Malhotra, she focused on getting funding for Kireet Joshi, Devan Nair, and possibly Dave Frawley.

Patel wrote to Malhotra that the speakers sponsored by Infinity Foundation were preparing remarks on the 2001 theme: *Realizing the New Creation: Revolution, Evolution, Manifestation*. She mentioned that Infinity Foundation would be named as the conference sponsor in the program, website, and other related literature, and thanked Malhotra: 'We appreciate your willingness to assist in the important work of making the 2001 AUM unforgettable'.[1]

He responded with the suggestion to add certain themes to the conference, including specific challenges to Wilber's theory. Malhotra wanted the speakers to focus on how Wilber had not truly understood Sri Aurobindo's work. As an example, he wanted to highlight that Sri Aurobindo's concept 'Ascend and Integrate' had been appropriated by Wilber as 'Transcend and Include', and that his portrayal of Sri Aurobindo's work was limited to individual sādhana and ignored collective transformation.

Malhotra explained to Patel and other Aurobindonians that his concerns about Wilber must be considered by the conference organizers in designing the panel topics. He felt that 'the anti-intellectual mentality of many Sri Aurobindonians, especially Indian' had emboldened Wilber to blatantly distort Sri Aurobindo. He wrote: 'AUM (All-USA Meeting) and AIM (All-India Meeting) are opportunities to debate the big issues as they pertain to the teachings of Sri Aurobindo and the Mother's teachings and practice. I humbly submit to your committee that the following are very critical matters that must be on the agenda'.

The first issue Malhotra wanted covered was to affirm that Sri Aurobindo does not consider the higher states of consciousness to be devoid of rationality:

> **PRE VERSUS POST**: Is supramental irrational, or does it include rationality while not being limited by it. Is it like a black & white movie upgrading to color, in which case black and white are still available as colors? Or is it that upon upgrade to color, black and white get discarded and eliminated from the scene and only other colors remain? Wilber's big slogan on this is "transcend and include", meaning the former interpretation: we don't cease to be rational upon being suprarational. But that has also been Sri Aurobindo's teaching all along. The implication is that one should not become anti-intellectual to transcend rationality, because the transcending includes rationality even at the new level. (When Shakti descends subsequently, then the transformation might be more radical than suggested here, but that still does not bypass this stage.) Wilber has claimed original discovery of this principle, especially given many Indians' fixation against intellectual development because they feel that stopping rational thought equates to spiritual advancement. He has claimed that this is one reason why Sri Aurobindo must be left behind and has justified setting up his own new integral institute. This is also the basis of Western stereotyping of Indic civilization as backward while the West is seen as scientific and progressive because they routinely come across Indians who say things like 'we don't believe in intellectual stuff because we are so spiritual'.[2]

Malhotra's second issue was that Sri Aurobindo's teachings are not confined to the individual level while ignoring the collective societal aspects:

> **SOCIAL VERSUS MERELY PRIVATE**: The other charge Wilber uses to justify his breaking off from the (sic) Sri Aurobindo and Mother's tradition (and now openly marginalizing their importance), is that Sri Aurobindo worked only at the individual level, and that the collective social aspect was missing in his

> teachings. This plays well into the stereotype that Indians are socially inactive, unconcerned, renouncing, and hence another reason why they are in need of the West to help them progress. This is baloney, for why else would they have created Auroville? The whole emphasis is on collective evolution and not for just an individual. This is utterly dishonest...[3]

Malhotra requested that the topics he raised become priority themes of the conference 'to debate these matters and help clarify for the benefit of all of us'.[4] He also invited knowledgeable Aurobindonians to post their views on these issues on the e-group. Patel wrote that she would 'keep your suggestions on the specific topics that may be covered' but was non-committal.

Sadly, the AUM organizers showed no interest in discussing these critical issues, while some dismissed them as too 'intellectual'. Other lofty and condescending Aurovillians cited excuses that they wanted to focus on spiritual 'truth' and avoid challenging Wilber's appropriations because that was at the 'mental' level. This view was a disservice to Sri Aurobindo, who had extensively written on the collective and social aspects of man and had authored some of the finest expositions on the importance of taking action in his analysis of the *Bhagavad Gīta*.

A typical example of this was Bhavana, an American Christian lady living like a long-term Aurobindonian. She considered Wilber to be an original thinker on par with Sri Aurobindo and blithely condoned the appropriation:

> Arguments such as these will also have to be put forth and understood, so long as we are working on the **mental level**, which does indeed need to be worked on. I find that the essence of Hindu religion is its acknowledgement of para-mental ways of knowing and of Truth which transcends all descriptions. Those who are serious about its practice, there are tried-and-true methods to access the states of consciousness where these higher truths or even The Truth Itself become known to the practitioner. **With a little practice and a few experiences, there is no surprise in finding that wise persons of many different cultures are saying the same things.** The most basic moral percepts and the most sublime attempts to point our minds toward the spiritual truth beyond the intellect **will sound**

> **the same, and even the metaphors will ring similarly, without anyone ever having to have heard it from someone else.** Wise persons have accessed those states of consciousness and they come back and report about the qualities and characteristics — and their reports sound similar. This is a better argument for the Universality of the Highest Truth, than for the inter-mixed heritages of various traditions. With all due respect and also delight in the play of ideas on this forum, and support for the goal of getting the image of Hinduism clearer and truer in America.[5]

Malhotra recognized this argument as one frequently used by Western appropriators. Bhavana was merely echoing them. He responded:

> I learnt recently that Teilhard de Chardin did indeed visit India, studied Ramanuja extensively and other Indian scriptures, and wrote about these, but explained his claim of originality on the basis that Indians were world negating and into renunciation. **The exact same argument was used also by Jung to first appropriate so much from India but then to reject the source as world negating, thereby setting the stage for his own movement, whose members today never heard of his sources such as Patanjali, Kundalini etc. Has Wilber reached this stage now?**[6]

The connection between Sri Aurobindo and Teilhard de Chardin, as mentioned in the exchange, was of particular interest to Malhotra. The two aforementioned were contemporaries and considered to have reached their insights without any influence on each other. This was very useful to Wilber because he could copy Sri Aurobindo's ideas and refer to de Chardin, even though the latter did not develop them in depth and had only a superficial understanding.

Malhotra was keen to understand the Indian influences on de Chardin and had personally met the philosopher and poet, K.D. Sethna, when the latter was in his final years at age ninety. Sethna had authored a book drawing comparisons between Sri Aurobindo and de Chardin and was glad that Malhotra had taken up the pertinent topic.

Another scholar Malhotra corresponded with in the same year was David Brookman, who had studied the connections between Sri Aurobindo and de Chardin. Brookman was a Presbyterian minister, and his master's thesis compared the visions of Sri Aurobindo and de Chardin. When Malhotra learned of Brookman's work, he wrote to him and requested a copy so that Infinity Foundation could consider developing it further. Brookman wrote back confirming his background in studying this important connection between the two philosophers. He expressed interest in applying to Infinity Foundation for a grant on 'the way in which transpersonal psychology has been informed by Indic sources'. He confessed, 'I did not know that Teilhard read Ramanuja and commented upon his texts. This is new to me'.[7]

Julian Lines, an Aurobindonian based in Woodstock, New York, also expressed interest in probing these Indian influences on de Chardin. He mentioned that the past president of CIIS, Robert A. McDermott, had been mentored by Thomas Berry; this was in response to the post wherein Malhotra had stated that Berry had been deeply influenced by Hindu and Buddhist thought. He mentioned that the book *Six Pillars: Introductions to the Major Works of Sri Aurobindo* had articles by both Berry and McDermott.[8]

Malhotra persisted in his request that AUM 2001 should have a session focused on these important influences in the past. To compare the teachings of Sri Aurobindo/The Mother with Ken Wilber, he proposed various speakers including Brant Cortright and Kundan Singh. For a comparison between Sri Aurobindo and Teilhard de Chardin (including Teilhard's study of Śrī Rāmānujācārya), he proposed Harold Coward of Calgary University and Thomas Berry. Malhotra offered to contact them and introduce them to the AUM organizers.[9]

Many such important Indian influences were ignored by the organizers and other Aurobindonians. This became Malhotra's passion – to take up such investigations as his personal research.

## Broadening the Debate with Aurobindonians

Given this Aurobindonian anti-intellectualism, and the implicit consent given for the appropriation of Sri Aurobindo's work into Wilber's institutes, Malhotra started a public debate on the importance of proper representation of various cultures in modern scholarship.

In one of his many position papers posted on the IndicTraditions e-group, he captured the common issues Hinduism faces in the USA, along with some of the most oft-cited responses given by Hindus when he brought such issues to their attention. He explained that Catholics, Protestants and Jews had forged a new Judeo-Christian ideology in the USA by engaging in constructive dialogue, which had previously not happened in Europe. Because tens of millions of Americans are now of Asian origin, Malhotra asked:

> Has the time come for Indic traditions in America (which includes Hinduism, Buddhism, Jainism, Sikhism) to similarly engage in a constructive dialog with the American mainstream cultures? For instance, will the new American culture respect images as representations of the divine, and as means to access the ultimate reality? Will it respect (not just tolerate) multiple views and representations of the ultimate reality (and hence multiple paths to it), or will it insist on a single worldview with all the others seen as varying degrees of backwardness? In what language will the new rules of the game be defined?[10]

He felt that Indian Americans are either cynical or reluctant to assertively negotiate in this American melting pot phenomenon or unskilled in the American due process required. Therefore, they cite the following kinds of excuses for their disinterest:

- There is no such problem, or it does not affect me since I am doing well with a nice job, house, and children in good schools.
- Hinduism is the same as all other religions. Hence, it does not matter what anyone believes. (This is caused by confusing Hinduism's pluralism/inclusiveness with sameness.) This has created many 'nominal' Hindus who know little about their faith.
- Our faith is so superior to others that we need not bother trying to explain anything to others. (Unfortunately, they have failed to explain it to their children as well.) Let us move forward and avoid past issues, because we must bypass negative vibrations. (This is tantamount to saying that the teaching of history is useless. If history has a purpose, then it is important to have history be truthful.)
- The problem of an authentic portrayal of our heritage should

be dealt with by someone else, such as the government or the guru-s.
- The problem is inevitable and unsolvable, so it is better to ignore it.

Malhotra went on to argue that despite numerous temples coming up in the USA, there is an unconscious and involuntary assimilation that the community leaders are not driving. On the one hand, there is a tremendous thirst for Indian ideas and culture, while on the other, there is a taboo about the traditions. One must ask if there is a subtle and indirect form of racism, especially with many Christian evangelists trashing Hinduism.

He wrote that in America, what is portrayed about culture in education and media, is negotiable. Native Americans, African Americans, Islamic groups, women, and the LGBTQ+ community are among those who are actively and publicly engaged in negotiating their fair portrayal by the mainstream. The sociological consequences of not participating in such activism are damaging for the next generation raised in the USA.

Interestingly, Malhotra found that many Indians considered such activism as 'negative'. They preferred to lead a cocooned life.[11]

This was a lengthy article and it provoked rebuttals from Aurobindonians who thought that it was unimportant to counter people like Wilber. A typical example of such a voice was David (Dave) Hutchinson, who advocated that Wilber simply be ignored. He did not want to accept that Wilber had already become the biggest name in consciousness studies and hence ignoring him would not serve any purpose. Hutchinson then wrote that it was not for Aurobindonians like him to counter Wilber, and the job was best left to people like Rajiv Malhotra.

Hutchinson was confident about his dismissal of Wilber:

> Very few of the people I speak with about spiritual topics are familiar with Wilber ... and honestly, a single writer like Wilber just doesn't have much sway. ... very few people are attracted to this kind of presentation, ... In a deeper sense, what "influence" is Wilber likely to have? ...Writers such as this latch onto one or a hundred ideas and promote them...and their intellectual star shines for a few years or a decade. Then their star declines, and other writers take their place.

> Their books go the way of most of the hundreds of thousands of books that are published each year, hidden in libraries or second-hand bookstores... **The force of the Integral Yoga – and in this, I include its ability to move out among the masses, find new persons to manifest in, grow in new channels – is not essentially affected by misinterpretations such as Wilber's. ... To sum up, countering a writer like Wilber is part of life's work – for you, not for me!** ... It is not critical for the future of the Integral Yoga or for spiritual advancement of the world at large.[12]

David Hutchinson's response was typical of those who do not understand how ideas become embedded in society; they fail to differentiate between random pop cultural influences and the kind that enter institutions of learning and become the dominant paradigms taught to the next generation. Malhotra pointed out that Wilber was in fact becoming a force among serious scholars, giving him long-term leverage.

Hutchinson was convinced that Integral Yoga had its own agency as a standalone force regardless of how it was represented or misrepresented. This seemed like a form of fatalism, whereas Sri Aurobindo emphasized the importance of individual puruṣārtha-s (yogic works).

Though he withdrew from the task of protecting Sri Aurobindo's work, Hutchinson went on to discuss funding for his activities, including setting up an office that would co-ordinate Infinity Foundation's USA-based activities related to Sri Aurobindo studies. He wrote to Malhotra, showing interest in some kind of collaboration:

> Dear Rajiv – I was wondering if the scope of the Infinity Foundation would include projects that are specific to integral yoga. The question arises because last year a "national office" was discussed that would coordinate public relations, travel of speakers from India, national and regional meetings, and support various projects such as web sites, journals, newsletters, and new books. The impetus was to create a mechanism for better cooperation and collaboration among the various centers (mainly in the US) that do work related to integral yoga, Auroville, or the Pondicherry Ashram. Blocking the project was mainly funds: we saw the office as having a full-time paid worker, with a decent modern salary ($45,000/year). The various people and organisations involved didn't see where or

how to raise the money, and the idea was shelved. Would Infinity possibly fund such a position? Or is that outside its scope?[13]

He went on to close the chapter of Malhotra's proposal for a discussion by Aurobindonians on such matters at the AUM conference when he posted the following:

> Rajiv has suggested holding such a session on Wilber at next year's AUM, but I think that's not optimal for two reasons. First, those who attend the AUM are largely sadhaks of the Integral Yoga. They're not likely to be directly misled by Wilber into his personal version of "integral psychology." So the effect of such a panel would be minimal. Second, the AUM exists to bring people together to look at the yoga itself, more than to compare and contrast it with other elements in the world.[14]

## 'Navel-Gazing Aurobindonians': Devan Nair

Fortunately, there were other voices present in these discussions. One was that of Devan Nair, former president of the Republic of Singapore and a devout follower of Sri Aurobindo. He posted the following online:

> **Dear Rajiv, This is to inform you that I not only read your postings with considerable interest and admiration**, but am also forwarding them to persons whom I know. **Living practitioners of Indian spiritual disciplines both in India and elsewhere in the world would be happy to know that an invaluable instrument like you is doing for them what they themselves are unable to. A highly valuable undertaking like yours deserves all the support and encouragement it can get. You have mine. All strength to your arms.**[15]

A vibrant dialogue ensued between Devan Nair and Rajiv Malhotra on the e-group and served as an important rejoinder to the anti-intellectual Aurobindonians. They explored serious questions and topics:

1. What changed in the positions of scholars from the time of the eighteenth-century French philosopher Voltaire to later scholars during colonial times, who went from being Indophiles to Hinduphobic?

2. Did the colonial scholars leave behind the first road map for the appropriation of Indic wisdom that became the guide for later scholars?
3. The sad state of Sri Aurobindo studies at the time in India.

**Rajiv:** Given that in Voltaire's time, it was OK for intellectuals to respect India, what made European scholars change their position later? One theory I heard is that **once India's nationalism started to be taken seriously, the British started to trash India, whereas earlier they regarded it and all its material and intellectual wealth as theirs.**[16]

**Devan Nair**: The difference was that in Voltaire's time Imperialism was not yet in full stride. In the 19th Century it was. It was during this period that Macaulays and their ilk helped to secure generous funding from the East India Company for scholars like Max Muller to persuade innocent Indian Pandits to teach them Sanskrit to enable them to trash India's Vedic heritage. Just as Big Business today helps to set the agendas of any administration after the ongoing American election campaign by dispensing huge sums of money to both the Republican and Democratic parties. The difference between Democrats and Republicans is that between tweedledum and tweedledee... Does that remind you of certain Aurobindonians you met during your visit to India?[17]

**Rajiv:** This is a key point about big business' influence on Indian history, and this should be understood as part of what led to the world-negating stereotype. So, **in a sense, Jung, Teilhard, and Wilber are thankful to Macaulay, Max Muller, etc. for laying the ground for co-opting. By establishing this world-negating picture of Indian civilization so deeply in the psyche of the West and, more dangerously, in Indians themselves, the door was open for modern Westerners to appropriate from India.** This was then repackaged as scientific discoveries by the West as contrasted with the world negating ideas of the East. This appropriation is also being justified openly in many cases as helping save the world-negating Indians by bringing them progressive Western ideas, which their own civilization is portrayed as being incapable of providing. These scholars who co-opt also convince Americans why they should stay away from Indian ideas and practices, although what they are selling is the very same Indian ideas repackaged supposedly in a more 'positive and world affirming' way. What a scam! Reclaiming the appropriated know-how requires countering this world negating interpretation as the very nexus of the conspiracy.

...it was a disappointment to learn from Dr. Karan Singh that the chair for Sri Aurobindo Studies at Varanasi University has been vacant for 5 years for lack of a qualified person. ...Matthijs showed me a beautiful building in the Aurobindo Ashram in Delhi, which is supposed to house a new world-class institute for advanced studies, but which is waiting for a right candidate to head it. I concluded that there was too much anti-intellectualist mentality. **This mentality does two things: First, people turn emotional in defending their views; being unable to do so intellectually (we saw some of that here, too). Second, it becomes tempting for the Wilberites of the world to fill this intellectual vacuum with their own agenda.**

**My case for intellectual activism remains on the table.** I am glad to have the quotes from you, Julian, Don, Kundan, which I shall incorporate into my next draft. More such quotes would be welcome, especially from sources other than Sri Aurobindo, as I wish to show that this is not some recent idea imported into India by Sri Aurobindo, which is another allegation that is often being made. Many Westerners, once caught in the corner, with their world negating excuse being countered using Sri Aurobindo's writings, then take the stand that he brought these ideas into India based on his study of Western thinking in England! So we are back to Indian civilization being stereotyped as world negating. My position is that, as interpreter of Vedas, Yoga, Upanishads, Gita, Sri Aurobindo was confirming the real meaning of Indian civilization and not westernizing it as alleged.

**Devan Nair**: Dear Rajiv, may I point out that "cognitive disorder" is not peculiar to any single nation. Americans, Europeans as well as people of other nations are not immune to this disorder.

> How else do we explain the stubborn efforts of modern Western scholars to paint Indian traditions in a most negative and dismissive manner? **It's intellectual dishonesty of a most repellent kind.** The only therapy for that deplorable condition is the kind of shock therapy that can be delivered most effectively by Indian academics themselves, provided they wake up in good time. **Your effort in this direction is the only palpable sign at present that this realization may not be too far off.** Some very good minds are already present on this forum. To focus them on your main objectives is the only real problem on your plate. Some formulae have already been put forward. I look forward very much to the implementation of one such formula in the not-too-distant future.

Devan Nair became very enthusiastic about supporting Malhotra's work. He admonished the 'navel-gazing Aurobindonians', as he called them. We quote this important piece below.

> Aurobindonians in Auroville gave a magnificent two page spread in the latest issue of their monthly journal AUROVILLE TODAY to an interview with Rajiv when he recently visited Auroville. They were rightly enthusiastic about his visit, his exposition and his work as a means of clarifying the minds of the human collectivity (including the Indian) about the genesis and nature of Indian tradition.
>
> Sri Aurobindo himself never talked of abolishing the intellect or the vital. When he repeatedly affirmed that 'ALL LIFE IS YOGA', he meant it in every sense of the word. In short, the worm would not wriggle, nor reptilian ecstasies thrash the slime, were it not for the unconscious Yoga of Life on earth. SUPREME TRUTH in its individual, universal and transcendent totality does NOT cancel the physical, the vital or the mental, but fulfills them. Their transformation, not their abolition, is the clearly stated aim of Integral Yoga. What Sri Aurobindo insisted upon was the clarification, enlightenment and ultimate transformation of Body, Life, Heart, Mind and whatever may lie below or above these. That's precisely what Integral Yoga is. Otherwise, it wouldn't be Integral.

Sri Aurobindo also wrote a good deal about collective yoga. ... he held that a critical number of human beings need to be prepared before the leap to the ultimate Transformation can possibly take place. And how could one prepare any collectivity if one neglects the intellectual side of what we call the Sanātana Dharma? Aurobindonians should encourage initiatives like that taken by Rajiv to correct misperceptions about Indian traditions and civilization in both the West and in India. Several aberrations have occurred in the Indian collectivity...There are no doubt quite a few in all Yogas who believe that the be-all and end-all of Yoga is ***to concentrate on one's own navel and ignore the rest of the universe.*** That's a fundamental fallacy that needs to be rejected out of hand. As did Krishna when he exhorted Arjun on the battlefield of Kurukshetra to see the world as it really was. And what it really IS and WAS presents anything but a pretty picture. His injunction to Arjun on that field of carnage was uncompromising.

Julian has already sent to this forum Sri Aurobindo's masterly chapter significantly titled "Kurukshetra" from the very hand of the supreme yogi of our times. The so-called Aurobindonians who appear to have suggested to you that we can look at the world as it really is by merely gazing at our own navels seem to have forgotten one of the most potent chapters ever written by the Master.

Encouraged by Nair, another comment supporting Malhotra came from a prominent Flemish writer on Sri Aurobindo, Georges van Vrekhem:

> Dear Mr. Malhotra, It was a pleasure getting acquainted with you during the last AUM meeting. I would not be surprised if we meet more often in the future. I do appreciate your efforts in making Sri Aurobindo and the Mother – and the traditions behind them – better known worldwide. If I do not participate in the exchanges concerning "Indic traditions", it is simply because I have an enormous pile of work ahead of me...I will always be interested in the work you do and in receiving some information about it.[18]

The support for Malhotra's cause slowly built on and the debate was clearly divided: a small group led by Rajiv Malhotra, Devan Nair and

Kundan Singh actively challenged Wilberization, while the majority was comfortable having conferences and discussing esoteric topics but ignoring the danger clawing through Sri Aurobindo studies.

Chapter 6

# Betrayal by the California Institute of Integral Studies

## CHAPTER SUMMARY

- This chapter describes the origins and role of the California Institute of Integral Studies, founded in 1968 by Haridas Chaudhuri and his wife, Bina, who were serious devotees of Sri Aurobindo.
- Infinity Foundation had been involved in extensive discussions and collaborations with multiple scholars from CIIS. From the faculty, these included Brant Cortright and Bahman A.K. Shirazi (then dean of graduate studies), both considered important Aurobindonians, as well as Stuart Sovatsky, a Tantra practitioner and scholar.
- These individual relationships led Rajiv Malhotra to explore collaborating with CIIS, with the hope that the institution would help bring an authentic portrayal of Indian spiritual traditions into American academia.
- To his dismay, Malhotra discovered that CIIS had undergone its own U-Turn away from Sri Aurobindo and Indian spirituality.
- After numerous discussions with Sovatsky and Singh, Malhotra entered into direct discussions with Joseph (Joe) L. Subbiondo, then president of CIIS. At first, CIIS appeared to share Malhotra's concerns and wanted help from Infinity Foundation to restore its focus on Sri Aurobindo.

- However, a serious disagreement broke out between Kundan Singh and Angana P. Chatterji, an influential faculty member at CIIS. This episode revealed to Malhotra that CIIS had turned anti-India and Hinduphobic under the influence of Chatterji. Malhotra publicly criticized this aspect of CIIS.
- The foundation eventually backed away from its projects with CIIS but developed a long-term friendship and relationship with Sovatsky and Singh.

## Academic Institute for Disseminating Sri Aurobindo's Teachings in the United States of America

In 1951, the *American Academy of Asian Studies* was founded in San Francisco with the explicit purpose of studying Eastern philosophy, literature, and psychology. Frederic Spiegelberg, professor of Asian religions at Stanford University, was its first director. He had spent time traveling and meeting guru-s in India including Sri Aurobindo, and wrote to the sage asking for his recommendations on those who could join the academy. Sri Aurobindo recommended Haridas Chaudhuri, who was steeped in Indian yogic tradition but also a professor of Western philosophy at Presidency College in Calcutta, (now Kolkata).

Spiegelberg wrote: 'Aurobindo is the guiding spirit of this earth and the prophet of our age'.[1] Haridas Chaudhuri, an accomplished scholar of Sri Aurobindo's work, pioneered the implementation in a Western educational institution, the integral approach to education that he had developed as a student of Sri Aurobindo.

In parallel with this, in 1951, Chaudhuri and his wife Bina established the Cultural Integration Fellowship, and eventually its educational branch became the California Institute of Integral Studies.

These beginnings at the academy in 1951 emerged as a precursor to the 1960s' spiritual New Age and counterculture movements in California, attracting several scholars including the famous Alan Watts, who became dean of the American Academy of Asian Studies. Another Indian philosopher on the faculty was C.P. Ramaswami Iyer, former diwan of the state of Travancore and later vice-chancellor of the University of Banaras.

Spiegelberg described that these developments 'became something of a society event in San Francisco, where artists and literates and important people of many ways of life were drawn, particularly to the weekly colloquium, where the teachers discussed simple questions, simple problems in the most inspiring and elaborate way before we opened the meeting to the general audience'.[2]

Under Chaudhuri's leadership, the academy became renowned as a place where lively debates and discussions were held. Michael Murphy, co-founder of the Esalen Institute, was a student during the time and recounted his experience:

> One of the great events of those early days was a colloquium held every Friday night that was chaired by Frederic Spiegelberg, Alan Watts and Haridas Chaudhuri. You had to get there about an hour early to get into the room... the electricity was really enormous.[3]

Murphy wrote in glowing terms of the influence this movement had on an entire generation, remarking that much of the inspiration for the poetry of the post-Second World War (1939-45) literary movement, the Beat Generation, came from it.

Watts recalled that this academy was

> one of the principal roots of what later came to be known, in the early sixties, as the San Francisco Renaissance, ... Between, say, 1958 and 1970 a huge tide of spiritual energy in the form of poetry, music, philosophy, painting, religion, communications techniques in radio, television, and cinema, dancing, theater, and general life-style swept out of this city and its environs to affect America and the whole world...

He described it as 'a transitional institution emerging from the failure of universities and churches to satisfy important spiritual needs'. Being free from the 'elaborate nonsense of accreditation, degrees, and academic status', it attracted young people seeking 'the thing variously called moksha, bodhi, kaivalya, or satori in the Asian religions, which is the wisdom of a transformed consciousness, of liberation from that exclusive identification of oneself with personality which overlays and conceals the basic sensation in the very back of the mind: the sensation of being identical with the universe...'.[4]

Chaudhuri brought the work of Sri Aurobindo with authenticity and fidelity to Western scholars and the public. He taught that in Integral Yoga, Sri Aurobindo had given the world 'a complete art of integral living. It points the way to dynamic integration of the material and spiritual values of life. It is a call to the reconstruction of human life and society on the basis of abiding spiritual values'.[5] Active projects and studies were started on Sri Aurobindo's work being applied to the fields of education, psychology, and social impact.

## The Hijacking of CIIS and Attempts at Course Correction

Infinity Foundation had already started working with several people from CIIS in their individual capacities: Brant Cortright and Bahman Shirazi (faculty members and considered serious Aurobindonians), and Stuart Sovatsky; and Kundan Singh (follower and scholar of Sri Aurobindo and The Mother, and a student at CIIS).

These individual relationships led Malhotra to explore possible collaboration with CIIS, with the hope that the institution would help bring about an authentic portrayal of Indian spiritual traditions into the American academia.

However, upon closer scrutiny of CIIS, Malhotra learned that after the untimely demise of Chaudhuri, CIIS had been commandeered by its president, Robert McDermott, who was keen to bring in the teachings of Rudolph Steiner. Steiner heavily borrowed Indian spiritual traditions into Theosophy, including key components like karma, reincarnation, unity of consciousness, etc., but claimed it as his own original system which he called 'Anthroposophy', when he split from the Theosophical Society and it named J. Krishnamurti as its successor rather than him. His influence in Europe was immense across a wide range of disciplines.

Another Western thinker whose influence had replaced Sri Aurobindo's framework was Carl Jung. Jung, too, had digested a lot of Indian spirituality into his work including Sr Aurobindo's seminal ideas like Tantra, cakra, maṇḍala, and so forth. These are, however, regarded as Jung's original insights.

Malhotra was vocal in bringing all this to the attention of everyone he encountered at CIIS. There was a sincere overture from Joe Subbiondo, then president of CIIS, to remedy the situation and restore

Sri Aurobindo's legacy at the institute. Malhotra and he had several promising email exchanges brainstorming these ideas.

Subbiondo then visited Malhotra's home in Princeton for detailed discussions. Several potential projects emerged where Infinity Foundation could provide funding. These included establishing the Haridas Chaudhuri Chair to bring back Sri Aurobindo's teachings as well as fellowships for funding researchers, and conferences on topics relevant to the foundation's goals, and an annual award to an exemplar who embodied the ideas championed by the foundation.

## Clashes with Angana P. Chatterji: Hinduphobia at CIIS

The discussions fell apart in the year 2002 when Singh, then a Ph.D. student at CIIS, brought some disturbing news to Malhotra's attention. This concerned Angana Chatterji, an overzealous activist on the faculty who taught social and cultural anthropology.[6] She had completed her Ph.D. from CIIS where Richard Shapiro was her colleague and partner. There are detailed write-ups on the 'psychological abuse, manipulation, exploitation and dysfunction' that some of her students experienced at CIIS.[7]

Chatterji was known for her extreme Hinduphobic views and was eventually fired from CIIS along with Shapiro due to their unprofessional conduct.[8] All these developments though, took time to come to light, and in the interim she had an adverse impact on Kundan Singh and the larger cause of Sri Aurobindo studies at CIIS.

Singh wrote to the Indic Traditions e-group, without mentioning names, about a seminar titled *Dialogue for Peace on Hindu Fundamentalism in India* being organized at CIIS against the backdrop of the Godhra riots (communal unrest that led to a violent clash between Hindus and Muslims in the state of Gujarat in 2002) that had recently taken place. He believed that a one-sided perspective of the issue was being presented and wanted to counter it; for this, he sought help from the knowledge base of the collective e-group, including historical information and statistics concerning Hindu-Muslim riots in India. Malhotra responded by introducing Singh to certain experts on the issue. Malhotra also encouraged him to stand up to any one-sided activism. He wrote:

> Do not fail to mention that the religious violence in India started in the 1980s, and one must correlate this with a huge influx of Arab petro-dollars to change the identity of Indian Muslims to be Arabized. Regarding Christianity, funding from foreign sources has gone sky high. Indians could and for centuries did, integrate every kind of religion harmoniously. But now these indigenous issues got internationalized and Indian Mosques and Churches are foreign subsidiaries.[9]

Singh wrote back saying he had already begun to face repercussions for his stand against Chatterji's Hinduphobic views. Someone had shared the e-group discussion with Chatterji, and she had summoned him to her office for a dressing-down, accusing him of using Hindu organizations to threaten her. She made an official complaint against Singh to the director of his program, who, upon investigation, found the charges baseless and completely speculative. Malhotra wrote back offering support to Singh:

> Your posts on the egroup were well within the bounds of academic debate. You are not rude or abusive to her at all. ...you are saying that you want to go well prepared to the event with FACTS to have a balanced discussion. Anyone who loves the truth would want to see that. I find her reaction to be that of someone wanting to force a one-sided view and to avoid an opposing perspective at all. You could turn the tables around and paint her as totalitarian and using intimidation to suppress the truth. ... you do not take ANY stand on Godhra but ask for the facts from every side. The only word you use to describe her is "leftist" ... – it's a common way to describe many persons. She is potentially using scary tactics in an unprofessional way. It would be an abuse of power if she used her higher position to suppress free thinking. You are the best judge and you must do what you think is right. Perhaps, consult Stuart Sovotsky (sic) who is a real friend, and get his advice.[10]

In addition, Infinity Foundation offered him legal support. Singh was grateful for Malhotra's support but called upon him not to intervene directly at CIIS. Malhotra continued debating the larger issues that were not related to Singh's controversy.

Chatterji's moot point was that the Hindutva movement was creating new mythology about the Hindu past and called it fascism. In response, Malhotra wrote an article titled *India's Crisis of Myth,* in which he explained that Jung considered the West's fundamental crisis to be the lack of a modern and believable myth to replace the old Christian dogma. This was why Jung had substantially appropriated Hindu material to help him create a new myth that he could sell to the West. Nobody accused him of fascism. By the same yardstick, why should Hindus not be allowed to reimagine their past and bring their narratives into the context of modernity? He wrote that 'the principle of rethinking the past, making the new myth more scientific, and compliant with social demands, is perfectly legitimate'. He added that Jungians at CIIS ought to understand that those like Chatterji were denying Hindus their old narratives and imposing imported narratives under the garb of secularism. 'Jungians should understand this as the basis for Hindus' anger'.[11]

The moderators of the e-group discovered that a mole had become a member and was responsible for sharing Singh's posts, and was immediately removed from the e-group.

To exacerbate the fight, Chatterji published another article titled *A Grave Confrontation* in the *Dawn,* Pakistan's oldest English newspaper.[12] The entire article was essentially an attack against Hinduism and aimed to damage its image in the West; it was shared with CIIS's community email received by the entire campus.

Malhotra countered the article with his response, pointing out that selective outrage during any inter-community violence served no purpose. He accused brown sepoys like Angana Chatterji of spreading misinformation while also talking about decolonization:

> Angana Chatterjee, a junior faculty member of The California Institute of Integral Studies, California, posted the letter copied below to Pakistan's newspaper, "Dawn." While there are many interesting and important points in it, its overall misguided, and imbalanced nature is typical of a pathology that bedevils many self-alienated Indian Americans. This person is simply trying to become another Somini Sengupta, who propelled herself into journalism, despite having little prior background, by supplying *The New York Times* with the "caste, cows, and curry" myth of

India as part of the continual reconfirmation of the superiority of the West.

This is the syndrome called "impressing the whites." It is what Enrique Dussel, Frantz Fanon, and Edward Said explained as the process of the dominant culture appropriating a tier of intellectuals from the dominated culture to become their proxies in ruling over the masses. In exchange for this loyalty to the dominant culture, they receive a considerably enhanced position, rewards, and a sort of neo-white status. Over 95% of all police firings and other forms of control during the British Empire was done by Indian Sepoys. Interestingly, the Chinese did not make good sepoys because they were not so willing to sell out to the masters.

Today, the Indian Sepoy archetype is found in academics in the West especially in the humanities. Their role on behalf of the dominant culture is to supply the myth of the "other" to fit into the dominant culture's grand narrative of itself.

As Edward Said pointed out, the West was defined only in relation to the "others." To sustain this self definition, an obsessive Indological scholarship has been carried out since the time of William Jones in the 1700s.

But today, it is these brown-skinned Kiplings who supply the "caste, cows, and curry" theory of India – the eternal land where nothing changes except with foreign importation, which therefore, legitimizes colonization, the multinationals' takeover on the indigenous, and Christian Proselytizing.

...I do agree that any inter-religious violence, such as that in Gujerat (sic), is a terrible reflection upon local governance. But I would not so simplistically rush to a one-sided explanation. ... Chatterji fails to acknowledge the 50,000+ madrassas operating in India, many with Saudi petro-dollars, and promoting "cultural imperialism" of Arabism, as V. S. Naipaul so eloquently described.

... the greater issue I take with this young Indian-turned-American trying to "impress the whites" is her ignorance about Kashmir. Is she aware of the edicts concerning dar-ul-islam and the fate of dar-ul-harb? Or does she interpret 9/11 as a Marxist economic class struggle with no understanding of how a Pre-

> Modern Islam plays out when confronted with Modernity? How about the plight of the Kashmir Pandits who got ethnically cleansed? In Pakistan, the 12% who were Hindus in 1947 per British census are now cleansed down to under 1%, whereas the 12% Muslims in India are now 14%? Is her stance an implied endorsement of General Musharraf's military dictatorship, Pakistan's ISI's hosting the Taliban and Al Qaeda, and its atrocious human rights record? Or is the strategy behind posting her piece in Dawn a way to seek accolades from ISI?
>
> For someone still trying to make her mark, she is making a fool of herself. Rather than name-calling her opponents, she should show some sophistication: The left/right dialectic that has grown up on her is too simplistic and obsolete. The view that tradition and modernity are necessarily in mutual opposition is too reductionistic. In a place like CIIS, I recommend that she take yoga and meditation lessons from one of the many qualified faculty members such as Stuart Sovatsky or Carol Whitfield. This would give her a better sense of dignity, calm, self respect, and less Hinduphobia.[13]

After this showdown with Chatterji, Singh, though still a student at CIIS, continued to politely oppose her Hinduphobic views. Malhotra helped him privately in dealing with the situation at CIIS. Unfortunately, Singh had very few voices of support among the faculty and fellow students at CIIS. He wrote to Malhotra:

> I feel that there is a larger purpose why I have come here. I have to set right certain things that have gone astray and do many things that have been left unfinished by Dr Chaudhuri. This school must go back to the vision with which it was started – we must reclaim our heritage. We must make it a flourishing center with India-related studies the way it was originally. Your support becomes very important consequently. I know that you are working with Prof. Thurman to establish the Second Renaissance Institute, and your further involvement with CIIS will revitalize this place as well.[14]

Singh met Subbiondo, and they tried to take a more balanced view of matters instead of Chatterji's one-sided narrative. Meanwhile, Malhotra introduced Singh to contacts in the San Francisco Bay Area to get some local support and also encouraged him to call upon seniors like Bina Chaudhuri and explain the entire situation at CIIS. Singh wrote to Malhotra:

> I am planning to take a copy of the mail that you sent regarding the U-turn of CIIS. In the backdrop of the conversations that I have had with her, I know that she is still quite aggrieved at the fact that CIIS took a turn away from the vision of Dr Chaudhuri, and by the manner in which she was humiliated and fired by McDermott almost immediately after he assumed the presidentship of the Institute.[15]

Malhotra continued to draw attention to Angana Chatterji's Hinduphobic articles publicly. Sovatsky wrote to Malhotra suggesting he try to resolve the issues concerning Chatterji directly with Subbiondo. Malhotra responded:

> We have far too many choices from universities of much higher calibre than CIIS to bother. Joe could have called first to chat about his "uncomfortable position" concerning Angana Chatterji. You should give him your personal assessment as you know Infinity Foundation. If he is still genuinely interested, only then would there be a point in pursuing further.
>
> You might point out to him the distinction between an institution and a cult – is CIIS behaving like a cult when it cannot separate a faculty's personal political stance from its own? Is CIIS turning into a political lobby? What precedence does this set for any faculty to go public (like Chatterji did) like a loose canon and ASSUME institutional support for his/her position.
>
> If CIIS wants to take a position on India's events, does it have the skills to do justice to this? Would CIIS be better off staying apolitical institutionally and decoupling its faculty's politics from itself? Frankly, there is little chance that CIIS will now be able to create any unique offer to the spiritual segment of the Indian community in the Bay Area to attract funds. Has CIIS not burnt its bridges?[16]

Yvette C. Rosser, a staunch supporter of Infinity Foundation's campaign against Hinduphobia, chimed in on the e-group to offer support. The team at IF compiled the following questions expressing their concerns:

- Does CIIS want to enter Indian politics for the sake of Ms. Chatterji, given that it does not specialize as a center for political activity?
- Does CIIS have the moral obligation to give equal time and coverage to opposing views?
- Is CIIS wandering away from its spiritual heart, rooted in Sri Aurobindo's work?
- Does CIIS run the risk of slipping further into a U-Turn that started when McDermott was its president?

This situation rapidly deteriorated into an all-out fight with Chatterji continuing to publish venomous, one-sided, anti-India, and Hinduphobic articles. For instance, the Pakistani newspaper *The Information Times*, published from Lahore, made its case against India by citing Angana Chatterji as their news reporter.[17]

Cortright responded by trying to distance Chatterji from CIIS, 'Dear Rajiv, I just want you to know that Angana and her husband Richard do not represent the whole of CIIS. In fact, they represent only a small minority of faculty and students'.[18]

Sovatsky responded as well, thanking Malhotra for sharing these updates regarding Chatterji's activities: 'Rajiv – Your continued efforts to share these points is very helpful. You may also know that Kundan has had some good conversations with key faculty. I also just received a very positive response from the East/West Psychology Chair to teach a semester-long course for Fall 2003 on what is happening to Yoga and Hinduism, Vedanta, Tantra, as they have gotten U-turned, misappropriated, commodified, unacknowledged, distorted, in the US'.[19] Behind the scenes, Sovatsky also tried to help Singh's relationship with Subbiondo.[20]

Despite Malhotra's attempts to educate serious thinkers, many Aurobindonians remained in denial. For example, Bindu from Auroville applied for funds from Infinity Foundation to cover her course fees at CIIS. She wrote to Malhotra:

> I have just started writing the paper, "*An Indic perspective for Ken Wilber's theories of evolution*", for which I had received funds from

> the Infinity Foundation. I needed to ask you about further funding prospects from the Infinity Foundation...I have gained admission to the East-West Psychology program in CIIS, San Francisco. ...I was wondering if it would be possible for Infinity Foundation to pay for my tuition fees at CIIS.[21]

Malhotra responded that he had serious reservations about the way CIIS had marginalized Indian traditions with Angana Chatterji as its lead Hinduphobic. Bindu replied:

> Some Aurovilians made the same critique as you when the CIIS President, Joe Subbiondio (sic) was visiting Auroville. Joe commented that while Angana had made herself unpopular with the Indian community in CA because of her stance, her opinion was hers alone. If I remember Joe correctly, I believe CIIS even gave funds to the construction of a Hindu temple in that area.[22]

Malhotra wrote back, asking Bindu to take a deeper look:

> Subbiondo is manipulative like most of these folks. He desperately wants credibility with Indians and Hindus, both to legitimize CIIS and to get money from rich Silicon Valley desis. So, these are games. I am copying this to Kundan, who knows all the games of Angana and how CIIS supports her without giving the opposing voice equal forum. Brant etc are minority voices there and won't stick their necks out in defense but rather remain private and let the Hinduphobia continue. **A major untold story is the way CIIS, as Sri Aurobindo's USA institution, got hijacked by liberal chauvinism and Christianity when McDermott took it over. From a 100% Aurobindo based curriculum, now it has less than 5% curriculum on Aurobindo or Indic culture.** What a disgrace! I point this out loud and clear every chance I get. So, they want to protect their image. Regarding CIIS funding a Hindu temple, it is a VERY TRIVIAL SUM and not even 1% of their budget. So, it's a token to fool gullible people at Auroville. Sorry to demolish their myth, but that's the truth.[23]

Tragically, the California Institute of Integral Studies had itself become an unfortunate example of the U-Turn model. As a result, Infinity

Foundation discontinued further active engagement with the institute but continued to maintain a good relationship with Singh, who moved on to other career opportunities outside CIIS once he completed his studies.

Chatterji continued her nasty campaigns, and this helped Malhotra spread awareness to the broader Hindu diaspora. Eventually, Chatterji got fired from her post at CIIS due to a scandal reported as follows:

> Chatterji and Shapiro were suspended in July 2011 and dismissed in December 2011 after 14 and 25 years of service respectively, after the CIIS received student complaints against them. The CIIS Faculty Hearing Board found them guilty of failure to perform academic duties and violation of professional ethics.[24]

The matter was later settled, but the couple exited CIIS. Chatterji went on to make her career attacking India on issues concerning Muslims and started co-authoring with Christophe Jaffrelot, another notorious Hinduphobic.

# Conclusion of Part 1

The first decade of Infinity Foundation proved to be a steep learning curve. Mapping the kurukṣetra and discerning the various forces and players involved in it, understanding who had sincere and supporting intentions towards the cause of dharma and its proponents on the one hand, and identifying the lapses that exist in the representation and preservation of dharma and its various aspects on the other, all required astute observation, agility, and innovative responses.

Rajiv Malhotra's interactions with American academia regarding this matter clarified that neither Indians nor practicing Hindus teaching Hinduism courses in the universities had any say in the way the studies of dharma and its history were being portrayed. Thus, Hinduism and India were subject to anthropological studies through Marxist lenses to derive critical conclusions, resulting in castigatory social justice allegations instead of any attention being paid to the larger issue of co-opting.

Insights from dhārmic philosophies, which were central to India's own civilizational identity and narrative, were being appropriated with little credit and taught as results of Western scientific discovery or Western thinkers.

The guru-s of dharma were amongst the greatest scientists the world had seen; as practitioners, they had demonstrated the results that were now being understood partially and being distorted and disseminated in the West. However, they were not even acknowledged in footnotes. The insights from Hinduism and India were being force-fitted into Abrahamic networks and used to champion liberal versions of their religions and propped onto the world stage under the umbrella of 'sameness' of all religions.

While many aspects of the above are interlinked with colonization and should ideally be actively studied as part of decolonization studies, Malhotra found that the response from India and Indians was disappointing and fell short of the action needed to meet the challenges. Most Indians were hesitant to understand the phenomenon and participate as negotiators and champions for the cause of dharma.

The state of Sri Aurobindo studies was one of the most pressing and challenging cases that exemplified all the aforementioned aspects. Ken Wilber started out as an interested student of Indian philosophy with appreciation for its profound insights into consciousness. He then translated these for his Western peers, and gradually incorporated key elements from Sri Aurobindo's works on the involution-evolution of consciousness as his own. Initially, he gave some credit, then moved the vague references as footnotes, and finally dropped any acknowledgment.

This is a perfect specimen of Malhotra's U-Turn Theory. Wilber not only appropriated Sri Aurobindo's core aspects of Integral Yoga but went on to posit deficiencies in the sage's body of work, which are the result of his own lack of understanding in the first place. Repackaging many of the concepts as his own, Wilber has positioned himself as the premier thinker of the century in consciousness studies, with his 'original' work finding applications in domains of mind sciences, psychology, education, and a whole range of allied subjects.

After discovering Wilber's guile handiwork, Malhotra turned to fellow Aurobindonians to examine if others were aware of the issue. To his surprise and increasing dismay, not only were most people in the community unaware of the depth of the distortion that had taken place of their guru's work but were disinterested in helping him respond. Numerous kinds of excuses were offered for their apathy.

Malhotra embarked on a purposeful tour of Auroville and Pondicherry to try and convince the leading Aurobindonians. Over the next few years, between 1998-2004, he put forward solid work and became the only counterforce to Wilber's appropriations. He sponsored individuals to research on the matter and provided grants and financial aid to several key Aurobindonians both in India and in the USA. He even tried to engage with scholars in France and other parts of Europe where Sri Aurobindo's work was known due to The Mother's influence.

As seen in the preceding chapters, a home team emerged around a few scholars who stood by Malhotra. Part 1 has summarized the discussions and work that took place and the substantial outcomes achieved by Infinity Foundation.

What remained undone was a comprehensive study of Wilber's work through the lens of a true Aurobindonian. This would entail a systematic analysis comparing Sri Aurobindo's original work on the evolution of human consciousness at both the individual and social level with that of Wilber's. Eventually, Malhotra decided to undertake such a project himself, along with the co-authors, Manogna Sastry and Kundan Singh.

PART TWO

# Reclaiming The Integral Movement

Chapter 7

# Predator Project to Hijack Sri Aurobindo's Work

## Challenging Ken Wilber, 'the Einstein of Consciousness' Studies

In Part 1 of this volume, we considered how Ken Wilber, the self-proclaimed genius of consciousness studies, had appropriated core concepts on a large scale from Sri Aurobindo's work and distorted them and other Indian traditions. Thereafter, Wilber repositioned himself and his institutes to be the foremost in the Integral movement, even if that meant subsuming core Aurobindonian organizations in India and across the world.

Also considered was how the community of the sage's followers failed to rise to the challenge of actively studying and refuting Wilber, including career Aurobindonians and leaders of the movement. *Infinity Foundation was the first to recognize, educate, work, and lead the efforts to counter the Wilberization of Sri Aurobindo studies.*

Wilber had studied and appropriated many ideas from Vedānta, Sri Aurobindo, Mādhyamaka Buddhism, and Kāśmīrī Śaivism. By the mid-1990s, Rajiv Malhotra had studied Wilber's wide range of works and found that some of the earlier ones explicitly acknowledged Sri Aurobindo's experiences as sources. This was during a phase when Sri Aurobindo and other Indians were widely quoted in the West as authoritative sources on higher states of consciousness. However, as Wilber's reputation and confidence grew, so did his ego's ambition. He started marginalizing his Indian sources, even outrightly ignoring them and in some instances, criticizing them to establish his superiority. His intellectual journey morphed into heroic claims of originality to position himself in the lineage of great Western thinkers.

When this book project began in 2000, Malhotra was unable to find any prior Indian scholar willing to take up a project of this kind in such a comprehensive way – namely, to challenge Wilber's superficial mappings and highlight that he failed to study the Indian material which he uses so confidently and his sole reliance *on second-hand interpretations.* Unfortunately, most traditional Indian scholars are unable to understand his use of several different Western frameworks and theories, nor have they invested the enormous time and energy required, and in many cases, lack the courage to challenge him.

As for Western scholars, there had been some serious attempts to critique Wilber. However, they were limited in their breadth and depth of understanding Indian thought, to which Wilber offers a bridge.

With copious amounts of work written over four decades, Wilber today holds a very significant place in Western studies of consciousness and human evolution. His earliest work presents a picture of a person aiming to bring the profound realizations of Eastern knowledge systems to the Western world of materialism and synthesize the two.

Undoubtedly, Wilber was once a serious student of Indian spiritual philosophy, and he began to map Sri Aurobindo's ideas on the evolution of consciousness into Western terminology. His initial purpose was to educate Western psychologists who felt Western thought on psychology and cognitive sciences had reached a dead end. There was a frenzied search for new ideas. Many individuals came to India looking for answers, but they lacked knowledge of Sanskrit in order to have direct access to Indian texts. Sri Aurobindo's writings were in English and served as a great bridge for Westerners to access Indian thought. Wilber positioned himself as a middleman manning the bridge on which considerable traffic was passing in those days.

Wilber's first two books, *The Spectrum of Consciousness* and *No Boundary,* were his early attempts at translating Indian ideas for Western consumption. His subsequent book, *The Atman Project,* formalized his movement to appropriate Sri Aurobindo's theories on human consciousness. The theme refers to the way the *Ātman* (the real self) has evolved and must continue to evolve.

This is how Wilber's career began, as a sort of intermediary between the dharma traditions as the source of great new knowledge for the West on the one hand and the Western disciplines of psychology and cognitive sciences on the other.

This Part 2 of the book explains the Wilberization of Sri Aurobindo studies, pointing out how Indian discoveries of the Ātman have been hijacked by the Predator Ego (a deluded self) of Ken Wilber. His *The Atman Project* has in effect become a Predator Ego project.

Wilber might have read some of Sri Aurobindo's works, but much of his knowledge came indirectly filtered by way of others' summaries and interpretations, such as the writings by Haridas Chaudhuri and other individuals like Robert McDermott. Wilber lacks the Sanskrit knowledge to access the original sources and did not study under a learned guru. As a result, his knowledge of Indian philosophy was flawed right from the very beginning.

He started out by equating all Indian traditions with perennialism, a superficial construct over the past century developed largely by Western followers of Swami Vivekananda. Perennialism diluted Indian thought into a common denominator of generic mysticism for Western consumption in three ways:

- Disembodiment: It removed the embodied 'this-worldly' emphasis found in the puruṣārtha-s, yoga, Tantra, dance, music, socio-political karma, and anything that might compete against Western approaches to worldly activities and social theories.
- Other-worldliness: The false stereotyping of Indian traditions as other-worldly mystical escapism served as a justification for the Predator Ego to take over.
- Museumization: Many diverse Indian traditions have been desacralized, and collapsed into a single homogeneous approach and turned into generic substitutes. This approach of showing all traditions as inter-changeable paves the way for Indian traditions to be placed into museums, because their usefulness as living traditions can be replaced with Western substitutes.

In an effort to demonstrate that Indian traditions are flawed and that he is the doctor offering cures, Wilber sometimes sprinkles his later writings with innuendos of abuses and 'primitiveness' in India based on unreliable secondary and tertiary sources. However, he does not cite Sri Aurobindo's writings which contradict his thesis. In sharp contrast, he superficially mentions the much larger archive of abuses by the West. He quickly moves on without exposing his Western icons. For instance, he heavily relies upon Hegel without examining how and why he had endorsed genocide, slavery, and colonialism.

The chapters ahead explore in detail Ken Wilber's series of appropriations from Indian civilization to bolster Western civilization, a project in which he serves as the intermediary that selects, filters, censors, recontextualizes, interprets, and reframes. The current chapter summarizes some of the key issues discussed in detail in subsequent ones.

In many instances, Wilber credits the West with traditions it did not have, or if it did, they were not developed in the manner and for the purpose he claims they were; he does this even where Indian sources are far more explicit and well developed. He connects the dots of various Western traditions, filling in the huge gaps in Indian appropriations without attribution. He is silent on the fact that many of his Western sources obtained their core ideas by studying Indian thought. A few examples illustrate this:

- He respects Carl Jung who was known to be anti-Semitic. He fails to examine Jung's view that yoga is dangerous for Westerners – a radical claim that ought to be examined in light of the huge success of yoga in the West.
- He builds his system using the notion of Panentheism which is credited as a development to the American philosopher, Charles Hartshorne. However, he fails to point out that Hartshorne had studied and relied upon Śrī Rāmānujācārya (tenth century Indian thinker) as well as the subsequent philosophies of Jīva Goswāmi (sixteenth century Vaiṣṇava philosopher), which he learnt through his Indian Ph.D. student at the University of Chicago.
- He collaborates with Christian theologians such as Father Thomas Keating, the American Catholic monk who U-Turned from Maharishi Mahesh Yogi's Transcendental Meditation (TM), and reformulated it into Christian Centering Prayer.

- He collaborates with Western cognitive scientists and neuroscientists, many of whose claims of 'originality' are based on unacknowledged appropriations from Indian traditions.

This drift towards self-assertion made Wilber patronizing and disrespectful towards the Indian sources of his inspirations and revelations. It led him to many mistaken conclusions and corrupted his original intention of creating a system in which Western and Eastern paradigms would converge with mutual respect. Instead, he built yet another Western paradigm with the borrowed ideas from original Indian thought. This project has brought him considerable financial sponsorship and clout and hence deserves our independent scrutiny.

Wilber's extensive writings since the early 1970s have evolved through several stages, which he has named Wilber-I, Wilber-II, Wilber-III, Wilber-IV, Wilber-V, and so forth.

We will begin with a critical analysis of his major theories and ideas in the chronological sequence of his books: *The Spectrum of Consciousness; No Boundary: Eastern and Western Approaches to Personal Growth*; *The Atman Project: A Transpersonal View of Human Development*; *Up from Eden: A Transpersonal View of Human Evolution*; *A Sociable God: Toward a New Understanding of Religion*; *Eye to Eye: The Quest for a New Paradigm*; *Transformations of Consciousness: Conventional and Contemplative Perspectives on Development*; *Sex, Ecology, Spirituality: The Spirit of Evolution*; *A Brief History of Everything*; *The Eye of Spirit: An Integral Vision for a World Gone Slightly Mad*; *The Marriage of Sense and Soul: Integrating Science and Religion*; *One Taste: Daily Reflections on Integral Spirituality*; *Integral Psychology: Consciousness, Spirit, Psychology, Therapy*; and *Integral Spirituality*.

We will briefly summarize the highlights of Wilber's career in terms of where he started and how he morphed at various stages. The later chapters detail the changes and errors in his assumptions and conclusions at each stage.

## Key Ideas in Each Phase of Ken Wilber's Career

### *Wilber-I (1977-9)*

Ken Wilber's first phase of writing comprises ideas published in his 1977 book, *The Spectrum of Consciousness.* The central tenet of this work was similar to English writer and philosopher Aldous Huxley's idea of *philosophia perennis* i.e. 'perennial philosophy', that there exists a *psychologia perennis,* a 'perennial psychology'. Wilber's 'insight' in this book is that, similar to the spectrum of electromagnetic radiation observed in physics, a human being is also a 'multi-leveled manifestation of a single Consciousness'. Wilber considers major levels of this spectrum, including that of the mind and the ego. The spectrum of consciousness is borrowed from the levels described in various Indian and Eastern traditions that Wilber has acknowledged here.

He attributes the existence of the levels to māyā and dualism. He refers to several Mahāyāna Buddhism-based works in this book while considering the parallel with Western therapeutic methods. Social therapies, psychoanalysis, Jungian analysis, and Gestalt therapy (a kind of psychotherapy founded by the German psychiatrist Fritz Perls) are all considered in terms of their fundamental belief, i.e. 'that pathology results from some sort of breakdown in communication between the conscious and the unconscious processes of the psyche, from a split between the persona and the shadow, however the latter may be conceived'.[1]

Each level of the spectrum is associated with a particular school of thought. For example, Wilber associates Jungian psychology with the 'Transpersonal Band' of his spectrum and Gestalt therapy with the 'Existential Band'. As a person moves across the spectrum, he moves from personality to ego to the entire cosmos in an expansion of identity. He sees parallels between his spectrum and Abraham Maslow's (American psychologist) hierarchical needs.

At this initial phase, Wilber describes himself as a Romantic Jungian and suffers the typical Western confusion which he rectifies in Wilber-II i.e. the pre-trans fallacy.

In this first book, he creates a place for himself as a librarian and curator, bringing together ideas that he sees as complementary from the

East and the West. However, he perpetuates the idea that the East was only concerned with the levels of the mind and not how pathologies played out in the human being and the larger collective, a presumption that is manifestly untrue:

> ..the overriding concern of the Eastern explorers of consciousness has always been with the Level of Mind, and thus they gave little, if any, attention to the pathologies that could develop on the other levels. This is understandable, for the perennial psychology maintains that all pathology stems from ignorance (avidya) of Mind. Thus, although they were perfectly aware of the various levels of the Spectrum, and although they mapped them in detail, they felt that 'curing' a pathology on any of these levels was not much more than a waste of time, for the root ignorance of the subject-object dualism would still remain.[2]

### *Wilber-II (1980-3)*

The *Atman Project* is Wilber's third major book, and this phase is characterized by his work on the ideas of involution-evolution, the evolution of consciousness from sub to self to superconsciousness, and resolving the pre-trans fallacy among others further discussed. This fallacy goes as follows: Most Western interpretations of Eastern philosophy misunderstand and misrepresent the highest state of spirituality as one where the seeker returns to a childlike state seen during infancy. Nirvāṇa and transcendence of the East are thus presented as a return to a primitive state of consciousness. This is rooted in the Western outlook of seeing human life as suffering a fall from the primordial spirit and Godhead and spiritual fulfillment as a return to this primitive state. Wilber recognized this misunderstanding in Western works, including that of Jung, and called out the difference between transpersonal states, where the seeker transcends the individual ego, and the pre-personal states of an infant. The pre- and trans-states may show superficial similarities, but they are different. Wilber called this the pre-trans fallacy.

The *Atman Project* further established Wilber as a compiler, with him admitting that his entire book was based on phenomenological and direct evidence of hundreds of people across Eastern and Western traditions. He extensively appropriates without acknowledgment concepts from Sri Aurobindo's work in this stage and uses it to create a thirteen-stage development model for consciousness.

### *Wilber-III (1983-7)*

Wilber continues with his development theory and introduces the ideas of distinguishing between lines of development and stages of development, as well as between enduring and transitional structures. These lines of development are to show that a human being can develop his different faculties at different paces, i.e. a person may be more emotionally developed than mentally or vice versa. Wilber appropriated both these sets of ideas from Sri Aurobindo; however, he wrote quite categorically that Sri Aurobindo did not make the distinctions that he was making. While appropriating Sri Aurobindo's ideas in Wilber-II, he fails to acknowledge the sage. But, when he realizes the errors of his limited understanding in Wilber-III, he conveniently attributes his misunderstanding of the appropriated ideas to the sage. He further claims to supersede Sri Aurobindo by using his corrected understanding as the solution to the issues in the previous stage of his work, while continuing to project limitations onto Sri Aurobindo's ideas. It is astonishing that at every stage of his own work, he borrows ideas from Sri Aurobindo's writings to correct his models, while attributing his initial mistaken understanding to the sage's work!

### *Wilber-IV (1987-2001)*

After a hiatus of a few years, Wilber published *Sex, Ecology, Spirituality* (1995), that marks the beginning of his new phase. Other key works in this stage include *The Eye of Spirit* (1997), *Integral Psychology* (2000), and *A Theory of Everything* (2000). During this stage, Wilber begins to associate the term Integral entirely with his own work and no longer refers to Sri Aurobindo.

The most significant aspect of Wilber-IV is the creation of his four-quadrant model that seeks to bring together in a single framework individual and collective aspects of the development of consciousness. Inner individual and inner socio-cultural aspects of the development of consciousness comprise the upper and lower left quadrants, respectively, of his model. The upper right quadrant expresses the individual development externally through behavioral aspects. The lower right quadrant refers to collective social systems that express external development. Plato, Karl Popper (Austrian-British philosopher), Immanuel Kant, and Jürgen Habermas (German philosopher) are all located across the quadrants, while Wilber limits Vedānta and other dhārmic systems into the upper left quadrant, that of the interior 'I' only.

He thus continues to perpetuate this fundamental falsity that Eastern traditions had systems only for inner development while Western systems champion all other external transformations. This characterization is especially problematic, considering the fundamental work done by Sri Aurobindo which focuses on the significance of external and collective systems.

Wilber adds to the All Quadrants All Levels (AQAL) model from this phase, incorporating dimensions to the states of consciousness to include more complexity. He uses Arthur Lovejoy's work on the Great Chain of Being in a new way, referring to his model as the *Great Nest of Being*. He continues to use Koestler's holons as the primary terminology, with each holon described through each of the four quadrants for its complete understanding. Consciousness is thus distributed across these four quadrants. Each quadrant though, uses its own language, validity claims, and domains to characterize itself.

In trying to bring together concepts such as science, arts, spirituality, individual, collective, and their respective dominant schools of thought, Wilber also places Sri Aurobindo and the Buddha, whose works stem from a place of deep and highly complex experiences, on the same plane as Jung, Jean Piaget and Freud. This is deeply problematic, for Wilber creates an artifice that has no integral unity but synthetically brings together a mishmash of ideas and people. He critiques postmodern thinking but ends up creating a scheme that is itself a classic example of the erroneous use of postmodern thinking.

### *Wilber-V (2001-current)*

Wilber now completely rejects all metaphysics, calling it unnecessary. The resultant post-metaphysical AQAL model is called the Integral Post-Metaphysical model. He introduces methodological perspectives for each of the quadrants and brings in Rupert Sheldrake's (spiritual-biologist) morphogenetic fields and Don Edward Beck's Spiral Dynamics.

This phase sees Wilber working on several off shoots like Integral Mathematics, and Integral Buddhism, the latter especially being very surprising, for he began his entire premise borrowing heavily from the dhārmic systems and now claims to add to them new material.

The following table is a small subset of the new offshoots from the application of AQAL and Integral Methodological Pluralism (IMP) to diverse domains. Each of the perspectives associated with the four quadrants of AQAL can be studied through two major methodological families, i.e. from a first- or a third-person perspective. This results in eight distinct zones of human inquiry and comprises what Wilber calls Integral Methodological Pluralism.

The following sample indicates the extent to which Wilber's system has propagated and the need to acknowledge and highlight the primary issues with it, even as it expands to more horizons.

| Domain | Movements based on AQAL |
|---|---|
| Businesses and Management Studies[3] | Integral Methodological Pluralism for transformation of business organizations,<br>Integral Agile, Integral Investing |
| Ecology[4] | Ecological entities studied as holons and through AQAL |
| Education[5] | Applying Integral Methodological Pluralism to research methodologies and education models |
| Interpersonal Studies[6] | Conflict Management, Gender Studies |
| Religions[7] | Integral Buddhism, Integral Christianity |

The key ideas from each of the phases of Wilber's work are summarized in the following table, showing how he went from being a scholar acknowledging Sri Aurobindo to airbrushing him out of any credit due.

Core ideas from Wilber's Phases (1-5 and onwards)

| Phase of Career | Early Wilber Position | Later Wilber Position | Key Writings |
|---|---|---|---|
| **Wilber-I (1977–9)** | Indian idea of non-dual consciousness is the basis of all existence. | Perennialism used to collapse all Indian conceptions. | *The Spectrum of Consciousness; No Boundary* |
| | Defends India against colonial ideas of 'other-worldliness'. | Reduces all Indian traditions to naïve spirituality with no worldly engagement. | *Quantum Questions* |
| | Spiritual transformation is a return to original perfect state. | Corrects his pre-trans fallacy; acknowledges that spiritual growth leads to increased complexity and not a return to the past. | *Spiritual Growth* |
| **Wilber-II, III (1980–7)** | Homogenous, linear evolution through planes of consciousness. | Borrows the idea of lines of development from Sri Aurobindo to explain evolution. | *The Atman Project; Up from Eden; Transformations of Consciousness; Eye to Eye* |
| | Involution-Evolution borrowed from Sri Aurobindo's work but perennialized to all mystics. | No acknowledgment at all about the extent to which the theory was already completely developed by Sri Aurobindo; attributes idea instead to Sheldrake. | |
| **Wilber-IV (1995–2001)** | Reductionist Quadrant Model | Begins to focus on the neurological changes seen in development; the quadrants represent individual-collective binaries and their relationships. Introduces holons, which are also borrowed from Sri Aurobindo. Newer insights on Immanence-Transcendence. | *Sex, Ecology, Spirituality; Integral Psychology* |
| **Wilber-V (2001 onwards)** | | Retains only a few concepts from perennialism and Involution-Evolution. Focus is on worldly applications. | *Integral Spirituality; Integral Life Practice* |

Each of these phases of Wilber's works uncovers layers of appropriations, distortions and misrepresentations of Sri Aurobindo's key concepts and insights as well as those from the larger Indic knowledge systems. Below, we summarize some of the key issues that will be discussed in detail in later chapters.

## Summary of Wilber's Distortions

1. Wilber uses perennialism from the beginning of Wilber-I to dilute all Indian thought into a superficial framework of generic mysticism, and positions it for Western consumption through disembodiment, other-worldliness, and museumization.
2. Wilber charges that Eastern explorers were only concerned with the mind and the levels beyond it, which is false. He assumes dualism is responsible for all pathologies of the mind, which in the first place, shows his limited understanding of dualism.
3. In Wilber-III, he borrows from, and then distorts, Sri Aurobindo's model of evolution and consciousness involuted into various forms of existence. Wilber did not comprehend that Indian tradition did not follow a linear model of development and requires a far more complex understanding of it.
4. In Wilber-II, he conflates Veda with Vedānta, Vedānta with Advaita Vedānta, and simply ignores everything else in Indian traditions. He then uses Sri Aurobindo's critique of other-worldly aspects of Advaita Vedānta and Buddhism and applies it to the entire Indian tradition. Wilber uses Sri Aurobindo's work to supersede the model of Charles Alexander but claims to supersede all Indian traditions as well.
5. Wilber-III charges that Sri Aurobindo's model does not have a separate development line for spirituality. His confusion stems from not having understood the Vedic ideas of immanence completely, and he slips back to his monotheistic background. *In the Vedic system, it is not only the transcendent that is being sought but also a positive relationship with the immanent.* He fails to understand that all 'developmental lines' are *involuted* in matter and life and mind. Further, we show how Wilber's 'lines of development' were derived from Sri Aurobindo's work.

6. In Wilber-IV, he creates AQAL and contains and localizes Eastern traditions only in the upper left quadrant, which deals with individual, and interior. This is problematic not only from a dhārmic perspective but also specifically because Sri Aurobindo has focused his yoga on work done in the world and on social systems of the collective. He categorizes Sri Aurobindo into the same group as Jung, Piaget, and Freud, which is a gross misrepresentation of a yogi who embodied integrality in his entire approach.
7. Wilber attributes typical conflicts seen in Western systems such as science versus spirituality and empiricism versus embodied knowledge, to all systems. Thus, he downgrades the more developed dhārmic model into a sub-category of Western systems.
8. Wilber's model may seem to be an integration of modernity and postmodernity, but in reality is a replication of modernity. Despite heavily critiquing reductionism on various occasions, he is blind to the fact that he has built an expanded version of the very same thing he has critiqued, i.e. reducing the understanding of the epistemological, ontological and metaphysical underpinnings of our cosmos and existence into an interaction of four quadrants.

## Summary of Wilber's Appropriations

1. In Wilber-II, he borrows from Eastern thought to fix a Western fallacy, but turns back and boxes Eastern traditions into the same category as those originally with the problem.
2. Wilber's entire involution-evolution is appropriated from Sri Aurobindo's and Swami Vivekananda's work. He uses this to reinterpret the West's fall from spirit as the spirit evolving in the human being through involution and evolution.
3. He uses Sri Aurobindo's detailed model and creates a thirteen-stage development schema for consciousness, but attributes insights to Westerners like Jung and Sheldrake. In Wilber-III, he professes to give a new definition of spirituality by reframing Sri Aurobindo's concept of the psychic being as his own.
4. During this phase, he attributes the lines of development to Gardner, whereas decades ago Sri Aurobindo used the exact same

phrase as well in the context of evolutionary development having various vertical and horizontal hierarchies.

5. He casts his evolutionary model of consciousness as borrowed from Koestler's holonic paradigm, while Koestler's work itself can be traced to ancient dhārmic texts. His tenets on holons are borrowed almost verbatim from Sri Aurobindo.
6. In Wilber-IV, he refers to generic theories of consciousness while postulating that higher stages of growth are possible. But none, save the loosely termed 'Eastern and Other Contemplative Tradition', contain any postulates, assumptions, mechanisms, or results that consider the evolution of man and envisioning future paths. Thus, Wilber attributes certain claims to Western knowledge systems that they do not make. Sri Aurobindo's Integral Yoga explicitly calls man a transitional being, with a 'Superman' being the next stage for human evolution. Wilber does not even mention, let alone credit, the idea to Sri Aurobindo.
7. In Wilber-IV, he mines Arthur Lovejoy's work on the *Great Chain of Being* in a different way from his previous phases. He uses Lovejoy's accounts of how transcendence and immanence were viewed in the West since the time of the Greeks and positions himself as the one bringing an innovative model by using Sri Aurobindo's core ideas.
8. In Wilber-V, he uses terms that are native to the dhārmic traditions while stripping them of their comprehensive framework, and plucking out the portions he wants as isolated ideas. Karma is an example, where Wilber explains the term through holons and credits Whitehead, Sheldrake, Peirce, the German philosopher Martin Heidegger and the Swiss philosopher Jean Gebser for reference. However, he repeatedly ignores what Sri Aurobindo wrote extensively on the concept of karma and rebirth and its relation to Integral Yoga.
9. Wilber maintains that only shamans and sages can know the outcomes of an event. Without a word on the yogic traditions of India Wilber credits Alfred Whitehead: 'This "transcend-and-include" relationship, grounded in Whiteheadian prehension, is the basis, on the feeling-side, of the gentle tilt of the Kosmos towards greater and greater complexity and depth, a tilt that by any other name is Eros'.[8]

## Summary of Wilber's Misunderstandings

1. Wilber misunderstands even the basic definition of Integral found in Sri Aurobindo's work. In Sri Aurobindo's model, subjective and objective (or interior and exterior) arise out of the concepts of involution-evolution of the Absolute Consciousness, which includes unity and multiplicity. In Wilber's model, because he rejects metaphysics, these concepts are not the result of a process but selected/imposed lenses with no basis. Evolution in Wilber's model refers to a mechanical process with no explainable cause or agency.
2 In dhārmic perspectives, direct experience is a fundamental process of yoga, and the witness perspective is a consequence. Wilber simply presumes this without the accompanying cosmological framework.
3. With his use of purely intellectual models without any grounding in the subjective experience of yoga and his rejection of all metaphysics, Wilber begins with non-dualism and introduces a fundamental flaw in his AQAL: There is no agency within the quadrants. Evolution without involution cannot generate causality and hence, agency. The only solution to this is Sri Aurobindo's involution-evolution model. Wilber misses the central point by mixing up two different frameworks: In dhārmic systems, consciousness is not the product of evolution; rather, evolution, along with its twin process of involution, manifests Absolute Consciousness, which exists independent of the processes themselves.
4. There is no gradation of consciousness at all in the choice of the holon, i.e. an atom is placed at the same level as a cell. The 'depth' that Wilber attributes to the various levels of the same quadrant again has no causality. There is no explanation for what actually produces the higher states of consciousness. This demonstrates his lack of understanding of the levels of Sri Aurobindo's model of consciousness – Matter, Life, and Mind – with each representing a leap.

   Wilber's work on Kosmic karma also exposes his flawed understanding of science, and he merely borrows vocabulary to prop up his assertions while ignoring the underlying concepts and their relevance. He conveniently creates a safety net for himself by claiming similarity and synthesis with modern science. Furthermore, he drops names of renowned thinkers of the past to leverage them as support for his model by extrapolating beyond their work.

Chapter 8

# Wilber-I: The Mining Expedition Begins

## Learning from India to get Credibility

Ken Wilber began his career as a student of Eastern traditions. He was initially heavily influenced by the works of Sri Ramana Maharshi, Sant Kirpal Singh (a proponent of *sabda* yoga, the yoga of sound), and Tibetan Dzogchen Buddhism. He also became a serious student of Zen Buddhism and later studied under many Tibetan teachers.[1]

He then became a disciple of another Westerner named Adi Da 'Free John', who had been a major disciple of Swami Muktananda (founder of *siddha* yoga) but had U-Turned from his Indian guru to proclaim himself the avatāra of this age and set up his massive ashram in Fiji. He was hero-worshipped by Wilber as 'the greatest sage of this century', and even the Buddha and Ramana Maharshi were presumptuously placed on a lower rung. Swami Muktananda was a very influential proponent of Kāśmīrī Śaivism with extraordinary abilities to transmit *Śaktipāt* (initiation) that made him famous in the West. He played a pivotal role in spreading Kāśmīrī Śaivism outside India.

The *Spectrum of Consciousness* was Wilber's first book. It explains Eastern mystical traditions to his Western readers and places them alongside different Western schools of psychology such as Freudian, Jungian, Existential, Humanistic, and Gestalt. His basic contention at that stage was:

- Consciousness is a 'spectrum' of different levels.
- The Western systems lack knowledge of the higher states of consciousness provided by Eastern traditions.
- The Eastern traditions do not deal with the lower states of consciousness because they assume a healthy ego as their starting point, and their goal is to transcend the ego. Hence, they are deficient in methodologies to strengthen the ego of one who has psychological disorders. On the other hand, the West has developed methodologies in the field of psychology that develop a healthy and strong ego.
- In other words, Eastern systems are strong in higher states of consciousness and Western systems strong in lower states of consciousness, but neither is strong in both.
- Therefore, Wilber's project is to integrate all the Western schools that function at the lower levels of consciousness with the Eastern traditions that have understood the upper levels in detail. He feels that their unification into a single comprehensive system is desirable.
- Wilber does not consider the different schools of Eastern and Western psychology and therapy when they are contradictory because he says that consciousness is multi-dimensional and multi-layered, and hence all schools are complementary and address different levels.

At this early stage, Wilber wanted to position himself as an authority on Indian thought to his readers who are mostly Western psychologists and lack access to Indian knowledge. This role as the middleman between civilizations gives him credibility with his readers, which he needs at this stage as a newcomer on the scene.

He drops names and quotes from Ramana Maharshi, Ādi Śaṅkarācārya, Nāgārjuna, Aśvaghoṣa, and Vasubandhu and from the traditions of the *Upaniṣad*-s, Advaita Vedānta, Mādhyamaka, Yogācāra, Ch'an, and Zen Buddhism. In almost every key chapter, he defines the framework using Advaita Vedānta, then elaborates and illustrates with Buddhist thoughts.

His work evolves haphazardly as he keeps discovering and importing all kinds of systems into his organizing principle. He mixes works from conflicting sources by doing a copy-paste to coalesce them into one taxonomy. Initially his sources are mainly Eastern but he steadily moves towards Western sources. He fails to reject, or reconcile, aspects of the different systems that are in conflict with each other.

He is more like what a librarian does to fit many works into a classification system. It is akin to curating items from a flea market of ideas and thereby ending up with a pastiche that lacks consistency. His is an artificial unity, a superficial one, and a façade hiding the deep ruptures and schisms of various schools of thought that have often been at loggerheads for centuries.

This is in contrast with the integrality of approach of Sri Aurobindo, which is described in his seminal work, *The Synthesis of Yoga*. Sri Aurobindo combines different approaches to consciousness and human development, from Haṭha Yoga to Rāja Yoga, including Karma, Bhakti, and Jñāna Yoga. He also presents them as complementary and the components of a single unified integral system.

The major difference is that all the systems being put together by Sri Aurobindo emanate from a common structure. They all have their roots in the *Veda*-s, the *Upaniṣad*-s and the *Gītā* and not taken from an assortment of diverse systems. Articulating a genuine Integral Unity requires a deeper understanding of the *Veda*-s, the *Upaniṣad*-s, the *Gītā* and even Tantra as the major contributors to integral knowledge.

Unlike Sri Aurobindo's system, Wilber did not start out with a unified foundation but was the result of a forced unity that fell apart under closer examination. A fundamental issue is what Wilber calls integral is, in fact, a synthetic unity and not an integral unity.

## Wilber's *The Spectrum of Consciousness*

The very first chapter of *The Spectrum of Consciousness* speaks in the Advaita Vedāntic language such as 'witness as springboard' and 'dissolution of dualism' and actively uses Buddhist notions to expand on them. He explains that Vedānta 'metaphorically speaks of the Ātman-Brahman as the Seer, Knower or Witness', but has a way of distinguishing between the Seer and the Seen. He says that systems aimed at this level include 'Mahayana Buddhism, Taoism, Vedanta Hinduism, Sufism, and certain forms of Christian mysticism', and that these address the dissolution of the duality between the subject and the object.

While admitting that most of his knowledge is borrowed from Indian traditions, Wilber believes that Western psychologists have an important role in healing the pathologies that arise in the various pathological levels, where he claims the West has special expertise:

> ...where every metaphysical tradition has described the levels of pluridimensionality, these levels are in substantial agreement with those outlined in the Spectrum (e.g., the Buddhist vijnanas, the Hindu koshas, Gurdjieff''s vibratory levels, etc.). I have only extended the psychologia perennis by suggesting that not only do these levels apparently exist, as maintained by the perennial psychology, but also that pathology can occur on any of these levels (except, of course, on the Level of Mind), and thus the great contribution of Western psychologies lies precisely in addressing themselves to these pathologies.[2]

When a serious scholar starts to unpack such statements point by point, it becomes clear that Wilber has failed to prove several assumptions and conclusions. Sadly, his Western audience did not challenge him and instead encouraged him to build his later stages.

His borrowings from Eastern traditions begin by adopting the infinite non-dual consciousness as the foundation for our existence. This borrowing serves as his foundation till date.

Wilber does not claim to have ever read the primary sources on Indian thought from which he borrows to build his foundation. He relies upon his *secondary readings* of Ādi Śaṅkarācārya to explain that there is a Self, it alone exists, and that the absolute subjectivity is Brahman, whose validity does not rely on any external source. It is the absolute subject or the absolute witness. His writing in his early years is quintessentially Vedāntic:

> In sum, there is "within" you that which knows, the Witness Absolute Subjectivity, and it is none other than Mind, the Godhead. But this Absolute Subjectivity is not the separate subject we habitually know and feel ourselves to be, for this sense of separate subject is an illusion, demonstrated by the fact that whenever

> you look for subject you find only objects of perception. Thus, the real Knower is one with its universe of knowledge: everything you observe is none than you who are observing it. When you go right down to the very base of your consciousness, you find the universe—not the false universe of objects out there, but the real universe which is no longer imagined as split into a subject vs. an object. At the very bottom of yourself you fall out of yourself into Reality.[3]

Using Vedāntic terms and framework, he explains the phenomenon of māyā and how it enables the absolute subjectivity to manifest as multiplicity: the non-dual oneness manifests as different levels of consciousness or a spectrum.

He cites numerous examples from Vedānta and various schools of Buddhism, but does not at any point mention the various sub-schools within the Indian systems such as *Dvaita*, *Viśiṣṭādvaita* or even the Tantra and *Cārvāka* systems. He uses broad brushstrokes to borrow big ideas which he claims are universal across all systems.

## Defending Indian Traditions Against Charges of 'Other-worldliness'

A common bias against India has been the allegation that Indian systems are inherently other-worldly and not engaged in socially positive ways. However, at this early stage, Wilber does *not* consider Indian spirituality to be other-worldly. This is important to note because he later reverses his position and accuses Indian traditions of being other-worldly: The allegation of 'other-worldliness' will later serve as one of his excuses for claiming to supersede Indian traditions.

At this initial stage, however, he is severely critical of Western scholars who allege Eastern thought to be other-worldly:

> Even though our scholarship in the field of pure mysticism, Eastern and Western alike, has dramatically improved over the past few decades, there are those who continue to distort its "doctrines" in all manner of idiotic ways, claiming mystics are otherworldly, totally out of touch with everyday reality (whatever that means), self-centered, constantly immersed in trance, and so on. This tells us nothing about

> mysticism but quite a bit about ignorance of those who subscribe to such incredible views; and furthermore, it completely overlooks the saying of the great masters of every tradition that 'your everyday and ordinary consciousness, that is the Tao.'... the highest ideal of the mystic that is expressed by the Bodhisattva, who in Mahayana Buddhism is one who sees Godhead everywhere and everywhen, in every person, place, and thing, and thus does not have to retire into solitude and trance in order to find "god".[4]

In the above quote, he is aware of the Eurocentric bias against Indian spirituality and mysticism and is mocking such biased Westerners as 'idiotic'.

At this stage of his career, he lacks credibility and makes his borrowed Indian ideas seem credible by showing a correspondence between quantum physics and the insights of mystics in general. He gives considerable space to this mysticism-science association in his book *Quantum Questions: Mystical Writings of the World's Greatest Physicists* by highlighting the writings of eminent quantum physicists such as Schrödinger, Heisenberg, Einstein, and Wolfgang Pauli.

What he avoids mentioning is that Indian thought had influenced many modern Western physicists, including those he cites, and were not Western philosophical ideas to begin with. For instance, he fails to inform his readers that Schrödinger was highly influenced by the *Gītā* and the *Upaniṣad*-s and had quoted from the *Māṇḍūkya Upaniṣad* in his *Meine Leben Meine Weltansicht*:

> This life of yours which you are living is not merely a piece of this entire existence, but in a certain sense the whole; only this whole is not so constituted that it can be surveyed in one single glance. This is what the Brahmins [wise men or priests in the Vedic tradition] express in that sacred, mystic formula which is yet really so simple and so clear; tat tvam asi, this is you. Or, again, in such words as "I am in the east and the West, I am above and below, I am this entire world".[5]

Walter Moore, in his biography of Schrödinger, writes about the new paradigm created by the two pioneers of Quantum Theory and the influence of Vedāntic thought on them:

> In 1925, the world view of physics was a model of a great machine composed of separable interacting material particles. During the next few years, Schrodinger and Heisenberg and their followers created a universe based on super imposed inseparable waves of probability amplitudes. This new view would be entirely consistent with the Vedantic concept of All in One.[6]

Werner Heisenberg, the American physicist J. Robert Oppenheimer, and the Serbian-American futurist Nikola Tesla have all acknowledged that the *Veda*-s and the *Upaniṣad*-s have influenced their work. Fritjof Capra, in conversation with the planetary scientist Renee Weber in *The Holographic Paradigm*, discusses how Heisenberg was hugely influenced by Indian philosophy:

> I had several discussions with Heisenberg. I lived in England then [circa 1972], and I visited him several times in Munich and showed him the whole manuscript chapter by chapter. He was very interested and very open, and he told me something that I think is not known publicly because he never published it. He said that he was well aware of these parallels. While he was working on quantum theory he went to India to lecture and was a guest of Tagore. He talked a lot with Tagore about Indian philosophy. Heisenberg told me that these talks had helped him a lot with his work in physics, because they showed him that all these new ideas in quantum physics were in fact not all that crazy. He realized there was ... a whole culture that subscribed to very similar ideas. Heisenberg said that this was a great help for him. Niels Bohr had a similar experience when he went to China.[7]

None of these profound Indian influences on the pioneers of quantum physics are mentioned by Wilber.

## Shallowness of Wilber's Indian Knowledge in Phase 1

From the very outset, Wilber's approach to Indian traditions shows the frog in a well syndrome:

1. Wilber had no guru in the true sense for any sustained period of tutelage. He did not begin his studies alongside a serious sādhana/

practice that would allow him to directly experience the states of consciousness he discusses.

2. His knowledge is almost entirely through reading. He has essentially been a bookworm experimenting with clever maps and convoluted use of language. Only later did he start practicing various Hindu/ Buddhist systems.
3. He limits his understanding of Hindu and Buddhist thought to a small subset of these systems – mainly Ādi Śaṅkarācārya's Vedānta and Mādhyamaka Buddhism. His inquiry into them is insufficient to let him differentiate among the finer aspects of the various schools. He relies solely upon secondary readings of them, which results in numerous misunderstandings and shallowness in his work.
4. He completely ignores the social/external dimensions built into Indian systems such as *Dharmaśāstra*-s, *Arthaśāstra* and *Nāṭyaśāstra*, for example. He incorrectly concludes that Indian thought lacks knowledge of the lower realms of consciousness. He brings in Western social thought concerning the external world to cure this presumed flaw. He seems unaware of the Indian *śāstra*-s that discuss in detail the social/external world, which evolves and changes according to the context. This allows him to reinforce his premise that Western systems are necessary to address worldly matters because the Eastern systems address *only* the spiritual aspect.
5. A glaring deficiency is that Wilber's foundation and the subsequent system built upon it are devoid of the goddess or feminine divinity. He utterly fails to consider the interplay between Puruṣa and Prakṛti or Śiva and Śakti or any kind of treatment of the masculine and feminine energies found in every Indian system. All his work is male-dominated – a feature he inherits from Judeo-Christianity. This stands in clear contrast to the Indian paradigms, which not only focus on the Goddess but also celebrate all forms of Her manifestation.

These blind spots lead him astray as he goes deeper. Once he has formulated his core ideas using Indian systems, he makes the Indian sources seem nothing more than one instance of 'generic' mysticism. While there are references from Vedānta and Buddhism in his early works, he intersperses them with superficial references from

Tao, Christian, and Islamic mysticism. As a result, he creates the aura that all mysticism is the same.

His elimination of subtle nuances and sophisticated distinctions of the various Indian systems is a serious violence, and he collapses all Indian thought into reductionistic categories.

In this early phase, there are few examples from Christianity and Islam, and these are picked out of rare instances of random mystics outside the mainstream of both religions. Later, as he gains self-confidence and a larger following, he starts downplaying the Eastern sources and emphasizing the Western ones.

In *No Boundary* (1979) and *The Atman Project* (1980), he increasingly dilutes the Indian sources and their distinctiveness, replacing them with (i) a mishmash of Western spiritual traditions, which he claims say the same thing; and (ii) Western psychology frameworks as the desired map to relocate everything. He starts to claim that he independently created his system and only casually found similarities with Indian systems.[8]

His assessment of his work of integrating the East and West at this stage is as follows, described in his Introduction to Volume 1 of the *Collected Works of Ken Wilber*:

> The general ideas themselves are still sound: the existence of a spectrum of consciousness, consisting of different levels or dimensions of awareness, ranging from matter to body to mind to soul to spirit. These different levels have different characteristics, values, needs, self-sense, motivations, and so on; and they also have different pathologies, which respond to different treatments. This spectrum of consciousness is consistent with the perennial philosophy, from Vedanta to Christian mysticism to Buddhism to Taoism, which gives us a cogent way to integrate Eastern and Western approaches to consciousness, psychology, and therapy. All of these ideas are still quite valid, I believe—and, in fact, they would be the seminal ideas that most of my subsequent writing would elaborate ...[9]

Wilber's approach has three important patterns:

- He relies on Indian frameworks for his spiritual ideas and combines them with Western frameworks for worldly ideas.

- When he reaches his limits of understanding Indian thought, he considers it to be the limitation of Indian thought. This is when he quickly switches over to Western thought and digests the Indian thought into some Western substitutes.
- He is fond of building hierarchies. When his knowledge of an idea X faces his limited understanding, he replaces it with Y and places X *under* Y. In other words, nothing gets rejected. This results in many contradictions in his scheme because he forces artificial harmony just to fit all ideas. Everything has a place in his overarching scheme, some lower than others. This hierarchy is not based on an honest and complete understanding of the various components.

Wilber insists that the explanations made in Vedānta can be found in multiple traditions, including Christianity. For instance, he argues that at every level across the spectrum of consciousness, dualism gets generated which further increases through a subtle process of dualism-repression-projection. It is the same understanding, he claims, in Christianity as in Indian systems.

## Wilber's First Stomach for Digestion: Freud and Jung

Wilber finds Indian systems deficient in addressing the ego's mundane problems. For instance, let us examine how he interprets māyā. He says that the *Gītā* explains two kinds of māyā: one that masks the truth (repression) and the other that projects the false. Wilber explains this at many levels. In the final level, he maps the nature of the Self onto the Freudian framework:

1. At the first level of dualism, a dichotomy between organism and environment is created. This produces the notion of space and time, hence the notion of past, present, and future. Our real nature, which is beyond time and space, gets suppressed, and a space-time universe gets projected.
2. Next, the mind-body harmony is repressed and replaced by the ego.
3. Finally, the ego evolves into the next level of consciousness, the shadow level, comprising persona and shadow.

The final step mentioned above is in terms of Freudian concepts, and this is how Wilber creates his framework for working with the ego through its persona and shadow.

Clearly, he has no knowledge about the sophisticated Sāṃkhya system that explains the mind as comprising buddhi (the discerning aspect of the mind), ahaṃkāra (ego consciousness), and manas (the aspect of the mind which is associated with the sense organs). Later, another dimension was added known as citta, which is the unconscious aspect of the mind comprising saṃskāra-s. These models not only describe the mind but also allow for working with the unconscious and conscious aspects of it. Clearly, Wilber is woefully uninformed of Indian theories and practices of therapy, so he quickly switches to the framework of Freud to describe unconscious desires.

He brings in various schools of Western psychology to show how to heal the problems of humans at different levels of the spectrum. He feels that Freudian psychoanalysis can be extremely beneficial for therapies at the shadow and ego levels, whereas existential psychotherapies can be used at the centaur or the existential level. Using these terms from Western psychology, he tries to evaluate Indian systems.

He ends up creating a muddled system in which Indian systems supply the theories for understanding consciousness, and Western psychology supplies the therapies. He disregards the therapeutic power of Indian systems. At times, he erroneously looks at yoga and Transcendental Meditation in the same category as Jungian analysis. At other times, he limits them and denies their healing roles. He ignores the widespread research in the West that shows the benefits of yoga and TM in physical, emotional, mental, and psychological ways. It is a serious blunder that he reduces Indian systems as being only 'spiritual' without the ability to address psychological problems.

The following table summarizes our review of Wilber's treatment of dhārmic systems based on his Figure 1 in his book *No Boundary.*

| Systems | Level | Our Response |
|---|---|---|
| Mahāyāna and Vajrāyana Buddhism | Nondual, Unity Consciousness | Clubbing dhārmic systems with fundamentally different systems like those based on Abrahamic faith is a gross misrepresentation of both.<br>Vedānta is only one among the six *darśana*-s/schools of Indian philosophy. Wilber cherry-picks one school out of six, reduces all of Hinduism to it, while using Western theories for issues he feels are not covered in Indian thought. Wilber confines dhārmic thought to only higher spheres and ignores their understanding of the lower levels of human psychology. He also substitutes Western equivalents to Vedānta and Buddhism. He introduces many misunderstandings of Indian knowledge systems and mixes them with an assortment of other systems. |
| Vedānta Hinduism | | |
| Taoism | | |
| Esoteric Judaism, Christianity, Islam | | |
| Jung's Analytical Psychology, Maslow | Transpersonal Bands | |
| Humanistic Psychology, Gestalt Therapy | Centaur/Total Organism | |
| Psychoanalysis, Ego Psychology | Ego | |
| Simple Counseling | Persona | |

## Wilber's Second Stomach for Digestion: Perennialism

From the beginning of his work, Wilber starts to map Vedānta and Buddhism into the popular framework known as Perennialism, which is a philosophical system developed by Aldous Huxley, a devout follower of Swami Vivekananda. His book, *The Perennial Philosophy*, became a classic in which perennialism is described as 'a perspective in modern spirituality that views all of the world's religious traditions as sharing a single, metaphysical truth or origin from which all esoteric and exoteric knowledge and doctrine has grown'.[10] Huxley elaborates further:

> *The Perennial Philosophy* is an attempt to present this Highest Common Factor of all theologies by assembling passages from the writings of those saints and prophets who have approached a direct spiritual knowledge of the Divine.

He was politically correct in this era when Europe had been destroyed by Nazi extremist ideology, and the world needed something to foster harmony among all faiths. The following list shows the major philosophies Huxley quotes to make all of them look the same:

> Aquinas, Augustine, St. Bernard, Bhagavad-Gita, Buddha, Jean Pierre Camus, St. Catherine, Christ, Chuang Tzu, "Cloud of Unknowing," Contemplation, Deliverance, Desire, Eckhart (five lines, the most quoted person), Eternity, Fénelon, François de Sales, Godhead, Humility, Idolatry, St. John of the Cross, Knowledge, Lankavatara Sutra, William Law (another four lines), Logos, Love, Mahayana, Mind, Mortification, Nirvana, Prayer, Rumi, Ruysbroeck, Self, Shankara, Soul, Spirit, "Theologia Germanica," Truth, Upanishads (six different ones are quoted), Will, Words.[11]

Huxley had spent much of his adult life actively learning the teachings of the Ramakrishna Mission. There, his intellectual and spiritual foundation matured, and he wanted to digest these ideas and present them for Western consumption.

Perennialism became Huxley's system to make Vedānta appear the same as other systems from various traditions around the world. This is typical of Westerners who lack the rigor of understanding the Indian systems and believe they are doing Indian thought a favor. Using the perennial framework allows him to claim equivalence between Indian ideas and those of several Westerners. However, Huxley's knowledge of Indian sources was limited to the staple teachings meant for Westerners at the Vedanta Society in the USA. In effect, perennialism became a stomach for digesting Vedānta and stripping it of deeper levels of understanding.

Huxley was nominated seven times for the Nobel Prize in Literature and was considered one of the eminent intellectuals of his generation.

Wilber's sole basis for equating Indian practices with numerous other perennial practices is the second-hand conjectural interpretations by prior Western U-Turners such as Huxley. Wilber studied perennialism and used it as a stomach to digest everything he was learning about Indian philosophical systems. In other words, a prior digestor (Huxley) served as the foundation for Wilber's further digestion of Vedānta and Buddhism.

Our goal is to uncover the pipeline of digestion: Western scholar A digests Indian thought; this digested version is later used by a future digestor B as his source; B digests the ideas further into his own 'original' framework. And so forth. Many of Wilber's so-called 'original' ideas have undergone multiple stages of digestion carried out previously by other famous Westerners.

Wilber's motive is twofold: Indian frameworks must be translated into a simple terminology accessible by Westerners, and Western schools of psychology must be placed on par with Indian schools. In sweeping generalizations, he positions carefully curated Indian concepts with what he sees as equivalent ideas from different ages and cultures. Wilber-II onwards he applies this to Sri Aurobindo's work: Instead of quoting and presenting Sri Aurobindo authentically, he tries to borrow bits and pieces and blend them within scattered sources. Indeed, in his Wilber-I stage, his familiarity with Sri Aurobindo is almost negligible. Since his appropriations of Sri Aurobindo begins at Wilber-II stage under the cover of perennialism, it becomes pertinent for us to discuss Sri Aurobindo's stance on perennialism and how distorting him as a perennialist has had a catastrophic effect on the sage's integral worldview and its digestion by Wilber.

## Sri Aurobindo Against Perennialism

Sri Aurobindo did *not* accept the perennialist view that all religions are the same or that all paths lead to the same outcome. This is not because he lacked a proper understanding of Western thought. In fact, he received the finest Western education available during his formative years, mastered Greek and Latin, and went through an intense study of Sanskrit and its original texts.

In his anthology of essays titled *The Foundations of Indian Culture*, he finely elaborates on the fundamental differences in the very nature of people from the East and the West. This difference has often played out in political, economic, social, and cultural arenas repeatedly in history. To set aside the distinct features of Indian civilization in the name of perennialism, as Wilber does, is simplistic and misleading. Naturally, one finds many commonalities across cultures without needing any help from perennialism. However, it is disingenuous to use perennialism as the excuse and the mechanism for wholesale reduction and co-opting of distinct concepts from India.

Sri Aurobindo was far from being a perennialist. His lucid exposition holds that all manifestation proceeds from Brahman (or sat-cit-ānanda, translated as Existence-Consciousness-Bliss), which transcends, and is not bound, by its manifestation. Brahman has two aspects — static and dynamic, or nirguṇa, without qualities, and saguṇa, with qualities, and neither can be ignored. Sat-cit-ānanda can be experienced in many ways depending on one's plane of consciousness, including worldly/mundane and 'other-worldly' lenses. He maintains that when one sees the Spirit at the heart of every sphere of human endeavor, then Matter, Life, and Mind reveal their truest meaning.

Thus, the individual embodies all the planes of existence: physical, vital, mental, and spiritual. Each of these cosmic planes finds a corresponding mapping within the individual. At the levels of the Mind and beyond, he introduces new terminology for the various levels of experience, such as Supermind, Overmind, Intuitive Mind, Illumined Mind, Higher Mind, and Mind, among others. In other words, even within an individual there are multiple mechanisms at work, uniquely defined by the Indian system; therefore, mapping all world religions into one view is ridiculous.

We can broadly explain three kinds of levels in his framework:

- The Supermind comprises all the different manifested aspects of the Divine; for example, the impersonal and personal, static and dynamic, are united and seen in their non-dual forms. The contradictions and conflicts of different traditions are experienced as one. *But this unified experience is only true at that level.* The Supermind forms the link between the sat-cit-ānanda and Manifestation.[12]
- The level of the Overmind is below the Supermind. Here, the diversity and differences of the different aspects of the Divine

begin to express, and the multiplicity of the One begins to manifest. Different facets of Truth begin to individuate and become independent truths.

- In the lower planes – Intuition, Illumined Mind, Higher Mind, etc., – the unity, which is known and accessible at the Overmind, gets masked, giving rise to conflicting traditions and practices, where their own vision and exclusive contentions are emphasized.

Sri Aurobindo explains how this differentiation intensifies because of the way the Overmind manifests at increasing levels of fragmentation:

> The Overmind takes these Truths and Powers and sets each working as a force in itself with its necessary consequences—there can be harmony in their actions, but it is rather synthetic and mostly partial than inherent and inevitable and as one descends from the highest overmind, separation, collision and conflict of forces increase, separability dominates, ignorance grows, existence becomes a clash of possibilities, a mixture of conflicting half-truths, an unsolved and apparently unsolvable riddle and puzzle.[13]

This implies that even if we assume that all religions emanate from a single source and are different facets of one Integral Truth, they would each provide access to this Truth from their own distinct vantage points, and hence there is diversity among their views. This uniqueness of a religion gets contextualized and digested in that religion's specific historicity. Hence, the diversity of claims cannot be easily mixed and matched.

Sri Aurobindo emphasizes the multifaceted Divine rather than collapsing the profound diversity into a single homogeneous 'sameness' of all traditions. Behind all of them is a unifying Truth of existence that can be experienced by the seeker, where all the diverse presentations of the Truth may find their real and unique place. He pierces through this confusion and writes:

> For the seeker of the Integral Yoga no single experience, no one Divine Aspect,—however overwhelming to the human mind, sufficient for its capacity, easily accepted as the sole or the ultimate reality,—can figure as the exclusive truth of the Eternal. For him

> the experience of the Divine Oneness carried to its extreme is more deeply embraced and amply fathomed by following out to the full the experience of the Divine Multiplicity. All that is true behind polytheism as well as behind monotheism falls within the scope of his seeking; but he passes beyond their superficial sense to human mind to grasp their mystic truth in the Divine. He sees what is aimed at by the jarring sects and philosophies and accepts each facet of the Reality in its own place, but rejects their narrownesses and errors and proceeds farther till he discovers the One Truth that binds them together.[14]

Many spiritual traditions do show some remarkable similarities, for example, in explaining the limitation of logical and discursive thinking or the need to transcend subject/object and seer/seen dichotomies. However, there is also tremendous diversity, which needs to be appreciated, not as a problem but as a resource to be harnessed for integral understanding. Every legitimate tradition could be considered as a manifestation of Integral Truth, but from varied vantage points at varied levels of consciousness. As a result, there are profound structural differences among the religions.

A second problem is that not all truth claims made by religions are necessarily true. Hence, not all such claims are even valid from some vantage points; many are outright false. A common illogical argument is that since there can be only one ultimate truth, all religions must be valid. The confusion here is between truth and truth-claim. There can be numerous human conceptions of a given truth, including false conceptions.

For instance, a patient may receive many different diagnoses, but one cannot say all are valid merely because some doctors examined the body of the same patient. Though there is one reality (the body of the patient), the various doctors' conceptions of it are not the same. Truth claims are human perceptions about some reality. Each faith is a true claim that has been propagated through a long history by various individuals and institutions.

Wilber does not appreciate this elementary logic until much later in his career. He conflates a vast array of traditions simply because they espouse some form of non-dualism. This is like saying that all fruits are the same if they are sweet – as if sweetness were their only attribute. This over-simplification collapses centuries of debates among various Indian schools, which have been at the heart of Indian spiritual development and progress to a single reductionist notion of non-dualism.

As an example of opposing such naïve reductionism, Sri Aurobindo emphasizes that Buddhism and Vedānta are not talking about the same experience of non-dual reality in different terminologies even though they do have many similarities. He explains the differences among various kinds of non-dual experiences:

> The impressions in the approach to Infinity or the entry into it are not always quite the same; much depends on the way in which the mind approaches it. It is felt first by some as an infinity above, by others as an infinity around into which the mind disappears (as an energy) by losing its limits. Some feel not the absorption of the mind-energy into the infinite, but a falling entirely inactive; others feel it as a lapse or disappearance of energy into pure Existence. Some first feel the infinity as a vast existence into which all sinks or disappears, others as an infinite ocean of Light above, others as an infinite ocean of Power above. If certain schools of Buddhists felt it in their experience as a limitless Shunya, the Vedantists, on the contrary, see it as a positive Self-Existence featureless and absolute.[15]
>
> The feeling of the Self as a vast peaceful Void, a liberation from existence is one that one can always have, Buddhist or no Buddhist. It is the negative aspect of Nirvana—it is quite natural for the mind, if it follows the negative movement of withdrawal, to get that first, and if you lay hold on that and refuse to go farther, being satisfied with this liberated Non-Existence, then you will naturally philosophise like the Buddhists that Shunya is the eternal truth. Lao Tse is more perspicacious when he spoke of it as the Nothing that is All. Many have the positive experience of the Atman first, not as a void but as pure unrelated Existence like the Adwaitins (Shankara) or as the one Existent.[16]

At this stage, Wilber is very much a perennialist and contends that the truths of all esoteric traditions are the same except for cultural and linguistic variations. This serves as a convenient framework for him to deny important distinctions of experiences, methods of practice, and results. He needs to work hard and study the variety of Indian traditions before making sweeping statements or bother to practice various kinds of techniques before passing judgment on them. After all, by declaring them to be perennial, he can mix and match the attributes of all sorts of religions and replace one with another freely.

Wilber is completely ignorant of what Sri Aurobindo wrote in the remarkable chapter, *Indian Spirituality and Life*, in *The Renaissance in India and Other Essays on Indian Culture*. He is very clear about the distinctiveness of Indian spiritual traditions:

> **The whole root of difference between Indian and European culture springs from the spiritual aim of Indian. It is the turn which this aim imposes on all the rich and luxuriant variety of its forms and rhythms that gives to it its unique character. Even what it has in common with other cultures gets from that turn a stamp of striking originality and solitary greatness. A spiritual aspiration was the governing force of this culture, its core of thought, its ruling passion. Not only did it make spirituality the highest aim of life, but it even tried, as far as that could be done in the past conditions of the human race, to turn the whole of life towards spirituality...**[17]

Interestingly, at a later stage in his *A Sociable God: Toward a New Understanding of Religion*, Wilber appropriates Sri Aurobindo's explanation of why perennialism is incorrect. At this stage, he suddenly turns against perennialism as his common framework for all traditions. However, he does not acknowledge and credit Sri Aurobindo for this insight.[18]

Things get even worse: Wilber writes that perennialism and everything Indian must get superseded by 'a more critical, less metaphysical approach, incorporating some of the important insights of post-Kantian and postmodern thought'.[19] This is a major distortion: His dismissal of perennialism lumps all Indian thought, and he dismisses all Indian systems with one sweep as perennial. He calls all Indian thought 'metaphysical' and declares this category to be inferior to his own system.

In fact, Indian thought is rejected in totality not only as perennialism, but worse, Wilber considers all Indian thought as the 'premodern' version of perennialism.

## Distorting Sri Aurobindo as a Perennialist

Wilber's distortion of Sri Aurobindo's Integral Yoga is at least two-fold. Firstly, Integral Yoga is comprehensively and emphatically *this-worldly* whereas Wilber conflates it with other-worldly mysticism by assuming perennialism's superficial premise that all mysticisms are the same. As we shall see later, this error perpetuates and magnifies as Wilber continues his journey.

Secondly, he fails to note Sri Aurobindo's core argument that the realization of pure undifferentiated consciousness is not the ultimate goal because, while it leads to liberation, it cannot bring about transformation. There are many other realizations possible *after mokṣa* is achieved, which he describes as the experience of active Brahman, Truth-Consciousness, Dynamic Truth, and so forth. Sri Aurobindo wrote:

> In our yoga the **Nirvana [or moksha] is the beginning of the higher Truth, as it is the passage from the Ignorance to the higher Truth**. The Ignorance has to be extinguished in order that the Truth may manifest.[20]

Sri Aurobindo had ascended and integrated various kinds of higher states, including realizations depicted in Vedānta (Advaita, Viśiṣṭādvaita, and Dvaita) and Tantra, and moved on to still higher states. Thus, he integrated not only the non-dual static Self as emphasized by Vedānta, but also the dynamic consciousness-force of Tantra, which transforms the mind, body, and all the other aspects of being. *Wilber has completely ignored this critical integration of Vedānta and Tantra into Integral Yoga.*

Prior to colonialism, Vedānta and Tantra were not separated and certainly not cast in mutual opposition. This unity of Vedānta and Tantra is evident in the writings of many exemplars, including Śrī Rāmānujācārya, Abhinavagupta, and Jīva Goswāmi among others. A sanitized version of Vedānta became emphasized in the colonial era. Tantra got demonized and linked with thugs and other so-called 'criminal tribes' as something uncivilized. Vedānta could be seen as abstract and disembodied, while Tantra was too embodied and hence 'pagan' for European sensibilities, especially after the Inquisition had eradicated the feminine from spiritual life.

Sri Aurobindo formulated his yoga based on personal experience and emphasized that Vedānta and Tantra when kept separate, captured only partial truths:

- Advaita Vedānta leads towards realizing the Lord as the non-dual Self, and Sāṃkhya aspires to liberation of Puruṣa from Prakṛti and becoming her master. The soteriological emphasis in both of these is transcendence from the realm of manifestation and union with the Lord/Self/Puruṣa. Sri Aurobindo considers this the *static aspect of the Divine*.
- However, Tantra sees the world as Śakti, which is the *dynamic power of the Divine*. It seeks perfection, mastery, and beatitude in the world rather than transcendence out of it, hence placing an emphasis on the dynamic aspect of the Divine: Prakṛti, Śakti, Nature, Nature-Soul, Force, and Will-in-Power.

Whereas Advaita Vedānta or Sāṃkhya leads to the inactive witness and the silent Puruṣa or the Self, Tantra takes the practitioner to the dynamic Śakti or Prakṛti which is feminine and is the force necessary to seek transformation within and without. Śrī Rāmānujācārya's Viśiṣṭādvaita had already combined both transcendence and immanence into what Westerners like Charles Hartshorne have called Panentheism. Malhotra has written extensively on its Indian origins.[21]

Sri Aurobindo explains how both these aspects are important to experience:

> We have in this central Tantric conception one side of the truth, the worship of the Energy, the Shakti, as the sole effective force for all attainment. We get the other extreme in the [Advaita] Vedantic conception of the Shakti as a power of Illusion and in the search after the silent inactive Purusha as the means of liberation from the deceptions created by the active Energy. But in the integral conception the Conscious Soul is the Lord, the Nature-Soul is his executive Energy. Purusha is of the nature of Sat, the being of conscious self-existence pure and infinite; Shakti or Prakriti is of the nature of Chit,—it is power of the Purusha's self-conscious existence, pure and infinite. **The relation of the two exists between the poles of rest and action. When the Energy is absorbed in the bliss of conscious self-existence, there is**

> **rest; when the Purusha pours itself out in the action of its Energy, there is action, creation and the enjoyment or Ananda of becoming.**[22]

Wilber has considerably watered-down Sri Aurobindo's philosophy under the cover of perennialism, while not even bothering to mention Tantra. At the same time, he falsely insinuates a lack of this-worldly spirituality in the Indian traditions so that he could freely co-opt ideas from Sri Aurobindo pertaining to the external world. Wilber's strategy is to reduce and collapse everything non-Western about higher states as generic perennialism, and then appropriate Indian ideas to make them appear as his own innovations:

> If we take all these higher stages and add them to the lower and middle stages/levels which have been so carefully described and studied by Western psychology, we would then arrive at a fairly well-balanced and comprehensive model of the spectrum of consciousness.[23]

In the above quote, Wilber is 'containing' and ignoring Indian systems that address the ordinary (i.e. lower and middle levels). This enables him to bring such ideas from Western psychology as his contribution.

Sri Aurobindo dealt with the psychology of the lower states of consciousness and elaborated a great deal on the transformations of these lower levels that should occur upon ascent to the higher levels. We will discuss these in detail in subsequent chapters to show that Wilber's claims of remedying the shortfalls in Sri Aurobindo's model are disingenuous.[24] We also show that his so-called solutions are blatantly appropriated from Sri Aurobindo.

Sri Aurobindo contends that spiritual practice of the Buddha and Ādi Śaṅkarācārya signified liberation *from* nature rather than liberation *of* nature and *in* nature.[25] Nature and body were seen as stumbling blocks in the process of self-realization and were viewed as something to be discarded when the objective was attained. Advaita Vedānta holds that once liberation is attained, the body which has come into existence due to its past karma will continue to exist till it works out its karma. The jñānī who has attained the knowledge will know that he or she is not the body; the body is unreal or mithya and will leave the terrestrial existence once the karma is worked out. The vital being—which is the seat of all desires, demands, cravings, sensations, passions, lust, greed, pride, and arrogance—needs to be bypassed in order to have the knowledge of the Self. Since terrestrial existence is unreal, there is no point in transforming the body. The emphasis was on transcendental liberation (mukti, mokṣā or nirvāṇa).

According to Sri Aurobindo, such yoga of liberation releases from the fetters of lower prakṛti but fails to transform the lower nature (*aparā*) into the higher (*parā*) so that the body-mind becomes a perfect instrument for *parā* prakṛti.

Sri Aurobindo's Integral Yoga is different from this. It states that release from lower prakṛti is only the first step. The next step is to bring the glories of the spirit not only into life and mind but also into the very cells of the body to transform and divinize it. (See Appendix for further discussion on Sri Aurobindo's ideas of transformation). An Integral yogi is not to remain static in transcendental realization; s/he must pull down the spiritual force for its fuller manifestation in the world.

Ascent and descent form the two-fold principle of Integral Yoga. Sri Aurobindo's symbol, comprising two triangles, represents this: the one pointed upwards, and the other projecting downwards, represent ascent and descent respectively. The aim of Integral Yoga is the complete transformation of the body, which he referred to as supramentalization, as well as that of the Mind and Life itself.

Many Indian spiritual systems such as the various systems of yoga, provide methodologies and epistemic frameworks for transcending the limits of the body-mind complex. Sri Aurobindo is emphatic that the spiritual journey continues beyond that transcendence. The puruṣa, upon experiencing its universal and transcendental nature, is then able to master prakṛti. Such a puruṣa can work in unison with the Śakti in complete freedom. In turn, Śakti can then seize upon all the parts of the sādhaka—the physical, the vital, and the mental—and transform them according to her light and power and the individual truths present in the being.

Sri Aurobindo's *The Synthesis of Yoga* studies the minute details, including the approaches based on an individual's primary disposition, such as Rāja Yoga, Karma Yoga, Jñāna Yoga, and Bhakti Yoga. He shows how his Integral Yoga uses all these methods and much more. The life-affirming Integral Yoga requires Divine energy through our being; only then can yoga carry out the work of world transformation. Indian traditions go into immense detail to explain these higher realms of the journey, which Wilber has completely sidelined.

## Wilber's Strategy to Contain Sri Aurobindo

While Wilber does express appreciation and regard for Sri Aurobindo in his early books such as *The Atman Project*, his understanding is limited and distorted. Wilber classifies Sri Aurobindo as a metaphysician and places him in the same slot as the philosopher Plotinus. This is a grave misinterpretation and unfair comparison. Though there are similar ideas in their work, the aims, methods and structures espoused are very different.

Wilber presents himself as the one who will move past the limitations of all these past great minds. Clearly, he does not understand Sri Aurobindo when he writes the following about all thinkers prior to himself:

> ... all of them are pre-quadratic attempts to derive the essentials of the Kosmos from a starting point that prejudicially has already collapsed the essentials out of existence and thus must attempt to recover those essentials with epicycles of further abstractions. ...am not saying that aspects of their work are not true; ...they have abstracted their conclusions out of the matrix of indigenous perspectives and then presented them as "the way things are," oblivious to the perspectives in which their "views from nowhere" actually arrive. This is certainly the case with "metaphysics" in general, whether we find it in Plotinus, Shankara, Asanga, Padmasambhava, Gurdjieff, Hegel, Rudolph Steiner, Carl Jung, William James, or the greatest of recent metaphysicians, Aurobindo.[26]

In the Indian traditions, one sees brilliant debates between the Advaita and Dvaita philosophies, yet Wilber sets aside all this diversity of perspective to lump Ādi Śaṅkarācārya and Sri Aurobindo in the same category with William James, Rudolph Steiner, and Hegel. He maintains that he 'supersedes' them all!

Wilber brushes aside dismissively under the term 'metaphysics' several aspects of supra-physical realities, which Sri Aurobindo has explained in intimate detail in his work. For instance, according to Sri Aurobindo, life on earth needs to be *transformed* and not merely *transcended*, which is unlike the Buddhist understanding of nirvāṇa as the goal. Though Wilber claims to know Buddhism, he fails to understand this key distinction.

M. Alan Kazlev, a critic and theorist, has scrutinized the references Wilber provides to Sri Aurobindo's quotes. He finds serious lapses which indicate a couple of possibilities: Wilber has not read Sri Aurobindo, as evidenced by his misquotes from secondary sources, or he does not consider it necessary to accurately refer to the sage's work while professing to transcend him.[27]

Wilber's placement of Sri Aurobindo in the upper left and upper right quadrants of his classification grid is incorrect. Wilber further charges that:

> **Although he had many important insights on the social and political system, he did not seem to grasp the actual interrelations of cultural, social, intentional, and behavioural. Nor did his analysis at any point proceed on the level of intersubjectivity (Lower Left) and interobjectivity (Lower Right). He did not fully assimilate the differentiations of modernity.**[28]

Such a sweeping and nonsensical statement is being made against a sage whose work ranges from prolific writings on colonization, freedom, economy, education, social issues to philosophies of yoga, the *Veda*-s and the *Upaniṣad*-s, the *Gītā*, and masterpieces such as *Savitri*. His works inspired thousands of people, and the city of Auroville was founded upon his vision.

Wilber is ignorant that Sri Aurobindo's important work, *Savitri*, describes man's spiritual journey until the very highest Supramental vision; it explains that man's life, in every sphere of activity, needs to be transformed by divinizing the terrestrial life.

In *The Life Divine*, the chapter titled *The Double Soul of Man*, explains the three stages of Integral transformation. The first stage is about the individual soul, the psychic being; the second is about the universal Self; and the third is about the transformation of all Nature. He calls them psychic, spiritual, and supramental transformation, respectively.

The individual psychic being 'is a flame born out of the Divine and, luminous inhabitant of the Ignorance, grows in it till it is able to turn it towards the Knowledge'. It is a deputy of the unborn Self or Ātman 'in the forms of Nature, the individual soul,... supporting mind, life and body, standing behind (them) ... watching and profiting by their development and experience'. He continues:

> If it can come forward into the front and govern overtly and entirely... this outer nature of mind, life and body, then these can be cast into soul images of what is true, right and beautiful and in the end the whole nature can be turned towards the real aim of life, the supreme victory, the ascent into spiritual existence.[29]
>
> The Psychic being can by the spiritual influx enlarge itself and embrace the whole world... in an intimate communion or oneness. Or it may become aware of its eternal Companion and elect to live for ever in His presence, in an imperishable union and oneness as the eternal lover with the eternal Beloved, which of all spiritual experiences is the most intense in beauty and rapture. All these are great and splendid achievements of our spiritual self-finding, but they are not necessarily the last end and entire consummation; more is possible.[30]
>
> The psychic transformation after rising into the spiritual change has then to be completed, integralised, exceeded and uplifted by a supramental transformation. In Supermind is the integrating Light, the consummating Force, the wide entry into the supreme Ananda: the psychic being uplifted by that Light and Force can unite itself with the original Delight of existence from which it came: overcoming the dualities of pain and pleasure, delivering from all fear and shrinking the mind, life and body, it can recast the contacts of existence in the world into terms of the Divine Ananda.[31]

In the last chapter of *The Life Divine,* these three stages of transformation are once again emphasized:

> It is, then, this spiritual fulfilment of the urge to individual perfection and an inner completeness of being that we mean first when we speak of a divine life. It is the first essential condition of

> a perfected life on earth, and we are therefore right in making the utmost possible individual perfection our first supreme business. The perfection of the spiritual and pragmatic relation of the individual with all around him is our second preoccupation; the solution of this second desideratum lies in a complete universality and oneness with all life upon earth which is the other concomitant result of an evolution into the gnostic consciousness and nature. But there still remains the third desideratum, a new world, a change in the total life of humanity or, at the least, a new perfected collective life in the earth-nature. [32]

Sri Aurobindo wrote about a truly Integral Life, embracing and synthesizing all aspects, and living in a way that divinizes man's earthly life. What Wilber sees as shortcomings in the sage's work are reflections of his limited understanding because Sri Aurobindo was explicit in his emphasis on outward transformation.

## A Compromised Middleman

After using Indian sources to secure his own credibility, Wilber steadily decreases citing them. He shifts to corroborating his positions by citing only Western sources, including many Westerners who had previously digested Indian traditions. Eventually, the Indian sources disappear completely. They get lost in his voluminous, generic, and non-Indian references. His statements start to discuss 'all traditions', with occasional patronizing statements about 'Eastern wisdom'.

Wilber has made personal claims of having experienced higher states of consciousness. However, when he was formulating his major ideas, he did not claim to have experiences of the higher states using any Abrahamic religious practices. As per his own writings, his entire empirical basis for making claims relies upon his sādhana/practice of Indian traditions *only*. Yet, he flippantly equates these as being the same as other traditions in which he did *not* have any direct experience. Most of the compilation of ideas he considers common across cultures are taken from books and not based on his actual experiences.

To clarify, if he wants to claim that systems X and Y produce similar results, he must practice both X and Y to be able to verify their equivalence based on direct experience. Or else he cannot equate them authentically.

A major shift in his work comes when he gradually starts parroting a standard Eurocentric claim: Indian spiritual systems are deficient in knowledge and application about the lower planes of existence, which deal with mundane life in the external world. He simply perpetuates this bias without supplying any supporting argument or data:

> The Ego Level and existential Level together constitute our general feeling of being a self-existent and separate individual, and it is to these levels that most Western approaches have addressed themselves. Eastern disciplines, on the other hand, are generally more concerned with the Level of Mind, and thus tend to completely bypass the levels of egocentricity. In short, Western psychotherapies aim at "patching up" the individual self while Eastern approaches aim at transcending the self. So while we find ourselves at the Ego Level or the Existential Level, let us avail ourselves of the existing methods—largely "Western"—of creating healthy egos, of integrating projections, of coming to grips with unconscious drives and wishes, of structurally realigning our body postures, of accepting responsibility of being-in-the-world, of dealing with neuroses, of living up to our full potentials as individuals.[33]

This is false because:

- It is only Advaita Vedānta and Theravada Buddhism among the Indian traditions that have some interpretations one may potentially consider to be other-worldly; the discovery of transcendental consciousness and becoming aware of it does not cancel the validity of the embodied state of consciousness.[34]
- Even within Advaita Vedānta, many interpretations are not other-worldly. Ādi Śaṅkarācārya himself did not live an other-worldly life.
- The emphasis of both Buddhism and Advaita Vedānta on renunciation was only for monastic life, while there were other lifestyles of dharma, artha, and kāma for those in need of developing the positive ego before being ready to seek liberation.

- The systems of Viśiṣṭādvaita and Dvaita, and the systems of Mādhyamaka and Vajrāyana in Buddhism, are certainly not 'other-worldly'.
- There are numerous other Indian traditions such as Tantra, Kāśmīrī Śaivism and Nyāya among others, which are profoundly this-worldly and pragmatic.
- Most of the *Upaniṣad*-s and *Yoga-vāsiṣṭham* begin with a discourse that is 'this-worldly'. The *Bhagavad Gītā* is entirely about responsible action in the world, set in the context of a truly human condition and realistic scenario – war.

In actuality, Wilber does not supersede the Indian traditions but a rather limited and digested version. He is unfamiliar with well-known Indian thinkers who had rejected ideas of escaping from the ego without first purifying it into a sāttvic ego. There have been many debates within the Indian system that challenge escapist understandings.

Having not been properly challenged, Wilber claims that his ostensible personal experiences in higher states of consciousness are the same as what a few sporadic Westerners wrote about. He also does not have contemporary testimonies from any Western exemplar that could be subject to due diligence or critical analysis.

Chapter 9

# Wilber-II: Appropriating Sri Aurobindo's Theory of Evolution

The previous chapter explained how Wilber-I adopted perennialism as the framework into which much of the diversity of non-Western spiritual traditions collapsed. Generic theoretical descriptions replaced distinct insights drawn from experiences. This was an extreme case of reductionism based on Wilber's synthetic foundational principles, and led to wrong equivalences such as equating the various interpretations of non-duality in Indian systems with one another and with all kinds of miscellaneous and irreconcilable mystical traditions from around the world.

With perennialism as his strawman to characterize the length and breadth of what he trivializes as 'Eastern traditions', Wilber became poised to supersede them with his own theories.

In *The Spectrum of Consciousness,* at least he is candid enough to cite examples from many Indian traditions. He chooses not to go deeper into these and instead becomes a compiler of broad knowledge at the expense of depth.

Things change significantly in *The Atman Project,* where he not only uses vague and generic statements like 'mystics have said...,' or 'perennial philosophy holds...,' but also seems to validate them by quoting superficially from Sri Aurobindo. Thus, the specific contributions of Sri Aurobindo get diluted into generic statements to be sprinkled for the purpose of giving Wilber authenticity, which he lacked in his early stages. Concurrently, he appropriates Sri Aurobindo's deeper and unique contributions by expressing them in modern Western idiom mixed with

Greek references. This is the phase he refers to as Wilber-II, in which he describes himself as 'evolutionary' Wilber.

Wilber-II is characterized by appropriating Sri Aurobindo's entire theory of involution-evolution and several of his other signature ideas. He maps this model of human development onto Western psychology, religion, and perennial philosophy. We expose this in detail in this chapter.

Swami Vivekananda first explained the concepts of involution-evolution to the Western audience in the late 1800s, which was later elaborated by Sri Aurobindo. This was an extraordinary and unique contribution pioneered by both of them. Wilber's *The Atman Project* and *Up from Eden* are based on this fundamental idea.

## Swami Vivekananda Introduces Involution-Evolution to the West

When Charles Darwin's (1809-82) theory of evolution suddenly entered the Western intellectual arena, it created a huge impact and controversy. It was based on strictly material assumptions devoid of spirituality. The theory was vehemently rejected by Christian scholars who could not accept there was no role for God in the scheme of things. During this conflict, Swami Vivekananda articulated the Hindu thesis of involution and evolution as a process of Divine Consciousness manifesting as the entire cosmos. This became one of his major contributions, and he spoke about it in detail year after year in many of his lectures delivered in the West.

Some of his most well-known lectures on this topic include: *Maya and Illusion*; *The Cosmos: The Microcosm*; *Realization*; *The Absolute and Manifestation*; *The Real Nature of Man*. He cited Hindu *śāstra*-s to explain the notion of involution as the *prerequisite* and necessary ingredient in evolution.

*Swami Vivekananda deserves credit for bridging the violent conflict in the West between biological materialism, which believes in evolution without any spiritual role, and Christianity, which rejects mechanical evolution and attributes the creation of the world to God only. In his interpretation of Vedic cosmology, both aspects are integrated: consciousness (spirituality/God) is the agent for involution, and biology that appears mechanical is the agency for evolution.*[1]

Many years later Sri Aurobindo, who acknowledged Swami Vivekananda as his guide and mentor, developed this idea further and made it a central part of his theory of the evolution of humans, and the future of man to evolve to a higher level of consciousness.

Since involution-evolution is such a foundational principle in Wilber's works, we will extensively review some of Swami Vivekananda's writings first followed by those of Sri Aurobindo. We will show how Wilber has appropriated these and also where he falls short.

Swami Vivekananda explains:

> **Every evolution is preceded by an involution.** The seed is the father of the tree, but another tree was itself the father of the seed. The seed is the fine form out of which the big tree comes, and another big tree was the form which is involved in that seed. **The whole of this universe was present in the cosmic fine universe. The little cell, which becomes afterwards the man, was simply the involved man and becomes evolved as a man.**[2]

Swami Vivekananda introduced the idea of involution-evolution in the USA, England, and India on numerous occasions. He clearly showcases how the concept of involution-evolution has been built into Indian thought since ancient times; he was merely restating this in modern scientific terms for his audiences.

The following excerpt is from a lecture titled *The Vedanta Philosophy*, where he uses Sāṃkhya terms to explain involution and evolution as a core Hindu tenet. This lecture was delivered in the USA after he attended the World's Parliament of Religions in 1893:

> All matter throughout the universe is the outcome of one primal matter called Akasha; and all force, whether gravitation, attraction or repulsion, or life, is the outcome of one primal force called Prana. Prana acting on Akasha is creating or projecting* the universe. At the beginning of a cycle, Akasha is motionless, unmanifested. Then Prana begins to act, more and more, creating grosser and grosser forms out of Akasha – plants, animals, men, stars, ...**After an incalculable time this evolution ceases and involution begins, everything being resolved back through finer and finer forms into the original Akasha and Prana, when a new cycle follows.**

> Now there is something beyond Akasha and Prana. Both can be resolved into a third thing called Mahat – the Cosmic Mind. **This Cosmic Mind does not create Akasha and Prana, but changes itself into them.**
>
> *The word which is "creation" in the English language is in Sanskrit exactly "projection," because there is no sect in India which believes in creation as it is regarded in the West as something coming out of nothing. What we mean by creation is projection of that which already existed.[3]

Swami Vivekananda then traveled to Europe, and the following two passages are from his lectures in London, the first of which was *The Real Nature of Man* followed by *Realisation*:

> Behind all these stories we find one idea standing supreme – that man is a degeneration of what he was. ...modern research seems to repudiate this position absolutely. Evolutionists seem to contradict entirely this assertion. According to them, man is the evolution of the mollusc; and, therefore, what mythology states cannot be true. **There is in India, however, a mythology which is able to reconcile both these positions. The Indian mythology has a theory of cycles, that all progression is in the form of waves. Every wave is attended by a fall, and that by a rise the next moment, that by a fall in the next, and again another rise. The motion is in cycles.** ... even on the grounds of modern research, ...man cannot be simply an evolution. ***Every evolution presupposes an involution.*** The modern scientific man will tell you that you can only get the amount of energy out of a machine which you have previously put into it. Something cannot be produced out of nothing. If a man is an evolution of the mollusc, then the perfect man – the Buddha – man, the Christ – man – was involved in the mollusc. If it is not so, whence come these gigantic personalities? Something cannot come out of nothing. Thus we are in the position of reconciling the scriptures with modern light. That energy which manifests itself slowly through various stages until it becomes the perfect man, cannot come out of nothing. It existed somewhere; and if the mollusc or the protoplasm is the first point to which you can trace it, that protoplasm, somehow or other, must have contained the energy.[4]

If we are developed from animals, the animals also may be degraded men. How do you know it is not so? You have seen that the proof of evolution is simply this: you find a series of bodies from the lowest to the highest rising in a gradually ascending scale. But from that how can you insist that it is always from the lower upwards, and never from the higher downwards? **The argument applies both ways, and if anything is true, I believe it is that the series is repeating itself in going up and down. How can you have evolution without involution? Our struggle for the higher life shows that we have been degraded from a high state.**"[5]

The following extract is from his lecture, *The Cosmos and Self*:

Everything in nature rises from some fine seed – forms, becomes grosser and grosser, exists for a certain time, and again goes back to the original fine form. Our earth, ...has come out of a nebulous form which, becoming colder and colder, turned into this crystallised planet upon which we live, and in the future it will again go to pieces and return to its rudimentary nebulous form. This is happening in the universe, and has been through time immemorial. This is the whole history of man, the whole history of nature, the whole history of life.

Every evolution is preceded by an involution. The whole of the tree is present in the seed, its cause. The whole of the human being is present in that one protoplasm. The whole of this universe is present in the cosmic fine universe. **Everything is present in its cause, in its fine form. This evolution, or gradual unfolding of grosser and grosser forms, is true, but each case has been preceded by an involution. The whole of this universe must have been involute before it came out, and has unfolded itself in all these various forms to be involved again once more.** Take, ... the life of a little plant. We find two things that make the plant a unity by itself – its growth and development, its decay and death. These make one unity the plant life. So, taking that plant life as only one link in the chain of life, we may take the whole series as one life, beginning in the protoplasm and ending in the most perfect man. Man is one link, and the various beasts, the lower

> animals, and plants are other links. Now go back to the source, the finest particles from which they started, and take the whole series as but one life, and you will find that every evolution here is the evolution of something which existed previously.[6]

Swami Vivekananda repeatedly and unambiguously laid out the most fundamental Indian principles concerning the emergence, role, and mechanisms of Life and its relationship with Man. Alongside, he positioned these ideas in the context of the fierce debate on evolution versus creation that was taking place in the West at that time.

Because Wilber had already collapsed all Indian thought into perennialism, and made it appear the 'same' as all mysticism, he wants his readers to become blind to the uniqueness of anything specific from this tradition. He failed to recognize and attribute to Swami Vivekananda the rightful claim of introducing involution-evolution as a cosmic process built deep into Indian thought.

### *Sri Aurobindo elaborates Involution-Evolution further*

Following in Swami Vivekananda's footsteps, Sri Aurobindo further explained this idea to his English language readers. Both these Indian exemplars extensively detailed how evolution can take place *because* the Divine Consciousness is already involuted in matter. The universe came into existence because pure consciousness underwent involution, unfolding in the process many different levels of consciousness, the lowest of which is what we experience as matter.

Unlike Western science's notions of consciousness evolving out of dead matter, Indian worldviews insist that consciousness pre-exists and manifests in the form of matter. In other words, *consciousness becomes matter and is involuted into matter. This is why the evolution of the cosmos is natural.* Sri Aurobindo developed his entire evolutionary spiritual philosophy and psychology based on these ideas. He explains the unfolding from Matter to Life, Mind, and Spirit:

> This Divine by his power has created the world or rather manifested it in his own infinite Being. But here in the material world or at its basis he has hidden himself in what seem to be his opposites, Non-Being, Inconscience and Insentience. This is what we nowadays call the Inconscient which seems to have created the material universe

> by its inconscient Energy, but this is only an appearance, for we find in the end that all the dispositions of the world can only have been arranged by the working of a supreme secret Intelligence. **The Being which is hidden in what seems to be an inconscient void emerges in the world first in Matter, then in Life, then in Mind and finally as the Spirit. The apparently inconscient Energy which creates is in fact the Consciousness-Force of the Divine and its aspect of consciousness, secret in Matter, begins to emerge in Life, finds something more of itself in Mind and finds its true self in a spiritual consciousness and finally a supramental Consciousness through which we become aware of the Reality, enter into it and unite ourselves with it. This is what we call evolution which is an evolution of Consciousness and an evolution of the Spirit in things and only outwardly an evolution of species.**[7]

This was radical for the West, where there has been (and still is) a fierce fight between two extreme poles:

- Evolutionary biologists believe in a strictly mechanical process with no prior consciousness or purpose and claim that consciousness arises out of random chance.
- At the other extreme, the Biblical creationists believe that man was a direct creation of God and attack the notion of evolution. The Bible does not accept the notion of God becoming the world or entering the world. He is considered to have entered the world only in one instance in history – in the form of Jesus Christ, but never before or after.

In Indian thought, there is no such dichotomy because both aspects have always been integrated into one unified worldview. There are many Indian systems incorporating this in their own ways: examples include the purāṇ-ic idea of evolution manifested by the ten *daśāvatāra*-s (incarnations), each representing a stage of evolutionary jump and Śaivism's view of cosmology that Śiva is everything that exists, including the material world. This difference between Indian and Abrahamic systems is a very serious and non-negotiable premise for both sides. Wilber's reduction of all systems into perennialism does serious violence to the integrity of Indian systems.

Sri Aurobindo's work details how the planes of consciousness are involuted and progressively evolve into the cosmos. Life emerges out of involuted matter, the mind emerges from involuted life, and all other levels of consciousness beyond the mind emerge from the involuted mind. This gives rise to a nested series or a chain of ascendance. Sri Aurobindo explains:

> We speak of the evolution of Life in Matter, the evolution of Mind in Matter; but **evolution is a word which merely states the phenomenon – without explaining it. For there seems to be no reason why Life should evolve out of material elements or Mind out of living form, unless we accept the Vedantic solution that Life is already involved in Matter and Mind in Life because in essence Matter is a form of veiled Life, Life a form of veiled Consciousness.** And then there seems to be little objection to a farther step in the series and the admission that mental consciousness may itself be only a form and a veil of higher states which are beyond Mind. ...**the unconquerable impulse of man towards God, Light, Bliss, Freedom, Immortality presents itself in its right place in the chain as simply the imperative impulse by which Nature is seeking to evolve beyond Mind, and appears to be as natural, true and just as the impulse towards Life which she has planted in certain forms of Matter or the impulse towards Mind which she has planted in certain forms of Life.** As there, so here, the impulse exists more or less obscurely in her different vessels with an ever-ascending series in the power of its will-to-be; as there, so here, it is gradually evolving and bound fully to evolve the necessary organs and faculties. **As the impulse towards Mind ranges from the more sensitive reactions of Life in the metal and the plant up to its full organisation in man, so in man himself there is the same ascending series, the preparation, if nothing more, of a higher and divine life.** The animal is a living laboratory in which Nature has, it is said, worked out man. Man himself may well be a thinking and living laboratory in whom and with whose conscious co-operation she wills to work out the superman, the god. Or shall we not say, rather, to manifest God? ***For if evolution is the progressive manifestation by Nature of that which slept or worked***

> ***in her, involved, it is also the overt realisation of that which she secretly is.*** We cannot, then, bid her pause at a given stage of her evolution, nor have we the right to condemn with the religionist as perverse and presumptuous or with the rationalist as a disease or hallucination any intention she may evince or effort she may make to go beyond. If it be true that Spirit is involved in Matter and apparent Nature is secret God, then the manifestation of the divine in himself and the realisation of God within and without are the highest and most legitimate aim possible to man upon earth.[8]

## Wilber Appropriates Involution-Evolution

To show that the quintessential idea of involution-evolution of Sri Aurobindo and Swami Vivekananda is appropriated by Wilber and digested into perennialism, we will first critically examine *The Atman Project* and then turn the lens to *Up from Eden.*

Explaining the plan of *The Atman Project,* Wilber writes:

> The theme ...is basically simple: development is evolution; evolution is transcendence (Erich Janstch's marvelous phrase: "Evolution as self-realization through self-transcendence"); and transcendence has as its final goal Atman, or ultimate Unity Consciousness in only God.... If men and women have ultimately come up from amoebas, then they are ultimately on their way towards God, but ...are under sway of the incredible half way house known as the Atman project. And this entire movement of evolution simply continues from unity to unity until there is only Unity, and the Atman project finally dissolves in the impact of very Atman.[9]

Wilber is quick to quote Erich Jantsch (1929-80), the astrophysicist and author of *The Self Organizing Universe: Scientific and Human Implications of the Emerging Paradigm of Evolution,* but does not care to mention Swami Vivekananda from whose work Jantsch had taken the concept. Swami Vivekananda was popular in the West, especially in the USA. In other words, Wilber has cleverly replaced Swami Vivekananda and the Indian sources with Jantsch, as if Jantsch had been the pioneer.[10]

It is a serious breach of academic integrity that Wilber's *The Atman Project* dilutes the contributions of Sri Aurobindo regarding involution-evolution by making it seem like a generic feature of perennial philosophy. When Wilber explains involution-evolution, he makes only two passing references to Hinduism in the entire book:

- The first is in the preface, where he states that he has brought his ideas of involution and evolution 'in accord with' those of Sri Aurobindo, as if his own ideas on the subject had pre-existed independently.[11]
- The other reference is in the last chapter in an obscure and inconsequential endnote.

This is in sharp contrast with the way he meticulously cites all his Western sources and authors throughout the book. Even his quotes on Ādi Śaṅkarācārya and yoga are not referenced, making it difficult to check his sources for misrepresentations and misunderstandings. His entire scholarship is filled with such double standards in treating Indian sources.

For instance, on pages 76 and 126 of *The Atman Project,* he states the idea of involution-evolution as some generic knowledge of all mystics. Later, he elaborates the point by giving a lengthy quote on page 60, which is from Sri Aurobindo, but ***does not name him as the source*** and refers to it merely as 'according to many sages'. The passage is as follows:

> [Evolution] has already brought forth humans from amoebas—why on earth should we think that after that prodigious feat lasting billions of years, evolution just petered out and wound down? And if the ratio "amoeba to human" is repeated, the result could only be God. The mystics simply show us the stages of higher evolution leading to that Summit. "Certainly, if that body, life and consciousness were limited to the possibilities of the gross body which are all that our physical senses and physical mentality [gross ego] accept, there would be a very narrow term for this evolution," says Aurobindo. However, **according to many sages**, "there are behind our waking mentality vaster ranges of consciousness... superconscient to it of which we become sometimes abnormally aware, [and] there are behind our gross physical being other and subtler grades of substance with a finer law and a greater power...;" by our entering into the ranges of consciousness belonging to

> them [we can] substitute their purer, higher, intenser conditions of being for the grossness and limitation of our present physical life and impulses and habits. Thus, our present gross "mind, life and body" are an inferior consciousness and a partial expression which strives to arrive in the mould of a various evolution at that superior expression of it-self already existent to the beyond-mind [the "beyond-mind" is simply the realms beyond body, mind, and centaur]. That which is in the beyond-mind is the ideal which in its own conditions it is labouring to realize. (Note 306)[12]

The reference 306 given for this quotation in Wilber's book leads to Radhakrishnan, S. and Moore, C., *A source book in Indian philosophy,* which has a chapter specifically on Sri Aurobindo's metaphysics. However, Wilber refers to it as '...according to many sages...'. as though it is something generic. It should be noted that Wilber does not quote Sri Aurobindo directly from *The Life Divine.*

The fact is that Wilber has lifted the following passage from the chapter titled *The Ascending Series of Substance* from *The Life Divine*:

> Behind all these terms of ancient psycho-physical science lies the one great fact and law of our being that whatever be its temporary poise of form, consciousness, power in this material evolution, there must be behind it and there is a greater, a truer existence of which this is only the external result and physically sensible aspect. Our substance does not end with the physical body; that is only the earthly pedestal, the terrestrial base, the material starting-point. As **there are behind our waking mentality vaster ranges of consciousness suboscine and superconscient to it of which we become sometimes abnormally aware, so there are behind our gross physical being other and subtler grades of substance with a finer law and a greater power which support the denser body and which can by our entering into the ranges of consciousness belonging to them be made to impose that law and power on our dense matter and substitute their purer, higher, intenser conditions of being for the grossness and limitation of our present physical life and impulses and habits.** If that be so, then the evolution of a nobler physical existence not limited by the ordinary conditions of animal birth and life and death, of difficult

> alimentation and facility of disorder and disease and subjection to poor and unsatisfied vital cravings ceases to have the appearance of a dream and chimera and becomes a possibility founded upon a rational and philosophic truth which is in accordance with all the rest that we have hitherto known, experienced or been able to think out about the overt and secret truth of our existence.[13]

Having erased the Indian underpinnings for his entire involution-evolution idea, on pages 185-6 Wilber uses Sri Aurobindo's cosmological explanation of Brahman's manifestation but again does not name the latter as the source. Instead, he renames it as 'a process of kenosis' and refers to it as 'according to perennial philosophy'.

At a later stage in his writings, Wilber seems to be aware of Sri Aurobindo's involution-evolution and rephrases it thus:

> Sri Aurobindo, India's greatest modern sage, has written on just this viewpoint - Brahman getting lost in involution and then evolving back - from matter to prana to mind to over-mind to super-mind and Atman, and he sees it occurring cosmologically as well as psychologically.[14]

Wilber further begins to prefix his statements in such manner, 'as theologians have long known', even though he is borrowing a key point specifically from Indian thought that is *diametrically opposed* to conventional Judeo-Christian theology. In fact, he begins the chapter with ideas copied from Hinduism. This is a sleight of hand to whitewash the difference between Indian involution-evolution and Biblical ex-nihilo creation (i.e. creation out of nothing).

In other words, he quietly assumes there is nothing new or distinct about discarding the theory of ex-nihilo creation in the Bible and replacing it with Hinduism's involution-evolution. *It is a well-known fact that Christian theologians have a long history of opposing any alternative worldview to ex-nihilo because this is necessary to defend the Bible against what they call pantheism.* This is not a trivial point because anything resembling the idea of manifestation of God-as-matter was rejected as idolatry.

Brad Reynolds, a biographer of Wilber, attests that 'the evolutionary theorist who exerted the most profound influence on Wilber at this time was the great synthesizer of Eastern philosopher and Western science, Sri Aurobindo'.[15] However, Reynolds removes Sri Aurobindo's framework, which was explicitly from the *Veda*-s, *Gītā*, yoga, and other Indian texts, and he mischaracterizes Sri Aurobindo as someone who was 'synthesizing Eastern philosophy and Western science'.

This dilution and simultaneous appropriation of involution-evolution serves as the backbone for Wilber's evolutionary and integral theories beginning with Wilber-II. A comparison of his ideas in *The Atman Project* with those of Sri Aurobindo suggests that he has lifted Sri Aurobindo's ideas mentioned in *The Essential Aurobindo: Writings of Sri Aurobindo* by Robert McDermott (a compilation of chapters from various works of Sri Aurobindo), and *A Source Book in Indian Philosophy* by S. Radhakrishnan and Charles A. Moore which has a chapter on Sri Aurobindo. Both books are listed as references in *The Atman Project,* but the specifics of what was borrowed are not mentioned. Wilber appears to have read *about* Sri Aurobindo only through these third-party summaries and not *directly*.

The extent of Sri Aurobindo's influence becomes evident as we put several paragraphs of the first chapter of *The Atman Project* alongside the writings of Sri Aurobindo. This borrowing will become even clearer as we proceed further in our analysis. Primary among the appropriated ideas is that evolution takes place through the ascending planes of consciousness or a chain of consciousness, leading to greater complexity and differentiation. The table on the following two pages makes this explicit. The bold font emphasizes phrases that indicate the similarity of ideas between Sri Aurobindo and Wilber.

| Sri Aurobindo's Original |
| --- |
| There is...an **ascending series in the scale of substance from Matter to Spirit**, it must be marked by **a progressive diminution of these capacities most characteristic of the physical principle and a progressive increase of the opposite characteristics which will lead us to the formula of pure spiritual self-extension**. This is to say that they must be marked by less and less bondage to the form, more and more **subtlety and flexibility of substance and force**, more and more interfusion, interpenetration, power of assimilation, |

power of interchange, power of variation, transmutation, unification. Drawing away from durability of form, we draw **towards eternity of essence**; drawing away from our poise in the persistent separation and resistance of physical Matter, we draw near to the highest divine poise in the infinity, unity and indivisibility of Spirit. **Between gross substance and pure spirit substance this must be the fundamental antinomy**.... Between these two poles there is the possibility of an **infinite gradation**.... Even within the formula of the physical cosmos there is an ascending series in the scale of Matter which **leads us from the more to the less dense, from the less to the more subtle**.... There must be and there are grades between inconscient substance and utterly self-conscious self-extension, as between the principle of Matter and the principle of Spirit...

The principle which underlies this continually ascending experience and vision uplifted beyond the material formulation of things is that all cosmic existence is **a complex harmony** and does not finish with the limited range of consciousness in which the ordinary human mind and life is content to be imprisoned. Being, consciousness, force, substance descend and ascend a many-runged ladder on each step of which being has a **vaster self-extension**, consciousness a wider sense of its own range and largeness and joy, force a greater intensity and a more rapid and blissful capacity, substance gives a more subtle, plastic, buoyant and flexible rendering of its primal reality. For **the more subtle is also the more powerful**,—one might say, the more truly concrete; it is less bound than the gross, it has a greater permanence in its being along with a greater potentiality, plasticity and range in its becoming. Each plateau of the hill of being gives to our widening experience a higher plane of our consciousness and a richer world for our existence.

But how does this ascending series affect the possibilities of our material existence? It would not affect them at all if each plane of consciousness, each world of existence, each grade of substance, each degree of cosmic force were cut off entirely from that which precedes and that which follows it. But the opposite is the truth; **the manifestation of the Spirit is a complex weft and in the design and**

**pattern of one principle all the others enter as elements of the spiritual whole.** Our material world is the result of all the others, for the other principles have all descended into Matter to create the physical universe, and **every particle of what we call Matter contains all of them implicit in itself**; their secret action, as we have seen, is involved in every moment of its existence and every movement of its activity. **And as Matter is the last word of the descent, so it is also the first word of the ascent; as the powers of all these planes, worlds, grades, degrees are involved in the material existence, so are they all capable of evolution out of it.** It is for this reason that material being does not begin and end with gases and chemical compounds and physical forces and movements, with nebulae and suns and earths, but evolves life, evolves mind, must evolve eventually Supermind and the higher degrees of the spiritual existence. **Evolution comes by the unceasing pressure of the supra-material planes on the material compelling it to deliver out of itself their principles and powers which might conceivably otherwise have slept imprisoned in the rigidity of the material formula.** This would even so have been improbable, since their presence there implies a purpose of deliverance; but still this necessity from below is actually very much aided by a kindred superior pressure.[16]

**Ken Wilber's Mapping**

Everywhere we look in nature, said the philosopher Jan Smuts, we see nothing but *wholes.* And not just simple wholes, but **hierarchical ones: each whole is a part of a larger whole which is itself a part of a larger whole.** Fields within fields within fields, stretching through the cosmos, interlacing each and everything with each and every other.

Further, said Smuts, the universe is not a thoughtlessly static and inert whole—the cosmos is not lazy, but energetically dynamic and even creative. It tends (we would now say teleonomically, not teleologically) to **produce higher- and higher-level wholes,**

**evermore inclusive and organized.** This overall cosmic process, as it unfolds in time, is nothing other than *evolution.* **And the drive to ever-higher unities, Smuts called *holism*.**

If we continued this line of thinking, we might say that **because the human mind or psyche is an aspect of the cosmos, we would expect to find, in the psyche itself, the same hierarchical arrangement of wholes within wholes, reaching from the simplest and most rudimentary to the most complex and inclusive.** In general, such is exactly the discovery of modern psychology. As Werner put it, "Wherever development occurs it proceeds from a state of relative globality and lack of differentiation to a state of increasing differentiation, articulation, and hierarchical integration." Jakobson speaks of "those stratified phenomena which modern psychology uncovers in the different areas of the realm of the mind," where **each stratified layer is more integrated and more encompassing than its predecessor**. Bateson points out that even learning itself is hierarchical, involving several major levels, each of which is "meta" to its predecessors. As a general approximation, then, we may conclude that the psyche—like the cosmos at large—is many-layered ("pluridimensional"), composed of successively higher-order wholes and unities and integrations.

The holistic evolution of nature—which produces everywhere higher and higher wholes—shows up in the human psyche development or growth. The same force that produced humans from amoebas produces adults from infants. That is, a person's growth, from infancy to adulthood, is simply a miniature version of cosmic evolution. Or, we might say, **psychological growth or development in humans is simply a microcosmic reflection of universal growth on the whole, and has the same goal: the unfolding of ever higher-order unities and integrations.** And this is one of the major reasons that the psyche is, indeed, stratified. Very like the geological formation of the earth, psychological development proceeds, stratum by stratum, level by level, stage by stage, with each successive level superimposed upon its predecessor in such a way that it includes but **transcends it** ("envelops it," as Werner would say).[17]

Wilber makes a few random changes of terms here and there (like substituting wholes for planes) and connects the ideas to Western thinkers like Jan Smuts, Roman Jakobson, and Gregory Bateson. Consider the example of the Chain of Being, which is a concept that casts all matter, including plants, animals, and natural elements, in a continuous and graded structure. Wilber repackages the Chain of Being as the Great Nest of Being by taking each link of the chain, discarding the metaphysics associated with it, and casting it as a result of practices that are derived from evolution. In his later renditions, he credits the idea of the Chain of Being to Arthur Lovejoy and Huston Smith, while in fact, it is *based on Sri Aurobindo's description of the chain of nested ascending series of planes.*[18]

## Appropriating Evolution from Sub- to Self- to Super-Consciousness

Wilber further appropriates Sri Aurobindo's idea that psychological evolution takes place from sub-consciousness to self-consciousness to super-consciousness. This is a principle that cogently sits in Sri Aurobindo's entire scheme. The following comparison of their writings makes the appropriation clear.

| Sri Aurobindo's Original | Ken Wilber's Mapping |
|---|---|
| In cosmos, [the Transcendent] uses its liberty of self-formation, its Maya, to make a scheme of itself in the complementary terms of unity and multiplicity, and **this multiple unity it establishes in the three conditions of the subconscient, the conscient and the superconscient.** For actually we see that the Many objectivised in form in our material universe start with a subconscious unity which expresses itself openly enough in cosmic action and cosmic substance, but of which they are not themselves superficially aware. **In the conscient the ego becomes the superficial point at which the awareness of unity can emerge**; but it applies its perception of unity to the form and surface action and, failing to take account of all that operates behind, fails also to realise that it is not only one in itself but one with others. This limitation of the universal "I" in the divided ego-sense constitutes our imperfect individualised personality. **But when the ego transcends the personal consciousness, it begins to include and be overpowered by that which is to us superconscious; it becomes aware of the cosmic unity and enters into the Transcendent Self which here cosmos expresses by a multiple oneness.**[19] | We...find that—if all the higher stages reported by the mystics [no citing of evidence based data or even who he means by these mystics, for, in the Indian context, these are clearly documented pieces] are real—**the life cycle moves from subconsciousness (instinctual, impulsive, id-ish) to self-consciousness (egoic, conceptual, syntactical) to superconsciousness (transcendent, transpersonal, transtemporal).**[20] |

These appropriations are at the heart of Wilber's formulation of his developmental and dynamic transpersonal view of human evolution and psychology, as opposed to the structural view of transpersonal psychology that was espoused earlier in *The Spectrum of Consciousness* and *No Boundary*. Sri Aurobindo's elaboration on the psychological and spiritual evolution through the planes of matter, vital, mind, higher mind, and planes beyond up to sat-cit-ānanda are co-opted by Wilber. He substitutes this with various developmental and psychoanalytic components picked up from Jean Piaget, Jane Loevinger, Silvano Arieti, Abraham Maslow, Lawrence Kohlberg, Sigmund Freud, Erik Erikson, Carl Jung, and Erich Neumann amongst others.

Wilber's mappings of the higher planes are inaccurate because of his perennialist orientation, which does not differentiate various planes, and because of his lack of adequate spiritual experience. He starts out with a dichotomy between higher levels of existence as 'described by the mystics' and lower levels as studied by Western psychologists. This makes his system an artificial synthesis between these separate and independent starting points of two diverse traditions.

Wilber does not acknowledge Sri Aurobindo's detailed knowledge of the lower levels of existence—the physical, vital, and mental—from which he has borrowed these ideas; neither does he mention Sri Aurobindo's extensive writings on the matter of developing a strong and transformed vital body that forms the basis of any further work such as:

> The vital is an indispensable instrument – no creation or strong action is possible without it. It is simply a question of mastering it and of converting it into the true vital which is at once strong and calm and capable of great intensity and free from ego.[21]

Instead, Wilber writes:

> If we take all these higher stages [as described by the mystics] and add them to the lower and middle stages/levels which have been so carefully described and studied by Western psychology, we would then arrive at a fairly well-balanced and comprehensive model of the spectrum of consciousness. This, exactly, is the nature and aim [of the Atman Project].[22]

Thus, Wilber perpetuates the colonial mechanism of appropriating from Indian sources.

## Appropriation of Ascent and Integration

Another major concept on which Wilber's entire future work rests is unabashedly lifted straight from the works of Sri Aurobindo. Sri Aurobindo explained that there is an 'ascent with integration' at each stage of evolution, which means that while the prior level of consciousness is transcended, it is not left behind but taken forward as a subset integrated into the higher level. This is the truly integral and all-encompassing nature of his theory.

Sri Aurobindo wants to explicitly and forcefully differentiate his system from the standard and run-of-the-mill 'spirituality' where the seeker is asked to purify and awaken himself. He is teaching a much higher pursuit:

> If it is the sole intention of Nature in the evolution of the spiritual man to awaken him to the supreme Reality...then in the essence her work has been already accomplished and there is nothing more to be done....But we have supposed that there is a farther intention, - **not only a revelation of the Spirit [i.e. traditional Liberation], but a radical and integral transformation of Nature**...[23]

Wilber repackages 'ascent and integration', without considering the deeper aspects of transformation, by coining 'transcend and include'. This becomes one of the key features of his theory and one of his most crucial appropriations. He calls this an original discovery, even though he has not understood the underlying metaphysics that necessitates a transformation as posited by Sri Aurobindo.

The key difference Sri Aurobindo repeatedly emphasizes in considering Integral Yoga with other spiritual attempts is that 'the ascent to the Divine', which other spiritual systems also talk about, is not enough. '**There must be too a descent of the Divine to transform all the energies of the mind, life and body**'.[24]

Sri Aurobindo's Integral Yoga has the unique feature that the ascent of Matter, Life, and Spirit towards the highest consciousness is always accompanied by the descent of the consciousness into each stage of man's pursuit of yoga, and this descent brings the complete transformation of the being: '**The supramental Yoga is at once an ascent towards God and a descent of Godhead into the embodied nature**'.[25]

In order to properly comprehend the dual role of ascent and descent, one must understand the transformation taking place – and this is what Wilber has missed. Sri Aurobindo introduced the term 'transformation' to refer to something very different from mere purification:

> Transformation is a word that I have brought in myself (like supermind) to express certain spiritual concepts and spiritual facts of the integral Yoga. **People are now taking them up and using them in senses which have nothing to do with the significance which I put into them.** Purification of the nature by the "influence" of the Spirit is not what I mean by transformation; purification is only part of a psychic change or a psycho-spiritual change — the word besides has many senses and is very often given a moral or ethical meaning which is foreign to my purpose. **What I mean by the spiritual transformation is something dynamic (not merely liberation of the self, or realisation of the One which can very well be attained without any descent). ... It means a bringing down of Divine Consciousness static and dynamic into all these parts and the entire replacement of the present consciousness by that.**[26]

He clarifies further:

> **... transformation is not the central object of other paths as it is of this Yoga — only so much purification and change is demanded by them as will lead to liberation and the beyond-life.** The influence of the Atman can no doubt do that — a full descent of a new Consciousness into the whole nature from top to bottom to transform life here is not needed at all for the spiritual escape from life.[27]

In Sri Aurobindo's system, an ascent into a higher level of consciousness creates an opening for the descent of the Divine, and this allows the integration of the lower level of consciousness into the higher level. Relying solely on the ego and its efforts through the mental and vital planes is insufficient. One must also call down the light of the higher consciousness (i.e. descent) into one's purified receptacle by 'vigilant surrender'. Thus, every ascent to a higher stage must be accompanied by a transformation of the plane by the Divine light and not by the ego, which requires the help of the descent.

### *Absence of a role for the Divine in Wilber's model*

*Wilber's scheme lacks a very important feature: the absence of a role for the Divine.* In contrast, Sri Aurobindo holds Divine Grace as an important means for spiritual ascension and progress.

The lack of the role of the Divine in Wilber's work stems from two factors: his work rejects metaphysics inherently and is based on a synthetic unity of borrowed knowledge. Wilber talks about higher and trans-mental states of consciousness, but his own knowledge is mental. The mental knowledge, by its very nature is limited, and his discussions of higher states and stages are speculative and the result of stitching disparate ideas together. In dhārmic canons, there is scope for both theories that reject the Divine and those that embrace it. This multiplicity in approaches is at the heart of an integrally unified model. The same does not hold true for Wilber's scheme.

Wilber's method of mixing, matching, and curating all sorts of intellectual systems has produced a hotchpotch collection that can, at best, lead to synthetic unity. As a result, there are contradictions in his 'Transcend and Include' mechanism of evolution. In Sri Aurobindo's model, every ascent and descent must culminate in a harmonious integration and transformation of all elements and forces that have been transcended. Only then can one transcend to the next higher level. Wilber's system does not involve the descent and integration required before transcending to the next higher level.

Sri Aurobindo also warns of the perils of yoga where this transformation does not take place, in which case the process is guided by egoistic mental ideas:

> This descent, this working is not without its possibility of calamitous fall and danger. If the human mind or the vital desire seizes hold on the descending force and tries to use it according to its own limited and erring ideas or flawed and egoistic impulses, ... stumblings and deviations, hard and seemingly insuperable obstacles and wounds and suffering cannot be escaped and even death or utter downfall

> are not impossible. **Only when the conscious integral surrender to the Divine has been learned by mind and life and body, can the way of the Yoga become easy, straight, swift and safe.**
>
> **And it must be a surrender and an opening to the Divine alone and to no other.** For it is possible for an obscure mind or an impure life force in us to surrender to undivine and hostile forces and even to mistake them for the Divine. There can be no more calamitous error. Therefore, our surrender must be no blind and inert passivity to all influences or any influence, but sincere, conscious, vigilant, pointed to the One and the Highest alone.[28]

Sri Aurobindo repeatedly cautions his disciples against the dangers of not transforming each plane from which one is ascending into higher planes. One does not blindly carry forward all impulses, emotions, forces, and thoughts associated with any plane into the higher plane without first transforming the plane from which one is ascending and harmonizing it with the rule of the Divine Will and not the ego. In the absence of the transformation of each plane, there are grave dangers in the path of yoga including a complete derangement:

> Although there is no ego in the spiritual planes, yet by the spiritual experience the ego on the lower planes may get aggrandised through pride and wrong reception of the experience. Also, by entering into the larger mental and vital planes one may aggrandise the ego. **These things are always possible so long as the higher consciousness and the lower are not harmonised in the being and the lower transformed into the nature of the higher.**[29]
>
> There are also wrong voices and experiences. The people who have gone mad, went mad because they were egoistic, began to think themselves great sadhaks and attach an exaggerated importance to themselves and their experiences; this made them get a wrong consciousness and wrong voices and visions and inspirations.[30]

Considering the absence of these vital guardrails for safety and caution in such serious pursuits, Wilber's model, built by selectively taking concepts without their accompanying deeply considered and original structures and philosophies, can become a recipe for misadventures for individuals.

The following shows how Wilber cannibalizes Sri Aurobindo's ideas to map onto his own:

| Sri Aurobindo's Original | Wilber's Mapping |
|---|---|
| An evolution of forms of Matter more and more subtly and intricately organized so as to admit the action of a growing, a more and more complex and subtle and capable organization is the indispensable physical foundation. *An upward evolutionary progress of the consciousness itself from grade to higher grade, an ascent, is the evident spiral line or emerging curve that, on this foundation, the emerging curve must describe.* ***A taking up of what has already been evolved into higher grade as it is reached and a transformation more or less complete so as to admit of a total changed working of the whole being and nature, an integration, must be also part of the process, if the evolution is to be effective.***[31] | At each point in growth or development, we find: (1) a higher-order structure emerges in consciousness; (2) the self identifies its being with that higher structure; (3) the next higher-order structure eventually emerges; (4) the self dis-identifies with the lower structure and shifts its essential identity...to the higher structure; (5) consciousness thereby transcends the lower structure; (6) and becomes capable of operating on that lower structure from the higher-order level; (7) such that all preceding levels can then be integrated in consciousness, and ultimately as Consciousness. *We noted that each successively higher-order structure is more complex, more organized, and more unified—and evolution continues until there is only Unity, ultimate in all directions, whereupon the force of evolution is exhausted, and there is perfect release in Radiance as the entire World Flux.*[32] |

## Wilber's *Transformation and Translation*

By co-opting 'ascent and integrate', Wilber can explain psychological evolution through the process of differentiation, emergence (of the lower plane into the higher), and integration (into the higher plane). He uses this to explain how the process can backfire: When the 'ascent and integrate' fails, psychopathologies emerge either as the result of dissociation of two planes that failed to integrate or from the suppression of the lower plane by the higher. Wilber avers that evolution occurs through the processes of *transformation* and *translation*. Transformation happens when one moves vertically from one plane or level of consciousness to the next, whereas *translation* is the horizontal process of seeking substitutes for one psychological process with another. Consequently, Wilber gives the following principle: 'When translation fails, transformation ensues'.[33]

There is a serious discrepancy here. Sri Aurobindo holds that the higher levels of consciousness in manifestation emerge due to (i) them being previously involuted in matter; and (ii) the pull from the higher realms present in the cosmos. However, Wilber contends that they emerge in due course of time by simply being involuted in matter. In other words, Wilber only considers the first of the two principles explained by Sri Aurobindo.

For example, Sri Aurobindo would describe the emergence of the mind in life due to the concurrence of two factors: the mind was already involuted in life, and the unmanifest level of mind pulls life from above. On the contrary, Wilber would describe the emergence of life from matter *only* because it is already involuted in matter. *This removes the spiritual component involved in the process of evolution and aligns it with the already present mechanistic Western view. This also enables his theory to be useful in Western psychological therapy.* This is another consistent practice of Wilber: to substitute the spiritual contents of Sri Aurobindo with the secular knowledge of the West while conveniently taking credit for the 'originality' of the idea. (Later in his intellectual journey, Wilber collaborates with Christians to develop what he calls 'Integral Christianity'. There, the 'pull from the higher realms', which is present in Sri Aurobindo's system but absent in Wilber's, becomes an important issue to resolve with the Christian notion of God.)

In the following table, we address each point of Wilber's mechanism described previously.

| | Ken Wilber's Transcend and Include | Issues | Sri Aurobindo's model with built-in solutions |
|---|---|---|---|
| 1. | Higher order structure emerges in consciousness. | Because he wants to avoid any metaphysical premise, the question arises: Why should higher order structure emerge in consciousness? | Vedic metaphysics provides the basis: Brahman is the sat-cit-ānanda, the highest Absolute Consciousness and Transcendental Spirit. It is unmanifest in its form but already possesses all attributes of multiplicity in its non-dual form. Also, the higher planes of consciousness, even when unmanifest, are already involuted. Evolution only manifests what is latent and unmanifest. |
| 2. | Self-identifies its being with the higher structure. | Why should it? What drives this identification? | Consciousness is already involuted in Matter, Life, and Spirit, and the spirit ascends to the consciousness through evolution. Each individual possesses an ego, which is a transitional device used for the process of evolution. While the ego is subject to all the qualities and attributes because of interaction with prakṛti, there is a portion of the consciousness that remains untouched, i.e. the psychic being. With each ascent and transformation, the ego is given a back seat, and the psychic being is brought forward, resulting in identification with the Absolute Consciousness. |
| 3. | Next higher-order structure eventually emerges. | Does Wilber mean that the process of emergence is entirely a mechanistic model which takes place due to evolution?<br>a) If so, what are the factors that lead to the emergence?<br>b) If not, why should higher-order structure emerge? | The higher planes of consciousness are increasingly unveiled as matter ascends to Life, then Mind, and then planes beyond the Mind. But throughout this entire process, the most active component is that of human effort which involves:<br>a) Aspiration of the seeker for higher consciousness.<br>b) Rejection of lower (in the sense of guṇa-s) tendencies.<br>c) Active willingness of the ego to the background and bringing forward the psychic being. |

| | Ken Wilber's Transcend and Include | Issues | Sri Aurobindo's model with built-in solutions |
|---|---|---|---|
| 4. | The 'self' disidentifies with a lower structure and shifts its essential identity to a higher structure. | If the same 'self' has attributes that can make it identify with lower and higher planes, how does the self distinguish between the two levels?<br>What constitutes the identity of this 'self' in any structure? | There is a clear distinction between the ego and the psychic being. The psychic being, which is a *microcosm of the Absolute Consciousness*, remains unchanged throughout any transformation as it is untouched by external contacts. The ego is a device used for evolutionary purposes in the creation of an individual. The ego is subject to sattva, rajas and tamas guṇa-s. With each ascent, the psychic being comes to the forefront, and the rule of the higher plane directs the workings of the psychic being. The transformation of the plane from which one is ascending ensures the ego transforms to drop negative attributes. The functions of the lower planes are carried in light of the higher law. |
| 5. | Consciousness thereby transcends the lower structure. | What happens to the lower structure when consciousness ascends to the higher one? | There must be transformation with every ascent. |
| 6. | Consciousness becomes capable of operating on lower structures from higher order levels. | How? | Each structure has its own relevance and position; with the transformation of each plane, it operates from the highest principle of the plane in light of the higher law. |
| 7. | All preceding levels are integrated into consciousness | How? | Each ascent and transformation is accompanied by a corresponding descent of consciousness into the plane. It is this that brings in the law of the highest consciousness. Sri Aurobindo refers to this as a 'pull' that is experienced in his practice of yoga. |

| | Ken Wilber's Transcend and Include | Issues | Sri Aurobindo's model with built-in solutions |
|---|---|---|---|
| 8. | When 'ascent and integrate' fails, psychopathologies emerge. | Psychopathologies emerge not only because of the reasons Wilber mentions but because there is a fundamental absence of a clear device or an agent that ascends in the first place. The ascent of the ego will necessarily bring about pathologies because the ego is subject to interactions with the outside world unless Wilber proposes that his system takes place in isolated conditions from the world. | Apart from all that has been elucidated in the previous points, including the role of the effort of the seeker, the most important element in the entire mechanism is spiritual, which in Sri Aurobindo's model is of two kinds: 1) through the guidance of an enlightened guru; 2) through Divine Grace. The latter has no role at all in Wilber's work, while the former is given bad precedence through Wilber's endorsement of questionable guru-s like Adi Da 'Free' John. |

### *Other fundamental issues in Wilber-II*

Wilber's work is replete with several other basic misunderstandings which cause danger to the practitioner. Sri Aurobindo, in his *Letters on Yoga III,* writes about the paramount importance of differentiating between experiences and realizations:

Experiences are usually temporary, occur in flashes, and do not remain as a permanent insight. Experiences can take several forms including symbols, visions, waking of one's kuṇḍalinī force, the opening of cakra-s in the body, and so on. Experiences can aid and support one to achieve realizations.

Realizations refer to:

> the reception in the consciousness and the establishment there of the fundamental truths of the Divine, of the Higher or Divine Nature, of the world-consciousness and the play of its forces, of one's own self and real nature and the inner nature of things, the power of these things growing in one till they are a part of one's inner life and existence, – as for instance, the realisation of the Divine Presence, the descent and settling of the higher Peace, Light, Force, Ananda in the consciousness, their workings there, the realisation of the divine or spiritual love, the perception of one's own psychic being, the discovery of one's own true mental being, true vital being, true physical being, the realisation of the Overmind or the supramental consciousness, the clear perception of the relation of all these things to our present inferior nature and their action on it to change that lower nature.[34]

If one is ignorant about this distinction and is driven by half-truths, *one mistakes experiences for realizations*. This can result in a downward path:

> If one is more concerned with the ego or being a big Yogi or becoming a superman than with meeting the Divine or getting the Divine Consciousness which enables one to live in or with the Divine, then a flood of pseudos or mixtures comes in, one is led into the mazes of the intermediate zone or spins in the grooves of one's own formations ... you have not to make experiences your main aim, but the Divine only your aim; ... you are more likely to get the true helpful experiences and avoid the wrong ones. If

> one seeks mainly after experiences, his Yoga may become a mere self-indulgence in the lesser things of the mental, vital and subtle physical worlds or in spiritual secondaries, or it may bring down a turmoil or maelstrom of the mixed and the whole or half-pseudo and stand between the soul and the Divine. That is a very sound rule of sadhana.[35]

Sri Aurobindo emphasizes on the proper guidance of a guru and cautions against letting the ego take matters into its own hands:

> In this process of the descent from above and the working it is most important not to rely entirely on oneself, but to rely on the guidance of the Guru and to refer all that happens to his judgment and arbitration and decision. For it often happens that the forces of the lower nature are stimulated and excited by the descent and want to mix with it and turn it to their profit. It often happens too that some Power or Powers undivine in their nature present themselves as the Supreme Lord or as the Divine Mother and claim the being's service and surrender. If these things are accepted, there will be an extremely disastrous consequence. If indeed there is the assent of the sadhak to the Divine working alone and the submission or surrender to that guidance, then all can go smoothly. This assent and a rejection of all egoistic forces or forces that appeal to the ego are the safeguard throughout the sadhana. But the ways of Nature are full of snares, the disguises of the ego are innumerable, the illusions of the Powers of Darkness, Rakshasi Maya, are extraordinarily skilful; the reason is an insufficient guide and often turns traitor; vital desire is always with us tempting to follow any alluring call. This is the reason why in this Yoga we insist so much on what we call samarpana – rather inadequately rendered by the English word surrender. If the heart centre is fully opened and the psychic is always in control, then there is no question; all is safe. But the psychic can at any moment be veiled by a lower upsurge. It is only a few who are exempt from these dangers and it is precisely those to whom surrender is easily possible.[36]

The guru must not only provide an unimpeachable ethical standard but also bring in his own realizations to discriminate between true realizations and ego-driven experiences. If the guru is not equipped with his own realizations, which have been tested against an established framework, the path of yoga will be ridden with very serious negative ramifications, including falling for mirages in the path. The real danger is that the ego-controlled mind is 'taking hold of love, Ananda, the sense of Beauty and using it for its own purposes, for vital human relations or interchange or else some kind of mere enjoyment of its own'.[37]

Against these powerful foundations of Sri Aurobindo's Integral Yoga, the model posited by Wilber suffers the following glaring deficiencies:

1. Sri Aurobindo writes with the sure-footedness of one with personal experience on each step along the yogic path. He describes the characteristics of every stage of ascent, the problems one encounters and the way ahead, the corresponding forces of descent, and the transformation that occurs with each ascent and descent. Wilber mines out a small and limited portion of this and repackages it as his own. He touches merely a fraction of the experiences that Sri Aurobindo delineates but lacks in the accompanying Vedic metaphysics that underlies the sage's entire system. The counterfeit copy of Wilber crumbles when closely scrutinized.
2. Sri Aurobindo is very clear that one does not simply ascend or to use Wilber's knock-off phrase, 'Transcend and Integrate', but at each stage there is a necessary transformation of the plane one is transcending to ensure harmonization of all elements in the plane. That is why the ascent is simultaneous to the descent of the higher spirit to transform the plane. *Any ascent is incomplete and potentially dangerous if it does not produce the transformation of the plane from which it is ascending.*
3. Sri Aurobindo repeatedly cautions the seeker against the pitfalls of letting the ego retain control over any plane when ascending to a higher plane. The ego's control must be replaced with an ever-arching will that obeys only the Divine. Or else, the ego misdirects the seeker onto a path where it tries to use the spiritual powers gained for further aggrandizing the ego.
4. To safeguard against the perils of half-baked pursuits, Sri Aurobindo emphasizes the role of a true guru, one who has not only realized his own experiences but is without the shackles of the ego. In the

context of dhārmic traditions, the guru has parameters from within the system that put checks and balances in place.

5. Sri Aurobindo's map of Integral Yoga is steeped in quintessential Vedic metaphysics. His *Record of Yoga* includes a detailed account of his practices including the following: Each stage of *Sapta-catuṣṭaya* – Śānti, Śakti, Vijñāna, Śarīra, Karma, Brahma, and Siddhi.[38] There are detailed accounts of the nuances and gradations of each of these seven catuṣṭaya-s, which are deeply rooted in Yogāṅga. Wilber has scant documentation of his experiences as the basis for his model, and his work is not rooted in any metaphysics. Clearly, he was able to take only a very small portion of Indian metaphysics and Sri Aurobindo's work, which he tries to pass off as his own.

Sri Aurobindo writes in detail about his experiences of the removal of ahaṁkāra (the ego), his work with various siddhi-s in thorough detail.[39]

## Fabricating the Pre-Trans Fallacy

The appropriation of involution-evolution and the 'ascent and integration' tenets also helped Wilber resolve what he calls the pre-trans fallacy, positing it as one of his most 'original' contributions.

He says that resolving this fallacy catapulted him to new heights in the fields of transpersonal psychology and other related domains. The impact was so momentous that Wilber writes, 'perhaps no other idea of mine has caused such turmoil'.[40] His biographer, Brad Reynolds, seconds it by stating:

> The pre/trans fallacy and its implications may be Wilber's most profound, novel, and yet most misunderstood idea. After establishing the pre/trans differentiation as a fundamental tenet of a true integral vision, Wilber has become intent on both promoting its insight and critiquing the fallacy, wherever it may appear.[41]

This fallacy is based on the notion that human development proceeds in the following stages:

Child (Pre-rational) → Adult Ego (Rational) → Higher State (Transcendence)

The child (first stage) and the enlightened yogi (third stage) often manifest similar egoless awareness: feelings of spacelessness, timelessness, and objectlessness. We must appreciate the difference: A child feels this way because s/he has not yet learned to fully cognize and rationalize himself/herself or the environment. An enlightened person, however, manifests some similar attributes because s/he is connected with a state of consciousness, which *includes* fully developed cognition of time, space, and causation but is not bound by them. The enlightened person has the faculties of the adult ego but is not limited by them. For instance, he has not forgotten to tie his shoelaces or forgotten his name; he is not limited by the ego, but he has not forgotten to function in pragmatic ways.

Due to the superficial similarities between the child and the higher states, many Western psychologists such as Freud, conflated the child state with what they called the 'mystic' state, concluding that spirituality or mysticism is a regressive child-like state. This problem is indeed common in Western thought because it does not understand the higher states adequately. Western traditions were not developed by people who practiced yoga; hence they have never adequately understood the higher states of consciousness. Wilber simply assumes that this problem is universal, and therefore considers it to be a fallacy in Indian traditions as well.

Many of the early European Romanticists of the eighteenth-nineteenth centuries also mistakenly imagined that spiritual enlightenment meant going backwards to some original state of primitive childlike perfection that has become blemished over time. They glorified Indian spirituality as that state of childlike perfection in the past. Europeans looking for their lost past felt they had found it in India, and hence distorted Indian philosophy to make it seem like a return to a golden past. India is often used as the premodern 'other' in the West's countercultural movement, as was the case of the naïve/romantic hippies of the 1960s.

However, this was not Indians' own view of the nature of spiritual advancement – as explained in the avatāra narratives and the yuga theories of time. Indian thought had no confusion between pre-rational and supra-rational states. For instance, non-dualism transcends dualism but includes the dualistic faculties to live in a practical sense.

Wilber understood this blunder in most Western thinkers who espouse non-dualism. He stated that though there may be superficial similarities between the egoic, verbal, and personal states of the child and the 'mystic', it is a huge mistake to conflate the two states. One cannot collapse the child state and mysticism. He calls the former the state of 'Pre' ego and the latter the state of 'Trans' ego. He writes, 'To return to the Divine, one doesn't regress to infancy. Mysticism is not regression in service of the ego, but evolution in transcendence of the ego'.[42] He starts to explain the ego's entire journey of evolution from pre to trans.

*While this is no doubt an important correction to most Westerners' ideas of spirituality, it is not a problem Wilber can superimpose on Indian traditions.* The pre-rational and trans-rational states have not been mixed up in India, and hence spiritual enlightenment is not seen as a return to a child state. After enlightenment, the Buddha did not become a child but went on to teach in profound ways. Nor did, upon enlightenment, Ādi Śaṅkarācārya, Śrī Rāmānujācārya, Pāṇini, Bhartṛhari, Abhinavagupta or any of the modern masters like Swami Vivekananda or Sri Aurobindo end up as dysfunctional imbeciles in society.

Wilber has blundered here because he has adopted the perennial tradition and removed the distinctive frameworks of Indian culture. He is irresponsible in projecting this pre-trans fallacy upon the Indian traditions. This is an absurdity because he has collapsed all Indian traditions into perennialism and applied the deficiencies with a broad brush to everything Indian.

Wilber's pre-trans resolution has distinct roots in Sri Aurobindo. Wilber prefers to recast it in terms of the Outward Arc and the Inward Arc. We will illustrate this by citing two passages by Sri Aurobindo.

The first passage describes the differences between the consciousness of peace and tranquility in matter and in the higher planes. Matter's peace and tranquility are inconscient, ignorant, and inert. However, the peace and tranquility in the higher planes come from self-awareness and knowledge. There has been an evolution between these two states. He writes:

> **Matter below life and mind contains in itself the balance between a perfect poise of tranquility and the action of an immeasurable energy, but does not possess that which it contains.** Its peace

> wears the dull mask of an obscure inertia, a sleep of unconsciousness or rather of a drugged and imprisoned consciousness. Driven by a force which is its real self but whose sense it cannot yet seize nor share, it has not the awakened joy of its own harmonious energies.
>
> Life and mind awaken to the sense of this want in the form of a striving and seeking ignorance and a troubled and baffled desire which are the first steps towards self-knowledge and self-fulfillment. But where then is the kingdom of their self-fulfilling? It comes to them by the exceeding of themselves. **Beyond life and mind we recover consciously in its divine truth that which the balance of material Nature grossly represented,**—a tranquility which is neither inertia nor a sealed trance of consciousness but the concentration of an absolute force and an absolute self-awareness, and an action of immeasurable energy which is at the same time an out-thrilling of ineffable bliss because its every act is the expression, not of a want and an ignorant straining, but of an absolute peace and self-mastery. In that attainment our ignorance realises the light of which it was a darkened or a partial reflection; our desires cease in the plenitude and fulfillment towards which even in their most brute material forms they were an obscure and fallen aspiration.[43]

He is clear about the huge difference between the pre-ego and trans-ego states.

The second passage compares intuition between the lower and higher realms of existence, which he calls sub-conscience and super-conscience respectively. In the lower realm of sub-conscience, intuition is involved in action, whereas it is free in the super-conscience and contains action instead of being contained by it. Between these two states, mind and reason serve as intermediaries that help liberate the involuted intuition in the sub-conscient to an evolved state in the super-conscient. Sri Aurobindo elucidates:

> The subconscient and the superconscient are two different formulations of the same All. The master-word of the subconscient is Life, the master-word of the superconscient is Light. **In the subconscient knowledge or consciousness is involved in action, for action is the essence of Life. In the superconscient action re-enters into Light and no longer contains involved knowledge**

> **but is itself contained in a supreme consciousness. Intuitional knowledge is that which is common between them and the foundation of intuitional knowledge is conscious or effective identity between that which knows and that which is known**; it is that state of common self-existence in which the knower and the known are one through knowledge. But in the subconscient the intuition manifests itself in the action, in effectivity, and the knowledge or conscious identity is either entirely or more or less concealed in the action. In the superconscient, on the contrary, Light being the law and the principle, the intuition manifests itself in its true nature as knowledge emerging out of conscious identity, and effectivity of action is rather the accompaniment or necessary consequent and no longer masks as the primary fact. **Between these two states reason and mind act as intermediaries which enable the being to liberate knowledge out of its imprisonment in the act and prepare it to resume its essential primacy**. When the self-awareness in the mind applied, both to continent and content, to own-self and other-self, exalts itself into the luminous self-manifest identity, the reason also converts itself into the form of the self-luminous intuitional knowledge. This is the highest possible state of our knowledge when mind fulfils itself in the supramental.[44]

Because Wilber's audience is Western, he can claim anything he understood ahead of other Westerners as 'original', as though the prior discoveries by Indians and his borrowing from them simply did not matter. This points to a racist mindset.

We find the following pattern repeated throughout his work:

- When he recognizes the limited understanding in his earlier works, he blames the Indian tradition for being flawed.
- When he resolves the issue by borrowing insights from the Indian tradition (which has resolved it already), he calls it his original discovery. Thus, he projects himself to be an insightful, original thinker who is 'synthesizing' and creating a new path that supersedes both the East and the West.

Worse, the pre-trans fallacy enabled Wilber to plant a seed that he later used to claim that Hinduism lacks ethics and morality: Because they lack the differentiation between pre- and trans-rational states, according to him, the Hindu spiritual paths abandon rationality and, along with it, ethical and social responsibilities. He has borrowed this idea from Hegel and other Western thinkers that Indians are still in the childlike pre-state, and hence have not yet developed a robust idea of ethics and morality. Such ideas were crucial to colonist propaganda. Wilber uses this ploy to debunk the very traditions he has used to build his career.

## Digesting Sri Aurobindo's Model of Consciousness

The *Atman Project* has three parts, each focusing on digesting a certain portion of Sri Aurobindo's explanation of consciousness and its evolution. A detailed description of these levels is provided in Sri Aurobindo's *The Life Divine* that serves as Wilber's foundation on which he superimposes an assortment of Western psychological theories.

Wilber uses mostly Greek mythological references to replace Sri Aurobindo's vocabulary. The corresponding stages in Sri Aurobindo's description are reduced to a table in the appendix and are lost amidst a long list of other theorists and traditions. Wilber consistently co-opts the ideas of Sri Aurobindo while reducing him to obscure footnotes and tables, or leaves him out entirely, while giving prominence to all sorts of miscellaneous sources from Western traditions.

We will now discuss each of the three parts of this digestion of Sri Aurobindo's ideas into his own system.

### *Digesting the lower planes of existence – Matter, Vital, and Mind*

The first part of *The Atman Project* maps the three lower planes of existence in Sri Aurobindo's system: Matter, Vital, and Mind. The following table shows Wilber's scheme for mapping these.

| Sri Aurobindo's Framework | Wilber's Mapping |
|---|---|
| Matter | Pleromatic |
| Vital | Typhonic |
| Mind | Piaget's 'concrete operational thinking' |

The following three comparisons show how Wilber maps each of the above levels of consciousness.

Table 1: **Consciousness in Matter Mapped to Pleromatic Consciousness**

| Sri Aurobindo's Original | Wilber's Mapping |
|---|---|
| **Matter, like Mind and Life, is still Being or Brahman in its self-creative action. It is a form of the force of conscious Being, a form given by Mind and realised by Life. It holds within it as its own reality consciousness concealed from itself, involved and absorbed in the result of its own self-formation and therefore self-oblivious.** And, however brute and void of sense it seems to us, it is yet, to the secret experience of the consciousness hidden within it, delight of being offering itself to this secret consciousness as object of sensation in order to tempt that hidden godhead out of its secrecy.... Matter is Sachchidananda represented to His own mental experience as a formal basis of objective knowledge, action and delight of existence.[45] | For the neonate there is no real separation whatsoever between inside and outside, subject and object, body and environment.... In a special sense, his self and his physical environment are one and the same. **The self is "pleromatic," as the alchemists *[unclear who he is referring to]* and Gnostics would put it, which essentially means that the self and the *material* cosmos are undifferentiated** [In other words, because it is identified with matter it is involved, absorbed, self-oblivious and devoid of sense]. Piaget himself says as much: "During the early stages the world and the self are one; neither term is distinguished from the other... the self is material, so to speak." The self is embedded in the *material prima*, which is both the primal chaos of the physical matter and the material matrix of Prakriti from which all creation was fashioned.[46] |

Table 2: **Consciousness in Vital Mapped to Typhonic Consciousness**

| Sri Aurobindo's Original | Wilber's Mapping |
|---|---|
| In the next grade of substance the initial, dominating, determining fact is no longer substantial form and force, but life and conscious desire. Therefore the world beyond this material plane must be a world based upon a conscious cosmic vital Energy, a force of vital seeking and a force of Desire and their self-expression and not upon an inconscient or subconscient will taking the form of a material force and energy. **All the forms, bodies, forces, life-movements, sense-movements, thought-movements, developments, culminations, self-fulfillments of that world must be dominated and determined by this initial fact of Conscious-Life to which Matter and Mind must subject themselves, must start from that, base themselves upon that, be limited or enlarged by its laws, powers, capacities, limitations; and if Mind there seeks to develop yet higher possibilities, still it must then too take accountof the original vital formula of desire-force, its purpose and its demand upon the divine manifestation.**[47] | It is out of this primordial fusion state...that the separate self emerges and, as Freud said, the self emerges first and foremost as a body, a bodyself. The mind—itself very fledgling and undeveloped—is almost totally undifferentiated from the body, so that the self's approach to the world is almost totally through bodily categories and schemes.... **The self, then, is one of an undeveloped mind—operating only with images—which is undifferentiated from the body.... out of primitive material unity emerges the first real self-sense: the bodyego....** The infant identifies with the newly emergent body, with its sensations and emotions, and gradually learns to differentiate them from the material cosmos at large. Notice that the bodyego, by differentiating itself from the material environment, actually transcends that primitive state of fusion and embeddedness. The bodyego transcends the material environment, and thus can perform physical operations upon that environment. Towards the end of the sensorimotor period (around age 2), the child has differentiated the self and the not-self to such a degree that |

| | |
|---|---|
| | he has a fairly stable image of "object constancy" and so he can muscularly coordinate physical operations on those objects. He can coordinate a physical movement of various objects in the environment, something he could not easily do as long as he could not differentiate himself from those objects.... At this bodyego stage(s), then, the self no longer is bound to the pleromatic environment—but it is bound to, or identified with, the biological body. The self, as bodyego, is dominated by instinctual urges, impulsiveness, the pleasure principle, involuntary urges and discharges—all the id-like primary processes and drives described so well by Freud et al. This is why we also call the bodyego the "typhonic self'—the typhon, in mythology, is half human, half serpent (uroboros). In physiological terms, the reptilian complex and the limbic system dominate the self at this stage.[48] |

Table 3: **Mental Consciousness Translated in Piaget's terms**

| Sri Aurobindo's Original | Wilber's Mapping |
|---|---|
| The next in the series must be governed by the dominating and determining factor of Mind. **Substance there must be subtle and flexible enough to assume the shapes directly imposed upon it by Mind, to obey its operations, to subordinate itself to its demand for self-expression and self-fulfillment. The relations of sense and substance too must have a corresponding subtlety and flexibility and must be determined, not by the relations of physical organ with physical object, but of Mind with the subtler substance upon which it works.** The life of such a world would be the servant of Mind in a sense of which our weak mental operations and our limited, coarse and rebellious vital faculties can have no adequate conception. There Mind dominates as the original formula, its purpose prevails, its demand overrides all others in the law of the divine manifestation.[49] | A fairly coherent mental-ego eventually emerges (usually between ages 4 and 7), differentiates itself from the body, transcends the simple biological world, and therefore can to a certain degree operate upon the biological world (and the earlier physical world) **using the tools of simple representational thinking. This whole trend is consolidated with the emergence (usually around age 7) of what Piaget calls "concrete operational thinking"—thinking that can operate on the concrete world and the body using concepts.** This cognitive mode dominates the middle ego/persona stage.<br>By the time of adolescence—the late ego/persona stage—another extraordinary differentiation begins to occur. In essence, the self simply starts to differentiate from the concrete thought process. **And because the self starts to differentiate itself from the concrete thought process, it can to a certain degree transcend that thought process and therefore operate upon it.** It is not surprising, then, that |

| | |
|---|---|
| | Piaget calls this—his highest stage—"formal operational," because one can operate upon one's own concrete thought (i.e. work with formal or linguistic objects as well as physical or concrete ones), a detailed operation which, among other things, results in the sixteen binary propositions of formal logic.[50] |

One clearly sees how Wilber uses several Western names to cover up his digestion of the various concepts that he has picked up from the detailed accounts of Sri Aurobindo.

### *Digesting inconscient, subconscient, and superconscient*

The second part of *The Atman Project* repackages Sri Aurobindo's foundational concepts of Inconscient, Subconscient, and Superconscient into Western psychoanalytic terminology *without any acknowledgment* of Indian sources. Wilber wants to impress his Western readers by claiming to re-interpret and supersede the ideas of Freud and Jung. He presents these mappings as though they are his original contributions to psychology.

The sleight of hand, however, is apparent once we put Sri Aurobindo's descriptions alongside Wilber's. There are three major mappings in this part of the book, which are shown in the table below:

| Sri Aurobindo's Framework | Wilber's Mapping |
|---|---|
| Inconscience | Ground-Unconscious |
| Subconscience | Archaic-Unconscious and Submergent-Unconscious |
| Superconscience | Emergent-Unconscious |

These three mappings are explained in the following three tables:

Table 4: **Inconscience Mapped to Ground-Unconscious**

| Sri Aurobindo's Framework | Wilber's Mapping |
|---|---|
| The **Inconscience** is an inverse reproduction of the supreme superconscience: it has the same absoluteness of being and automatic action, but in a vast involved trance; it is being lost in itself, plunged in its own abyss of infinity. Instead of a luminous absorption in self-existence there is a tenebrous involution in it, the darkness veiled within darkness of the Rig Veda, *tama āseet tamasā guhayam*, which makes it look like Non-Existence; instead of a luminous inherent self-awareness there is a consciousness plunged into an abyss of self-oblivion, inherent in being but not awake in being...**it carries in it the awareness of all the truths of existence [including the planes of life, mind, and beyond-mind] hidden in its dark infinite and, when it acts and creates,—but it acts first as Energy and not as Consciousness,—everything is arranged with the precision and perfection of an intrinsic knowledge.**[51] | **[Ground-unconscious] is all the deep structures existing as potentials ready to emerge, via remembrance, at some future point. All the deep structures given to a collective humanity—pertaining to every level of consciousness, from the body to mind to soul to spirit, gross, subtle, and causal—are enfolded or enwrapped in the ground-unconscious.** All of these structures are unconscious, but they are not repressed because they have not yet entered consciousness.... Development—or evolution—consists of a series of hierarchical transformations or *unfoldings* of the deep structures out of the ground-unconscious, starting with the lowest (pleroma and body), and ending with the highest (God and Void). When—and if—*all* of the ground unconscious has emerged, then there is *only* consciousness: all is conscious *as* the All.[52] |

Table 5: **Subconscient Mapped to Archaic-Unconscious and Submergent-Unconscious**

| Sri Aurobindo's Framework | Wilber's Mapping |
|---|---|
| The **subconscient** is universal as well as individual like all the other main parts of the Nature. But there are different parts or planes of the subconscient. All upon earth is based on the Inconscient as it is called, though it is not really inconscient at all, but rather a complete "sub"-conscience, **a suppressed or involved consciousness, in which there is everything but nothing is formulated or expressed. The subconscient lies between this Inconscient and the conscious mind, life and body. It contains the potentiality of all the primitive reactions to life which struggle out to the surface from the dull and inert strands of Matter and form by a constant development a slowly evolving and self-formulating consciousness; it contains them not as ideas, perceptions or conscious reactions but as the fluid substance of these things. But also all that is consciously experienced sinks down into the subconscient, not as precise though submerged memories but as obscure yet obstinate impressions of experience, and these can come up at any time as dreams, as** | The **archaic-unconscious**...is simply the most primitive and least developed structures of the ground-unconscious, associated with the pleroma, the uroboros, and the typhon. **They are finally unconscious but unrepressed, and some tend to remain unconscious, never clearly unfolded in awareness except as rudimentary deep structures with little or no surface content.... On the whole, the archaic-unconscious is not the product of personal experience; it is initially unconscious but not repressed; it contains the earliest and most primitive structures to unfold from the ground-unconscious, and, even when unfolded, they tend towards unconsciousness. They are preverbal, and most are subhuman.**"[53]<br>"Once a deep structure has emerged from the ground-unconscious and taken on some sort of surface structure, it can for various reasons be returned to a state of unconsciousness. That is, once a structure has emerged, it can be submerged, and the total of such structures we call the |

| Sri Aurobindo's Framework | Wilber's Mapping |
|---|---|
| **mechanical repetitions of past thought, feelings, action, etc., as "complexes"....** All too that is suppressed without being wholly got rid of sinks down there and remains as seed ready to surge up or sprout up at any moment.[54] | **submergent-unconscious.** The submergent-unconscious is that which was once conscious, in the lifetime of the individual, but is now screened out of awareness.[55] |

Table 6: **Superconscience Mapped to Emergent-Unconscious**

| Sri Aurobindo's Framework | Wilber's Mapping |
|---|---|
| In the **superconscience** beyond our present level of awareness are included the higher planes of mental being as well as the native heights of supramental and pure spiritual being.[56] | At any point on the developmental cycle, those deep structures which have not yet emerged from the ground-unconscious [as yet as one has not reached the corresponding developmental and evolutionary stage when they should become available] are referred to as the **emergent-unconscious.** For someone at the ego (or centaur) level, the low-subtle, the high-subtle, the low-causal, and the high-causal are emergent-unconscious.[57] |

Sri Aurobindo has written in great detail on how to transform inconscience and subconscience, as they are the unconscious repository of saṃskāra-s and indelible impressions that stealthily influence the personality. Wilber ignores citing these and instead uses them as his own analysis.

| Sri Aurobindo's Framework | Wilber's Mapping |
|---|---|
| The subconscient retains the impressions of all our past experiences of life and they can come up from there in dream forms: most dreams in ordinary sleep are formations made from subconscient impressions.<br>The habit of strong recurrence of the same things in our physical consciousness, so that it is difficult to get rid of its habits, is largely due to a subconscient support. The subconscient is full of irrational habits.<br>When things are rejected from all other parts of the nature, they go either into the environmental consciousness around us through which we communicate with others and with universal Nature and try to return from there or they sink into the subconscient and can come up from there even after lying long quiescent so that we think they are gone.<br>When the physical consciousness is being changed, the chief resistance comes from the subconscient. It is constantly maintaining or bringing back the inertia, weakness, obscurity, lack of intelligence which afflict the, physical mind and vital or the obscure fears, desires, angers, lusts of the physical vital, or the | The meditation practice begins to break the present egoic translation by either halting it (koan) or watching it (shikan).... As the present egoic translation begins to loosen, then the individual is first exposed to the subliminal-submergent unconscious (the nonrepressed submergent unconscious in general), which includes, among other things, the "innumerable unnoticed aspects of experiences, aspects tuned out due to habit, conditioning, or the exigencies of the Situation." All sorts of odd memories float up, screen memories, insignificant memories, memories that are not repressed, merely forgotten or preconscious. Months can be spent "at the movies" watching the subliminal-submergent reemerge in awareness and dance before the inward eye....<br>The embedded-unconscious, by being "interfered with," starts to shake loose its habitual hold. Now recall that the embedded-unconscious translations were the unrepressed but repressing aspects of the self-system of a given level. Naturally, then, as the repressor is relaxed, the repressed tends to emerge. That is to say, the repressed-submergent unconscious now tends to float—or |

| Sri Aurobindo's Framework | Wilber's Mapping |
|---|---|
| illnesses, dullnesses, pains incapabilities to which the body-nature is prone.<br>**If light, strength, the Mother's Consciousness is brought down into the body, it can penetrate the subconscient also and convert its obscurity and resistance.**<br>When something is erased from the subconscient so completely that it leaves no seed and thrown out of the circumconscient so completely that it can return no more, then only can we be sure that we have finished with it for ever.[58] | sometimes erupt—into awareness. The individual confronts his shadow (and, on occasion, primal or archaic phantasies from the archaic-unconscious). An individual can spend months or even years wrestling with his shadow, and this is where orthodox therapy can certainly complement meditation.[59] |

### *Digesting the process of Jīva's evolution and unity with the Divine*

The third part of *The Atman Project* takes Sri Aurobindo's explanation of the jīva-s process of evolution and unity with the Divine and restates it in Western psychoanalytic terms. Wilber's appropriation is obvious, yet no credit has been given to Sri Aurobindo. The following table summarizes the mapping, which we shall next explain.

| Sri Aurobindo's Framework | Wilber's Mapping |
|---|---|
| **Aspiration** of the soul to know its true nature | ***Atman telos*** |
| Pull of ignorance leading to **denial** of the Divine | ***Atman denial*** |
| The tension or *dvandva* between the above two (i.e. aspiration and ignorance) | ***Atman project*** |
| This *dvandva* is resolved by a combination of two ways – that of the **calm Self** and that of the **psychic being** | **Eros and Thanatos** or incest and castration |

Wilber's *Atman telos* is a restatement of the following from Sri Aurobindo:

> For the fulfillment of life or for transcendence of life, and whether purity, calm and freedom in the spirit be our aim or puissance, joy and perfection, Sachchidananda is the unknown, omnipresent, indispensable term for which the human consciousness, whether in knowledge and sentiment or in sensation and action, is eternally seeking.[60]

Wilber's *Atman denial* is a restatement of Sri Aurobindo's following description of how the pull of ignorance leads to the denial of the Divine or Brahman:

> Awakened to a profound self-knowledge than his first mental idea of himself, Man begins to conceive some formula and to perceive some appearance of the thing that he has to affirm. But it appears to him as if poised between...negations of itself.... In the world, in himself, and around himself, he is met always by the opposites of his affirmation. Death is ever with him, limitation invests his being and his experience, error, inconscience, weakness, inertia, grief, pain, evil are constant oppressors of his effort. Here also he is driven to deny God, or at least the Divine seems to negate or to hide itself in some appearance or outcome which is other than its true and eternal reality.[61]

The *Atman project* is a restatement of Sri Aurobindo's following description of the dialectic between aspiration and ignorance:

> For Life, these things that seem to deny God, to be the opposites of Sachchidananda, are real, even if they turn out to be temporary. They and their opposites, good, knowledge, joy, pleasure, life, survival, strength, power, increase, are the very materials of her workings.... Because that which he has become is out of harmony both with what the world of his habituation is and what he himself should be and is to be, therefore man is subject to these contradictions of the secret Truth of things. ... they are not the punishment of a fall, but the conditions of a progress. They are the first elements of the work he has to fulfill, the price he has to pay for the crown which he hopes to win, the narrow way by which

Nature escapes out of Matter into consciousness; they are at once her ransom and her stock. For out of these false relations and by their aid, the true have to be found. By the Ignorance we have to cross over death.... It would be, then, not when he has excised the evil In Nature out of himself by an act of moral surgery or parted with life by an abhorrent recoil, but when he has turned Death into a more perfect life, lifted the small things of human limitation into the great things of divine vastness, transformed suffering into beatitude, converted evil into proper good, translated error and falsehood into their secret truth that the sacrifice will be accomplished, the journey done and Heaven and Earth equalized join hands in the bliss of the Supreme.[62]

Table 7: **Sri Aurobindo's Evolutionary Process Mapped onto Western Psychoanalytic Terms**

| Sri Aurobindo's Framework | Wilber's Mapping |
|---|---|
| When the soul draws towards the Divine, **there may be a resistance in the mind and the common form of that is denial and doubt**—which may create **mental and vital suffering.** There may again be **a resistance in the vital nature whose principal character is desire** and the attachment to the objects of desire, and if in this field there is conflict between the soul and the vital nature, between the Divine Attraction and the pull of the Ignorance, then obviously there may be much suffering of the mind and vital parts. **The physical consciousness** also may offer a resistance which is usually that of a **fundamental inertia**, an obscurity | From the very beginning, all creatures intuit God. From the start, man and women intuit their prior Atman nature, and this acts like a huge unconscious magnet, so to speak, drawing them onward and upward toward that perfect release in the superconscious All [the Atman **telos**]. **But it also forces them, as a temporary and remedial measure, to fashion all sorts of substitutes for Atman**—substitute subjects, substitute objects, substitute gratifications, substitute sacrifices, immortality projects, and cosmocentric designs, and tokens of transcendence [the Atman **denial**]. Under this pressure, successive |

| Sri Aurobindo's Framework | Wilber's Mapping |
|---|---|
| in the very stuff of the physical, an incomprehension, an inability to respond to the higher consciousness, a habit of helplessly responding to the lower mechanically, even when it does not want to do so; both vital and physical suffering may be the consequence. There is, moreover, **the resistance of the Universal Nature** which does not want the being to escape from the Ignorance into the Light. This may take the form of a vehement insistence in the continuation of the old movements, waves of them thrown on the mind and vital and body so that old ideas, impulses, desires, feelings, responses continue even after they are thrown out and rejected, and can return like an invading army from outside, until the whole nature, given to the Divine, refuses to admit them. This is the subjective form of the universal resistance, but it may also take an objective form, - opposition, calumny, attacks, persecution, misfortunes of many kinds, adverse conditions and circumstances, pain, illness, assaults from men or forces. There too the possibility of suffering is evident. There are two ways to meet all that - first that of the Self, calm, equality, a spirit, a will, a mind, a vital, a physical consciousness that remain resolutely | structures of consciousness are created and then abandoned, fashioned and then transcended, constructed and then passed by. ***They are created as a substitute for Atman, and abandoned when those substitutes fail.*** And evolution proceeds by a series of such abortive attempts to reach Atman-consciousness—proceeds, that is, via the Atman **project**, with each step, as it were, getting a bit closer.... Once a new level of evolution—a new but higher-order substitute self—is created by a vertical transformation of the deep structure of the previous level, the Eros of the new level proceeds by means of horizontal translations to integrate the surface structures of that stage into some sort of higher-order wholeness. Since it cannot have true and real Union, it at least attempts (as a substitute) to unify self. These **Eros** translations proceed to organize and develop the emergent characteristics and surface structures of the new level, to stabilize and preserve that level by *integrating* the new and higher symbolic substitutes. And this overall translative process continues until—for various reasons—this type of translation is found inadequate. And then? And then translation fundamentally fails and transformation ensues. Now the |

| Sri Aurobindo's Framework | Wilber's Mapping |
|---|---|
| turned towards the Divine and unshaken by all suggestion of doubt, desire, attachment, depression, sorrow, pain, inertia.... There is also the way of the psychic,—when the psychic being comes out in its inherent power, its consecration, adoration, love of the Divine, self-giving, surrender and imposes these on the mind, vital and physical consciousness and compels them to turn all their movements Godward. If the psychic is strong and master throughout, then there is no or little subjective suffering and the objective cannot affect either the soul or the other parts of the consciousness—the way is sunlit and a great joy and sweetness are the note of the whole sadhana.[63] | reasons for the failing of translation are numerous, and they differ from level to level of the spectrum. In general, however, we may state that whenever **Eros** (of that level) exceeds **Thanatos** (of that level), translation proceeds and stabilization occurs. The seeking and grasping of that particular level is happy with its substitute gratifications, which present as fulfilled the desire for Unity. When Thanatos exceeds Eros, however, the particular translation involved winds down and is eventually surrendered, and transformation to a different mode of self and a different type of translation ensues: a new deep structure is remembered so that new surface structures can be learned.[64] |

Thus, the major rungs of Wilber's schema are co-opted from Sri Aurobindo's work, where they have been developed with exceptional clarity.

An important highlight of Sri Aurobindo's work is his explanation that the evolution of Matter, Life, and Spirit are one process of prakṛti (the other process being yoga); this evolution occurs because the divinity is already involuted in matter. Matter is shown to be the manifestation of the same spirit and constitutes the very first step of the ascent.

Apart from creating alternative monikers such as Pleromatic and Typhonic for Sri Aurobindo's categories of Matter and Vital, all Wilber does is take specific points and details from the sage's work and pass them off as his own. Wilber's Atman denial is nothing but a restatement of Sri Aurobindo's writings on the denial of the Brahman; the sage's work on the various gradations of the vital, mental, and higher planes including the physical and sensational gradations of each of them is ignored. The resistance offered by the physical vital to any attempts to ascend, the polarities of aspiration and ignorance seen in the manifestation of sat-cit-ānanda, all clearly seen in Sri Aurobindo's work, are presented as though these were genuinely Wilber's own insights. He hides his hubris and appropriation by couching them in convoluted Western psychoanalytic jargon.

He actively uses terms such as Brahman and Ātman without explaining the systems in which they are embedded and without fully explicating their meaning in the Vedic systems. Such terms serve as intellectual ornaments to impress those Western readers who are even less informed about Indian thought than he is.

## Wilber's *Up from Eden*

While *The Atman Project* was Wilber's mapping of Sri Aurobindo's theory of individual development, his other book, *Up from Eden*, deals with the evolutionary process of groups as distinct from individuals. In the latter book, Wilber discusses the collective human evolution from Australopithecus to possible future godheads, once again copying Sri Aurobindo's ideas.

Wilber dilutes Sri Aurobindo's ideas by replacing them with generic perennialism, and he connects them to ancient Greek or more recent Western philosophers like Joseph Campbell, Earnest Becker, L.L. Whyte and Erich Neumann. He sprinkles a few technical Indian words to show off his mastery but digests them into Western frameworks. He emphasizes that India has nothing to contribute beyond other-worldly 'mysticism'.

In *Up from Eden*, Wilber considers eight stages as part of the 'collective human development': nature, body, early mind, advanced mind, psychic, subtle, causal, and ultimate. He confidently proclaims that we are in the fourth stage of the 'high mental-egoistic stage' that began around 1500 C.E. during the Renaissance and Enlightenment movements in Europe. In other words, the collective evolution of humanity is something being led by Europeans and marked by milestones in European history. What is conveniently sidelined is that Eastern civilizations, both Indian and

Chinese, have existed for millennia and have seen brilliant intellectual activity in every sphere of human endeavor.

### *Appropriating Sri Aurobindo's Theory of Future Evolution*

Sri Aurobindo considered humans transitional beings between inconscient matter and *future* superconscient beings. His work, *Man: A Transitional Being,* is devoted to this. He developed this notion in complex detail, challenging the materialists' position, which considers humans as the final product of evolution, and the Abrahamic religions which consider man God's highest creation. Wilber adopts this pioneering theory of Sri Aurobindo, which states that humans are intermediaries in the evolutionary process.

Sri Aurobindo explained in minute detail, starting from matter all the way to sat-cit-ānanda—when the mind emerged from the lower planes of matter and life, the result was the human being, in a plane that is predominantly mental. The higher planes beyond the mind are still unmanifest in the collective evolutionary process, and our collective purpose is to evolve to beings higher than humans.

Just as Nature evolved the human from an animal, it will also work out the superman. Sri Aurobindo explains that just as human beings, while having evolved from animals, are significantly different from other animals, the superhuman will be different from humans in the same measure:

> Supermanhood is not man climbed to his own natural zenith, not a superior degree of human greatness, knowledge, power, intelligence, will, character, genius, dynamic force, saintliness, love, purity or perfection. Superman is beyond mental man and his limits; it is a greater consciousness than the highest consciousness proper to human nature.[65]

This is a radical insight by Sri Aurobindo vis-à-vis all spiritual traditions before him which had only talked about liberation from the present human condition, but had no claim of an entirely new being evolving out of the conscious collective humanity. This is a new kind of teleology replacing ideas of Heaven, escape from Damnation, or merger with God or living in the state of nirvāṇa.

Sri Aurobindo further maintains that Nature will work out her evolutionary mechanism into superhuman if left alone, but yoga is a process of accelerating this endeavor. Thus, Sri Aurobindo not only provides the framework in his thought, but also highlights the active role played by man through his sādhana and yoga in realizing this goal.

Wilber appropriates these tenets as a part of generic perennialism. However, this was never a claim made by Huxley or other perennialists. Wilber incorporates Sri Aurobindo's ideas into his own fabricated version of perennialism and writes:

> According to perennial philosophy, the path of transcendence follows what is called the "Great Chain of Being," which is said to be a universal sequence of hierarchic levels of increasing consciousness. The Great Chain of Being moves, to use Western terms, from matter to body to mind to soul to spirit. Thus history, from this viewpoint, is basically the unfolding of those successively higher-order structures, starting with the lowest (matter and body) and ending with the highest (spirit and ultimate wholeness).[66]
>
> The earliest stages of humankind's evolution were dominated by, although not defined by, subhuman and subconscious impulses. And it was out of this subconscious state—dominated by physical nature and animal body—that men and women eventually evolved a self-reflexive and uniquely human mode of consciousness that we know today as the mental-ego.... According to the perennial philosophy, the mental-ego, apart from all its shortcomings, is nonetheless something of a halfway mark on the path of transcendence. That is, egoic self-consciousness is halfway between the subconsciousness of nature and the super-consciousness of spirit. The subconsciousness of matter and body gives way to the self-consciousness of mind and ego, which in turn gives way to the superconsciousness of soul and spirit—such is the "big picture" of evolution and history, and such is the context of man's history as well.[67]

While appropriating the central tenets of Sri Aurobindo's evolutionary philosophy, Wilber is cautious not to be explicit about proposing the emergence of new beings that Sri Aurobindo called supramental beings because that would be irreconcilable with the Abrahamic religions.

The following extracts compare the words of Sri Aurobindo and Wilber. Wilber appropriates the idea that humans are transitional beings.

He mentions this in the opening sentence of *Up from Eden*, but credits it to Plotinus. Sri Aurobindo gets only a casual mention, clubbed with Teilhard de Chardin in a lesser role.

**Sri Aurobindo**

MAN is a transitional being; he is not final. For in man and high beyond him ascend the radiant degrees that climb to a divine supermanhood. There lies our destiny and the liberating key to our aspiring but troubled and limited mundane existence.

We mean by man mind imprisoned in a living body. But **mind is not the highest possible power of consciousness; for mind is not in possession of Truth**, but only its ignorant seeker. **Beyond mind is a supramental or gnostic power of consciousness that is in eternal possession of Truth**. This supermind is at its source the dynamic consciousness, in its nature at once and inseparably infinite wisdom and infinite will of the divine Knower and Creator. **Supermind is superman; a gnostic supermanhood is the next distinct and triumphant evolutionary step to be reached by earthly nature.**

The step from man to superman is the next approaching achievement in the earth's evolution. **It is inevitable because it is at once the intention of the inner Spirit and the logic of Nature's process.**

**The appearance of a human possibility in a material and animal world was the first glint of some coming divine Light, the first far-off promise of a godhead to be born out of Matter. The appearance of the superman in the human world will be the fulfilment of this divine promise.** Out of the material consciousness in which our mind works as a chained slave is emerging the disk of a secret sun of Power and Joy and Knowledge. The supermind will be the formed body of that radiant effulgence.... Man is a mental being whose mentality works here involved, obscure and degraded in a physical brain. Even in the highest of his kind it is baulked of its luminous possibilities of supreme force and freedom by this dependence, shut off even from its own divine powers, impotent to change our life beyond certain narrow and precarious limits; it is an imprisoned and checked force, most often nothing but a servitor or caterer of interests or a purveyor of amusement to the life and the body. But divine superman will be a gnostic spirit. Supermind in him will lay hands on the mental and physical instruments and, standing above and yet penetrating our lower already manifested parts, it will transform mind, life and body.[68]

**Ken Wilber**

'Mankind,' said Plotinus, 'is poised midway between the gods and the beasts' .... If men and women have come up from the beasts, then they will likely end up with the gods. The distance between man and the gods is not all that much greater than the distance between beasts and man. We have already closed the latter gap, and there is no reason to suppose that we shall not eventually close the former. **As Aurobindo and Teilhard de Chardin knew, the future of humankind is God-consciousness, and we will want to examine this future in the entire context of human history.**

But if men and women are up from the beasts and on their way to the gods, they are in the meantime rather tragic figures. Poised between the two extremes, they are subjected to the most violent of conflicts. No longer beast, not yet god—or worse, half beast, half god: there is the soul of humankind. Put another way, humankind is an essentially tragic figure with a beautifully optimistic future—if it can survive the transition.[69]

Besides explaining the nature and evolutionary processes of individual and society, Sri Aurobindo also wrote extensively on the nature of future levels of evolution. His work, *The Supramental Manifestation* explains the future of the individual, whereas *The Human Cycle: The Psychology of Social Development* explains the collective future. Evolution is a zigzag path with a forward trajectory. Human society has moved through symbolic, typal, conventional, and individualistic stages.[70]

The stages in collective evolution will be manifested in the future and will radically change the human condition. There will be a greater reign of peace, harmony, art, and beauty in everyday life; human relations will be dictated by psychic love rather than demands of the vital. Unity and freedom will override division and oppression, with a harmonious balance between the individual and the collective without one dominating the other. The arts, sciences, education, social and political structures will be geared towards finding and manifesting the inner divine.

Such ideas are extensively discussed in the later chapters of *The Human Cycle* and specifically in *The Conditions for the Coming of a Spiritual Age,* which was included by Robert McDermott in his compilation of Sri Aurobindo's writings, *The Essential Aurobindo.* Wilber has read these works and includes McDermott's book in his bibliography.

The following quotations show similarities in Wilber's chapter, *In Prospectus: The Future.* He acquires the prophetic tone of a social scientist and states:

> If our overall hypothesis is correct, then what we see in the stages of present-day meditation is the same thing we saw in the stages of the historical evolution of the *advanced tip* of consciousness; we see the unfolding of the higher levels of the Great Chain of Being. And *therefore* we also see the probable *future stages* of the evolution of the *average mode* of consciousness, consciousness of the whole. In simplistic terms we see humanity's future.[71]

**Sri Aurobindo**

A spiritualised society would live like its spiritual individuals, not in the ego, but in the spirit, not as the collective ego, but as the collective soul. This freedom from the egoistic standpoint would be its first and most prominent characteristic. But the elimination of egoism would not be brought about, as it is now proposed to bring it about, by persuading or forcing the individual to immolate his personal will and aspirations and his precious and hard-won individuality to the collective will, aims and egoism of the society, driving him like a victim of ancient sacrifice to slay his soul on the altar of that huge and shapeless idol.... **Therefore a society which was even initially spiritualised would make the revealing and finding of the divine Self in man the supreme, even the guiding aim of all its activities, its education, its knowledge, its science, its ethics, its art, its economical and political structure...**

A spiritualised society would treat in its sociology the individual, from the saint to the criminal, not as units of a social problem to be passed through some skilfully devised machinery and either flattened into the social mould or crushed out of it, but as souls suffering and entangled in a net and to be rescued, souls growing and to be encouraged to grow, souls grown and from whom help and power can be drawn by the lesser spirits who are not yet adult. The aim of its economics would be not to create a huge engine of production, whether of the competitive or the cooperative kind, but to give to men—not only to some but to all men each in his highest possible measure—the joy of work according to their own nature and free leisure to grow inwardly, as well as a simply rich and beautiful life for all. In its politics it would not regard the nations within the scope of their own internal life as enormous State machines regulated and armoured with man living for the sake of the machine and worshipping it as his God and his larger self, content at the first call to kill others upon its altar and to bleed there himself so that the machine may remain intact and powerful and be made ever larger, more complex, more cumbrous, more mechanically efficient and entire. Neither would it be content to maintain these nations or States in their mutual relations as noxious engines meant to discharge poisonous gas upon each other in peace and to rush in times of clash upon each other's armed hosts and unarmed millions, full of belching shot and men missioned to murder like war-planes or hostile tanks in a modern battle-field. **It would regard the peoples as group-souls, the Divinity concealed and to be self-discovered in its human collectivities, group-souls meant like the individual to grow according to their own nature and by that growth to help each other, to help the whole race in the one common work of humanity. And that work would be to find the divine Self in the individual and the collectivity and to realise spiritually, mentally, vitally, materially its greatest, largest, richest and deepest possibilities in the inner life of all and their outer action and nature.**[72]

**Ken Wilber**

The Nirmanakaya Age will mean a society of men and women who, by virtue of an initial glimpse into transcendence will start to understand vividly their common humanity and brother/sisterhood; will transcend roles based on bodily differences of skin color and sex; will grow in mental-psychic clarity; will make policy decisions on the basis of intuition as well as rationality; will see the same Consciousness in each and every soul, indeed, in all creation, and will start to act correspondingly; will find mental-psychic consciousness to be transfigurative of body physiology, and adjust medical theory accordingly; will find higher motivations in men and women that will drastically alter economic incentives and economic theory; **will understand psychological growth as evolutionary transcendence, and develop methods and institutions not just to cure emotional disease but foster the growth of consciousness; will see education as a discipline in transcendence, body to mind to soul, and regear educational theory and institutions accordingly, with special emphasis on hierarchic development**; will find technology an appropriate aid to transcendence, not a replacement for it; will use mass media, instant telecommunication, and human/computer linkages as vehicles of bonding-consciousness and unity; will see outer space as not just an inert entity out there but also as a projection of inner or psychic spaces, and explore it accordingly; will use appropriate technology to free the exchanges of the material level from chronic oppression; will find sexuality to be not just a play of reproductive desire but the initial base of kundalini sublimation into psychic spheres—and will adjust marriage practices accordingly; will see cultural-national differences as perfectly acceptable and desirable, but will set those differences on a background of universal and common consciousness, and thus view radical isolationism or imperialism as criminal; will view all people as ultimately one in Spirit, but only potentially one in Spirit, and thus provide incentives for each individual to actualize that Spirit, hierarchically, thus limiting mindless and undeserved "entitlement"; will realize fully the transcendent unity of all Dharmakaya religions, and thus respect all true religious preferences while condemning any sectarian claim to possess "the only way"; **will realize that politicians, if they are to govern all aspects of life, will have to demonstrate an understanding and mastery of all aspects of life—body to mind to soul to spirit.**[73]

### *Contesting the interpretation of the Bible*

In his evolutionary framework, Sri Aurobindo offers a novel interpretation of the Biblical notion of man's Fall. He contends that the Fall occurred with the involution of the spirit, and the cause of suffering is the ego's persistence on its separation instead of unity and oneness. He writes:

> It is the division, the separation, the principle of isolation from the Permanent and One that brought [Fall] about; it is because the ego set up for itself in the world emphasising its own desire and self-affirmation in preference to its unity with the Divine and its oneness with all; it is because instead of the one supreme Force, Wisdom, Light determining the harmony of all forces each Idea, Force, Form of things was allowed to work itself out as far as it could in the mass of infinite possibilities by its separate will and inevitably in the end by conflict with others. Division, ego, the imperfect consciousness and groping and struggle of a separate self-affirmation are the efficient cause of the suffering and ignorance of this world. Once consciousnesses separated from the one consciousness, they fell inevitably into Ignorance and the last result of Ignorance was Inconscience; from a dark immense Inconscient this material world arises and out of it a soul that by evolution is struggling into consciousness, attracted towards the hidden Light, ascending but still blindly towards the lost Divinity from which it came.[74]

Christian theologians have contended that once human beings walked out of the Garden of Eden, they were burdened with suffering and sin due to the damnation by a transcendental divine living strictly outside the cosmos. Sri Aurobindo disagrees. He contends that the Divine is present and involuted in our being and in the universe, thereby supporting the evolution from ignorance to knowledge:

> It is not, as some religions suppose, a supra-cosmic, arbitrary, personal Deity himself altogether uninvolved in the fall who has imposed evil and suffering on creatures made capriciously by his fiat. The Divine we know is an Infinite Being in whose infinite manifestation these things have come—it is the Divine itself that is here, behind us, pervading the manifestation, supporting the world with its oneness; it is the Divine that is in us upholding itself the burden of the fall and its dark consequence. If above It stands for ever in its perfect Light, Bliss and Peace, It is also here; its Light, Bliss and Peace are secretly here supporting all; in ourselves there is a spirit, a central presence greater than the series of surface personalities which, like the supreme Divine itself, is not overborne by the fate they endure. If we find out this Divine within us, if we know ourselves as this spirit which is of one essence and being with the Divine, that is our gate of deliverance and in it we can remain ourselves even in the midst of this world's disharmonies, luminous, blissful and free.[75]

Unlike the West, Indian science and spirituality have never been divided in a state of war. Therefore, Sri Aurobindo had no need to wrestle with his own tradition to make this interpretation. Such a view is built into the Vedic metaphysics.

Wilber, however, operates within the Western tradition through its war between science and spirituality. He wants to become the peacemaker between rival camps of Judeo-Christian theologians and scientists and thereby establish himself as a Western pioneer. To accomplish this, he distorts Sri Aurobindo's reinterpretation of the Fall: To make both sides of the West happy, he says that instead of one Fall, there have been two Falls: Theological and Scientific.

The Theological Fall occurred at the time of the Big Bang when, as a final step in the process of involution, the spirit exploded to gradually coalesce as matter, and the superconscience inverted to become completely oblivious of being inconscience, providing itself the illusionary ignorance of separation from the source. The Scientific Fall occurred with the emergence of the mind, which recognized its separation from superconsciousness. However, it was not a fall from superconsciousness but from involuted consciousness and subconsciousness, as consciousness in both planes of matter and life is oblivious of its separation from the source because it does not yet have the faculty to identify it, which only happens with the emergence of the mind. Wilber states that with the growth in consciousness came the knowledge of separation from superconscience, which led to guilt and vulnerability with the emergence of the mind.

The Scientific Fall is a fall from the pre-state and not trans-state of consciousness. In other words, the Scientific Fall is not the Original Sin but the 'original apprehension of original sin' occurring through the emergence of the mind through which humans gain an understanding of sin and separation.

According to Wilber, neither theologians nor scientists comprehend the distinction between the two Falls and thus have been in warring camps. Theologians believed, and many still do, that there was on earth an Eden in which all humans lived in a superconscious and enlightened state. Scientists, on the other hand, find no evidence of such an existence and maintain that we evolved from apes. This conflict continues.

Wilber's solution is that if the distinction between the two Falls is recognized, science can marry religion. He writes that 'the union of science and religion is union of involution and evolution'.[76] He proposes a win-win solution in which theologians are right because with the Big Bang, humankind did encounter a fall from superconscience, and scientists are right because we did evolve from apes as we were already involuted in them.

To support his reconciliation, Wilber extensively elaborates on the idea of involution-evolution in the chapter, *Original Sin*. Readers should verify for themselves the similarities between it and Sri Aurobindo's writings on involution-evolution cited earlier. Interestingly, Wilber credits the original description of involution to himself by citing the following sentence from *The Atman Project*: 'This whole downward movement, whereby Spirit playfully loses and forgets itself in lower levels, is called *involution*'.[77]

Wilber goes to great lengths to claim this as his own pioneering breakthrough, even though he writes this several decades after Sri Aurobindo, and admits to being influenced by him. He makes a condescending mention that Sri Aurobindo also held similar views along with others like S. Radhakrishnan, Haridas Chaudhuri and Gopi

Krishna, without citing any of their writings or acknowledging that he derived these ideas from them.[78]

### *Digesting into Hegel*

While giving occasional small and casual mention to Indians, Wilber spends considerable space in his writings to cite numerous Westerners. He credits Teilhard de Chardin for influencing his pioneering breakthrough, without acknowledging that de Chardin was heavily indebted to Indian sources, especially from his intense study of Śrī Rāmānujācārya.

He then maps the idea back to Hegel, Johann Gottlieb Fichte, and Friedrich Schelling (the latter both German philosophers), again without mentioning their debts to the study of Indian philosophy by their German peers with whom each of these scholars had extensive debates on Indian worldviews.[79] He cites Hegel's ideas on the relationship between the One and the Many, and adds that the Absolute is involuted in the process of its becoming. Development (evolution) is the result of a spiritual *telos* of the Spirit actualizing itself. Quoting Hegel, Wilber writes that the 'end-goal of history is "Spirit's return to itself on a higher level, a level at which subjectivity and objectivity are united in one infinite act"'.[80]

He then connects the process of evolution from subconsciousness to superconsciousness to the three stages enumerated by Hegel: *Bewusstsein* (subconsciousness), *Selbstbewusstsein* (selfconsciousness), and *Vernunft* (superconsciousness). The idea of 'Transcend and Include' is mapped to Hegel's *negation* of the movement of spirit to the next level along with the *preservation* of all previous levels or stages, with no mention of Sri Aurobindo's exact same ideas from which he originally sought to 'synthesize'. (Rajiv Malhotra has authored a book that shows Hegel's immense debt to Vedic thought both directly and through various Westerners whom he cites and who had studied Vedic *śāstra*-s in detail.)

He concludes the chapter by crediting the Russian Christian mystic, Nikolai Berdyaev, with ideas parallel to the evolution from subconsciousness to superconsciousness through self-consciousness. Thus, be it de Chardin, Hegel, Fichte, Schelling, or Berdyaev, the precursors to his ideas are from the Western arena, while the Indian sources he has drawn from do not get any credit.[81]

*Nature's rhythms made linear*

It is important to explain another major difference between Wilber and Sri Aurobindo on collective evolution. Wilber's description of human evolution is linear, and occurs in the following stages: archaic-uroboric, magical-typhonic, mythic-membership, mental-egoic, and so on. He does not leave any doubt that consciousness is more evolved and differentiated from one level to the next.

However, Sri Aurobindo clearly states that consciousness has a forward trajectory but that it moves in a zigzag path. Below are two self-explanatory passages from Sri Aurobindo:

> Development forms a sort of psychological cycle through which a nation or a civilisation is bound to proceed. **Obviously, such classifications are likely to err by rigidity and to substitute a mental straight line for the coils and zigzags of Nature.** The psychology of man and his societies is too complex, too synthetical of many-sided and intermixed tendencies to satisfy any such rigorous and formal analysis.[82]
>
> Nature effects her evolution through a rhythm of advance and relapse, day and night, waking and sleep; there is a temporary pushing of certain results at the expense of others not less desirable for perfection and to a superficial eye there may seem to be a relapse even in our advance. **Progress admittedly does not march on securely in a straight line like a man sure of his familiar way** or an army covering an unimpeded terrain or well-mapped unoccupied spaces. Human progress is very much an adventure through the unknown, an unknown full of surprises and baffling obstacles; it stumbles often, it misses its way at many points, it cedes here in order to gain there, it retraces its steps frequently in order to get more widely forward. The present does not always compare favourably with the past; even when it is more advanced in the mass, it may still be inferior in certain directions important to our inner or our outer welfare. But earth does move forward after all, *eppur si muove*. Even in failure there is a preparation for success: our nights carry in them the secret of a greater dawn. This is a frequent experience in our individual progress, but the human collectivity also moves in much the same manner.[83]

In later chapters, we see how this linear and absolute trajectory has facilitated Wilber's Eurocentrism. This is worrisome as his ideas have morphed into a new epoch of Western superiority.

## Wilber's Unethical Scholarship

This chapter has shown in considerable detail that the Wilber-II model has borrowed many quintessential ideas from Sri Aurobindo *in its entirety.*[84] Academic ethics demands that he should have suffused *The Atman Project* and *Up from Eden* with references to Sri Aurobindo. Instead, he cites Western thinkers almost exclusively. *It is the norm to explicitly cite when one is restating from established Western sources; there is no reason to give non-Western sources less credit and respect, especially if one uses them so extensively.*

Wilber would not have been able to get away with publishers, readers, and academia had he committed such large-scale acts of appropriation and misquoting from a prominent Western thinker, and his methods constitute nothing short of shoddy research!

Explicit acknowledgments and transparent discussions would have allowed experts on Sri Aurobindo to verify whether his mappings are valid, especially since these mappings have served as the foundation for the entire edifice of Wilber's work. His lack of transparency allowed numerous distortions to slip in unnoticed because there has been little to no due diligence by independent experts. Because of his linguistic and semantic disguises used to claim originality, nobody has adequately pointed out his numerous shortfalls. Meanwhile, he has misled a whole bandwagon of blind followers like the famous Pied Piper of Hamlin.

By giving not more than six or seven minor references to Sri Aurobindo in *The Atman Project* and even fewer in *Up from Eden*, Wilber claims to have assimilated and 'included' about forty volumes of the sage's writings. From Wilber-II onwards, he starts to marginalize Sri Aurobindo's ideas even further into mere footnotes, which are made generic by hiding him in long lists of 'mystics'. Then, Sri Aurobindo gradually fades out of sight altogether.

One of the most pertinent criticisms of Wilber's methods and his philosophy, especially regarding his understanding and representation of the work of Sri Aurobindo comes from the voice of a prominent

Aurovillian, the American, Rod Hemsell. Hemsell's essay *Ken Wilber and Sri Aurobindo: A Critical Perspective* is relevant even today. Hemsell points out that in spite of using the works of Sri Aurobindo so extensively in all the several books of Wilber, 'there is hardly a page all together of direct quotes from Sri Aurobindo, very little that is direct commentary on his work, and the references are usually to a list of names, among which Sri Aurobindo is included. And so, one might well ask what actually remains of Sri Aurobindo after his ideas are incorporated, along with all of the other many sources that Wilber's genius has so skillfully worked into his voluminous synthesis, and what is there that is truly Wilber's?'[85]

An important aspect of Wilber's unethical scholarship is his pattern of appropriation. Wilber does not acknowledge the source at the same stage where he appropriates. As we see in the chapters ahead, every stage of Wilber's contentions beginning with Wilber-II has a major imprint of Sri Aurobindo's ideas but they are not acknowledged during Wilber-II works. The acknowledgment appears much later down the line when Wilber has already appropriated them substantially and has decisively enunciated them as his own, making a name for himself as their original exponent. The acknowledgments also come when they do not threaten his intellectual standing and can bolster his reputation. Sometimes, his admissions happen when he is ready to supersede the source and at other times, the source is cited as an authority to win an argument against the opponents.

Though we do not see the recognition of Sri Aurobindo as a source in his Wilber-II thoughts, they appear much later in Wilber-III and consequent stages, which we study in the next chapter. Similarly, the acknowledgment of Sri Aurobindo's ideas to construct Wilber-IV happens towards the end of Wilber-IV. However, this does not mean that all the appropriated ideas are acknowledged in the subsequent stages—only those selective appropriations or his distorted versions are acknowledged that help Wilber to supersede Sri Aurobindo. If an appropriation or his distorted version has come under criticism and/or if he thinks he is enhancing it, he will be quick to dump it onto Sri Aurobindo, while sometimes even refining it with ideas borrowed from Sri Aurobindo himself.

The appropriated ideas that have helped him to either construct the future stages or refine previous stages that either have not come under criticism or he has not felt the need to revise, are kept discreet and under the carpet. The borrowed ideas that may have helped him supersede his ignorance will be touted as his own till they meet the same fate as his previously co-opted ideas. They remain Wilber's own till he can bask in glory.

For instance, principles and thoughts that were not acknowledged in Wilber-II have been partially acknowledged in Wilber-III, and fully acknowledged in Wilber-IV. By Wilber-IV, he had already earned a name for himself and had sufficiently distorted Sri Aurobindo to conflate him with Wilber-II. Conflating Sri Aurobindo with Wilber at this stage would not have hurt his career; in fact, he was at a stage where it would be enhanced by it.

Sri Aurobindo, as discussed in the Appendix, speaks of two active systems that describe a human being's parts and their organization. One of them is a vertical system of planes that show the gradations of consciousness, from the lowest Inconscient to the highest Saccidānanda. In *The Atman Project* (1980), a Wilber-II work we have seen in this chapter, Wilber elaborates upon the nature and characteristics of the planes, particularly the lower ones and it is clear that Wilber did not coincidentally develop them on his own, but was using Sri Aurobindo's schema, without any mention. In *Transformations of Consciousness* (1986), a Wilber-III work, there is a partial acknowledgment by Wilber regarding his detailed awareness of Sri Aurobindo's description of the planes of existence through which the psycho-spiritual growth takes place. Though at no stage here does Wilber concede that he first studied Sri Aurobindo, perennialized his ideas, renamed the planes in Western terms, and passed them as perennialized truths back in 1980 itself, in *The Atman Project*.

Wilber co-authored the *Transformations of Consciousness* along with Jack Engler and Daniel Brown. The book aimed to bring together contemplative traditions and contemporary psychology, for which they needed 'overview' models that could be rendered crude to which enhancements from contemporary psychology could be made. One such 'overview' model was that of Sri Aurobindo's; with Engler and Brown already using 'crude' overview models from Buddhism and Vedānta, Wilber, true to his pattern of appropriating a) becomes the expert on Sri Aurobindo studies among fellow Westerners and even quotes the sage in the book a few times; b) uses a version of Sri Aurobindo's model which he had distorted in 1980 (Wilber-II); and c) adds changes in 1986 (Wilber-III) to the distorted model and thus presents himself as one who supersedes the sage.

While Wilber concedes a partial acknowledgment in *Transformations of Consciousness,* in the Wilber-IV book *The Eye of Spirit,* on numerous occasions he uses 'Wilber-II/Aurobindo' to describe his thoughts in *The Atman Project,* thus revealing his complete hand seventeen years after first publishing the work! This pattern of appropriating seen in Wilber's work becomes clearer and more instantiated in the next chapters as well.

In Wilber-III, we also see Wilber's use of Sri Aurobindo's critique of Advaita Vedānta and Buddhism as a device for critiquing perennial philosophy – again without acknowledgment. This is a dramatic reversal of Wilber's posture on perennialism.

Chapter 10

# Wilber-III: Appropriating Lines of Development and Psychic Being

We saw that Wilber-I was built on Wilber's limited exposure to Indian traditions, mainly through Advaita Vedānta and Buddhism, which he erroneously reframed as perennialism, and hence declared as other-worldly. In Wilber-II, he encountered the transformative practices of Sri Aurobindo, which are explicitly this-worldly and socially engaged, so he should have corrected the premise of his framework that all Indian traditions are other-worldly. Instead, he continued to club Sri Aurobindo with various miscellaneous perennialists. He launched a program of blatant appropriations from Sri Aurobindo and built his entire framework.

In Wilber-III, he stoops further and claims to have resolved the 'defects' in Indian traditions. He writes:

> Because Wilber-II is essentially consonant with Aurobindo, Wilber-III constitutes my criticism and critique of Aurobindo (and Chaudhuri) as well. ... this is not a repudiation but a refinement. ... since the Great Chain of Being (the Great Holarchy) is essentially identical to Wilber-II, Wilber-III constitutes a significant part of my overall criticism and refinement of the perennial philosophy itself (including the basic psychology of Vedanta, Mahayana/Vajrayana Buddhism, the Kabbalistic sefirot, Plotinus and the Neoplatonic tradition, and so on). These Wilber-III refinements are, ... absolutely crucial, especially as we begin the actual and specific details of integrating Eastern and Western models. The Wilber-II types of models will no longer suffice for these details, useful as they were as a first orientation.[1]

Wilber did not really understand Sri Aurobindo's theory of evolution, i.e. the entity that is evolving and how. He mistook the evolution of forms of prakṛti for simple evolution following the Darwinian model; the spiritual vision of cyclical movement was only static and perennial for him. Wilber could not comprehend that Indian tradition did not follow a linear model of development but cyclical (*kalpa*-s, *manvantara*-s, yuga-s), and therefore, he concluded that the Indian developmental model lacked elements.

The common Western understanding fails to see that the cyclical movement is a tool helping the involuted consciousness grow and move forward, gradually changing the forms of prakṛti. The cyclical movement allows the spirit to recapture all the elements of prakṛti repeatedly, modifying the forms into a new order and in unison with the growing presence of the spirit within. It is the device used by prakṛti to gradually manifest the involuted divine being in her forms.

We will cite a specific example of Wilber mischaracterizing Indian thought: His *The Eye of Spirit* has a section titled *Vedic Psychology and Transcendental Meditation*, which attacks the work of Charles Alexander, a transpersonal development psychologist. Alexander had written a dissertation titled *Growth of Higher Stages of Consciousness: Maharishi's Vedic Psychology of Human Development* on the effect of Maharishi Mahesh Yogi's Transcendental Meditation on the ego development and personality change of prison inmates. Wilber contends that Alexander's model (based on the five *kośa*-s) is flawed. He portrays the kośa structure as 'another version of the Great Holarchy of Being and Consciousness'. He then appropriates Sri Aurobindo's critique of other-worldly aspects of Advaita Vedānta and Buddhism and applies it, superseding Alexander's model. This is how he claims to supersede all Indian traditions as well. He writes:

> The first difficulty is that they take their developmental levels (level 1: sensorimotor; level 2: prana-desire; level 3: representational mind; level 4: abstract mind; level 5: transcendental intuition; level 6: self or ego; level 7: pure Self)—and attempt to turn them into the important developmental lines as well, so that anything not found in their levels does not show up as a line. Obviously, music is not a particular level of consciousness; neither is ethics,

> nor aesthetics, nor dance, nor object relations, nor needs, nor worldviews, and so on. Those are all lines, not levels, and therefore, if you try to make your levels serve also as the major lines, then you will be forced to ignore all of those real lines—which is exactly what Alexander et al. do....[**Their**] **model actually has no domains that are moral and social (or musical, or dance, or artistic, etc.), because their domains are nothing but a horizontal unfolding of their vertical basic structures, This is why their diagram, which summarizes their model, has nothing listed on it that even vaguely corresponds to moral, interpersonal, artistic, worldview, musical, dance, and so forth.**[2]

There are several flaws in his approach. Firstly, Wilber seems to completely misunderstand the kośa-s of consciousness, especially the higher ones, naming them so ignorantly. Vijñāna, being the fourth level in the *Taittirīya Upaniṣad*, named by Sri Aurobindo the Supermind, is not the level of the abstract mind. The fifth level of the Divine Bliss, Ānanda, is not the level of transcendental intuition. The sixth level of Cit-Tapas, Consciousness-Power, is not the level of the self or ego at all.

Secondly, he seems to be unaware of the highly developed Indian art, music, dance, aesthetics, and ethics, their spiritual uses, and profound influences on the modern West. He ignores the transformational philosophy and practices of Sri Aurobindo and other Indian traditions and pretends they do not exist.

Furthermore, he ignores that the vision of the five puruṣa-s is found in the *Taittirīya Upaniṣad* where all the five selves (*annamaya*, *prāṇamaya*, *manomaya*, *vijñānamaya,* and *ānandamaya ātman*-s) are integrated into oneself. There is nothing other-worldly – if one integrates physical, vital, mental, supramental, and transcendental selves into one Self, there can be no other-worldliness. His knowledge of Vedānta is seriously flawed.

The demonization of Indian traditions becomes a feature of Wilber going forward. He writes:

> ...we all know of spiritual teachers who have glimpsed very high stages of spiritual and/or cognitive development, while their moral, affective, defense, object-relations, and interpersonal lines are very poorly developed—often with disastrous consequences.

> ... great traditions themselves often emphasize the spiritual line alone (particularly in its ascending mode), and ... severely neglect the interpersonal, affective, and psychological lines, so that they remain, as it were, the last place to look for help in these areas.[3]

However, the great spiritual traditions of India are very deeply committed to various lines including social and political laws, art, music, dance, tactile and dual-brain approaches to education, creative theater, etc., as transformative lines. For example, American 'accelerated learning' movements originated with the study of such methods in traditional Indian systems. Yet, Wilber dismisses Indian traditions saying, 'Spiritual teachers have no knowledge of the dynamics of borderline or psychoneurotic disorders, and their advice may be, "Intensify your effort!" which is precisely what triggered the problem in the first place'.[4]

Sri Aurobindo has written extensively on art and its role in transformation:

> Spirituality is a wider thing than formal religion and it is in the service of spirituality that Art reaches its highest self-expression. Spirituality is a single word expressive of three lines of human aspiration towards divine knowledge, divine love and joy, divine strength, and that will be the highest and most perfect Art which, while satisfying the physical requirements of the aesthetic sense, the laws of formal beauty, the emotional demand of humanity, the portrayal of life and outward reality, reaches beyond them and expresses inner spiritual truth, the deeper not obvious reality of things, the joy of God in the world and its beauty and desirableness and the manifestation of divine force and energy in phenomenal creation.[5]

Sri Aurobindo has further explained that the difference in the approaches between the Western and Indian mind has resulted in the former being unable to appreciate the true role and nature of the latter's artistic forms. What the British colonizer did in representing Indian art and sculpture as something barbaric holds true even now. Sri Aurobindo states:

> The canons of Western artistic creation were held to be the sole valid criteria and everything else was regarded as primitive and

half-developed or else strange and fantastic and interesting only by its curiosity.[6]

## Wilber-III: Differentiating Lines from Levels

Wilber states that the Wilber-II model failed to distinguish between levels/stages of development and lines of development and was hence flawed. This made the lines unilinear, unidirectional, and a monolithic one-dimensional spectrum; it failed to explain the enduring structures that were preserved and the transitional structures that were negated during evolution.

To remedy this, lines of development in Wilber-III refer to independent streams along which a person progresses into higher consciousness. Cognition, morals, creativity, and self-identity are all lines of development which can fall across any of the five levels and pass through as vertical lines in the Wilber-III model. He states:

> Wilber-III explicitly *distinguishes the different developmental lines that unfold through those seventeen levels.* These different developmental lines include affective, cognitive, moral, interpersonal, object-relations, self-identity, and so on, *each of which develops in a quasi-independent fashion through the general levels or basic structures of consciousness.* There is no single, monolithic line that governs all of these developments.[7]

For an all-encompassing spiritual development to take place, all these different developmental lines must reach the fourth stage. Wilber borrows the first three stages from Lawrence Kohlberg (1981) and adds the fourth:

1. Pre-conventional stage: The morality of children is determined by obedience, punishment, and self-interest.
2. Conventional stage: Adolescents and adults are morally driven by the need to maintain conformity and interpersonal accord, and social order and authority.
3. Post-conventional stage: The morality of adults is driven by social contract principles (concern for the general welfare and the welfare of the masses, usually within one's own nation) and

universal ethical principles (commitment to justice that includes the entire world).

4. Post-postcon stage: This is Wilber's addition.

He maintains that the evolution of morality must necessarily go through each of these stages in sequence. Defining holistic development of human beings through the above four stages is a highly debatable exercise; merely because Kohlberg claims something that does not make it sacrosanct, and Wilber fails to give a sound argument in its favor. For any development line such as cognition, affect, morals, and self-sense he claims that:

> Research to date strongly indicates that the developmental sequence is generally from precon to con to postcon to postpostcon, either in a "strong" or "soft" sense, but present nonetheless. Thus, in this sense, spiritual developments (post-postconventional developments) cannot stably emerge until the precon, con, and postcon waves have been, at least to a significant degree, secured.[8]

From an Indian perspective, this raises several issues which Wilber fails to address. These include:

1. The requirement of going through each stage in proper order assumes that every child is born in the same state, whereas each individual is unique with his/her own svadharma based on prior birth and karma. Therefore, some might be born at a higher state than others. This basic reality finds no place in Wilber's development sequence, even though he speaks of Kosmic Karma in his later work.
2. What is appropriate depends also on the *varṇā-śrama* of a given person and is not the same for all persons. Hence, what is good for youth might be inappropriate for the elderly and vice versa.
3. His stage three (social contract using so-called 'universal principles') has in the past encouraged Eurocentric universalism in which 'society' and 'masses' have meant White folks. For instance, the third president of the USA, Thomas Jefferson, famously proclaimed the universal principle, 'All men are created equal', while he owned 250 slaves.[9] Today, there is a new trend of neocolonialism driven by White evolutionary champions that

> evaluate different cultures along a matrix of advancement, with the West ahead of the rest. This is a kind of neo-Hegelianism all over again.

Wilber's new definition is that spirituality is a separate developmental line that can 'develop alongside, or behind, or parallel with development in the other lines, affective, interpersonal, moral, and so on'.[10] This can be dangerous: It can lead to non-spiritual development lines with the potential for turning racist or oppressive in the worst ways.

Wilber claims that Sri Aurobindo lacks the differentiation between spiritual levels and lines of development, and hence his model cannot account for moral, ethical, cognitive, rational, conative development, and transformation. The practice of Integral Yoga can give the experience of subtle and spiritual states, but since the developmental lines are not differentiated, they cannot be taken to the post-postcon level required for an integral ontogenetic human being. If we take Wilber's new definition of spirituality as a separate developmental line, there is nothing in Sri Aurobindo that can run parallel, along, or behind the other developmental lines in order to bring about their transformation.

Thus, there are four reasons why Wilber thinks that Sri Aurobindo's model can be collapsed into Wilber-II, and through this collapse, he is able to downgrade Sri Aurobindo (and all Indian traditions). His allegations may be summarized as follows:

1. Sri Aurobindo's model is unilinear, monolithic, and one-dimensional.
2. The developmental lines are not differentiated.
3. Since the developmental lines are not differentiated, they cannot be taken to any post-postcon equivalent stage.
4. There is no notion of any spiritual developmental line running parallel to other developmental lines, which would support transformation.

To evaluate such a sweeping dismissal of Sri Aurobindo's Integral Yoga, let us briefly examine what Sri Aurobindo means by Integral. In particular, we wish to highlight the following features, even as Sri Aurobindo explicitly says, 'All Life is Yoga':

- A seeker of Integral Yoga not only strives for a static release in Brahman but also aspires for a transformation of life, mind, body, and the conditions on earth. A Divine life on earth with full and active participation with the *dynamic* Divine (the supramental Truth-Consciousness) is the goal and not mere liberation from māyā and karma.
- A yogi therefore, embodies the dynamic Divine Śakti in order to overrule the workings of lower Nature, which maintains darkness, ignorance, suffering, poverty, and pain.
- Yoga is not to be practiced within the narrow confines of a monastery or an ashram but right here in the world, facing, encountering, transmuting, and transforming all the forces to bring about a Divine life on earth.

Wilber's confusion stems from not wholly understanding the Vedic ideas of Divine immanence. It is not only the transcendent that is sought but also a positive relationship with the immanent. Therefore, renunciation of life is not what Integral Yoga prescribes. In contrast to a monotheistic pursuit of God, Integral Yoga seeks the Divine here on earth, fulfilled in life. Renunciation is an inner one, of all the attachments, passions, and hankerings that prevent the Divine from descending into our human flesh.

Sri Aurobindo writes on these issues; in the first excerpt, the sage criticizes the escapist approaches to yoga, by those seeking to abandon the world and seek God as a refuge:

> **The difficulty of the task has led naturally to the pursuit of easy and trenchant solutions; it has generated and fixed deeply the tendency of religions and of schools of Yoga to separate the life of the world from the inner life.** The powers of this world and their actual activities, it is felt, either do not belong to God at all or are for some obscure and puzzling cause, Maya or another, a dark contradiction of the divine Truth...There appears at once the antinomy of a bright and pure kingdom of God and a dark and impure kingdom of the devil; we feel the opposition of our crawling earthly birth and life to an exalted spiritual God-consciousness; we become readily convinced of the incompatibility of life's subjection to Maya with the soul's

> concentration in pure Brahman existence. The easiest way is to turn away from all that belongs to the one and to retreat by a naked and precipitous ascent into the other. Thus arises the attraction and the necessity of the principle of exclusive concentration which plays so prominent a part in the specialised schools of Yoga; for by that concentration we can arrive through an uncompromising renunciation of the world at an entire self-consecration to the One on whom we concentrate.[11]

In the same passage, he explains that such escapist paths lead to world-negation, which he opposes:

> It is no longer incumbent on us to compel all the lower activities to the difficult recognition of a new and higher spiritualised life and train them to be its agents or executive powers. It is enough to kill or quiet them and keep at most the few energies necessary, on one side, for the maintenance of the body and, on the other, for communion with the Divine. **The very aim and conception of an integral Yoga debar us from adopting this simple and strenuous high-pitched process.** The hope of an integral transformation forbids us to take a short cut or to make ourselves light for the race by throwing away our impediments.[12]

In the next segment of the passage, he explains that the true goal of Integral Yoga is to complete the Divine manifestation on earth:

> We have set out to conquer all ourselves and the world for God; we are determined to give him our becoming as well as our being and not merely to bring the pure and naked spirit as a bare offering to a remote and secret Divinity in a distant heaven or abolish all we are in a holocaust to an immobile Absolute. The Divine that we adore is not only a remote extra-cosmic Reality, but a half-veiled Manifestation present and near to us here in the universe. ***Life is the field of a divine manifestation not yet complete:*** **here, in life, on earth, in the body,—*ihaiva*, as the Upanishads insist,—we have to unveil the Godhead; here we must make its transcendent greatness, light and sweetness real to our consciousness, here possess and, as far as may be, express it.**[13]

To achieve this, we must use yoga to work with and within the material world in order to help the cosmos evolve:

> **Life then we must accept in our Yoga in order utterly to transmute it; we are forbidden to shrink from the difficulties that this acceptance may add to our struggle.** Our compensation is that even if the path is more rugged, the effort more complex and bafflingly arduous, yet after a certain point we gain an immense advantage. For once our minds are reasonably fixed in the central vision and our wills are on the whole converted to the single pursuit, Life becomes our helper. **Intent, vigilant, integrally conscious, we can take every detail of its forms and every incident of its movements as food for the sacrificial Fire within us. Victorious in the struggle, we can compel Earth herself to be an aid towards our perfection and can enrich our realisation with the booty torn from the Powers that oppose us.**[14]

The West's deep divides between spirit and matter, spirituality and science, arts and spirituality, philosophical and practical life, sacred and profane, need to be healed. Because Brahman and the world are one, and the two ends of one spectrum of consciousness, the liberated soul in union with the Brahman should participate in the world in just the way the Divine participates, upholds, and sustains the world.

*In Integral Yoga, there is no earthly activity that has to be shunned or abandoned; rather, they have to be carried out with a God-centered consciousness as an offering to the Divine, so that the Divine uses our unique individuality and constitution to create heaven on earth.* **This is the exact opposite of Wilber's allegation that Indian spirituality is an escape into immoral inaction and other-worldliness.** Sri Aurobindo explains the life-affirming nature and role of the arts as a *line of development*:

> For all must be done as a sacrifice, all activities must have the One Divine for their object and the heart of their meaning. The Yogin's aim in the sciences that make for knowledge should be to discover and understand the workings of the Divine Consciousness-Puissance in man and creatures and things and forces, her creative significances, her execution of the mysteries, the symbols in which

> she arranges the manifestation. The Yogin's aim in the practical sciences, whether mental and physical or occult and psychic, should be to enter into the ways of the Divine and his processes, to know the materials and means for the work given to us so that we may use that knowledge for a conscious and faultless expression of the spirit's mastery, joy and self-fulfillment. The Yogin's aim in the Arts should not be a mere aesthetic, mental or vital gratification, but, seeing the Divine everywhere, worshipping it with a revelation of the meaning of its own works, to express that One Divine in ideal forms, the One Divine in principles and forces, the One Divine in gods and men and creatures and objects....***The spiritual life does not need, for its purity, to destroy interest in all things except the Inexpressible or to cut at the roots of the Sciences, the Arts and Life. It may well be one of the effects of an integral spiritual knowledge and activity to lift them out of their limitations, substitute for our mind's ignorant, limited, tepid or trepidant pleasure in them a free, intense and uplifting urge of delight and supply a new source of creative spiritual power and illumination by which they can be carried more swiftly and profoundly towards their absolute light in knowledge and their yet undreamed possibilities and most dynamic energy of content and form and practice.*** The one thing needful must be pursued first and always; but all things else come with it as its outcome and have not so much to be added to us as recovered and reshaped in its self-light and as portions of its self-expressive force.[15]

Since Integral Yoga aims to transform all life here on earth, a renunciation of earthly activities would be illogical. The arts, sciences, philosophical thinking, artistic creativity, music, dance, drama, poetry, literary activities, sports, games, etc., have to be pursued as an expression of Divine living which the sage embodied in his own life, from being a poet to a freedom fighter as well as a spiritual seeker. This is why different psychological functions, which Wilber translates as 'developmental lines', must be refined and perfected.[16] To achieve this, the differentiation among various psychological functions must first be recognized.

## Wilber Appropriates 'Lines of Development' from Sri Aurobindo's Work

Wilber has even appropriated the term 'lines of development' from Sri Aurobindo's work. Sri Aurobindo writes that lines of development are the potential ways prakṛti uses to advance a person towards spiritual realization. These lines could be in the form of a mindset that is drawn to higher spiritual pursuits or even religion, as in the case of dhārmic ones, where the whole structure is designed to help man fulfill his fundamental spiritual experience:

> In considering the achieved course of the evolution of the spiritual being, we have to regard it from two sides, — a consideration of the means, the lines of development utilised by Nature and a view of the actual results achieved by it in the human individual. There are four main lines which Nature has followed in her attempt to open up the inner being, — religion, occultism, spiritual thought and an inner spiritual realisation and experience: the three first are approaches, the last is the decisive avenue of entry. All these four powers have worked by a simultaneous action, more or less connected, sometimes in a variable collaboration, sometimes in dispute with each other, sometimes in a separate independence.[17]

Wilber's second allegation is that Sri Aurobindo fails to differentiate the developmental lines from the levels of spiritual evolution. This is untrue because Sri Aurobindo gives considerable importance to the differentiation, development, and perfection of human faculties. One can pick any work of Sri Aurobindo and find such ideas in abundance.

To illustrate, we consider just one chapter from his *Synthesis of Yoga*, titled *Integral Perfection*. Sri Aurobindo's yoga starts from the very basic and mundane levels of everyday living, encapsulating all the differentiated lines of psychological and sociological concerns: intellectual and rational faculties, artistic abilities, aesthetic sensibilities, ethics and morality, willpower, physical strength, and so on.

The key insight Sri Aurobindo brings is that in mundane human existence, the 'development lines' cater only to the needs of the ego. For a Divine life on earth, these mundane activities and their employed faculties and instruments have to be subordinated to the

Divine. Hence, nothing in ordinary life is rejected except for changes in attitude, intention, and direction towards different goals, purposes, and objectives. Sri Aurobindo examines the mundane pursuits, along with the well-defined workings of man's faculties, according to yoga. He appreciates them deeply but wants us to go further while pursuing them:

> This double character of our Yoga raises it beyond the mundane ideal of perfection, while at the same time it goes too beyond the loftier, intenser, but much narrower religious formula. The mundane ideal regards man always as a mental, vital and physical being and it aims at a human perfection well within these limits, a perfection of mind, life and body, an expansion and refinement of the intellect and knowledge, of the will and power, of ethical character, aim and conduct, of aesthetic sensibility and creativeness, of emotional balanced poise and enjoyment, of vital and physical soundness, regulated action and just efficiency. **It is a wide and full aim, but yet not sufficiently full and wide, because it ignores that other greater element of our being which the mind vaguely conceives as the spiritual element and leaves it either undeveloped or insufficiently satisfied as merely some high occasional or added derivatory experience, the result of the action of mind in its exceptional aspects or dependent upon mind for its presence and persistence.** It can become a high aim when it seeks to develop the loftier and the larger reaches of our mentality, but yet not sufficiently high, because it does not aspire beyond mind to that of which our purest reason, our brightest mental intuition, our deepest mental sense and feeling, strongest mental will and power or ideal aim and purpose are only pale radiations. Its aim besides is limited to a terrestrial perfection of the normal human life."[18]

He clearly recognizes the differentiation of the developmental lines and how humans try to develop and refine them using some correspondence of mental planes or ideals (i.e. the precon, con, and postcon levels of Wilber). He rarely rejects any mundane activity and always tries to give a broader and wider inclusion and synthesis, as evidenced by the following:

> **The object of our synthetic Yoga must, in this respect too as in its other parts, be more integral and comprehensive, embrace**

> **all these elements or these tendencies of a larger impulse of self-perfection and harmonise them or rather unify, and in order to do that successfully it must seize on a truth which is wider than the ordinary religious and higher than the mundane principle.** ***All life is a secret Yoga***, an obscure growth of Nature towards the discovery and fulfillment of the divine principle hidden in her which becomes progressively less obscure, more self-conscient and luminous, more self-possessed in the human being by the opening of all his instruments of knowledge, will, action, life to the Spirit within him and in the world.[19]

Thus, all psychological and developmental lines have to be perfected, transformed, and transfigured so that each becomes an instrument of Divine expression. They not only have to be taken to planes beyond the mental, but through the spiritual to the supramental, which is superior to the post-postcon level that Wilber champions from a purely intellectual plane. Sri Aurobindo is quite clear that none of the spiritual planes other than the supramental can bring about a complete perfection and transformation of the developmental lines. In addition, whereas Wilber advocates a complete nondual awareness as the ultimate state for a post-postcon perfection, for Sri Aurobindo it is only the beginning of transformation and perfection:

> **Nirvana in my liberated consciousness turned out to be the beginning of my realisation, a first step towards the complete thing, not the sole true attainment possible or even a culminating finale.**[20]

Wilber-III's description of differentiating 'levels' from 'lines' and recognizing that the lines move through different levels is not only explicitly recognized in Sri Aurobindo but also given a much more comprehensive treatment. The developmental lines that are imprisoned in lower levels of matter, life, and mind in ordinary human existence have to be freed and given a wider play by having them ascend through the planes that are beyond the mental: Higher Mind, Illumined Mind, Intuitive Mind, Overmind, and Supermind.

In their fullness of development and expression, the developmental lines do not remain a manifestation of the mental but become those of the supramental planes. The Overmind is the bridge between the higher supramental plane and the lower mental planes, but it is the supramental plane alone which has the power to spiritualize life on earth. Sri Aurobindo writes:

> A Yoga of integral perfection regards man as a divine spiritual being involved in mind, life and body; it aims therefore at a liberation and a perfection of his divine nature. It seeks to make an inner living in the perfectly developed spiritual being his constant intrinsic living and the spiritualised action of mind, life and body only its outward human expression. *In order that this spiritual being may not be something vague and indefinable or else but imperfectly realised and dependent on the mental support and the mental limitations, it seeks to go beyond mind to the supramental knowledge, will, sense, feeling, intuition, dynamic initiation of vital and physical action, all that makes the native working of the spiritual being. It accepts human life, but takes account of the large supraterrestrial action behind the earthly material living, and it joins itself to the divine Being from whom the supreme origination of all these partial and lower states proceeds so that the whole of life may become aware of its divine source and feel in each action of knowledge, of will, of feeling, sense and body the divine originating impulse.* ***It rejects nothing that is essential in the mundane aim, but enlarges it, finds and lives in its greater and its truer meaning now hidden from it, transfigures it from a limited, earthly and mortal thing to a figure of infinite, divine and immortal values.***[21]

Contrary to the perception that Wilber creates of Sri Aurobindo's work, the latter's lines of development span the entire gamut of corporeal and spiritual lives, with all the gradations and subtle shades of difference between each level captured in the categorization. And unlike Wilber's theories, which are speculations without experience, Sri Aurobindo's have emerged from his experiences as a yogi, also captured in the mantric poem, *Savitri*.

## Role of Supermind in Sri Aurobindo's Model

The transformation of these developmental lines discussed so far has to be illuminated by the supramental plane through the process of supramentalization. However, in order to understand what Sri Aurobindo means by supramentalization, we have to understand his notion of the Supermind.

Supermind (Vijñāna) is the plane connecting the lower three planes of existence—physical, vital, and mental (Anna, Prāṇa, and Manas)—with the higher three: Being, Consciousness, and Bliss (Sat, Cit, Ānanda). This is the plane of unity consciousness, which holds all diversities in itself for their manifestation in the lower planes. The Supermind is the plane of total knowledge. It knows the right relationship between the eternal absolute and the terrestrial relative. Unlike the mind, which knows by analysis and synthesis, the Supermind is a plane of direct knowledge.

All mental knowledge contains the Supermind's truth in latent form, but this latent truth is obscured and distorted by various impurities and by the mind's inherent limitations. When an aspirant ascends to the supramental plane,[22] ignorance disappears, and there is all-knowing: he or she acquires the capacity to act in the divine wisdom manifesting the Divine Will. The Supermind is described as follows:

> **The original nature of supermind is the self-conscience and all-conscience of the Infinite, of the universal Spirit and Self in things, organising on the foundation and according to the character of a direct self-knowledge its own wisdom and effective omnipotence for the unfolding and the regulated action of the universe and of all things in the universe. It is, ... the gnosis of the Spirit, master of its own cosmos, *ātmā, jñātā, iśwarah.*** As it knows itself, so too it knows all things—for all are only becomings of itself—directly, totally and from within outward, spontaneously in detail and arrangement, each thing in the truth of itself and its nature and in its relation to all other things. And it knows similarly all action of its energy in antecedent or cause and occasion of manifestation and effect or consequence, all things in infinite and in limited potentiality and in selection of actuality and in their succession of past, present and future.[23]

Therefore, deriving its power and existence from the Divine, the Supermind is its organizing principle and power informing all activities in the terrestrial sphere, though its full manifestation is concealed by the obscurities inherent in the lower planes. Since all developmental lines are involuted in matter and life, they too must find their utmost fulfillment and perfection in the Supermind. The differentiated developmental lines must be transformed and transmuted to their highest potential. The sage writes:

> *Opening from below* means this – that the supramental force descending awakes a response from below in the earth consciousness so that it is possible for a supramental activity to be formed in the material itself. All is involved as potentiality in the earth-consciousness, life, mind, supermind – but it is only when life force descended from the life plane into the material that active and conscious organised life was possible – so it was only when mind descended that the latent mind in Matter awoke and could be organised. The supramental descent must create the same kind of opening from below so that a supramental consciousness can be organised in the material.[24]

## Psychic Being Becomes Wilber's Second Definition of Spirituality

### *Two processes of development and transformation in Sri Aurobindo's model*

The foregoing discussion was in the context of Wilber's first definition of spirituality, that spirituality is trans-mental, trans-egoic, trans-rational, and so forth. But subsequently, by 1997, Wilber sees spirituality not only as a higher level of human existence (i.e. trans-egoic, trans-mental, trans-rational, etc.), but also as a separate line of development that runs parallel to other developmental lines. Such a spiritual line can bring about their transformation.

We now show that Wilber's new definition of spirituality is a reformulation of Sri Aurobindo's approach to transformation through the process of the psychic being.[25] According to Sri Aurobindo, the first step towards a spiritual change is the emergence of the psychic being from the cave of the heart—*hṛidaye guhāyām.*[26] It is the psychic in us that transmigrates from one lifetime to another until it finds its conscious union with the Divine, for, all other components of the individual constitution are perishable upon death, except under extraordinary circumstances. The psychic being contains all the possibilities of our human manifestation, affects our surface being, but is not constituted by it, as it is the ever-pure portion of the Divine within us.

When the psychic being is concealed and not in control of the activities of an individual, then the modes of Nature—mundane prakṛti with guṇa-s in flux—dominate the psychological constitution. In this mode, the vital ego and the physical mind, as opposed to the higher mind, obscure the manifestation of the higher life of peace, love, beauty, delight, etc.

In proportion to the opening of the psychic being, the Divine guides the individual towards the intended goal that the Divine Mother considers ideal, which is in accordance with the unique truth that the individual is meant to manifest. In addition, there is psychological and physical purification and transformation that makes one more self-aware. What is ugly, devoid of light, reprehensible, false, erroneous, and evil begins to disappear from one's psychological makeup. The Parā Prakṛti, or the Higher Nature, begins to take control, purifying the thoughts, perceptions, emotions, sensations, actions, and all the movements that assist in a greater manifestation of the Divine in our lives. It leads to the emergence of the soul-power within, making us luminous and intense, without the distortions caused by the turbid vital and mental activities.

Therefore, it is critical to awaken the psychic being and bring it forward so that it takes control of the intended transformation. Since the psychic being is involuted in the mental, vital, and physical, its awakening leads to an aspiration in these realms to change in order to become the perfect instrument of the Divine.

In other words, the lower facet of the mental, vital, and physical being obscures the movement of the Divine within an individual, whereas the higher facet expresses the Divine in all its power and fullness. When the psychic being comes forward, it begins to purify the lower and allows space for the higher to express itself, creating conditions for manifesting divinity on earth.

Thus, Integral Yoga has two processes taking place simultaneously—development and transformation:

- One is *vertical*, which is an ascent to the higher reaches of our existence and a consequent descent of Divine forces from the respective planes, commonly known as 'ascent and descent'.

- The second is *horizontal* which is the emergence of the *psychic being* from behind our surface nature—thus functioning as a separate developmental line—that consequently begins to align all the other psychological developmental lines around itself enveloping them in a parallel manner, bringing about personality changes like sweetness, empathy, unconditional love, compassion, forgiveness, nobility, etc.[27]

These are inter-connected movements, with growth in one facilitating growth in the other, and both are combined to anchor the person more robustly. The psychic being is not to be confused with the jīvātman. It is *antarātman*, man's portion of the Divine that builds into its experiences from life to life. It is the emergence of this psychic being that 'flowers as the saint, the sage, the seer; when it reaches its full strength, it turns the being towards the Knowledge of Self and the Divine, towards the supreme Truth, the supreme Good, the supreme Beauty, Love, and Bliss, the Divine heights and largenesses, and opens us to the touch of spiritual sympathy, universality, oneness'. A crucial milestone in Sri Aurobindo's yoga is to aspire and work for the emergence of the psychic being and to let it govern one's everyday actions.

### *Wilber's appropriation of the concept of psychic being*

Wilber appropriates Sri Aurobindo's notion that the emergence of the psychic being illuminates all other psychological processes and turns them into a *separate* line of development that runs parallel, behind, and above all other developmental lines. The considerable difference is that Sri Aurobindo is a seer and yogi who simultaneously sees the multivariate directions and processes of change and growth, whereas Wilber is a mere intellectual who postulates something he never experienced first-hand for the sake of building a model. The model builder conceptualizes from a lower level of consciousness by looking up in a speculative way using his imagination. When Wilber tries to see in one direction, he loses sight of the other.

In summary, we have shown that Wilber appropriated both his notions in Wilber-III: the notion of multiple development lines and his 'second definition' of spirituality. To transplant these notions into his Wilber-III model, he cunningly clubs Sri Aurobindo with all the other perennial philosophers so as to sideline him as a world-negating thinker. This is simply appalling!

## Wilber Projects Problems with his Wilber-II onto Sri Aurobindo

We now consider the two limitations of the Wilber-II model, which he superimposes upon Sri Aurobindo's model. He alleges that Sri Aurobindo's model:

1. Is unilinear, monolithic, and one-spectrum.
2. Fails to distinguish between transitional and enduring structures.

### *Non-linearity of Sri Aurobindo's Integral Yoga*

Sri Aurobindo's Integral Yoga is neither unilinear nor monolithic, as clarified by him in no uncertain terms:

> But all this must not be taken in too rigid and mechanical a sense. It is an immense plastic movement full of the play of possibilities and must be seized by a flexible and subtle tact or sense in the seeing consciousness. It cannot be reduced to a too rigorous logical or mathematical formula.... This plasticity [should] not be lost to our view.[28]

The sage elaborates on the non-linear journey visualized as a three-dimensional model, with two systems acting in parallel. The first system comprises the psychic being at the centre and a series of concentric sheaths surrounding it. A sādhaka must delve deep through these sheaths to find and access his psychic being. Then, he must increasingly draw out the psychic being to the various inner parts of the being, including the inner mind, vital, and physical, divinizing each aspect.

The second system comprises vertical movement between the planes, with the Supermind at the highest. The sādhaka ascends each plane while transforming the lower planes. Sri Aurobindo writes:

> There are in fact **two systems simultaneously active in the organisation of the being and its parts: one is concentric, a series**

> **of rings or sheaths with the psychic at the centre; another is vertical, an ascension and descent, like a flight of steps, a series of superimposed planes with the supermind-overmind as the crucial nodus of the transition beyond the human into the Divine.** For this transition, if it is to be at the same time a transformation, there is only one way, one path. ... **there must be a conversion inwards, a going within to find the inmost psychic being and bring it out to the front, disclosing at the same time the inner mind, inner vital, inner physical parts of the nature. ... there must be an ascension, a series of conversions upwards and a turning down to convert the lower parts. When one has made the inward conversion, one psychicises the whole lower nature so as to make it ready for the divine change. Going upwards, one passes beyond the human mind and at each stage of the ascent, there is a conversion into a new consciousness and an infusion of this new consciousness into the whole of the nature. ...** rising beyond intellect through illuminated higher mind to the intuitive consciousness, we begin to look at everything not from the intellect range or through intellect as an instrument, but from a greater intuitive height and through an intuitivised will, feeling, emotion, sensation and physical contact. ... **proceeding from Intuition to a greater overmind height, there is a new conversion and we look at and experience everything from the overmind consciousness and through a mind, heart, vital and body surcharged with the overmind thought, sight, will, feeling, sensation, play of force and contact. But the last conversion is the supramental, for once there—once the nature is supramentalised, we are beyond the Ignorance and conversion of consciousness is no longer needed, though a farther divine progression, even an infinite development is still possible.**[29]

Wilber acknowledged that the Wilber-II model was unilinear and could not accommodate a person who could simultaneously be at different levels of development of various faculties. For instance, it could not explain how a person could be intellectually advanced and simultaneously be aesthetically under-developed. Besides, it was also unable to account for the immense diversity among the spiritual growth of individuals.

However, Sri Aurobindo's system did not suffer from this, as shown thus far.

## Wilber Borrows 'Enduring' and 'Transitional' States from Sri Aurobindo

According to Wilber, enduring structures are permanent and result from transforming each lower stage from the higher stage:

> Once they emerge in development, tend to remain in existence, such as linguistic competence, cognitive capacities, spatial coordination, motor skills, and so forth. These enduring structures tend to build upon, and usually incorporate, previous structures in a larger and more integrated pattern. The most important of these enduring structures I call the *basic structures,* which are the basic holons of consciousness itself. *The basic structures of consciousness are essentially the traditional Great Holarchy of Being* (as presented by, say, Plotinus or Asanga or Aurobindo). ...the basic structures are simply the basic levels in the spectrum of consciousness—matter to body to mind to soul to spirit.[30]

On the contrary, transitional structures are

> those features that are relatively *transitional* or temporary; they come into existence but subsequently are phased out or replaced.... Once a particular transition structure is present, it is as important and as real as any enduring structure; it's just that transitional structures are destined mostly to pass, enduring structures mostly to remain.[31]

Highlighting the difference between these two, Wilber writes:

> The important difference between the enduring structures and the transitional structures can easily be seen in a comparison of, say, Piaget and Kohlberg. With cognitive development in general, each stage is *incorporated* into subsequent stages, so that the junior is a crucial *component* of the senior. Once images emerge, for example, the individual has full and constant access to the capacity to form images. And images themselves will be

> an indispensable ingredient in the higher symbolic, conceptual, and formal thought. But with moral development, the process is quite different: higher structures do not so much incorporate as *replace* previous ones. Thus, a person at moral stage 3 does not have open access to moral stage 1, for those stages are mutually incompatible.[32]

In Sri Aurobindo's evolutionary yoga, since the different planes from matter (annam) to the highest being (sat) are arranged in a hierarchical manner, every ascension brings knowledge and integrates the lower ones. Sri Aurobindo indicates:

> It must be observed that this ascent, this successive fixing in higher and higher principles, does not carry with it the abandonment of the lower grades, any more than a status of existence in the lower grades means the entire absence of the higher principles.[33]

Wilber appropriates this without acknowledgment. His enduring and transitional structures are borrowed from Sri Aurobindo as the following illustrates:

> Each plane has its own truths. **Some of them are no longer true on a higher plane;** e.g. desire and ego were truths of the mental, vital and physical Ignorance—a man there without ego or desire would be a tamasic automaton. As we rise higher, ego and desire appear no longer as truths, they are falsehoods disfiguring the true person and the true will. The struggle between the Powers of Light and the Powers of Darkness is a truth here—as we ascend above, it becomes less and less of a truth and in the supermind it has no truth at all. Other truths remain but change their character, importance, place in the whole. The difference or contrast between the Personal and Impersonal is a truth of the overmind—there is no separate truth of them in the supermind, they are inseparably one.[34]

The differentiation of lines from levels and enduring or basic structures from transitional structures is the foundation from which Wilber proposes that there is a unique trajectory for the spiritual growth of every individual. However, every genuine Indian guru teaches that two individuals with the same issues may be suggested different interventions, remedies, or practices because their constitutions, as well as their spiritual trajectories, may be different.

Given his large-scale appropriation of Sri Aurobindo's ideas, Wilber is not always able to conceal the trail in his writings, despite his best efforts. As a result, his attitude towards Sri Aurobindo's authority is full of contradictions. For instance, when Wilber gets cornered by a competing Western thinker, he plays the 'Sri Aurobindo card' by citing him as the authority in order to boost his own case.

Here is a clear example. Two years after Wilber had claimed that the distinction between developmental lines and levels was his personal innovation, Howard Gardner came up with similar conclusions in *Frames of Mind: The Theory of Multiple Intelligences* by refining Piaget's developmental theory and drawing upon huge experimental data. Wilber claimed that his own thought experiments were now being confirmed by experimental data but that Gardner fell short of taking the developmental lines to the post-postcon stage, which Wilber had done. To outdo Gardner and claim credit for himself, Wilber credits Sri Aurobindo and writes in a footnote:

> Following Aurobindo's lead, we can treat gross (frontal), subtle (psychic), and causal (higher and superconscient) development as ***three broadly distinct lines, which means that, within certain limits, they can each develop quasi-independently.*** This means that individuals (ontogenetically and phylogenetically) might make strides in psychic/subtle development while still being relatively undeveloped in frontal structures (ego, rationality, conventional verbal, etc.). This further points up why I believe these various streams are not stacked linearly on top of each other like bricks, but rather alongside each other like columns—and further, why progress in some lines might run ahead, or lag behind, others.[35]

Sri Aurobindo is now cited as his ally to lend credibility against a Western rival, Howard Gardner. Wilber contradicts his earlier allegations against Sri Aurobindo and accepts that Sri Aurobindo's system has 'distinct lines' that can 'each develop quasi-independently'. In effect, this voids his prior fifteen years of claims of superseding Sri Aurobindo because now he needs Sri Aurobindo to boost his stature against a Western competitor.

So, he positions himself as the expert on Sri Aurobindo's works to get this edge over Gardner. At the same time, he wants to assert his own superiority over Sri Aurobindo by claiming in other parts of the same book that the latter's developmental lines are not distinguished from spiritual stages. A low-profile footnote becomes adequate for doing the job without toppling his apple cart.

But once his clout in the West is secure, he does not mind acknowledging Sri Aurobindo occasionally, even in the main section of his work. For example, in *One Taste* Wilber writes:

> Although all sorts of regressions and temporary leaps forward are possible, the empirical fact remains as Aurobindo said: individual streams [lines of development] obey the law of successive unfolding (undulating through the waves of the Great Nest itself).[36]

Another example is when Wilber first pronounced his theory of 'Transcend and Include', there was no mention that it was replicated from Sri Aurobindo's 'Ascent and Integration'. However, when Brant Cortright confronted Wilber that his psycho-spiritual developmental model shows a sequential growth whereas Sri Aurobindo's enunciations do not, Wilber reproduced the identical paragraph from Sri Aurobindo's work to show how exactly it mapped.[37] At that moment it was critical to silence Cortright, who wrote in *Psychotherapy and Spirit: Theory and Practice in Transpersonal Psychotherapy*:

> Wilber's three transpersonal stages of fulcrums 7, 8 and 9 do not accurately reflect spiritual unfolding. ...some mystics experience psychic phenomena (fulcrum 7), many others do not. Both theistic-relational and nondual traditions generally hold that psychic experience may or may not come to the seeker. It is not a stage that all must or do pass through. And it may come before or after the realization of soul or spirit. ...experience of the soul and the subtle level (fulcrum 8) does not necessarily precede the nondual experience (fulcrum 9). Ramana Maharshi, whom Wilber holds out as an exemplar of nondual realization, emerged directly into the nondual experience without "passing through" either the psychic or subtle "stages." The Buddhist literature is full of many, many

> examples of people directly realizing the impersonal emptiness of the nondual. Additionally, in one school of interpretation of the Bhagavad Gita, the path that the Gita seems to prefer out of the several it teaches has the nondual atman realized first and then afterward the level of soul is realized; Sri Aurobindo would be an exemplar of this tradition.[38]

Wilber responded to Cortright in *One Taste* without citing sources for his information on Ramana Maharshi while also misrepresenting Sri Aurobindo's model:

> Cortright tries to give several examples to support his case, and they are all demonstrably inaccurate. "Ramana Maharshi, whom Wilber holds out as an exemplar of nondual realization, emerged directly into the nondual experience without 'passing through' either the psychic or subtle stages." In fact, Ramana's awakening was, ...a three—day ordeal, culminating in a thirty—minute climax, in which he passed through savikalpa samadhi (psychic and subtle forms) and nirvikalpa and jnana samadhi (causal formlessness), only then to awaken to sahaja (pure One Taste or nondual Suchness). That Cortright so confidently and cavalierly misreports this crucial event is typical, I'm afraid, of his reporting in general. He similarly misreports Aurobindo's model, and that of Vajrayana. He mentions Aurobindo as an "exemplar of this tradition," the tradition that, according to Cortright, does not believe in a specific sequence of spiritual development, overlooking Aurobindo's explicit statement that 'The spiritual evolution obeys the logic of a successive unfolding; it can take a new decisive main step only when the previous main step has been sufficiently conquered: even if certain minor stages can he swallowed up or leaped over by a rapid and brusque ascension, the consciousness has to turn back to assure itself that the ground passed over is securely annexed to the new condition; a greater or concentrated speed which is indeed possible does not eliminate the steps themselves or the necessity of their successive surmounting' (Aurobindo, The Life Divine, II, 2.6)[39]

This statement clearly goes to prove how far Wilber misunderstands the spiritual experiences of Sri Aurobindo and the nature of psychic awakening altogether, mixing it up with *savikalpa samādhi* and *nirvikalpa samādhi.* The very term samādhi, whether savikalpa or nirvikalpa, is a particular spiritual realization achieved through the concentration of mental consciousness on an object or without it, respectively. It has nothing to do with either psychic awakening, or any other fundamental realizations depicted by Sri Aurobindo as Silent Brahman (nirvāṇa), or Dynamic Brahman, which he experienced personally. It shows how vaguely and carelessly Wilber deals with the spiritual experiences, clubbing them together into his schemes.

## Preparing for Wholesale Appropriation of Sri Aurobindo's Theory

From this point onwards, Wilber begins to develop his own integral model, which garners immense support by the time he reaches his Wilber-IV stage. It is not surprising that his integral project is laced with unacknowledged borrowings from Sri Aurobindo. Even the very term 'integral' was first used by Sri Aurobindo in philosophy and spiritual practice to describe a system of yoga that he had devised for spiritual growth, realization, and transformation. He developed this using the central principles of different yoga systems like Haṭha, Rāja, Karma, Jñāna, Bhakti, and Tantra.[40]

Sri Aurobindo brought into an integral whole different aspects of Indic spiritual traditions like Advaita, Viśiṣṭādvaita, Dvaita, Sāṃkhya, Buddhism, Tantra, and so on, showing them as emerging from genuine spiritual experiences. However, because each of them was based on one development line and provided one kind of experience, it was limited. The integral philosophy reconciles their oppositions and weaves harmoniously their truths into a bouquet of unity. He not only achieved the aforementioned integration but also a host of many others, as mentioned in minute details in a section of *The Life Divine* titled *The Knowledge and Spiritual Evolution.*

We will limit ourselves to one portion which deals with the integration of objective and subjective realities. It will provide some background on Sri Aurobindo's vision and help understand Wilber's appropriation of the integral paradigm.

## Refuting Wilber's Charge on Sri Aurobindo's Lack of Empiricism

A major conception Wilber borrows is that there are two modes of knowing: One mode operates on the dichotomy of subject and object, while the other mode is where the subject-object dichotomy is transcended, and reality is experienced in a non-dual manner. He regards the non-dual mode of Indian thought as supreme because it reveals the *paramārtha-satya*, while he considers the dualistic mode of Western knowing as inferior.[41]

He considers the foundation of Western knowledge, rooted in Greek thought, as primarily dualistic. Only in the beginning of the twentieth century, he correctly says, did scientific discoveries begin to crumble the dualistic paradigm. Amongst others he cites Albert Einstein, Max Planck, Erwin Schrödinger, Werner Heisenberg, Louis de Broglie, Alfred North Whitehead, and William James to show that dualism is now obsolete.

Wilber paraphrases Indian traditions for his fellow Western psychologists to explain that real knowledge is gained by transcending subject/object, knower/known, and seer/seen dichotomies to reveal the experiential knowledge of Śūnyata, Void, Dharmadhātu, Brahman, and so forth. Knowledge gained through the subject/object dualism is 'not so much false as illusory, and the philosophies, psychologies, and sciences that depend on them are therefore not wrong but nonsensical'.[42]

He alleges that Sri Aurobindo lacks understanding of scientific empiricism because research from cutting-edge and frontier domains such as neuroscience was not available during his time. But we argue otherwise.

When Western positivism (attributed to the eighteenth-century French philosopher Auguste Comte) became popular, any phenomenon that could not be seen, tested, and verified by the five senses was declared non-existent and illusory. Mind and consciousness cannot be physically observed or empirically verified, and hence were considered non-existent and at best treated as epiphenomena. Positivist science thus, recognizes only an objective reality, considering all that is not physically observable as unreal or less real. Sri Aurobindo comments:

> If pushed to its extreme, it would give to a stone or a plum-pudding a greater reality and to thought, love, courage, genius, greatness, the human soul and mind facing an obscure and dangerous world and getting mastery over it an inferior dependent reality or even an unsubstantial and evanescent reality. For in this view these things so great to our subjective vision are valid only as the reactions of an objective material being to an objective material existence.[43]

Though not physically observable, Sri Aurobindo considers the mind to be an expression of the power of being or self in manifestation. It is primarily a percipient and interpreter and secondarily, a creator of some truth of the being in manifestation. All mental subjectivity, in some sense, reflects the truth of being in manifestation that will exist independent of that reflection.

Similarly, Sri Aurobindo further holds that the realm of the supraphysical, which is beyond the planes of senses and mind, is real too, and its exploration has to be conducted for an integral knowledge of our existence.

> There are different orders of reality; the objective and physical is only one order. It is convincing to the physical or externalising mind because it is directly obvious to the senses, while of the subjective and the supraphysical that mind has no means of knowledge except from fragmentary signs and data and inferences which are at every step liable to error. Our subjective movements and inner experiences are a domain of happenings as real as any outward physical happenings.[44]

Due to the opposition between the Western Church and science, the knowledge of the supraphysical or the occult was dismissed as superstition.[45] He writes:

> The subjective and objective are two necessary sides of the manifested Reality, and in the range of the objective itself the supraphysical object of consciousness has as much right to acceptance as the physical objectivity; it cannot be *a priori* set aside as a subjective delusion or hallucination.[46]

He proposes epistemology and ontology that incorporates planes of matter, life, and mind as well as the ones that lie beyond the mind—an integral and comprehensive knowledge that includes the physical, mental, and spiritual realms. A preoccupation with any one plane would lead to skewed knowledge and not integral knowledge:

> A solution to the whole problem of existence cannot be based on an exclusive one-sided knowledge; we must know not only what Matter is and what are its processes, but what mind and life are and what are their processes, and one must also know the spirit and soul and all that is behind the material surface: *only then can we have a knowledge sufficiently integral for a solution of the problem.*[47]

Thus, integral knowledge is a simultaneous knowledge of matter, mind, and spirit and of subjective reality and objective reality. The supraphysical and mental realms must be explored by the inner senses just as the objective is explored by the outer senses. He discusses the verification of subjective experience by its own methods and not by subjecting it to the outer senses:

> The more partial view concedes no substantive reality to anything which exists only in the consciousness, or, to put it more accurately, to anything to which the inner consciousness or sense bears testimony but which the outer physical senses do not provide with a ground or do not substantiate.... In each case, understanding, discrimination, verification are necessary; but the subjective and the supraphysical must have another method of verification than that which we apply successfully to the physical and external objective. Subjective experience cannot be referred to the evidence of the external senses; it has its own standards of seeing and its inner method of verification: so also supraphysical realities by their very nature cannot be referred to the judgment of the physical or sense mind except when they project themselves into the physical, and even then that judgment is often incompetent or subject to caution; they can only be verified by other senses and by a method of scrutiny and affirmation which is applicable to their own reality, their own nature.[48]

Sri Aurobindo held that there is Eternal Truth beyond the scope of the mind and materialism; at the same time, there are manifestations of the Truth revealed at various planes of matter, mind, and life according to the primary instruments of inquiry. The former (Eternal Truth) is not dependent on the latter (manifestations), and in fact, the latter is only a small subset of the larger, all-encompassing Eternal Truth. All scientific empiricism belongs to the latter level of truth available as per the limits of the instruments of knowing.

The following passages illustrate Sri Aurobindo's understanding of scientific empiricism and its limitations:

> For a long time, we have been asked not to believe in these [metaphysical] things, to put our trust only in the measuring rods of science and its calculations and crucibles, to accept only what is materially ascertamable (sic) and measurable. But these measurements are those of something that is limited — how can we ascertain by it whether there is or is not the Illimitable? **The instruments by which we question Nature in order to find out what is ascertainable have been proved to give only the results which are already contained in the question or in the questioner. Science gives us the measures and process of things within the physical limit, but it has failed [to] tell us what things are, their final origin or their reason of existence.**[49]

Next, Sri Aurobindo explains the importance of subjective yogic insight to resolve the limits of sense-based objectivity:

> **Why should we limit ourselves only to our responses to an outer evidence?** Let us explore ourselves and not only our sense or perception of what is around us. And in ourselves let us look not only at our surfaces but at the inner and the inmost of our being and nature. ... **This self-knowledge pursued far enough shows us a deeper than the surface mind and a deeper than the physical sense, a profounder than the outward life.** It shows us also a Beyond-Mind and Beyond-Sense, a Beyond-Life; the limited passes into [the] illimitable. If there were not this capacity of research, we would have to be content with an unsatisfied agnosticism; but the means is there by which we can know ourselves and this Alpha and

> X and Omega of things or if not absolutely It at any rate its status and its dynamis, the law of its being and the law of its nature quite as deeply and more deeply than Science can show us the law and process of the physical universe.[50]

In the following explanation, the Divine as the absolute manifests itself in all the various forms and states. What is experienced as unity from one side of the coin is experienced as multiplicity from the other. The first part of the quote is cited to explain the unity of the subjective/inner with the objective/outer as mere manifestations of the same Transcendental Reality:

> **Subjectivism and objectivism start from the same data ...**
>
> **...Objectivism proceeding by the analytical reason takes an external and mechanical view of the whole problem**. It looks at the world as a thing, an object, a process to be studied by an observing reason which places itself abstractly outside the elements and the sum of what it has to consider and observes it thus from outside as one would an intricate mechanism. The laws of this process are considered as so many mechanical rules or settled forces acting upon the individual or the group which, when they have been observed and distinguished by the reason, have by one's will or by some will to be organised and applied fully much as Science applies the laws it discovers. Life is to be managed, harmonised, perfected by an adjustment, a manipulation, a machinery through which it is passed and by which it is shaped. A law outside oneself, — outside even when it is discovered or determined by the individual reason and accepted or enforced by the individual will, — this is the governing idea of objectivism; a mechanical process of management, ordering, perfection, this is its conception of practice.
>
> **...Subjectivism proceeds from within and regards everything from the point of view of a containing and developing self-consciousness.** The law here is within ourselves; life is a self-creating process, a growth and development at first subconscious, then half-conscious and at last more and more fully conscious of that which we are potentially and hold within ourselves; the principle of its progress is an increasing self-recognition, self-realisation and a resultant self-shaping.[51]

The subsequent part of the same quote explains how the individual and the plural are mere manifestations from the same Divine ground of all existence:

> ... But also **we may enlarge the idea of the self and, as objective Science sees a universal force of Nature which is the one reality and of which everything is the process, we may come subjectively to the realisation of a universal Being or Existence which fulfils itself in the world and the individual and the group with an impartial regard for all as equal powers of its self-manifestation.** In this view neither the separate growth of the individual nor the all-absorbing growth of the group can be the ideal, but an equal, simultaneous and, as far as may be, parallel development of both, in which each helps to fulfil the other. **Each being has his own truth of independent self-realisation and his truth of self-realisation in the life of others and should feel, desire, help, participate more and more, as he grows in largeness and power, in the harmonious and natural growth of all the individual selves and all the collective selves of the one universal Being.** These two, when properly viewed, would not be separate, opposite or really conflicting lines of tendency, but the same impulse of the one common existence, companion movements separating only to return upon each other in a richer and larger unity and mutual consequence.[52]

The last two sentences reaffirm the harmony between individuality and plurality. Each individual 'has his own truth', and this individuality should 'feel, desire, help, participate more and more' in others and realize that all the individual and collective selves are manifestations of 'one universal Being'. These two views are ultimately not opposite or separate but are 'companion movements' which return to a richer and larger unity.

The first couple of chapters of Wilber's *Eye to Eye* are based on the aforementioned theme of seeking integral knowledge. Instead of acknowledging the role of Sri Aurobindo in developing his chapters as well as the well-established system of yoga where the workings of these parts are thoroughly studied, Wilber quietly appropriates these ideas. He maps them to St. Bonaventure's (the Italian Catholic bishop) three modes of knowledge or 'eyes' – the *eye of flesh, eye of reason,* and *eye of contemplation.*[53]

The three aforementioned eyes according to Wilber, are mutually exclusive, and a 'category error' occurs if any one of them tries to encroach upon the function of the other two. For instance, if the eye of flesh tries to capture the truths of the eye of reason or the transcendental realm, the knowledge gained is erroneous. Conversely, if the eye of spirit tries to investigate the realms of the senses or the mind, then too the knowledge is faulty.

In order to substantiate his contentions on the category error, Wilber uses Western history. In the process, Wilber causes two distortions due to his tendency to universalize the appropriated truths that have been transplanted within the Western context. One is primarily historical, and the other is primarily epistemological, though both are intertwined:

1. The first distortion results from the conflation of both Hinduism and Buddhism with Christianity. Further, perennial philosophers map the strengths of alien traditions, primarily Hinduism and Buddhism, onto their own (Christianity) without naming the source, while they are quite detailed and fastidious in junking the horrors of Christianity onto Hinduism and Buddhism.
2. Secondly, Wilber states that the three eyes were undifferentiated in all traditions, including Hinduism and Buddhism, before the advent of a Renaissance. This is his distortion. The three eyes in the Indian context were fully differentiated, unlike in the Western religions. The crucial difference is that Indian traditions consider the *sūkṣma indriya*-s or the subtle senses capable of giving knowledge not only of the subtle realms of existence but also of the gross realm and of the interaction of the subtle and gross, whereas Wilber considers the three eyes to be mutually exclusive. Wilber avers that a 'category error' occurs if different eyes confuse their functions and try to encroach upon the territories of others.[54] Indian spiritual traditions hold that if the lower eye encroaches upon the functions of the higher eye, ignorance will emerge. However, the higher eye can give insights into the lower, if it chooses to, for as the *Upaniṣad*-s say, 'by knowing That all is known'.

We assume that Wilber's reason to make these three eyes mutually exclusive is because of Europe's wars of science, philosophy, and religion. These three have been fighting battles, each trying to dethrone the other two while attempting to explain all the mysteries of human existence from its exalted perspective. When the Church was in power, it did not allow science and philosophy to flourish. When science gained recognition, it banished the Church and God from its province. Philosophy has been at loggerheads with both science and religion. Thus, the precedent for Wilber's work lies mostly in the Indian traditions and not in the Western paradigms, as he wants to highlight.

In India, contrary to Europe, knowledge of the material, intellectual, and spiritual realms have existed in a harmonious relationship with one another— jñāna (knowledge) and vijñāna (science) are not opposed to each other, and jñāna and bhakti are not contradictory. In fact, they feed each other with insights, each being an instrument used for its right, and well-defined purpose. Therefore, all individual spiritual experiences have been backed by comprehensive philosophies or darśana. At the same time, it is recognized that whereas reason can explain spiritual truths by someone who attains spiritual illumination, it cannot take someone to the spiritual realm. Thus, its status is always subordinate to the direct knowing through identity with the spirit. A philosopher or a pandit is given a lower status than a yogi who has transcended the intellectual knowledge of the mental realm.

Furthermore, Wilber states that the eyes of flesh, reason, and contemplation were not differentiated in pre-Renaissance humanity. It was Johannes Kepler and Galileo who differentiated the eye of flesh by using empirical-analytical methodology; it was Immanuel Kant who differentiated the eye of reason, showing it to be an insufficient instrument for transcendental reality. The entire range of knowledge pursuit had been held hostage under the authoritarian brutality of the Church. Wilber's assertion is absolutely correct, but this is relevant within European history and cannot be assumed as universal. Such statements by Wilber are teeming with a tone of Western supremacy.

Both these distortions—namely, that the three eyes were not differentiated and the conflation of Hinduism-Buddhism with Christianity—will gather steam as Wilber's march of a Hero continues.

### *Wilber's new epistemology for Integral knowledge*

Mapping Sri Aurobindo's critique and approach of modern science towards consciousness and spirituality, Wilber makes instrumental injunction (engagement of paradigmatic practices for gathering data), intuitive apprehension (a direct experience of data), and communal confirmation (confirmation of data by experts) the three strands of his epistemology for gaining an integral knowledge of the physical, mental, and spiritual realms. His contention is that if instrumental injunction, intuitive apprehension, and communal confirmation are extended to all the aforementioned realms, then the knowledge gained in each of the realms is scientific, and its integration will lead to an integral knowledge.

Of the three, two have distinct roots in the writings of Swami Vivekananda and Sri Aurobindo. Swami Vivekananda was one of the pioneers who attempted to bridge the gap between science and spirituality/religion in modern times. His contention was that direct experience of data is what makes an enterprise scientific and that spirituality, because it believes in direct experience of Truth, is science.

Since both science and spirituality have direct experience as the common thread, they can be brought together. Wilber is certainly aware of this pioneering contribution of Swami Vivekananda as he writes in the *Eye of Sprit*, fifteen years later, following his pattern of not acknowledging the source of information at the same stage when he appropriates, 'Vivekananda initiated the dialogue between physics and spirituality'.[55]

Similarly with *Instrumental Injunction*: Instrumental injunctions are the precepts and directions given to a researcher working within a framework for the generation and interpretation of data. The *Instrumental Injunction* is the second strand of Wilber's epistemology that he copied from Swami Vivekananda:

> The science of Raja-Yoga proposes to put before humanity a practical and scientifically worked out method of reaching this truth. In the first place, every science must have its own method of investigation... Each science must have its own methods. I could preach you thousands of sermons, but they would not make you religious, until you practised the method. These are the truths of the sages of all countries, of all ages, of men pure and unselfish,

> who had no motive but to do good to the world. They all declare that they have found some truth higher than what the senses can bring to us, and they invite verification. They ask us to take up the method and practise honestly, and then, if we do not find this higher truth, we will have the right to say there is no truth in the claim, but before we have done that, we are not rational in denying the truth of their assertions. So we must work faithfully, using the prescribed methods, and light will come.[56]

Not surprisingly, Sri Aurobindo echoes similar sentiments. He too, emphasizes the need for a guru and to carry out injunctions to attain spiritual knowledge. 'Direct Experience' is the cornerstone of integral knowledge for both Sri Aurobindo and Wilber. Wilber, however, does not explain the problems associated with direct knowledge obtained through senses and mind, which Sri Aurobindo considers mediated knowledge. Since the knowledge of *sensibilia* and *inteligibilia* is mediated through senses, sense-mind, and pure reason, differences in the constitutional make-up of researchers in their senses and reason will lead to different constructions in knowledge systems. That knowledge gained from senses and intellect cannot be trusted as 'true knowledge' is the subject matter of many Indian spiritual systems, which both Swami Vivekananda and Sri Aurobindo emphasize in their writings.

Wilber uncritically embraces the received view of science that empirical scientific knowledge are facts gained through a direct experience of data via senses and unprejudiced mind. Further, according to Wilber, knowledge can be considered true or false by domain experts through a peer consensus. But this practice is not failsafe and this third strand in the aforementioned epistemology further enhances its vulnerability.

Chapter 11

# Wilber-IV: Premodern-Postmodern and Appropriation of Immanence-Transcendence

The Wilber-III writings concluded in 1986, with his integral model arguing for a comprehensive knowledge gained through the *eyes of flesh, reason*, and *spirit*. In other words, he argued for knowledge that was a synthetic unity of facts of subjective and objective realities gained through a) occult and mystical means; b) reason; and c) the sense organs. Wilber's claims were trying to mimic the main arguments found in Sri Aurobindo's classic work, *The Life Divine*. These ideas also form the basis of Wilber-IV, which is a series of books claiming the following significant innovations:

- Integrating premodern-modern-postmodern tenets as something original;
- Integrating transcendence-immanence and claiming it to be a Western concept;
- Introducing holons;
- Introducing the twenty tenets of holarchical evolution; and
- Developing the taxonomy of four quadrants, a template into which he organizes different aspects of consciousness.

Since Wilber-II, his posture towards Indian sources was the five-pronged approach of diluting, distorting, appropriating, superseding, and demonizing. These five approaches went in parallel. However, the relative weightage progressed along this sequence from dilution to distortion to appropriation and so forth.

## Wilber-IV's Claim of Integrating Premodern-Modern-Postmodern

Wilber analyzes premodern, modern, and postmodern thought and claims that each of these suffers seriously in the following ways:

1. All premodern societies had the knowledge of the 'Great Nest of Being' which made them All-Level, but being other-worldly, they were upper-left quadrant only and hence were not All-Quadrants.
2. Modernity made the world view All-Quadrants by differentiating the arts, morals, and science which were previously undifferentiated under the control of the Church. However, the price paid was that differentiation turned into dissociation, as science and scientific materialism colonized the arts and morals. In other words, the right quadrants (outer) took over the left quadrants (inner). So, the All-Quadrants was not symmetrical.
3. Postmodernity tried to release the colonization of the left quadrants but the pendulum swung to the other side, with the right-hand quadrants being reduced to the left-hand quadrants.

Wilber presents his AQAL model as the result of integrating the best of premodernity, modernity, and postmodernity without including the above problems. We study this model in greater detail in the following chapter.

Wilber's evidence is entirely based on a Western intellectual journey, which he assumes must apply to Indian history as well. Malhotra has extensively discussed this syndrome that he calls Western Universalism – the fallacy of universalizing European intellectual history as the chronology of development all civilizations must follow. The implication is that societies lose their own specific cultural histories because once something is said of European chronology, it is then sweepingly applied to all other societies without providing any evidence that the European trajectory is necessarily applicable.[1] This is a Hegelian blunder.

Wilber claims that *only the modern West* has investigated the outer realms of individuals and societies. He applies perennialism as the lens to see the 'Great Nest of Being' idea, and concludes that all premodern societies (assumed to be perennialist) are other-worldly. All Indian history gets collapsed into the premodern West where only the inner-individual quadrant was important. We will challenge this in detail.

We also challenge Wilber's contention that postmodernism's central tenets (contextualism, constructivism, and integral aperspectivalism) are exclusively Western and recent origin. We show that Indian traditions contain these ideas and were digested by many Western postmodernists. We also point out that Wilber's use of postmodernism within his integral framework contains fundamental epistemic tensions between modernism and postmodernism.

Furthermore, he criticizes postmodernism as self-referential and hence self-refuting, and resolves this by resurrecting objectivist modern epistemology and metaphysics. This brings him back into modernity and Eurocentrism, and therefore is a contradiction.

To set the stage, we provide a brief outline of the distinction between modernity and postmodernity, then summarize Wilber's position on these and how he claims to supersede them. Thereafter, we respond from an Indian point of view.

### *Brief outline on modernity and postmodernity*

Western modernity, which produced European colonialism, capitalism, Marxism, and Nazism, has been dominated by monolithic master discourses, which became hegemonic and homogenized and thereby blocked true intellectual freedom. These grand narratives are characterized by the following beliefs: 1) scientific materialism, technology, and medicine; (2) universal, and general truths, which are usually capable of abstract and scientific statements; (3) the self as an atomic ego separated from all others and with a true existence beneath its several roles; (4) commitment to freedom, equality, liberty, social justice, and progress in accordance with its universal truths; (5) large unitary state and national purpose, be it liberal, conservative or Marxist; and (6) large corporations and/or state planning based on consumerism as the yardstick for wellbeing and on the assumption of indefinite growth. Clearly, this was a problem peculiar to Europe's history that cannot be universalized. Whatever did not fit this worldview was excluded or even ridiculed.

Relief came in the twentieth century with the spread of anti-authoritarian and anti-establishment movements in the West, such as anti-colonialism, anti-Vietnam War (1955-75) in the USA, and anti-fascism. These brought a whole range of counter-discourses among Western intellectuals to challenge modernity. These anti-modernity reactions became known as the 'post' discourses: post-structuralism, postmodernism, post-Marxism, postfeminism, post-capitalism, etc., and offered liberation and escape from modernity's reductionist discourses.

Jean Francois Lyotard, one of the founding fathers of postmodernism, called them *petit recites,* which suggests that they are small, local, fragmentary narratives, and not grand, totalizing, and therefore oppressive like modernity. Lacking any centers/nexuses and being minor theories, they are said to avoid the oppressive potential of the very large, monolithic, and hegemonic master narratives that they attack. Lyotard explains that a defining feature of postmodernism is its opposition to grand overarching stories as the templates by which specific situations get interpreted.[2] Postmodernity was the child of modernity, like a Frankenstein turned against its creator.

While postmodernism emerged as a loose collection of anti-narratives from uncoordinated multiple disciplines and domains of society, it solidified into having its own 'toolkit of theories' that is celebrated by intellectuals as having 'theory power'—ironically, contradicting its very stated purpose by replacing one set of power nexuses by another.

There is no consensus on defining it, but one reasonable definition is by the following qualities: (1) alienation from objective knowledge, sometimes to the point of epistemic anarchy; belief in uncertainty principle and chaos theory, skepticism, and a tendency toward relative or personal 'truths'; (2) plurality of sources of knowledge, which tends to be nonlinear and non-formal; (3) self as plural, moving freely among a number of independent identities; (4) stress on ecology; (5) fragmented society with a limited sense of common identity or goals; and (6) concern to incorporate those on the social margins.[3]

Postmodernism is a specifically Western response to what was a peculiarly Western problem. This makes it very Western-centric, contrary to its ideals. The frameworks of its debates were developed strictly in the context of the West's past and present conditions. These cannot be assumed to apply to all cultures any more than the grand narratives of history by Hegel – a pillar of modernity – can be universalized. It has created its own excesses, a supremacist outlook, and a new centralized authority.

Additionally, ideas traveling from the West to India get metamorphosized because of the receiving context. The Indian champions of postmodernism are Western-educated and promote themselves in the guise of helping victims of social injustice. Postmodernism becomes like a franchise operation of some Western franchisors that give opportunities and power to the middlemen who distribute it in the Third World. Indians serve as 'data hunter-gatherers' supplying case studies and examples – including fabrications or exaggerations to fit the sponsor's requirements – in order to help 'prove' the theories. In return, the West protects and nurtures its intellectual sepoys in India.

We agree that postmodernism is a welcome relief when it gets applied to Western egos for their own deconstruction, but it is imperialistic when being exported as a way to self-de[con]struct the Third World.

## Wilber, Postmodernism, and India

We use Wilber's three features of postmodernism[4] to discuss how Indian traditions relate:

1. *Constructivism:* Reality is not in all ways a priori, but in some significant ways a construction and an interpretation; the belief that reality is simply given and not also partly constructed is referred to as 'the myth of the given'.
2. *Contextualism:* Meaning is context-dependent, and contexts are boundless.
3. *Integral aperspectivalism:* Cognition must, therefore, not unduly privilege any single perspective.

Nāgārjuna (a Mādhyamaka Buddhist philosopher) not only refuted the 'myth of the given', but he also explicated in his philosophy of *pratītya samutpāda* or dependent co-origination. That meaning is also, always, generated within contexts and in the inter-related web of interconnections. He states that concepts, events, and entities, which he calls *svabhāva*, do not exist in isolation but exist in relation to one another and lack any intrinsic separate existence; any attempt to reduce them to having an independent status will lead to absurdity. Nothing exists in itself, and of itself, and no concept has any meaning independent of a relation to other concepts. The Realists' search for knowledge is grounded in language, presuppositions, and all those concepts and entities that are considered as a given in our everyday lives. They attach a transcendental and eternal value to these givens, which Nāgārjuna deconstructs by placing them in a sociolinguistic and historical context, thus paving the way for a spiritual seeker to transcend the rationalistic tendency to make sense of the truth through any epistemological or ontological suppositions.

The Buddhist scholar C.W. Huntington confirms this in his assessment:

> According to the Madhyamika, a...convoluted and subtle relationship holds between any two dichotomies of conceptual thought, whether expressed in ontological, epistemological, ethical or any other terms: Cause/effect, subject/object, substrate/predicate, absolute/relative, truth/error, good/evil, and all other dualistic concepts find their meaning in the context of their elusive relationship with each other and with an interrelated network of other such concepts. The structure that they give to all experience—a structure that seems "to emerge from the things themselves"—is also dependent on an illusion similar to the Necker cube where each image finds its meaning and existence only in the context of its relationship to partners that must always remain out of sight. The critical difference is only that the context of everyday life in which these other relationship are embedded is infinitely more complex, for it embodies an indeterminate number of historical and circumstantial factors shared by the sociolinguistic community in which this vocabulary is used and thought and perception take place.[5]

Thus, both constructivism and contextualism were known to ancient Indians in far greater depth than Western postmodernists.

Similarly, Jainism, with its theory of *anekāntavāda* or the doctrine of non-exclusivity, preceded Western integral aperspectivalism by several centuries. According to this theory, the notions of Reality and Truth are perceived differently from different standpoints; no standpoint gives the complete Truth or the view of Reality, and hence, no perspective has the privileged status of defining Reality or Truth. Jainism regards each entity as having infinite characteristics; just as different colors can exist in a lustrous gem without conflicting with each other, these diverse characteristics too can abide in reality. Hindus, Jainas, and Buddhists were in constant debates and dialogues with one another for many centuries; they understood each other's positions very well and borrowed from each other frequently.

But a critical difference between Indian and Western systems is that Indian systems ultimately lead one to a *positive* state (such as Self = Ātman = Brahman) after deconstructing the dualist ego. *Postmodernism does not offer a positive reality that would replace whatever it deconstructs* (even though this is sometimes postulated by thinkers such as Jacques Derrida) because it is not based on empirical spirituality to achieve such a result. *What prevents Western postmodernists from understanding and embracing positive non-dualism is their lack of yoga to experience states that are positive and yet beyond narratives.* Their worldview is limited to ego states filled with narratives.

Hence, postmodernists often end up as cynics or anarchists, and some of them slip further into nihilism. The yogic deconstructing leads to the discovery of Brahman, a transcendent non-discursive state of consciousness where there is no subject/object dualism and hence no 'thing' to deconstruct. Buddhism's deconstruction culminates in the emptiness of substance. However, this is fullness as radical interdependency, and therefore, not nihilistic. It becomes nihilistic for the mind to view it metaphysically, as it were, but psychologically it is a positive experience.[6]

### *Indian influences on Western postmodernism*

Indian philosophy has numerous sophisticated systems for the deconstruction of narratives, identities, boundaries, reasoning, and so forth. The American journalist Carl Olson's book *Indian Philosophers and Postmodern Thinkers: Dialogues on the Margins of Culture* explains many influences of Indian thought upon Western postmodernists and/or similarities between them. Another important book is by Harold Coward, *Derrida and Indian Philosophy,* devoted to examining closely the manner in which various Indian thinkers and schools predated

Derrida—an icon of postmodernism—by many centuries, and in many ways influenced these recent European developments. He has chapters on the postmodernism inherent in Bhartṛhari's *Vākyapadīya* on the origin of language and on the philosophy of speech and writing. There are separate chapters on Ādi Śaṅkarācārya, Sri Aurobindo, and Nāgārjuna, discussing their postmodern contributions to Derrida.[7]

For instance, in discussing one of the most important concepts of postmodern analysis on textual reading, Coward sees parallels between Derrida's thought and that of Bhartṛhari, who lived centuries before the former:

> The different parts or separations that characterize the written text are from the same dynamic that manifests itself in spoken words. ...Derrida is attempting to recover what is already present in language; thus Derrlda's (sic) often misunderstood statement, "There is nothing outside the text." Just as the dynamic of difference (separation, articulation) is beginninglessly present in the written text, so it is also present in speech. There is no metaphysical "other" outside of text or speech that starts language. This insight of Derrida's is nicely paralleled by Bhartrhari's view that the dynamics of separation into word (sabda) and meaning (artha) is beginninglessly present in language at all its levels - from the uttered or fully sequenced speech (vaikhari viik) to the apparently unitative intuition (pasyanti vak) in which sequencing is present only as a pregnant force. Between these two levels, says Bhartrhari, is the mental speech (madhyamii viik) with its thought separation into sentence meanings and sounds that have not yet been uttered. Bhartrhari, like Derrida, sees sequencing or difference as the characteristic dynamic of language in all its levels.[8]

Some pioneers that influenced later postmodern thought like Alexander von Humboldt, Arthur Schopenhauer, Nietzsche, Martin Heidegger, Ludwig Wittgenstein and Ferdinand de Saussure were influenced by translated or original texts of Hinduism and Buddhism. Clearly, the much-celebrated postmodern notions of plurality and multiplicity are not new in Indian thought.

In the following statement in an interview, Wilber dilutes these Indian ideas as 'a few similarities', and does not mention the profound

Indian influences on many Westerners whom he cites as his sources:

> The poststructuralists have a few similarities with the relative aspects of some of the Eastern traditions, such as nonfoundationalism, the contextuality of truth, the sliding nature of signification, the relativity of meaning, and so on.[9]

Given that Wilber has been a student of Buddhism for many years and every now and then drops Nagārjuna's name to impress his Western readers, one would expect a more thorough and honest account of the history of these ideas. But true to the U-Turn syndrome, he completely avoids any such acknowledgment in his main writings, and only occasionally hints at the mild significance of Indian philosophy in his minor interviews.

In Europe in the nineteenth and twentieth centuries, the discovery of Sanskrit language and linguistics and Indian philosophy created new disciplines like comparative philology, general and theoretical linguistics, the discovery of Indo-European languages, structuralism and post-structuralism, and so forth. The discovery of Indian scientific knowledge refashioned the entire body of the humanities in the West.

According to Sri Aurobindo, the Individualist Age is a result of the Renaissance in Europe, which led to the Industrial Age and democratic social order. This was exported to many other countries and brought power to the colonizers. It created an arrogant and superior attitude in the Western mind since they could finally break through the prerational mythical period of religious dogmatism. The conquest and victory over the cryptic and irrational dogmatism created a tendency to judge all forms of spirituality as other-worldly and inferior.

Western civilization has failed to evolve into the next stage of spirituality, for neither the Greco-Roman civilizations nor the Christian tradition has enough spiritual depth to establish a solid ground for the next stage of development: the Subjective Age. Therefore, many major Western thinkers turned towards Indian spiritual knowledge. Today, one cannot imagine the Western world without Indian influence and correlations with the spiritual stage of development. It is as if India is preparing for the next stage of development of the Subjective Age in the world.

## *Can India be classified in the premodern-modern-postmodern framework?*

There are two common notions we wish to contest concerning the assumptions about premodern, modern, and postmodern stages:

- Because these were sequential stages in Western history and were in mutual tension, i.e. mutually exclusive, therefore all societies are examined as though they must exhibit the same behavior of passing through these stages in the exact same chronological sequence.
- Only the West has had modernity, and hence its next stage is postmodernity, whereas all other societies have been premodern except to the extent they could copy the West and become partially modern.

We demonstrate that traditional Indian society, without the recent Westernization, (i) does have many qualities characteristic of modernity as well as postmodernity; and (ii) has its equivalents of premodernity, modernity and postmodernity all in parallel and simultaneously, not in mutual tension but in harmony.

Some Chinese scholars, led by Tu Weiming of Harvard, have been making a similar argument for the past few decades. Weiming argues that China has its own kind of modernity, which is based on Confucianism (teachings of the Chinese philosopher Confucius 551-479 BCE) and not on a Western model, and that its ancient civilization has been compatible with this Confucian modernity rather than being in tension with it. Furthermore, China has its own kind of postmodernity as well. We are sympathetic to this view and make the same claim on behalf of Indian civilization. The point is that *Western modernity is only one kind of modernity*, i.e. there are many kinds of modernity. Therefore, a society wishing to modernize does not necessarily have to Westernize itself.

It is unfortunate that one of the biggest outcomes of intellectual colonization and imperialism of the last millennium across the world has been the need to cast ancient cultures into the Western worldview. Unlike objective categories of science, the subjective domains of humanities cannot possibly do justice to cultures and societies such as

India. The Industrial Revolution (1760-1839) marked a high point in Western civilization for the massive improvement in livelihoods and wealth it created. To the Indian subcontinent, however, that made no difference, for India already had the riches of the world and a livelihood to which the Westerner could only aspire. Any study of the world's richest nations until the advent of European colonization will show the same – India was the richest, most prosperous nation until the seventeenth century. This is not jingoistic rhetoric but a statistical fact.

Western intellectual imperialism, however, boxes India into categories that are unnatural and unjust to it. The table below shows the standard differentiation between premodern, modern and postmodern societies:

| | Epistemology | Socio-Political Structure | Primary Occupations and Methods | Cultural Structure |
|---|---|---|---|---|
| **Premodern** | Faith, Mystic | Feudal, Collectivist | Agriculture, Individual Labor, Local Markets | Feudalist |
| **Modern** | Objective | Capitalist, Individualist | Industrial, Mass Manufactured, Global Markets | Bourgeois |
| **Postmodern** | Subjective | Socialist, Collectivist | Information-based revolution such as using the internet, Global Markets | Fragmented |

It is very difficult to categorize Indian history as passing through each of the above stages in time. Consider, for instance, the primary trait of the socio-political nature through each of these periods. While the importance accorded to the collective has always been the basis of Indian societies through each period, as seen in the framing of the stages of life of man – the āśrama system – the individual has enjoyed extraordinary freedom even in the midst of the collective! Contrary to the picture of a highly casteist society that has been painted of India since colonization, the svabhāva of an individual was a major factor in influencing his pursuit in life, even if it went against the collective grain. In light of this, studying India through this classification is erroneous and injudicious.

### *'Great Nest of Being': premodernity dismissed as static and other-worldly*

The 'Great Chain of Being', according to Wilber, is a nest of hierarchies of levels of existence, from matter to body, mind, soul, and spirit, organized like concentric spheres with the higher ones including and transcending the lower ones. To counteract the postmodern challenge to hierarchy, Wilber modifies this to his own 'Great Nest of Being' ('Nest' replaces 'Chain'), which is a hybrid of Lovejoy's and Smith's 'Great Chain of Being' combined with Arthur Koestler's 'holons'.[10] He states that levels are actually holons (wholes that are a part of larger wholes), forming the 'Great Nest of Being'.[11]

Wilber asserts that in premodern cultures such as India, a few highly evolved exemplars from traditional societies have embraced and realized the 'Great Nest of Being'. He writes:

> In premodern times, while it is true that much, or even most, of spirituality was magic, mythic, and prerational, nonetheless the most highly evolved yogis, saints, and sages had access to the transrational, transpersonal, transcendental realms—they embraced, in their own way and in their own terms, the entire Great Nest of Being, subconscious to self-conscious to superconscious.... And by and large they were supported by the entire culture in their attempts to do so. This is why we say that the *wisdom of premodernity* was embodied in the Great Nest of Being. And even if the *average* did not awaken to the higher levels in the Nest, it was clearly understood that these higher potentials were available to any who wished to pursue a path of awakening, liberation, or enlightenment.[12]

Wilber proceeds to list his issues with all premodern societies framed in terms of the Great Nest. He claims that the basic orientation of the

Great Nest was other-worldly societies that lacked knowledge of science, arts, culture, politics, etc.:

> Traditionally, every level above matter was usually viewed as "transcendent" to matter, *totally beyond it*, existing either in some sort of heaven or in some nonearthly state, and this gave the Great Chain its largely "otherworldly" feel.... The Great Chain invited a rejection and devaluing of *this* world.[13]

We do not accept this as a fair characterization of India. This description applies to Abrahamic religions' denial of the immanence of the Divine, and hence it applies to the premodern West. Indian worldviews, however, see the world as the sacred body of Brahman or Śiva's Śakti, and the same cannot be assumed.

In addition, Wilber insists that all societies were *static* prior to European modernity:

> It thus was a great, massive, *static* system, not yet clearly understood according to the differentiation of pluralistic cultural contexts, and their further integration into globally evolving systems—an understanding provided by modernity and postmodernity.[14]

But the 'pluralistic cultural contexts' which he claims were invented by Western modernity have already been built into Indian society, given its absence of centralized authority and canonized prophetic dictates.

Among the factors causing this static nature, Wilber states that these societies did not have the knowledge of how culture affected the consciousness of an individual:

> There was little or no understanding of how a person's view of the world—and a person's experience of the spectrum of consciousness—is profoundly colored and molded by the background cultural contexts in which the people live.[15]

This is false in the case of India. We show that Indian traditions have deeply understood how the state of consciousness of an individual effects his cognition.

In addition, Wilber says they lacked the understanding of how modes of production related to individual consciousness:

> There was little or no understanding of how the material mode of production (foraging, horticulture, agrarian, industrial, informational) deeply affects the contours of an individual consciousness and dramatically alters everything from gender roles to suicide rates to eating habits.[16]

Indians, however, have appreciated that individual consciousness is related to material modes of production, as is evident in all the arts using the same taxonomy and structures as the inner realms. The Indian notions of svadharma as individual purpose and potential, and varṇa as specialization, are in harmony with ideas of consciousness.

For Wilber, these limits prevented art, morals, and science from becoming differentiated:

> Premodernity...did not fully differentiate the value spheres [arts, moral, and science] at any of the levels in the Great Nest. Thus, among other things, objective-scientific investigation of the spectrum was hampered; the specific and often local cultural expressions of the Great Nest were taken to be universally valid; and the moral injunctions recommended to all were tied to those limited cultural expressions. Giordano Bruno might have experienced many of the upper levels of the Great Nest, but because the value spheres were not fully differentiated at large and their individual freedoms were not protected by law and custom, the Inquisition cheerfully burned him at the stake.[17]

Clearly, what he is saying applies only to his fellow Westerners and their history. There was no equivalent of the Italian philosopher of the 1600s, Giordano Bruno, being burnt at the stake in India. Indian traditions have nurtured the coexistence of a multiplicity of life forms, cultural patterns, and ways of life. Hence, there has been no need to 'reform' any laws and fight for freedom of expression because nobody has enforced such 'laws' upon the public. Europe had problems, and so needed these solutions, but Indians never fell under oppressive theocracies from which separation of Church/State was required.

Wilber attributes several major breakthroughs to European modernity, which led to what he calls the differentiations of art, morals, and science:

> The differentiation of "I" and "we" meant that the individual I would no longer be subservient to the collective We (church, state, monarchy, herd mentality): the universal rights of man were everywhere proclaimed, which eventually led to the liberation movements from abolition to feminism. The differentiation of "I" and "it" meant that objective reality could no longer crush individual choice and taste, with other things, freed art from representation. The differentiation of "we" and "it" meant that sciences investigation of objective truth was no longer subservient to dictates of church or state, which contributed to the stunning discoveries in physics, medicine, biology, and technology.[18]

Again, this history does not apply to India where the loose network of jāti-s comprised a decentralized social structure. The spiritual freedom of svadharma, with a library of texts and multiplicity of living guru-s as exemplars, was entirely different from an authoritarian Church or institution. India absorbed, changed, mutated, and domesticated foreign imports, and hence it has included both modernity and postmodernity. Wilber's understanding applies only to prophet-based (i.e. Abrahamic) religions with finality of canon in the hands of institutions of absolute power.

Furthermore, Indian theories of aesthetics and performing arts have always respected individual tastes. In fact, the science of Āyurveda is based on the cosmological principle that every individual is uniquely constituted in his or her prakṛti, which necessitates individualized treatments rather than the standard 'pill' approach of the West. So, to proclaim that the West brings individual freedom in the arts and scientific inquiry is indeed a chauvinistic assumption.

We question the sweeping generalizations of Wilber's attack on India being lumped together with 'all premodern societies' simply by assigning Western postmodernity for everyone to follow. Using these generalizations, he condemns all traditions for being resistant to change, hence frozen in time; for prohibitions and sanctions that disallow freedom; for being blind, mechanical, and unreflective.

We contest the Western category of premodern as a universal category applicable to all societies prior to the West's modernity.

## Indian Traditions in Wilber's Premodern/Modern Mapping

In this section, we respond to each of Wilber's main contentions about the premodern and modern as they apply to India. We summarize eleven major issues in his work on this topic and respond individually to each, showing how the systems in India have their own unique structures.

The column on the left lists Wilber's key positions on how premodernity was a problem in all cultures worldwide and how European modernity deals with these issues. The column on the right states whether his analysis of European history applies to Indian society.

| How European Modernity Differs from its Premodernity | Applies to India? |
|---|---|
| Premodernity was other-worldly. | No |
| Premodernity was devoid of science. | No |
| Premodernity was unable to appreciate that cultural contexts mold a person's experience. | No |
| Premodernity lacked understanding of how material modes of production (horticulture, agrarian, etc.) impact human life. | No |
| Premodernity was controlled by a Church-like or State-like central authority that regulated all the spheres of human activity. | No |
| Premodernity was without differentiation of science, arts, and morals. | No |
| Modernity helps arts and sciences in a manner that cripples the inner domain. | No |
| Premodernity was ignorant about childhood development. | No |
| Premodernity did not grasp the types of psychopathologies. | No |
| Premodernity was ignorant of Consciousness-Brain links. | No |
| Premodernity lacked the understanding of evolution. | No |

Wilber parrots the colonial discourse on India and the spiritual and intellectual history of Europe which becomes the history of the entire world, legitimizing the White man's burden to civilize others by colonizing them. If arts, morals, and sciences were undifferentiated in early Europe, that had to be the case everywhere. If the Church as the central authority controlled and regulated human affairs in Europe, it had to be the same story everywhere. If Europe was under the sway of the dark ages, then the entire world had to be dark as well. If these issues were resolved in Europe by its modernity movement at the expense of spirituality, it also had to apply to non-Western traditions.

All this is blatant Eurocentrism. India did not have violent conflicts between the organized institutions of Religion and State. Nor were there Indian authorities exerting control over pursuits such as science whereas in Europe there was a powerful theological domination over intellectual pursuits for centuries!

We refute each of Wilber's assertions in the case of Indian traditions by showing that this premodern/modern chasm cannot automatically be superimposed upon Indian civilization.[19]

## Response to Postmodern Charges Against Indian Traditions

A criticism levied against Indian thought is that it was developed largely to deconstruct the *individual* level of identity, whereas Western postmodernism was developed mainly to deconstruct the *collective* grand narratives of societies, religions, nations, etc. Thus, Indian thought is limited to being a personal tool for one's liberation from the *private grand narrative* of which the ego is the self-appointed 'owner', whereas Western postmodernism is a sociological tool to deconstruct collective egos. While the former can help an individual, the latter is required to liberate societies and evolve them further.

To give a fair response from an Indian perspective to this critique, one would have to examine Indian sociological writings concerning jāti, ethics (as in the *Mahābhārata*), and related texts.

Sri Aurobindo points out that the Subjective Age would be impossible to arrive at without Indian spiritual knowledge, which was developed, practiced, and refined over millennia. He writes:

Out of this awakening vision and impulse the Indian renaissance is arising, and that must determine its future tendency.

1. The recovery of the old spiritual knowledge and experience in all its splendour, depth and fullness is its first, and most essential work;
2. The flowing of this spirituality into new forms of philosophy, literature, art, science and critical knowledge is the second;
3. An original dealing with modern problems in light of the Indian spirit and the endeavour to formulate a greater synthesis of a spiritualised society is the third and most difficult. Its success on these three lines will be the measure of its help to the future of humanity.[20]

### *India is not other-worldly*

As already discussed in Chapter 8, India was not other-worldly as alleged. Sri Aurobindo reminds us:

> **If the Indian mind gave the highest importance to a spiritual release,—and whatever the positivist mood may say, a spiritual liberation of some kind is the highest possibility of the human spirit,—it was not interested in that alone. It looked equally at ethics, law, politics, society, the sciences, the arts and crafts, everything that appertains to human life. It thought on these things deeply and scrutinisingly and it wrote of them with power and knowledge.[21]**

### *The Indian mind is not void of a scientific approach*

Wilber insinuates that physical sciences did not flourish in premodern India, but this contradicts the overwhelming evidence on Indian contributions to the history of science and technology. To dismiss India as lacking knowledge of worldly subjects such as medicine, astronomy, physics, mathematics, etc. is Eurocentric hubris. Sri Aurobindo writes:

> **To say that Indian philosophy has led away from the study of nature is to state a gross unfact and to ignore the magnificent history of Indian civilisation. If by nature is meant physical Nature, ... no nation before the modern epoch carried scientific**

> **research so far and with such signal success as India of ancient times. That is a truth which lies on the face of history for all to read**; it has been brought forward with great force and much wealth of detail by Indian scholars and scientists of high eminence, but it was already known and acknowledged by European savants who had taken the trouble to make a comparative study in the subject.[22]

In his attempt to produce his 'theory of everything' (also the title of one of his important books) including the sciences, Wilber must clearly recognize the historical difference in approach towards science in India and the modern West. If it is only after the advent of the Renaissance that Western science found its due place of independence in Western society, Indian science has always enjoyed freedom from any religious dogmatism, because religious culture in India, in general, encourages freedom of inquiry and experiential knowledge. Any great religious breakthrough or spiritual discovery was followed by the flourishing of scientific advancement, as seen in India's contributions to astronomy, metallurgy, the physical sciences, mathematics, and the life sciences — the advancement had been in all walks of human life. The continuous perpetuation of this colonial bias, of either attributing anything worthwhile of practical application found in India to Greek influence or openly just co-opting it, finds a subscriber in Wilber.

It is also important to recognize and understand that Indian knowledge systems do not see metaphysical theorizing as the summit of intellectual activity, and unlike Wilber's usage of the term, in India, the highest philosophical thinking was based on experience of various kinds and not merely speculative reasoning. Modern scientific principles and standards are thus not radically new or different from ancient Indian thought, even as it intelligently recognized the boundaries of the scope of scientific validity and domains. Kant's distinction between noumena and phenomena has always existed as the *dṛṣṭa* and *adṛṣṭa,* and more so, the bona fides of adṛṣṭa also come from strong experience. Wilber, though, assumes that the ancient Indian sages did not have modern scientific knowledge and imperiously states:

> Part of the problem is that the relation of human consciousness to human neurophysiology is something that is not obvious (and not even available) to introspective phenomenology (i.e.,

> to meditation or contemplation), which means that items such as dopamine, serotonin, synaptic pathways, the Kreb's cycle, hypothalamic regulation, and so on, were not generally available to the ancients. Again, this does not mean that their spiritual realization was flawed or inadequate, but simply that they did not have the advantage of some of the finite facts that modern science has discovered. Were Plotinus alive today, you can bet that several chapters of the Enneads would be devoted to brain neurophysiology and its relation to spirit. Were Shankara alive today, his commentaries on the Brahma Sutras would no doubt have extensive discussions on the relation of the nadis to neurotransmitters.[23]

What Wilber presumes here is that knowledge continues to develop in time. Therefore, one can think of past development as outdated. What he does not understand is that the previous stages of development prepare the future ones and that the spiritual heritage of India is preparing the coming of the Subjective Age of humanity.

By picking out only metaphysical experiences as part of building a case for perennialism while rejecting the very distinctive features of the tradition in which it is set and considered, as shown earlier in the book, Wilber attempts to give a theoretical framework for states a priori.

Andrew F. Smith writes the following in his critique of Wilber's *Integral Spirituality*:

> Throughout all of Wilber's expanding and refining of his model, ...a fundamental problem remains. In attempting to develop a philosophical system that explicitly recognizes, let alone regards as one of its fundamental anchoring premises, higher consciousness, he confronts a dilemma. On the one hand, his system must be intellectually rigorous enough to enable scientists, philosophers, and other academics to take it seriously. On the other hand, mystical states, by definition, are beyond thought and difficult to describe in words. It would therefore seem to be impossible to construct a system that is completely accessible and transparent to the intellect and ...does justice to the experience of these states. ...Wilber is trying to please everyone, and we all know what generally becomes of attempts to do that.

> **As I and several others posting at this site have argued at length elsewhere, there are numerous inconsistencies, oversimplifications and misrepresentations in Wilber's treatment of the work of others, and many of these flaws, ...are ultimately rooted in his attempt to integrate these data or ideas smoothly with the notion of higher states of consciousness.** This is very evident in his four quadrant model, where human beings of different kinds of societies, such as magic, mythic and rational, are considered to occupy genuinely different levels of existence, levels that have the same relationship to each other—transcend and include—as still higher, trans-rational levels have to them. There is no reason in principle why Wilber could not have theorized that the relationship of higher levels of consciousness to any ordinary level is quite different from that the consciousness of a modern, Western individual has to, say, that of someone of several thousand years ago. But by proposing they are the same, he has been able to incorporate higher levels of consciousness very neatly into his philosophical system. They are basically an extrapolation of the levels of human/social development proposed by Piaget, Gebser and great many others....**he plays somewhat fast and loose with empirical facts to make them fit a model that includes higher states, so does his understanding of the role of these higher states suffer from his need to connect them to empirical phenomena**...This problem—what might be called Wilber's intellectualization or academization of higher states—is also very evident in his four-quadrant model, which makes higher, trans-rational stages a natural extension of the development of lower stages.[24]

He continues:

> Not only is the relationship of these higher stages to lower ones, ..., the same as the relationship of the latter among themselves, but meditation, the process by which higher consciousness is realized, is even viewed as a way of moving through these lower stages as much as it is a way of moving from them to the higher. ... Wilber states that "empirical research has consistently demonstrated that meditation can induce vertical transformation in adults"[2],

and more specifically claims that "if...people...meditate about an hour a day, then about four years later, they're two [SD] stages higher."[3] He also reports that 38% of meditators have reached the turquoise level, in the SD spectrum, compared to 2% of non-meditators.[4][25]

## *Indian traditions are not frozen but are evolving*

Dharma, which includes both inner and outer actions, is dependent on place, time, and person or deśa, kāla, and nimitta. This is the nature of smṛti-s, i.e. human constructions which are specific to time, place, and context and are meant to be amended and superseded for each new context. On the other hand, śruti is eternal truth. These two modes of knowledge are studied with the understanding of the distinct differences between them.

In contrast, in the Bible and Koran, both śruti and smṛti are collapsed into one book. So, what is eternal, and what is specific to a particular time and cultural milieu, are mixed up. This has made Christianity and Islam rigid because attempts to bring social change (which should merely require new smṛti-s) are seen as threats to God's words and edicts. Wilber is addressing religions where śruti-smṛti are merged as one and made indistinguishable.

Therefore, his analysis does not apply to the Indic traditions where these were always taught as separate so that change can occur via smṛti-s, and hence he needs to be mindful of this crucial difference while making sweeping generalizations.[26] In the West, change had to topple the frozen canon that combined smṛti in it, leading to discontinuities which Wilber rightly criticizes. However, given that change in the Indic system has taken place numerous times without the need to topple any regime or use violence, there has been greater harmony from one era of social evolution to another.

## *Jāti-Varṇa framework influences socio-economic specialization*

Vedic India used varṇa as the framework for modes of production to be based on one's inner nature or svadharma. Sri Aurobindo writes in *The Human Cycle: The Ideal of Human Unity, War, and Self-Determination* that with the passage of the yuga-s from Satya, Tretā, and Dvāpara to Kali, the spiritual and inner knowledge is progressively replaced by outer knowledge. The significance of varṇa is in the internal capability based on personal quality, guṇa, but man later became dependent on the economic mode of production located in the jāti. Indeed, Sri Aurobindo writes:

> In the evolution of caste, the outward supports of the ethical fourfold order,—birth, economic function, religious ritual and sacrament, family custom,—each began to exaggerate enormously its proportions and its importance in the scheme.[27]

With an increased emphasis on the economic function, the material mode of production and the jāti became co-determinants of an individual consciousness in collective folk knowledge. Ethnographically speaking, even today, it is not too difficult to find conversations in Indian villages involving the connection of individual consciousness with one's mode of production or the jāti to which one belongs.

### *No hegemony via centralized church in Indian systems*

Varṇa refers to different forms of social capital which by design, were not allowed to become concentrated in anyone's hands. There was never any Church-like central authority specifically because the various forms of social capital were not allowed to get consolidated. The Brahmins/ brāhmaṇa-s (spiritual capital), Kṣatriya-s (governance capital), and Vaiśya-s (commercial capital) were always kept as separate functions; none of these could be combined into a single person. This ensured that power remained unconcentrated and there could not be a European-style theocrat. Sri Aurobindo writes:

> The predominance from early times of the religious and spiritual tendency in the mind of the Indian people brought about at the top of the social system the growth of the Brahmin order, priests, scholars, legists, repositories of the sacred lore of the Vedas, a development paralleled elsewhere but here given an unequalled permanence and definiteness and supreme importance. In other countries with a less complex mentality this predominance might have resulted in a theocracy: but the Brahmins in spite of their

> ever-increasing and finally predominant authority did not and could not usurp in India the political power. **As sacrosanct priests and legists and spiritual preceptors of the monarch and the people they exercised a very considerable influence, but the real or active political power remained with the king, the Kshatriya aristocracy and the commons.**[28]

Interestingly, the king did not claim absolute powers. He was a custodian and guardian of dharma, which included the notion that each varṇa has its own varṇa-dharma.

It was dharma, the abstract operative principle, that regulated the inner and outer lives of Indians. Before rulers could assume the role of guardianship, their own lives had to be regulated in accordance with the rule of the dharma.

> A greater sovereign than the king was the Dharma, the religious, ethical, social, political, juridic and customary law organically governing the life of the people. This impersonal authority was considered sacred and eternal in its spirit and the totality of its body, always characteristically the same, the changes organically and spontaneously brought about in its actual form by the evolution of the society being constantly incorporated in it, regional, family and other customs forming a sort of attendant and subordinate body capable of change only from within,—and with the Dharma no secular authority had any right of autocratic interference. ***The Brahmins themselves were recorders and exponents of the Dharma, not its creators nor authorised to make at will any changes***, although it is evident that by an authoritative expression of opinion they could and did favour or oppose this or that tendency to change of principle or detail. The king was only the guardian, executor and servant of the Dharma, charged to see to its observance and to prevent offences, serious irregularities and breaches. He himself was bound the first to obey it and observe the rigorous rule it laid on his personal life and action and on the province, powers and duties of his regal authority and office.[29]

### *Science, arts, and morals were differentiated in India*

In the absence of a centralized Church or state, the creative and spiritual lives of people were free, only to be guided by the social rules of the varṇa-āśrama dharma and svadharma. There was absolute and total freedom in the way one wanted to know one's relationship with the Divine; Indian society recognized that one's relationship with the Divine was unique and had to be explored in accordance with one's inner dictates under the guidance of a guru of one's own choosing. There was no heretic to be burned at the stake, and different philosophies ranging from hedonistic materialism to lofty spiritual transcendence and everything in between existed in harmony. Consequently, the pursuit of science, arts, and morals was not undifferentiated in premodern India.

The *śāstra*-s are canons that showcase the massive strides India has taken in the past in pursuing various domains. Unlike the crippling impact of the Church on Western science, the ancient Indian used his freedom to push boundaries in every field: medicine, warfare, metallurgy, architecture, art forms of every type, being just a few among innumerable achievements. The fundamental freedom the Indian had enabled him to clearly distinguish between the central and timeless principles of his chosen domain and those forms that are subject to change and further advancement. Wilber's failure to understand this distinction perhaps leads him to believe that he is surpassing Sri Aurobindo by using modern discoveries of neuroscience and medicine, while clearly the sage based his work on the timeless and central principles that are not subject to change.

### *Indian arts and sciences do not cripple inner domains*

When modernity rescued arts, ethics, and science in Europe, Wilber rightly explains that it did so by privileging materialistic science at the expense of spirituality. Hence, one problem gets solved, and another gets created:

> Modernity, on the other hand, did manage to differentiate the Big Three of art, moral, and science, on a large scale, so that each began to make phenomenal discoveries. But as the Big Three dissociated, and scientific colonialism began its aggressive career...and thus all the interior stages of consciousness—reaching from body to mind to soul to spirit—were summarily dismissed as so much superstitious

> nonsense. The Great Nest collapsed into scientific materialism—into what we will be calling "flatland" and there the modern world, by and large, still remains. Our job, ... is to take the strengths of both premodernity and modernity, and jettison their weakness.[30]

Once again, this applies only to the West. Wilber's analysis of science throwing out spirituality is boxed within the West's historical clash between spirituality and science, but this dichotomy never existed in Indic traditions, and hence this imposition of Western history as the universal grid is not valid.

### *Indian traditions have been rich in developmental psychology*

Wilber feels that only Western modernity had knowledge about the stages of child development. All others get lumped as limited by perennial philosophy:

> [Another] inadequacy is that the level of mind itself needs to be subdivided in the light of its *early development*. Here the contributions of Western psychology are decisive. To put it in a nutshell, the mind itself has at least four major stages of growth: *magic* (2-5 years), *mythic* (6-11 years), *rational* (11 onward), and integral-aperspectival or *vision-logic* (adulthood, if then). Precisely because the infantile and childish origins of the *preformal* levels of magic and mythic were not clearly understood, the traditions often confused them with the *postformal* states of psychic and subtle, and this pre/post fallacy haunts most of the perennial philosophy, injecting it not only with truly enlightened wisdom, but substantial stretches of superstition.[31]

Concerning the first part of this passage, Indian epics provide lengthy explanations of the stages that even Śrīrāma, Śrīkṛṣṇa and the Buddha underwent, raised from childhood with the required training – emotional and intellectual. Sri Aurobindo explains that all the avatāra-s have to undergo a process of yoga or intense sādhana in order to experience the stages and planes of human existence in the evolutionary process, i.e. the avatāra has to evolve through the planes of vital and the various subdivisions of mind (citta, manas, and buddhi) that characterize the growth of a child into an adult.

The second part of the passage deals with the pre-post fallacy, which we responded to earlier in this book. For the development of post-rational faculties, the development of the rational mind as well as the understanding of its limits, was an important prerequisite. Spirituality was not a return to the past perfection of a child but an evolution into a trans-adult stage. It was a commonly held mistake of the European Romanticists (and by Wilber by his own admission) to conflate the childhood state with the mystic state, which Wilber now uses to characterize all premodern societies.

Another central feature that needs to be considered is the manner in which Indian societies cared for the stage of child growth. Piaget and Montessori have impacted Western thought in this regard, but India has always placed a huge premium on how a child and young adult were cared for. What is specialized knowledge today was common folklore – one reads and hears in stories such as that of the warrior Abhimanyu in the *Mahābhārata* learning about the *cakravyūha* (military formation) while in his mother's womb – understanding the intricacies of even infant psychology. Placing the young adult under the care of the ṛṣi-s – the noblest of men in the society – so that focused attention is given to strengthening the character, mental and physical faculties as well as several domains of practical and theoretical knowledge, shows the sophisticated and unique systems of India. To lump these under general categories or outright ignore them amounts to blindsiding in order to claim credit for ideas that have existed in more complex forms elsewhere.

Contrary to Wilber's charge that Eastern traditions do not grasp the various psychopathologies that arise in different individuals, Indian traditions in fact, have not only recognized their existence but also suggested several frameworks to heal the pathologies and create harmony and balance from the earliest stages. Remarkably sensitive observations have been made in Indian traditions concerning the behavioral traits from the unborn stage to those of advanced age. Wilber claims that:

> Because the traditional Great Chain theorists had a poor understanding of the early, infantile, prerational stages of human development, they likewise failed to grasp the types of psychopathologies that often stem from complications at these early

> stages. ... psychosis, borderline, and neurotic diseases often stem from problems at the early fulcrums of self-development, and can best be approached with an understanding of their developmental dimensions. Meditation—which is a way to carry development forward into the transpersonal—will not, as a rule, cure these prepersonal lesions (as hosts of American practitioners found out the hard way).[32]

It is even debatable whether the various psychopathologies such as psychosis, borderline and neuroses emerge from early childhood developments as claimed by some Western theories. As far as the etiology, classification, and treatment of psychological disorders including psychoses and neuroses are concerned, Āyurveda lists psychiatry as one of the eight branches of medicine and has a theory of mind based on the five kośa-s. It explains mental disturbances as kleśa-s and various meditations are ways of calming and cleansing the mind of past habits and deposits. Many modern cognitive science theories, neuroscientific research, and various wellness programs are based on Western research and appropriation of Indic spirituality. It is hardly fair to say that these are Western innovations when they are derived from Indic models and empirical research of yogi-s and Buddhist practitioners. Another project volume from Infinity Foundation will go into the U-Turns by Westerners in the fields of cognitive sciences, neurosciences, and health.

### *Indian knowledge includes consciousness-brain links*

Wilber appropriates the critique of materialism from Sri Aurobindo, which upholds the primacy of consciousness: it produces phenomena but is not caused by it; it has correlates in the brain and body but can exist independent of them. Wilber lacks understanding of the interaction of consciousness with matter and the mechanisms of manifestation, and not being a mystic, he appropriates Sri Aurobindo's experience in lieu of his own. There is a direct correspondence between Sri Aurobindo and Wilber on how the chemical interactions in the physical brain cannot explain higher cognitive processes.

The following table shows how Sri Aurobindo's ideas of the bi-directional relationships between consciousness and the body have been annexed by Wilber.

**Sri Aurobindo**

There is no doubt **a connection and interdependence between consciousness and the inconscient substance in which it resides and through which it seems to operate. Consciousness depends upon the body and its functionings, on the brain, nerves, gland-action, right physiological working, for its own firm state and action. It uses them as its instruments and, if they are injured or unable to act, the action of the consciousness may also be in part or whole impaired, impeded or suspended.** But this does not prove that the action of consciousness is an action of the body and nothing else. There is an instrumentation and if the instrument is impaired, the user of the instrument can no longer manifest himself rightly through it; if it is destroyed, he cannot operate any longer unless or until he can get another instrument. This then has to be seen whether the phenomena of consciousness are such that they make it necessary to suppose such a use or instrumentation of the body.... **Both sides of the phenomenon must be given their value; to reject Matter as an illusion of Consciousness or Consciousness as a freak or disease of Matter are equally one-eyed views which miss the true problem and are not likely to lead to a satisfying solution.... It is not sufficient to examine the material, the physiological processes accompanying the functioning of consciousness and attempt to explain the functioning by its physical processes. This leaves consciousness itself unexplained; if it accounts to some extent, but imperfectly, for sense phenomena or mechanical thinking, it does not account in the least for the most important powers of our conscious energy; it does not account for reason, understanding, will, creative thought, conscious selection, the conscious intellectual and spiritual action and self-development of the human being. Yet these are of capital importance, for it is here that consciousness begins to unfold itself out of its chrysalis or matrix of inconscience and a half conscious first working and reveal its true nature.**[33]

**Ken Wilber**

The interior waves of **the full spectrum of consciousness**, as they appear in an individual—from body (feelings) to mind (ideas) to soul (luminosity) to spirit (all-pervading)—are listed in the Upper-Left quadrant. **These cannot be reduced to material dimensions (because, unlike matter, they do not possess simple location).** Nonetheless, feelings, mental ideas, and spiritual illuminations all have physical correlates that can be measured by various scientific means, from EEG machines to blood chemistry to PET scans to galvanic skin response.... Thus, for example, certain archaic behavioral impulses have correlates in the reptilian brain stem. Various emotional states and feelings have correlates in states of limbic system arousal. Conceptual thinking shows activity particularly in the frontal cortex. Various meditative states show pronounced changes in brainwave patterns (e.g., high amplitude theta and delta waves, hemispheric synchronization). From bodily feelings to mental ideas to spiritual illuminations (Left Hand), there are at least some physical correlates (Right Hand) for all of the states and stages of consciousness evolution.

And why don't we simply go all the way and say that consciousness is therefore nothing but a byproduct of complex brain structures, connectionist systems, digital processes, computational biocircuits, or some such? Because none of those Right-Hand correlates have any value gradations, which are the essence of the Left-Hand domains themselves.

For example, different brainwave patterns can be registered by an EEG machine; but nothing on the machine says that one pattern is better than another, only that they are different. Thus, ethnocentric prejudice and worldcentric fairness will both register brainwave patterns on the EEG machine; but nothing on the machine says, or can say, that one of those brainwaves is better, or more valuable, or more beautiful than another. None of those value gradations show up, or can show up, on the machine registering the Right-Hand correlates, because in the Right-Hand world you only have gradations of size and simple location, not gradations of value, depth, and meaning.

> **Thus, to the extent that we reduce states of consciousness to brain states, we lose all values. We end up in the disqualified universe.** If we reduce joy to serotonin and morals to dopamine, if we reduce consciousness to neuronal pathways and awareness to connectionist systems, we completely erase value, meaning, depth, and Divinity from the face of the Kosmos itself: we fall into flatland, we fall into subtle reductionism.[34]

Despite Sri Aurobindo's insights into brain functioning and its links with the mind, Wilber writes:

> There was little or no understanding of the way in which consciousness is correlated with brain states, neurophysiology, and neurotransmitters.[35]

### *Indian systems comprise a profound understanding of evolution*

The development and change of the physical form are what the Western paradigm focuses on in its core understanding of evolution with the underlying assumption that evolution takes place mechanically. The role of consciousness is a novel contribution made by Indian thought, according to which consciousness involuted in matter is evolving, changing, and developing the outer garb of Nature for its embodiment. Trying to explain the development of the outer form without acknowledging its inner spiritual cause and driving force is to miss the critical point in evolutionary theory and the possibility of true integration of Spirit and Nature.

Wilber, however, continues to attribute to the Great Chain of Being this important concept:

> [The final] inadequacy in the traditional Great Chain is its lack of understanding of evolution, an understanding that is also a rather **exclusive contribution of the modern West.** This is easily remedied, because, as many theorists have pointed out, if you tilt the Great Chain on its side and let it unfold in time—instead of being statically given all at once, as traditionally thought—you have the outlines of evolution itself.[36]

Sri Aurobindo's work on evolution does not suffer from the problem he alleges. His model has been discussed earlier in the book.[37]

## Appropriation of Transcendence-Immanence

Wilber appreciates the importance of integrating patriarchal other-worldly religions with matriarchal this-worldly neopagan religions. The West has a horrific history of persecuting the practitioners of pagan traditions, including the ones that emphasized the Great Mother, reaching its nadir with the Inquisitions (established to suppress heresy) that lasted a few centuries. He incorrectly conflates 'spirituality = premodernity = other-worldliness' and 'science = modernity = Western'. He writes:

> If there is ever to be a truly integral psychology (or any sort of integral studies), this extraordinary rupture between premodernity and modernity—spiritual and material—needs to be confronted head on. Although there is a slow movement in the modern and postmodern world to reintroduce some sort of spirituality, nonetheless the "official" and most widespread worldview of the modern West is that of scientific materialism. ...we cannot have an integral view of the levels of consciousness if modernity and modern science denies the existence of most of them. "Integral" means, if it means anything, the integration of all that is given to humanity; and if modernity insists instead on trashing everything that came before it, then the integral enterprise is derailed from the start.[38]

Although this is a fair representation of a schism in Western history, the analysis cannot be applied to all civilizations. Sri Aurobindo has critiqued the other-worldliness of some Indian spiritual traditions such as Advaita Vedānta and Buddhism. He shows how Indian spirituality is this-worldly by bridging the gap between the Transcendent and the Immanent. He integrates the distinct spiritual experiences of Passive and Active Brahman and recovers the *Upaniṣad*-ic truth of 'All is Brahman' or *sarvam khalvidam brahma*, combining Vedānta and Tantra.[39] The spiritual goal of Vedānta and Tantra is liberation in Brahman, and they are not in mutual opposition. This is unlike monotheism's dichotomy between sacred and profane or God and World.

While premodern-modern refers to historical European periods with violent conflicts between their forces, in the Indian context, Sri Aurobindo explains how the Matter-Spirit aspects are complementary:

> In the cosmic consciousness [there is] a meeting-place where Matter becomes real to Spirit, Spirit becomes real to Matter.... Matter reveals itself to the realising thought and to the subtilised senses as the figure and body of Spirit,—Spirit in its self-formative extension. Spirit reveals itself through the same consenting agents as the soul, the truth, the essence of Matter. Both admit and confess each other as divine, real and essentially one.[40]

To solve this Western problem, Wilber borrows the Indian integration of the Transcendent and the Immanent without acknowledgment. He credits the concept to Charles Hartshorne, who had spent many decades in the early- and mid-twentieth century to bring to the West the philosophy of Transcendent-Immanent integration. He called this philosophy panentheism, which is how it is widely known in the West.

Panentheism, a combination and an integration of Transcendence and Immanence is a term coined by Hartshorne after borrowing the same from the work of his Indian doctoral student, Mahanambrata Brahmachari (1904-99). Brahmachari was a follower of Śrī Jīva Goswāmi, and his dissertation (*The Philosophy of Sri Jiva Goswami*) focused on the same. Śrī Jīva Goswāmi is an exemplar of panentheism.

Wilber furthers the typical model of the West – appropriating a key central idea from India, denying credit for the same to Indians, and further accusing India of not having the idea in the first place, and thereby presenting his appropriated ideas as the solution. Wilber credits Charles Hartshorne but not the Indian works that served as the basis for it.

Worldly and other-worldly are not binaries in Indian thought, but they are for Wilber. In his system, other-worldly equals premodern, and worldly equates with modern, and one supersedes, rejects and replaces the other. In the Indian system, the Transcendence, which Wilber would call other-worldly, without Immanence, is māyāvāda. This system looks at the world as an illusion, and the only reality is the other-worldly Transcendence. By boxing Ādi Śaṅkara as māyāvādin and the entire

Indian philosophy with māyāvāda, Wilber uses a sleight of hand to brand all Indian philosophy as one which is Transcendent but without Immanence.

Wilber's portrayal is manifestly false, for India has both nirguṇa Brahman and saguṇa Brahman. Prakṛti and puruṣa of the Sāṃkhyā philosophy expressly consider the relationship between man and nature and study its various manifestations. Wilber refers to the pair as Nirvāṇa and Saṃsāra, Heaven and Earth, Ascent and Descent, and patriarchal other-worldly religions and matriarchal this-worldly neo-pagan traditions. To relocate this into the lineage of Western thinkers, he cites the work of Arthur Lovejoy to show that this-worldly and other-worldly trends were in harmony in the thoughts of Plato and Plotinus,[41] and connects these ideas increasingly to Western sources such as Gottfried Leibniz and Friedrich Schelling.[42]

### *Arthur Lovejoy: the major link in Wilber's U-Turn*

A major link in Wilber's analysis of Transcendence and Immanence is Arthur Lovejoy. The Great Chain of Being, used by Wilber innumerable times in his Wilber-II stage had, at that point in time, not once been linked with Lovejoy. He is also not mentioned in *Eye to Eye*—a Wilber-III book. These were the stages when Wilber had used the Great Chain of Being idea to the hilt, as it was the skeleton on which he could graft various psychological and anthropological theories.

In Wilber-IV, he discovered the heart of the work of Lovejoy and mapped the idea of harmony between this-worldly and other-worldly binaries to the Greeks, for it was Lovejoy who proposed that the theory of continuity and gradation of Aristotle gave rise to the Great Chain of Being, which became particularly more sophisticated in the writings of Plotinus. The locus of this fundamental idea of bridging the Transcendent and the Immanent could now successfully be moved to the Western world.

In his book, *The Great Chain of Being: A Study of the History of an Idea*, Lovejoy argues the following regarding the Greek philosophers:

1. Contrary to the widespread notion, Plato is not an other-worldly philosopher. Despite not widely acknowledged, the emphasis on this world is strong in Plato, for the transcendental

god is the cause and the support of the terrestrial existence.

2. The balance between One and Many, and this world and other world is skewed in Aristotle as there are paradoxical emphasis in his writings: his philosophy is more this-worldly than Plato's, and at the same time, Aristotle's God is much more aloof and less involved in the world. Aristotle's God cannot explain the basis of the Many or the diversity found in this world—Lovejoy calls this the theory of plentitude.
3. It was in Plotinus that the 'Great Chain of Being' idea finds its maximum expression, when the Aristotelian theory of continuity got fused with the Platonian theory of plentitude—the idea that the ultimate Good or God gives rise to everything in the universe. A mere translation of that idea meant that the God as the highest existent was linked to the lowest in manifestation through a chain.

Lovejoy's writings enabled crucial actions for Wilber in his Wilber-IV phase; the first contention of Lovejoy regarding Plato helped Wilber show that in the ancient Western worldview, spirituality was integral and used Plato as the revised starting point for his integral vision.

The second point helps Wilber assert that it was in the writings of Aristotle that the balance between Ascent and Descent, One and Many, and Transcendent and Immanent, was upset. Aristotle's philosophy skewed the Greek world towards other-worldliness as his God generated nothing.

Further, Lovejoy's treatment of St. Augustine enabled Wilber to assert that it was St. Augustine who tilted the Western world in favor of other-worldliness for the second time—the first time by Aristotle.

The Great Chain of Being, during the Middle Ages and early modern period, was a static model, i.e. it came into existence by the design of God on a single occasion and stayed fixed without any evolution through the ages. This was mainly because of the dominant ideas of creationism or emanationism, both of which Christian Europe believed firmly. This conception changed with the thoughts of the German philosopher Gottfried Leibniz (eighteenth century), who argued that the 'Chain of Being must be construed as a process in which all forms are gradually realized in the order of time',[43] thus making the Great Chain of Being temporal. This was one of the first steps to introduce the idea of evolution in the Chain of Being in European history.

A decade later, Kant propounded the theory of cosmic evolution. With the Chain of Being temporalized, according to Lovejoy, God was not the cause of the universe but was the summit of the Great Chain of Being yet to emerge.

These different ideas found a comprehensive treatment in Schelling, according to whom there is the Transcendental God that is complete in itself, perfect, and which does not need anything for its existence; however, there is also a terrestrial God that evolves from its lower manifestation. These two Gods are not reconciled; they are not the one and the same God. He is not the Transcendental God who manifests himself in creation and rediscovers himself through evolution. There is a conflict in his writings regarding the Transcendent as well as Immanent God that is not resolved. Schelling's ideas on Transcendent and Immanent God exist side by side.

Wilber makes complete use of this entire history of the idea. He claims to have resolved the conflict in Schelling regarding the Transcendent and Immanent, and the One and the Many, as if to say that Schelling completely understood the process of involution through which the Transcendental Divine becomes involuted matter and then starts its evolutionary process to rediscover itself, developing through the levels or grades of Life, Mind, Higher Mind, and so on.

Since Schelling is considered a link between Fitze and Hegel, Wilber can now map the entire involution-evolution vision of Sri Aurobindo to the Romantics and spiritualize the Darwinian and materialistic evolution. Further, he distorts and misrepresents Sri Aurobindo's model to claim false equivalences with the Chain of Being as seen in Plotinus' work, including using the wrong nomenclature of Sri Aurobindo's model. We see in the next chapter how Wilber reduces Sri Aurobindo to a mere dot in one of his quadrants of AQAL and even claims to have superseded him, while in reality, having massively appropriated the structure and morphology of key concepts such as Immanence-Transcendence, Ascent-Integration and the process of evolution.

Over time, the evolution of the two core streams of this-worldly and other-worldly in Europe saw a history of one thousand years of one dominating the other and vice versa. The split of medieval Europe that

Lovejoy wrote of in his works becomes the conflict for Wilber (copying Sri Aurobindo) to reconcile, harmonize, and integrate. Instead of understanding what Sri Aurobindo had already written on this subject in *The Life Divine* and understanding the philosophical, metaphysical, and methodological approach adopted by Sri Aurobindo to reconcile and integrate the two opposing approaches to human existence, Wilber completely ignores it. By using the thesis of Lovejoy, Wilber could replace Sri Aurobindo's connection and continue with his approach of giving to the West an original lens of viewing an integrated world.

Wilber now does not need to refer to the *Veda*-s or Sri Aurobindo or Swami Vivekananda; the Western world itself could suffice for the promulgation of his integral worldview, of which the Great Chain of Being is a crucial component. Lovejoy's further contention that the Great Chain of Being idea remained alive even during the Middle Ages and up to the nineteenth century helps Wilber assert himself as an original Western thinker, furthering an original Western idea, which had an unmitigated continuity since the Greeks. By selectively reproducing Sri Aurobindo when necessary, Wilber aims to integrate the subjective and objective but names it as an integration of the best of premodernity, modernity, and postmodernity.

As he came to Wilber-IV stage, he kept mining *The Life Divine* for more ideas and the evolutionary morphology of Sri Aurobindo was repackaged as Twenty Tenets and his integral vision with modifications as the Integral AQAL model. The ideas of Ascent and Descent, the intricate balance between the play of the One and the Many, and the Transcendent and Immanent Divine were absorbed by Wilber into his vision without acknowledgment.

He completely discards Sri Aurobindo's view that the Spirit and Matter were not in opposition but two facets of one integral whole. Sri Aurobindo had a clear understanding of the problems faced by the modern West, and while lauding its achievements he also suggested the need to integrate its physically-oriented life with spirituality. He advocated reconciling spirit and matter, spirituality and science, philosophy and practical life, arts and spirituality, sacred and profane, etc. He wrote:

> Western civilisation is proud of its successful modernism. But there is much that it has lost in the eagerness of its gains and much which men of old strove towards that it has not even attempted to accomplish. There is much too that it has wilfully flung aside in impatience or scorn to its own great loss, to the injury of its life, to the imperfection of its culture.... But an unbiassed (sic) view will prefer to regard this age of civilisation as an evolutionary stage, an imperfect but important turn of the human advance. It is then possible to see that great gains have been made which are of the utmost value to an ultimate perfection, even if they have been made at a great price. There is...a greater generalisation of knowledge and more thorough use of intellectual power and activity in multiple fields. There is...the advance of Science and its application to the conquest of our environment, an immense apparatus of means, vast utilisations, endless minute conveniences, an irresistible machinery, a tireless exploitation of forces.... Much has been diminished or lost, but it can be recovered, eventually, if not with ease. Once restored to its true movement, the inner life of man will find that it has gained in materials, in power of plasticity, in a new kind of depth and wideness. And we shall have acquired a salutary habit of many-sided thoroughness and a sincere endeavour to shape the outer collective life into an adequate image of our highest ideals. Temporary diminutions will not count before the greater inner expansion that is likely to succeed this age of external turmoil and outward-looking endeavour.[44]

Sri Aurobindo wrote that there was always the material and pragmatic side alongwith the aspiration for Transcendence and that India would, in its post-British era, once again integrate and balance these like before. Furthermore, in *The Life Divine* he critiques Buddhism and Ādi Śaṅkarācārya's māyāvāda for their other-worldly emphasis, though never invalidating their spiritual experiences. He agrees that Buddhism and Ādi Śaṅkarācārya's Advaita had the other-worldly strain and that there was a minority tendency towards asceticism prior to them, but emphasizes that these are not the whole of Indian existence. His writings are conveniently ignored by most Westerners, especially those who rely upon a second-hand study of Indian civilization.

## Sri Aurobindo's Rebuttal of Other-worldly Stereotypes of India

The other-worldly discourse has been conclusively refuted by Sri Aurobindo in *The Foundations of Indian Culture,* later retitled *The Renaissance in India*. He wrote it in response to a book by a Western journalist, William Archer, that was teeming with European stereotypes of India being other-worldly.

Sri Aurobindo wrote that the *Veda*-s and the *Upaniṣad*-s are life-affirming, encouraging and showing the way towards a higher plane of this-worldly fulfillment:

> The European critic very ordinarily labours under the idea that this exaggeration in the direction of negating life was actually the whole of Indian thought and sentiment or the one undisputed governing idea of the culture. Nothing could be more false and inaccurate. The early Vedic religion did not deny, but laid a full emphasis on life. The Upanishads did not deny life, but held that the world is a manifestation of the Eternal, of Brahman, all here is Brahman, all is in the Spirit and the Spirit is in all, the self-existent Spirit has become all these things and creatures; life too is Brahman, the life-force is the very basis of our existence, the life-spirit Vayu is the manifest and evident Eternal, *pratyaksham brahma*. But it affirmed that the present way of existence of man is not the highest or the whole; his outward mind and life are not all his being; to be fulfilled and perfect he has to grow out of his physical and mental ignorance into spiritual self-knowledge.[45]

In *The Life Divine* Sri Aurobindo considers the age-old questions of man's relationship with the world around him as well as to the one within, the relationship between the Universe and the Infinite Beyond. He writes extensively on the materialist on one hand and the ascetic on the other. While the former negates the Spirit and the latter refuses Matter and sees its world as that of an illusion, what we need for harmony must transcend both, he says.

He observes that until the advent of Buddhism, the old Vedic mind had found harmony among the Vedic and *Upaniṣad*-ic central conceptions. With the rise of Buddhism, the negation of the world occupied a higher priority. Buddhism was primarily taught as a pragmatic method of achieving nirvāṇa.

> His [i.e. Buddha's] explanation of things was psychological and not metaphysical and his methods were all psychological, the breaking of the false association of consciousness which causes the continuance of desire and suffering, so getting rid of the stream of birth and death in a purely phenomenal [not real] world; the psychological method, the eight fold path developing right understanding and right action. His objects was pragmatic and severely practical and so were his methods; metaphysical speculations would only draw the mind away from the one thing needful.[46]

The fundamental differences between the positivist Vedic and the illusionist māyāvādin's templates lie where the mind stops in its quest for the Ultimate Reality. The highest conception of the mind – sat-cit-ānanda – was not only an intellectual pinnacle conceived through jñāna (knowledge) but also experienced as the ultimate expression of consciousness. The seers, however, did not stop there and went beyond to even the asat – non-being, remarks Sri Aurobindo. The *Upaniṣad*-s contain profound and remarkable insights into the unity of the Ultimate Consciousness and the multiplicity in which it manifests. While the ascetic may consider the pursuit of the ultimate unity as the main goal, the rejection of the multiplicity (worldly manifestation) as false and illusory only amounts to creating a block out of knowledge itself, says the sage. Thus, the dhārmic systems have both as central elements.

Sri Aurobindo not only moved past the māyāvādin conceptions but also highlighted the significant role played by Tantra as an attempt at a synthesis of yogic processes and profound spiritual transformation. He writes:

> Tantric discipline is in its nature a synthesis. It has seized on the large universal truth that there are two poles of being whose essential unity is the secret of existence, Brahman and Shakti, Spirit and Nature, and that Nature is power of the spirit or rather is spirit as power. To raise nature in man into manifest power of spirit is

> its method and it is the whole nature that it gathers up for the spiritual conversion.[47]

He highlights that Tantra works on many aspects that are especially worldly, such as human desires and actions, and brings to them balance, power and discipline. Tantra makes these worldly actions agents of spiritual ascension, with increasing purity becoming their feature. *Mukti* (liberation) and *bhukti* (enjoyment) have been equally important in Tantra since its inception. It is manifestly wrong to claim that Eastern spiritual traditions, especially the Indian, were world-negating, for that claim has set aside an entire profound and important approach to Indian spirituality.

## Integral Psychology from Sri Aurobindo's Lens

Sri Aurobindo's Integral Psychology is based on first-hand, and direct experience of the hidden layers of consciousness, including the occult and the subtle realms of human existence not visible to the ordinary human eye—*pratyakṣa pramāṇa* as the Vedāntic tradition describes it. It comes from beyond the mental and intellectual realms through the purification of mind and body by transcending logical and intellectual thought and stilling the mind within from all internal and external chaos and flux so that the knowledge of the subtle and the invisible becomes known. Indian traditions refer to this vision as the 'third eye'. Sri Aurobindo, based on years of intense sādhana, writes:

> Fundamentally, it [knowledge of the supra-intellectual] is not an expression of ideas arrived at by speculative thinking. One has to arrive at spiritual knowledge through experience and a consciousness of things which arises directly out of that experience or else underlies or is involved in it. This kind of knowledge, ... is fundamentally a consciousness and not a thought or formulated idea. ... my first experience...came after and by the exclusion and silencing of all thought—there was, first, what might be called a spiritually substantial or concrete consciousness of stillness and silence, then the awareness of some sole and supreme Reality in whose presence things existed only as forms but forms not at all

> substantial or real or concrete; but this was all apparent to a spiritual perception and essential and impersonal sense and there was not the least concept or idea of reality or unreality or any other notion, for all concept or idea was hushed or rather entirely absent in the absolute stillness. These things were known directly through the pure consciousness and not through the mind, so there was no need of concepts or words or names.[48]

Wilber himself claims to be a mere scholar of texts, i.e. he lacks the kind of experience described by Sri Aurobindo. He seems to have had intermittent experiences of witness consciousness in waking, dreaming, and deep sleep, which are preliminary steps in gaining a mystical knowledge of the world. *Thus, for Wilber, Integral Psychology is literally the intellectual study of consciousness, whereas for Sri Aurobindo it is directly experiencing and knowing consciousness as a concrete reality.*

Sri Aurobindo writes:

> **Direct and experiential and experimental psychology seems to be demanded if psychology is to be a science and not merely a mass of elementary and superficial generalizations with all the rest guesswork or uncertain conclusions or inference. We must see, feel, know directly what we observe; our interpretations must be capable of being sure and indubitable; we must be able to work surely on a ground of sure knowledge.**[49]

An intense spiritual practice of yoga becomes the method through which the knowledge of consciousness and its mode of operation is gained. Sri Aurobindo further elucidates:

> **It is only by Yoga process that one can arrive at an instrumentation which will drive large wide roads into the psychological Unknown and not only obscure and narrow tunnels. The field of psychology needs a direct inner psychological instrumentation by which we can arrive at sure data and sure results in ourselves verified [by] equally sure data [and] results in our observation of others and of the hidden psychological world and its play of unseen forces.** The physical is the outwardly seen and sensed and needs physical instruments for its exploration; the psychological is the physically

> unseen and unsensed, to be discovered only by an organisation of the inward senses and other now undeveloped and occult means. It is through consciousness, by an instrumentation of consciousness only that the nature and laws and movements of consciousness can be discovered—and this is the method of Yoga.[50]

The vast body of Western psychology has emerged from the methodology of physical sciences to observe, classify, and formulate laws. This methodology may suffice for concrete physical entities, but the instrumentation required for observing and studying the abstract cognitive processes is different. The Indian tradition is unanimous in stating that behind gross instruments (indriya-s) are subtle ones that provide knowledge of the invisible and the abstract. Those subtle or sūkṣma indriya-s have a wider capacity to study the laws of human behavior. A genuine yogi, because of the intensity and time invested in the purification of his gross and subtle levels, can comprehend the operative forces crucial to psychological laws. Western psychology has yet to find the right instrument for exploration of the internal human universe. Identifying that the basis of human behavior lies much deeper in the realm of consciousness and nothing much can be achieved merely by the outer aspects, Sri Aurobindo explains:

> Psychology is the science of consciousness and its status and operations in Nature and, if that can be glimpsed or experienced, its status and operations beyond what we know as Nature. It is not enough to observe and know the movements of our surface nature and the superficial nature of other living creatures just as it [is] not enough for Science to observe and know as electricity only the movements of lightning in the clouds or for the astronomer to observe and know only those movements and properties of the stars that are visible to the unaided eyes. Here as there a whole world of occult phenomena have to be laid bare and brought under control before the psychologist can hope to be master of his province. Our observable consciousness, that which we call ourselves, is only the little visible part of our being. It is a small field below which there are depths and farther depths and widths and ever wider widths which support and supply it but to which it has no visible access. All that is our self, our being, - what we see at the top is only our

> ego and its visible nature. Even the movements of this little surface nature cannot be understood nor its true law discovered until we know all that is below or behind and supplies it – and know too all that is around is and above.[51]

The limitations of a psychoanalytic approach were quite apparent to Sri Aurobindo, who categorically stated that only by knowing the whole can one know the parts and that any knowledge gained by only the lower planes cannot explain human behavior; for the secrets of human existence lie in supernal planes. Psychoanalysis cannot become a knowledge system, not only because it is partial in its approach but also because of the lack of proper methodology used:

> This new psychology [psychanalysis] looks to me very much like children learning some summary and not very adequate alphabet, exulting in putting their a-b-c-d of the subconscient and the mysterious underground super-ego together and imagining that their first book of obscure beginnings (c-a-t cat, t-r-e-e tree) is the very heart of the real knowledge. **They look from down up and explain the higher lights by the lower obscurities; but the foundation of these things is above and not below, *upari budhna esham.* The superconscient, not the subconscient, is the true foundation of things.** The significance of the lotus is not to be found by analysing the secrets of the mud from which it grows here; its secret is to be found in the heavenly archetype of the lotus that blooms for ever in the Light above. The self-chosen field of these psychologists is besides poor, dark and limited; you must know the whole before you can know the part and the highest before you can truly understand the lowest. That is the promise of the greater psychology awaiting its hour before which these poor gropings will disappear and come to nothing.[52]

Integral vision and theorizing require much more than mental gymnastics and reading spiritual accounts of mystics and integrating them with various schools of Western psychology. The planes of consciousness in Integral Psychology need to be discovered through inquiry into the nature of phenomena and things. This requires yogic development, which involves direct and intuitive experience into the very core of all aspects of Matter-Life-Mind-Spirit. Wilber needs to match the sage in the development of his consciousness and engage with his writings honestly and faithfully, address his arguments in a cogent manner, refute them with sound arguments wherever he disagrees, and systematically demonstrate before experts (who are not his personal fans) on how he surpasses Sri Aurobindo.

Furthermore, the accounts of postmodern psychologists who have shown that the claims of Western psychology are culturally restrictive have been dismissed too expeditiously as self-refuting. Wilber quickly dismisses the prodigious relevance of the postmodern critique to revive the modernist paradigm of objective knowledge, thereby contradicting his own claims of integrating the 'best of premodernity, modernity, and postmodernity'.

Chapter 12

# The Indian Influences on Arthur Koestler's Holons and Their Impact on Wilber-IV

## Indic Concepts in Arthur Koestler's Writings

In this chapter, we map the Hungarian author and journalist Arthur Koestler's concept of holons, their use by Wilber and show the Indian basis at the heart of this important framework.

Arthur Koestler has been hailed as one of the most brilliant writers in politics and science. His focus included Jean-Baptiste Lamarck's (French naturalist) theory of evolution, quantum theories of matter and nature, esoteric concepts such as extrasensory perceptions, Eastern spiritual teachings, and even levitation. His writings include *The Sleepwalkers: A History of Man's Changing Vision of the Universe* (1959); *The Ghost in the Machine* (1967); and *The Case of the Midwife Toad* (1971). The *Lotus and the Robot* (1960) is often treated as Koestler's seminal book on India, based on his travels. His works reveal his familiarity and knowledge of several quintessential Indian concepts.[1]

The Indian concept of a yogi is first seen in Koestler's 1945 work, *The Yogi and the Commissar and Other Essays*. Written in three parts, Koestler pits the commissar, driven by materialism and scientism, against the yogi, with the latter's worldviews characterized by extreme spiritual and metaphysical thinking. Koestler uses the term yogi from a colonial perspective; he paints the yogi as a paradigm of absolute non-violence.

Koestler perpetuates the notion that India was not concerned with external development and says the tide of human attitudes oscillates from the commissar to the yogi.

> On the other end of the spectrum, where the waves become so short and of such high-frequency that the eye no longer sees them, colourless, warmthless but all-penetrating, crouches the Yogi, melting away in the ultra-violet. He has no objection to calling the universe a clockwork, but he thinks that it could be called, with about the same amount of truth, a musical-box or a fishpond. He believes that the End is unpredictable and that the Means alone count. He rejects violence under any circumstances. He believes that logical reasoning gradually loses its compass value as the mind approaches the magnetic pole of Truth or the Absolute, which alone matters. He believes that nothing can be improved by exterior organization and everything by the individual effort from within; and that whosoever believes in anything else is an escapist. He believes that the debt-servitude imposed upon the peasants of India by the moneylenders should not be abolished by financial legislation but by spiritual means.[2]
>
> **In the post-pink or yogi decade the irrational dimension takes its revenge by outgrowing all others.**[3]

Not only does Koestler use broad brushstrokes to paint the yogi as a world renouncer, but he also defines yogi ethics as the following:

> **'Yogi-ethics' is the attempt to transfer the values derived from passive contemplation into practical action.** This is not an impossible undertaking, but extremely difficult. The Contemplative focuses his attention on the vertical aspect of the staircase and is apt to neglect the intricate factual relations on the horizontal planes. **This leads to a naive, amateurish, and often crankish; approach to social problems. Such dilettantism is fraught with dangers: the most obvious among them is the danger of quietism, escapism, of sinning by omission.**[4]

Koestler's knowledge of Indian works includes that of the fifteenth century yogi Svātmārāma, and the author of *Haṭha Yoga Pradīpikā*:

> **The Vedanta bores me to death** and Tao doesn't mean a thing to me. 'The practiser of Hathayoga', Swatmaram Sami informs me, 'should live alone in a small hermit-age or monastery situated in a place free from rocks, water and fire; of the extent of a bow's length and in a fertile country ruled over by a virtuous king where he will not be disturbed.' Think of the bus-driver.[5]

The next work of Koestler that clearly demonstrates his knowledge of Indian concepts is his 1949 *Insight and Outlook: An Inquiry into the Common Foundations of Science, Art and Social Ethics*. Koestler remarks that the earliest societies were pre-animistic and lived in 'a state of original self-transcendence of consciousness'. He believes Indians belonged to such a society and formulated the highest expression of consciousness through the concept of Ātman.[6]

It becomes clear that Koestler is intimately aware of:

1. The way Eastern traditions, in this case dhārmic, view the evolution of consciousness from the individual to the collective and the relationship between the two.
2. The dhārmic concepts of self-transcendence and cosmic consciousness.

He further writes in the same book that Indian mystics embody extreme forms of self-transcendence, in contrast to Western approaches:

> Some of the more extreme forms of visceral behaviour in self-transcending emotions have been observed in Indian mystics, but on the whole the symptomatology of the self-transcending emotions is still in its infancy; and their study is not made easier by the fact that in situations which lead to pronounced stress usually both basic tendencies are aroused, so that the resulting emotion reflects a blend or oscillatory cycle between two antagonistic reaction patterns.[7]

Koestler further writes that while basic survival instincts and emotions such as rage and fear dominate the psychology of Western civilizations, Eastern approaches look at self-transcendence as the summum bonum of existence. Even through such a clear understanding of Indian goals, Koestler continues to highlight only the extreme form of this philosophy and ignores everything else to paint a picture of Indians as pursuing only the heavens and ignoring earthly mastery and Westerners as seeking scientific development. How convenient it must be to forget the squalor most of Europe lived in until the twentieth century and its torturous relationship with science throughout much of its history.[8]

The progression in Koestler's work, from the domains of politics to science, is reflected in his works of the 1950s. While there is no explicit reference to any Indian works in his 1959 book *The Sleepwalkers*, Koestler refers to Werner Heisenberg and Erwin Schrödinger, both pioneers of quantum physics, without mentioning the deep influence of the *Upaniṣad*-s and the *Gītā* on them despite their own admission.[9]

Koestler also cites Alfred North Whitehead extensively throughout the book and refers to the latter's *Science and the Modern World*. The dependence on previous digesters such as Whitehead is only strengthened when one sees Koestler tracing everything to Greek sources: 'Professor Whitehead's famous remark: "the safest general characterization of the European philosophical tradition is that it consists in a series of footnotes to Plato" could be amended by: "Science, up to the Renaissance, consisted in a series of footnotes to Aristotle"'.[10]

A book by Koestler that focuses solely on the East is *The Lotus and the Robot*, published in 1961. His 1964 work, *The Act of Creation*, further demonstrates not only his bias but also his deep engagement with terms such as māyā, even from a linguistic perspective.[11]

The *Lotus and the Robot* not only documents Koestler's impressions about the squalor and terrible living conditions that he found in India but also the range of references in traditional Indian texts on yoga and the *Upaniṣad*-s. It also reveals his knowledge of Sri Aurobindo, as seen on page 36 of his book.

His extensive knowledge of Indian concepts is also seen in his biography (*Koestler: The Literary and Political Odyssey of a Twentieth Century Skeptic*) by Michael Schammel and in Koestler's contemporary Walter Terence Stace's 1961 book, *Mysticism and Philosophy*.[12] An important reference in Schammel's work, which contains extracts from Koestler's diary, demonstrates the latter's explicit belief that the cognitive processes of Easterners and Westerners diverge and that he did not believe in blanket perennialism.[13]

Stace recounts in his book Koestler's experiences in terms of *Upaniṣad*-ic knowledge, and also includes a conversation with Koestler. Stace is also aware of the teachings of the *Upaniṣad*-s and the Sāṃkhyā philosophy, and traces the Eastern roots and approaches to mysticism.[14]

Stace considers Koestler's experiences when he was imprisoned during the Spanish Civil War (1936-9) and placed in solitary confinement. Stace looks at this experience from the standpoint of mysticism.[15] In his interview, he refers to the descriptions in the *Upaniṣad*-s for such altered states. The exchange demonstrates Koestler's awareness of these extra-sensory experiences, and their explanations in light of the *Upaniṣad*-s.

> ... In the full-blown classical cases of introvertive experience, what we have is a total void, an undifferentiated unity in which, as **the Mandukya Upanishad expresses it, all "awareness of the world and of multiplicity are completely obliterated."** One phase of this total blotting out of all distinctions is the blotting out of the distinction between the "I" and the infinite unity in which it is sunk or merged. This phase is what Tennyson and Koestler report, but they do not report the total disappearance of *all* distinctions. For this reason their experiences would seem to be incomplete or partially developed introvertive experiences.
>
> Mr. Koestler has been kind enough to answer some questions which I addressed to him with a view to verifying this. They were as follows:
>
> Q. Am I right in supposing that during the experiences your physical senses were still in operation, so that you continued to perceive the various physical objects around you, the walls, window, objects outside the window, etc.?
> A. Yes.
>
> Q. Did they become dim or fuzzy at the edges?
> A. No. But they were just there in the margin of attention, but unattended to.
>
> Q. One of the Upanishads says: "It is pure unitary experience wherein awareness of the world and of multiplicity is completely obliterated." Have you had any experience like this? **Do you think that when the Upanishad speaks of the awareness**

> **of multiplicity being *"completely* obliterated" it is perhaps exaggerating?**
> A. No, I did not experience that. That must be a higher degree. But **somehow I believe that the experience exists and that its description is not exaggerated.**
> It will be seen that I am following Mr. Koestler in regarding his experience as not of a different type from the classical cases, but as an incomplete, or lower degree of it.[16]

## Holons and Open Hierarchical Systems Mapped from Indian Sources

### *Holarchy through a Vedic lens*

We now discuss holons, an important concept by Koestler, which features significantly in Wilber's writings from this stage onwards. Holons are wholes that are part of larger wholes. In this section, we understand the fundamental conceptions of Vedic thought vis-a-vis the features of Open Hierarchical Systems (OHS). Several diverse disciplines, including management studies, business administration, supply chain systems, economics, and engineering have been mapped into the language of holonic systems and networks.

Koestler, while introducing the word holon for the first time in his landmark work *The Ghost in the Machine*, begins with the following:

> This concept has a long and respectable ancestry. So much so that defenders of orthodoxy are inclined to dismiss it as "old hat" - and often in the same breath to deny its validity. Yet I hope to show as we go along that this old hat, handled with some affection, can produce lively rabbits.[17]

The precursor to understanding holonic systems is the concept of atomicity as a philosophy, which traces its roots to pre-Socratic Greece, when it became the primary Western paradigm to study the observed universe. The roots of using hierarchy as a method can be traced to the Greeks, in particular, Aristotle. The debate between wholism and atomism began in the twentieth century through the 1926 work of Jan Christiaan Smuts – *Holism and Evolution,* and Koestler's *The Ghost in the Machine*. Smuts, a South African statesman, wrote, 'the tendency in nature to form wholes that are greater than the sum of the parts through creative evolution'. While mechanism is the characteristic feature of atomism/reductionist view of matter, wholism has been the paradigm through which evolution has been studied in the West.

Koestler's writings on the subject began with his work on evolutionary theories, even as he had followed and written extensively on the preceding quantum revolution, especially the writings of Schrödinger and Heisenberg. As Koestler wrote through the decades of intense debate between Darwinism and Lamarckism, one can chronologically trace the primary issues he sought to address:

1. There was a need to reconcile the reductionist view of hard sciences with the views of Freudian and other psychologies. The hard sciences had successfully questioned Newtonian mechanics, and a new quantum revolution was forcing the West to look at the universe in a different way.
2. There was a need for a theoretical framework to apply recent results in evolutionary studies to the social sciences.
3. Koestler sought to examine reality through the different lenses that had dominated the West's ideas of physics and biology and focused on the relationship between the whole and the part.

Koestler coined the term holon to describe entities that straddled both the whole and the part; thus, holons are not objects themselves but a way of looking at entities. The observed Universe is a hierarchy of holons, i.e. a holarchy, where each holon is a node and is 'nested' or contained in a larger holon. Each holon is a part of the structure, operation, and mechanism of its superordinate one, even as it produces effects in its subordinate holons. Holarchy thus describes the relationship between self-contained and complete wholes and sub-parts that are dependent on others. With the possibility of infinite nested structures, the hierarchy of holons is open-ended. In Koestler's words:

> Parts and wholes in an absolute sense do not exist in the domain of life [...] The organism is to be regarded as a multi-levelled hierarchy of semi-autonomous sub-wholes, branching into sub-wholes of a lower order, and so on. **Sub-wholes on any level of the hierarchy**

> **are referred to as *holons*.** Biological holons are self-regulating open systems which display both the autonomous properties of wholes and the dependent properties of parts. This dichotomy is present on every level of every type of hierarchic organization, and is referred to as the Janus Effect [...] The concept of holon is intended to reconcile the atomistic and holistic approaches.[18]

Koestler's work has served as a bridge between wholism and atomism. The latter especially, has been the primary means of study of the material world in the West. Reductionism is the tool through which each part of a whole is brought into focus, and studied for its properties in isolation from its larger group. For instance, modern medicine typically treats an ailment by focusing exclusively on the pain point. By describing Reality this way, the Western lens arrives at the larger whole in a synthetic manner – individual parts, recursively connected with larger structures and mechanistic causality binding them.

Classical science relies on natural laws to frame theories of observable phenomena; this paradigm does not satisfactorily address the most complex questions of consciousness. It does not include the possibility of a meta and unified origin for both consciousness and complex phenomena such as evolution, quantum physics, and relativistic models. As the whole system is not under study, even the organization of the parts and their relation to each other and the whole is not the focus of classical studies. Quantum physics and evolutionary theories especially, have been points where the inherent inadequacy of Western science and its basic metaphysics have failed. In the words of theoretical physicist David Bohm:

> The prevailing tendency in science to think and perceive in terms of a fragmentary self-worldview is part of a larger movement that has been developing over the ages and that pervades almost the whole of our society today ... it gives [people] a picture of the whole world as constituted of nothing but an aggregate of separately existing "atomic building blocks," and provides experimental evidence ... that this view is necessary and inevitable. ...people are led to feel that fragmentation is nothing but an expression of "the way everything really is" and that anything else is impossible.[19]

Koestler was placed right in the eye of the breakdown that classical science faced in the twentieth century. He sought to present a holonic view, which is neither singularly wholistic nor atomistic. In his hierarchy, each holon is part of a larger whole while containing in itself sub-parts that constitute its form and function in the first place. The holon cannot be reduced to its sub-parts, but has properties that emerge from it in increasing complexity. This model has been the basis for understanding the structure and dynamics of biological and evolutionary systems.

### *Features of holons*

We consider here some of the key properties of Koestler's holons. These include survival and integration i.e. a holon has autonomy and is simultaneously part of a larger dependence. This creates a two-way arrow for influence between the sub- and super-structures. Koestler writes:

> Every holon has the dual tendency to preserve and assert its individuality as a quasi-autonomous whole; and to function as an integrated part of a larger whole. This polarity between the Self-Assertive and Integrative tendencies is inherent in the concept of hierarchic order; a universal characteristic of life.[20]

The above feature of self-preservation in connection with its sub- and super-structures is key to providing a stable form to each holon, even as it is nested in a larger whole. At the same time, the integrative tendency lets the holon be subject to the influence of the larger structure in which it is contained. The superordinate structure can set the behavioral objectives of the subordinate structure, which transmits the results of its activities to the higher level, resulting in emergent properties. The holon thus manifests aspects of both the whole and its parts.

The stability of the holon at each intermediate state of the holarchy is important, especially when one considers evolutionary holons. The emergence of complexity, leading to evolution, takes place faster with stable holons at each level. The stability also leads naturally to the structure of hierarchy. Koestler writes, 'the different levels represent different stages of development, and the holons ... reflect intermediary structures at these stages'.[21]

Koestler also refers to the holon as Janus-faced (the Roman god) because of the property to be able to observe its own interior (nested sub-parts) and exterior (the super-structure in which it is nested) while maintaining autonomy during self-observation.

The holonic paradigm thus provides a description of reality as not something that is made up of structures of interrelated entities, but one that is fundamentally based on relationships between included entities of a super-structure. Holarchy is a vertical structure of increasingly bigger units with increasing complexity and consciousness. The organization of reality in such a way forms the structure of Koestler's Open Hierarchical Systems. In particular, the representation of cognition and evolution as a holarchy, through the holonic principles, titled 'General Properties Of Open Hierarchical Systems (O.H.S.)', is treated in the appendix of *The Ghost in the Machine*. His principles form the basis for social development theory and general evolutionary theory.

Holons can also be perceived as units of information. They are self-similar. Because of these properties, holons provide a framework to understand Nature through relationships between holarchies.

While holarchy is described in terms of a vertical structure of nested holons with open-endedness on both upward and downward sides, holons can also form networks horizontally, with parallel holarchies. There is ability for self-organization at both horizontal and vertical levels, evident in the changes seen in super holons when changes are made in any sub holons. This feature of self-organization is also seen through the mechanism of feedback loops, which help each holonic level to adapt itself to changing levels of cognition.

With such properties, one can consider different types of holons for study, such as biological holons. With increasing complexity, consciousness is considered to emerge at the higher levels of holarchy. This view forms the basis for even Wilber's structure for development of consciousness, which we will see in the next section. Wilber has also been influenced by the work of Smuts on wholism, as seen in *The Atman Project*.

### *Vedic roots of holons*

One of the most significant distinctions between Western and Indian viewpoints is the role played by causality. Western metaphysics and resultant branches of study are firmly rooted in Aristotelian ideas of causality, which seek to answer the 'why' of any phenomenon and is of four types: material, efficient, formal, and final. Material cause refers to the material that makes up the object; formal cause refers to the arrangement or design of the object; efficient cause refers to the agent apart from the object that causes any change in the latter and final cause refers to the eventual purpose for which the object or phenomenon is designed. Consider the simple example of a chair: wood is the material cause of it, its design is the formal cause, the carpenter is the agent who brings in the efficient cause, and the final act for which it is meant, i.e. to be a seat, is the final cause. Western outlook reads a hierarchy in these four aspects, which constitute causality – the final cause is the highest and overarching one.

The Vedic outlook is different and sees causality as not something with a vertical hierarchy but as one which is cyclical. Cyclical causality closes the loop among the four causes.

The above important difference is also intimately tied to mechanism. Western mechanism is inherently dualistic and looks at the world as a machine, i.e. the world is mechanical with conscious observers who perceive the objective phenomena. In Vedic metaphysics, *wholeness and wholism are something transcendental to the system in which causality operates.* Brahman is this transcendental and Ṛta is the cosmic order of wholeness. What is seen as an add-on in the Western paradigm is a fundamental concept of Vedic metaphysics. Schrödinger, while considering the issues that arise from Western thought opined that:

> This is precisely the point where our present way of thinking does need to be amended, perhaps by a bit of blood-transfusion from Eastern thought.[22]

John Jay Kineman, the American scientist, further writes the following on these fundamental lacunae in the Western paradigm, unlike the Indian model which had already moved past these issues:

> This model of cyclical causality corresponds to the ancient meta-model described in the Vedas and Upanishads of India.......In Kantian terms, questions of the "noumenal" origin (existence) of natural systems may be distinguished from their "phenomenal" perception.

**In ancient times the Vedic orientation seems to have placed even mind-body dualism, as later characterized by Descartes, as components of perceived existence, with a common origin in Brahman, an indescribable whole existing simultaneously with and comprising both. In modern thinking we see subjects and objects generally ignoring their possible unity or conflating unity with the subject. But a "whole-part" dichotomy (or more formally 'universals' vs. 'particulars') is incomplete because it proposes only division** (Gare, 2011).

...the reductive/objective view of the material world, and especially its identification with mechanism, led naturally to measurement uncertainty and the requirement for at least two very different formalisms (mathematical structures) to describe natural phenomena. Essentially, we discovered system-dependency.

...modern science is still holding onto the idea that we are conscious observers of a fundamentally mechanical world, arrogating holism to the human intellect. Among systems thinkers this view became known as 'the machine metaphor'.

Mechanisms are by definition pre-established according to precise laws and conserved quantities (substances that can neither be created nor destroyed). Their origin is thus not considered or, if referenced, it is outside the system, as in the "big bang" origin of space and time or the original 'chicken-egg problem'. Such external origins are singularities, or exceptions, in the theoretical reality implied by the mathematical definition of a mechanism. **Mechanism also leads us to obscure our own identity, having no source for cognition. That profound absence creates psychological and social dissonance.** It may be characteristic of this dualistic age in human mental evolution that subjective experience is considered beyond understanding and that we consequently feel unwelcome in nature and without even a path of inquiry into our own existence. In such a disconnected world, internals do not correspond with externals and technological 'solutions' evade the experiential problems. ...**The essence of this problem in modern times is that our way of doing science does not allow it to model the causes of life and related complex phenomena. But the surprising evidence is that our present dualistic age of reason was pre-dated by more**

**holistic understanding in ancient times associated with the Vedas from India, presenting a philosophy and practice of metaphysical holism ("non-duality").**[23]

As the West struggled with the issues that had surfaced from a purely reductionist approach on the one hand and the synthetically developed ideas of wholism on the other, the Vedic model of existence had encountered and moved past the singularities introduced by the West's dualistic approach.

Sanātana dharma, as we have seen earlier in the book, is founded in an integral unity that binds all aspects of matter, life, and mind. An aspect of this integral unity is the idea of totality. The whole is always seen as that which is complete – pūrṇa. This concept of pūrṇa permeates every domain and is visible in its approach to perception. The whole is not a sum or totality of its parts. The Vaiśeṣika philosophy is the approximate equivalent of atomism of the West. Vaiśeṣika-s believed that all matter is reducible to the smallest indivisible entity – the *paramāṇu.* The combinations of the *aṇu*-s due to forces result in various types of objects, qualities, and experiences. Earth, water, fire, air, and manas are treated as being made up of the aṇu-s while space, time, ākaśa, and ātma are treated as *vibhu,* i.e. pervasive substances.

The West has struggled with atomism and wholism to a great extent because of the thematic clash between self and that apart from the self, subjectivism, and objectivism. This conflict forms the basis of much of Western philosophy. While the West sees atomism and wholism as opposites of a polarity, Nyāya–Vaiśeṣika-s recognize the connection between the two: if there is no perception of the parts, there is no perception of the whole.

The dialogue between Yājñavalkya and Maitreyī in the *Bṛhadāraṇyaka Upaniṣad* captures beautifully the existence of the Brahman alone and thus, the interconnectedness and totality of all existence. The precision and clarity in dhārmic tradition regarding totality is seen even in the choice of words – *viśva* (disseminated totality) and *sarva* (unified/integrated totality). The approximate Greek parallel to this is the difference between pan and holon.

Long before the work of Koestler, the composition of the whole and the relationship between it and the parts have been the focus of dhārmic philosophies. The French philosopher Christian Godin writes in *The Notion of Totality of Indian Thought*:

> ... the gift and the sacrifice are not seen as subtractions chipping away at an original totality but as points of radiating energy. (On the contrary, very early in the West the self is defined as an owner of goods and faculties, as an indirect consequence of which sacrifice and the gift are seen as reductions of the whole.) In India, the ascetic *deprives* himself of nothing, even though he *abstains* (from nourishment, from pleasures), yet he *pours out* – that is to say, into the universe from which he is never separated – the energy condensed within him.[24]

Vedic literature contains the term *skanda*, which means aggregate and a whole made up of constituent parts. In Buddhism, skanda refers to five types of aggregates. The *Bṛhadāraṇyaka Upaniṣad*, a text referred to by Koestler in his *The Lotus and the Robot,*[25] speaks about *vyaṣṭi-samaṣṭi prakriya,* i.e. individual and aggregate. Any entity can be individual (*vyaṣṭi*) or made up of smaller aggregates (*samaṣṭi*). Both ways of observing represent the same entity. An illustration of this principle, as found in the *Upaniṣad*, is also seen in Ādi Śaṅkara's *Brahmasūtra:* 'Vāyu is both the distributive pervasion (*'vyaṣṭi'* — aggregate or whole viewed as made up of many separate parts) and the collective pervasion (*samaṣṭi* — an aggregate which is considered as made up of parts, each of which is substantially the same as the whole) and one who knows that conquers death'.[26] The same ideas of nested aggregates make up the whole, as seen in Koestler's work.

Another characteristic feature of Indian metaphysics is the way it treats the individual. Inherent and fundamental indivisibility is the basis for defining the individual in dhārmic paradigms and not separateness.

While understanding totality, India has also sought to understand non-totality. The key concept that is associated with the latter is remainder, and Sāṃkhya philosophy addresses it:

> Experience is a transformation of the indeterminate Prakrti, a transformation that results from Purusa's illumination of Prakrti. Hence experience entails Purusa's bondage — the imprisonment of

> the pure intelligence in blind non intelligent matter. It is Purusa's light that accomplishes the indeterminate Prakrti into a world of experience. The union of Purusa and Prakrti in experience is however incomplete and artificial. The formless Prakrti the indeterminate given manifold cannot be completely transformed into the free unity of thought. Nor can the self-revealing intelligence truly find itself in the shifting forms of non-intelligent Prakrti. The given, the merely real in other words cannot be completely resolved into pure self revealing truth Intelligence is pure self revealing truth and given reality cannot be merged into pure truth without a remainder. Hence arise the contradictions of experience the miseries and sorrows of life the disappointments and baffled hopes that darken mundane existence.[27]

The remainder is not an unconscious and static trace, but the basis for a more conscious experience. The remainder can also be seen as the residue of the feedback system and is intricately tied to the concept of karma.

There exists a hierarchy in Indian metaphysics among concepts that are treated as universals across the entire canon. The highest, and at the top of the hierarchy, is Ultimate Consciousness (sat-cit-ānanda). There is also a hierarchy in the manner in which consciousness is increasingly realized and manifested in matter. Indian metaphysics bases itself on seeming contradictions – Unity and Multiplicity – and each of these manifestations of the same transcendental consciousness is based on a hierarchy.

The *Taittirīya Upaniṣad* speaks of a five-tiered hierarchy of states of being—kośa-s—from the grossest to the subtlest state. While the West thought primarily through Aristotelian and Newtonian cause and effect mechanisms of simple hierarchy, it took the quantum revolution to be the point of breakdown of this simplistic model. Indian metaphysics on the other hand, looks at cause and effect through the lens of tangled hierarchies (where the effect impacts the cause). As there is a feedback loop between the cause and the effect, tangled hierarchies are independent in their unit from the surrounding system. In that sense, they possess autonomy. The autonomous unit, when it becomes a locus of experience and observes the subject-object divide, is called the ego.

## *Features of Koestler's Open Hierarchical Systems and corresponding older Indian concepts*

The āstika schools of Indian philosophy accept the *Veda*-s as valid sources of knowledge and comprise Sāṃkhyā, Yoga, Nyāya, Vaiśeṣika, Mīmāṃsā, and Vedānta. The Nyāya-Vaiśeṣika schools primarily correspond with realism and naturalism/atomism. The latter reduces all physical objects to the indivisible aṇu, while the former focuses on epistemology. It is Sāṃkhyā, which is associated with dualism (puruṣa and prakṛti) and the three guṇa-s of sattva, rajas, and tamas. Yoga is closely linked with Sāṃkhyā, with the same basis in puruṣa and prakṛti. Advaita, Dvaita, and Viśiṣṭādvaita constitute the sub groups of Vedānta.

As we have seen in the previous chapters, Advaita philosophy holds the Brahman as the summum bonum of the cosmos. Brahman is the pure consciousness and is sat-cit-ānanda. The concept of Ānanda is considered the cause and effect of existence, i.e. it is both the efficient and the final cause. Brahman is the material and efficient cause of all manifestation. While Brahman is seen as the infinite universal, Ātman refers to particularity manifested in the individual. Several centuries before the West's discussions on the epistemology of wholism and atomism, the *Upaniṣad*-s have looked at models of cosmogony to understand the relationships between the microcosm and the macrocosm. Advaita philosophy (non-dualism) treats the Brahman as the same as the Ātman, thus presenting all reality as a single unified whole. Apart from Advaita, dualism and qualified monism are other ways to explore the relationships between the macro and the micro.

Vedānta looks at creation as a process of arising from the Brahman and returning to the Brahman, i.e. 'As the spider puts out and gathers in, as herbs spring up upon the earth, as hair of head and body grow from a living man, so here all is born from the Immutable'.[28] In each of these examples, the efficient and the final causes are one and the same, leading to a non-linear connection.

There are major differences between each of the three sub categories – Sāṃkhyā-Yoga, Nyāya-Vaiśeṣika, Mīmāṃsā-Vedānta – in terms of causation, accepted sources of evidence, methodology, and worldviews. This mammoth structure, with diverse and yet related subsets, is what makes Indian philosophical traditions integrally unified and all-encompassing.

The *Chāndogya Upaniṣad*, which Koestler quotes from, is the source of some of the most profound treatment of dualism. Specific to *Chāndogya Upaniṣad* and *Bṛhadāraṇyaka Upaniṣad* (also cited in Koestler's work) is the unique *madhu vidyā*, i.e. everything in the cosmos is related to everything else. The central theme of this vidyā is understanding the interrelatedness between the individual (prāṇa – the life breath that sustains an individual) and the nature (annam) around him. The realities of the individual and cosmic penetrate each other, creating an open-ended honeycomb and honey is the metaphor for this interrelatedness. S. Radhakrishnan translates the *Upaniṣad* verse as the following:

> This earth is honey for all creatures, and all creatures are honey for this earth.
>
> This shining immortal person who is in this earth and with reference to oneself,
>
> This shining, immortal person who is in the body, he indeed, is just this self.
>
> This is immortal, this is Brahman, this is all.[29]

In the succeeding verses, all elements and entities such as the sun, moon, space, and lightning, are described in connection with honey. The various manifestations of the Brahman are all connected to entities through the same principle. The seed is related to water, speech is related to fire, prāṇa is related to air, the eye is related to the sun, and the mind is linked to the moon. To use Koestler's language, each of these microcosms is a holon, existing independently, and asserting individuality, yet retaining the essence of a larger macrocosm. Honey is used as the metaphor to connect them all:

> *Ayam atma sarvesam bhutanam madhu; asyatmanah sarvani bhutani madhu*
>
> (This self is like honey for all beings and all beings are like honey for this self)[30]

The principal *Upaniṣad*-s (we consider only those Koestler refers to) have also been the source for not only Advaita (monism) but also dualism and qualified monism. The latter, Viśiṣṭādvaita, studies the relationship between the world and the Brahman as one between part and whole. The simile used for this relationship is the sea and waves. Brahman is the sea, and the world, both animate and inanimate entities, are like the waves. There are also other similes: when gold transforms into ornaments, it continues to remain gold in the new form; the relationship between clay and clay pots. *The Brahman is thus the material cause (upādāna kāraṇam) and the intelligent (nimitta kāraṇam) cause.*

Unlike Western analysis, hierarchy has never been linear but always cyclical and open-ended, culminating in the highest conceptions of infinity and transcendence. The seventh chapter of *Chāndogya Upaniṣad*, from sections two to twenty-six, presents a beautifully constructed hierarchy as Sanatkumāra journeys, through contemplation, from the objective outer world, characterized by fine knowledge, to the inner worlds of infinite knowledge. The process of contemplation, called *bhūma vidyā*, looks at reality from its grossest, and most tangible form to the subtlest, and highest form. Each degree and form of reality is presented as nested in its higher degree and form of manifestation, through the conversation between Sanatkumāra and Nārada, the musician and storyteller.

*This entire sequence of* Chāndogya Upaniṣad *is the mirror of Koestler's tenets of OHS, except these were composed millennia earlier. It is indeed very surprising that Koestler refers to the* Chāndogya Upaniṣad *but fails to mention these central portions, which find expression in his book in modified ways.*

We consider in the following table specific instances of similarity in thought between Indian sources which Koestler had cited and the tenets of Open Hierarchical Systems:

| Koestler | *Upaniṣad*-s 1 | *Upaniṣad*-s 2 |
|---|---|---|
| The **organism, in its structural aspect, is not an aggregation of elementary parts,** and in its functional aspects, it is not a chain of elementary units of behavior. | **Each entity of creation is connected to the Absolute Consciousness because it is That itself in reality.** This integrally unified whole is governed fundamentally by the principle of aspiring to merge with the highest reality but governed at each stage by the specific nature of the stage. ***Chāndogya Upaniṣad,* in section 6.9, compares individual beings and units to rivers that flow in different directions but culminate in the same ocean.** | The *Bṛhadāraṇyaka Upaniṣad* compares the structure of the individual parts of the whole to that of a spider and its web. Just as how a spider spins the thread and weaves a web, the individual ātman puts forth its various constituent organs and entities. Another analogy used is fire and the sparks it produces. **One cannot simply aggregate all sparks and create a fire.** |
| Parts and wholes in an absolute sense do not exist in the domain of life. The concept of the holon is intended to reconcile the atomistic and holistic approaches. | *Upaniṣad*-s use the analogy of the individual parts to be like the individual organs of a whole body, i.e. Brahma's body. Each organ, for example, the eyes, has its own principles and functions but exists only when part of the larger whole body with life. | *Upaniṣad*-s establish very clearly the following: a) the necessity and position of the universal as the substratum of all manifestation, inclusive of all entities and phenomena; and b) the tendency inherent in the absolute reality to manifest as finite and localized ātman and ahaṁkāra forms. |

| Koestler | *Upaniṣad*-s 1 | *Upaniṣad*-s 2 |
|---|---|---|
| Man's self-assertive tendency is the dynamic manifestation of his unique wholeness, autonomy, and independence as a holon. Its equally universal antagonist, the integrative tendency, expresses his dependence on the larger whole to which he belongs: his 'part-ness'. The polarity of these two tendencies, or potentials, is one of the leitmotifs of the present theory. | *Chāndogya Upaniṣad* 3.18. 1-2 considers how the various phenomena such as fire, sun, elements, life, and the activities of the individual self are parts of the Brahman. The same *Upaniṣad* in 6.3 speaks of how Brahman entered each creation after manifesting it. | *Bṛhadāraṇyaka Upaniṣad* 3.2.13 speaks of how, at death, each part of an individual life returns to its corresponding larger whole in nature, which is its source; for example, the Ātman returns to space. Here, Ātman is the holon nested in the larger holon of space. |
| **The hierarchy is open-ended in the downward and the upward directions. Every holon has the dual tendency to preserve and assert its individuality as a quasi-autonomous whole** and to function as an integrated part of an (existing or evolving) larger whole. **This polarity between the Self-Assertive (S-A) and Integrative (INT) tendencies is inherent in the concept of hierarchical order and a universal characteristic of life.** The S-A tendencies are the dynamic expression of the holon's wholeness, and the INT tendencies of its partness. | Chapter 6 of the *Chāndogya Upaniṣad* focuses on how **the individual emerges from the universal and sustains itself through essences of life.** The entire *Chāndogya Upaniṣad* constantly affirms that the individual is the manifestation of the universal i.e. the individual is the microcosm and the mirror of the whole. | **Individuation manifests the Absolute Consciousness locally**. The tendency and will to merge with the wholeness are inherent in every individual entity, for, it is its very nature. This whole universe is the Brahman. 'In tranquility, let one worship It, as Tajjalan (that from which he came forth, as that into which he will be dissolved, as that in which he breathes)'. — *Chāndogya Upaniṣad* 3.14.1 |

| Koestler | *Upaniṣad*-s 1 | *Upaniṣad*-s 2 |
|---|---|---|
| 6.2 **Conscious experience is enriched by the cooperation of several perceptual hierarchies in different sense-modalities and within the same sense-modality.** | All three principal *Upaniṣad*-s cited by Koestler present an architecture of the mind in terms of its mental experiences being two parallel branches and with hierarchy in each branch. **Jñānendriya-s are the sense organs, karmendriya-s are the organs of action, while buddhi, citta, and ahaṁkāra are the inner tools that govern and process them within.** | |
| 8. **Holons on successively higher levels of the hierarchy show increasingly complex,** more flexible, and less predictable patterns of activity, while on successively lower levels, we find increasingly mechanized, stereotyped, and predictable patterns. | *Katha Upaniṣad*, through verses 1.3.10 to 1.3.12, looks at Reality as a hierarchy, beginning from the grossest to the subtlest. **Those dependent on the senses, i.e. the indriya-s are at the lower rungs of hierarchy, ascending to artha (objects and means of life), then to the manas, then the buddhi (the discriminating and reasoning faculty), then ascending further to the Ātman (the individual self) and above it, to the puruṣa.** | |
| 8.4 **Each upward shift is reflected by a more vivid and precise consciousness of the ongoing activity**, and, since the variety of alternative choices increases with increasing complexity on higher levels, each upward shift is accompanied by the subjective experience of freedom of decision. | *Chāndogya Upaniṣad,* Chapter 7, discusses **the progressive shift in consciousness, with the accompanying change in acquiring liberation and freedom.** The various forms of yoga, especially karma yoga and Integral Yoga, focus on expanding the complexity through one's actions and interactions with the prakṛti outside. | |

| Koestler | *Upaniṣad*-s 1 | *Upaniṣad*-s 2 |
|---|---|---|
| 8.5 **The hierarchical approach replaces dualistic theories by a serialistic hypothesis** in which **'mental'**, and **'mechanical' appear as relative attributes of a unitary process**, with the dominance of one or the other depending on changes in the level of control of ongoing operations. | Advaita Vedānta speaks of exactly the same as its central tenet—**the Brahman is the all-pervading, and all-encompassing self of the universe. Everything is the Brahman, including the individual Ātman, which also has its individual identity. Attributes including mental, and mechanical are all a part of a reality which is either (i) pāramārthika – absolute, where everything is the One – metaphysical and ontological – the view of non dualism; or (ii) vyāvahārika – empirically true, phenomenal world with its materialism is valid and is true – the view of dualism; or (iii) prātibhāsika – apparent, mentally constructed reality.** | |
| **8.6 Consciousness appears as an emergent quality in phylogeny and ontogeny which, from primitive beginnings, evolves towards more complex and precise states. It is the highest manifestation of the Integrative Tendency (4.3) to extract order out of disorder, and information out of noise.** | **Consciousness is referred to as Brahman, prajñā, and citta. It can be either pure consciousness or self-consciousness, with the latter being a transitory locus in an individual.**<br>**Consciousness emerges into increasing complexity as one moves through its various gradations of manifestation – matter, life, and mind, with the last being the highest, and subtlest expression and the first the grossest.**<br>**Consciousness emerges because Everything is That itself, i.e. *Sarvam Khalu Idam Brahma and Tat Tvam Asi.* The principal *Upaniṣad*-s, including *Chāndogya*, *Muṇḍaka*, and *Bṛhadāraṇyaka*, all used by Koestler, refer to the various aspects of this consciousness.** | |

From the table, it is very clear that several features of the OHS that are attributed to Koestler's original insights are present in the texts he has referred to in his work but failed to credit.

## Tracing Ken Wilber's Holons to Indic Sources

Wilber refers to two major proponents of the holon theory in his works – Jan Smuts in *The Atman Project* and Arthur Koestler from *Eye to Eye* to *Sex, Ecology and Spirituality*. Wilber developed his twenty tenets based on the theory of holons, which forms a very important part of his AQAL model. Holons are the primary lens of viewing any quadrant of the AQAL system and thus, a way of looking at any part of reality while knowing that the holon always embeds the part in the whole.

The four quadrants of Wilber's AQAL have unique accompanying methodologies. By using the holonic view, one can understand and analyze any event in one quadrant without the reductionist view traditionally associated with that discipline. As the holon is a unit that describes the relation of the part with the whole, Wilber is able to use the holonic paradigm across quadrants, be it social or cultural, subjective or objective.

Mark Edwards, in *A Brief History of Holons*, constructs Table 1 to map Wilber's twenty tenets to the corresponding principles of Koestler's Open Holarchical Systems.[31] Each of these tenets has a basis in the *Upaniṣad*-s and mappings to our table seen in the previous section. While we have seen Koestler cite the *Upaniṣad*-s at specific places in his works, Wilber too refers to the *Chāndogya Upaniṣad* on several occasions, including page 267 of the same book where he uses holons for the first time, i.e. *Eye to Eye*, page 3 of his 1998 book *Body, Mind and Spirit*; he quotes from *Bṛhadāraṇyaka Upaniṣad* on page 279 of *Eye to Eye*. Wilber also refers to Sri Aurobindo's work, and the latter has extensively used the *Upaniṣad*-s as the basis to expand upon in his Integral Yoga.

*Both Koestler and Wilber in their respective works selectively attribute only pantheistic and universal elements to the* Upaniṣad-*s, while not referring to the same works for the attributes of nestedness, hierarchies, and open-endedness that have instead become signatures of their own works.*

Sri Aurobindo explains that consciousness manifests itself in an ascending series of planes, with each plane connected to other planes and subsumed by the higher ones; each plane is also

> a world in itself, with its own movements, forces, beings, types, forms existing as if for its and their own sake, under its own laws, for its own manifestation without apparent regard for the other members of the great series'.[32]

In other words, the planes are parts of wholes, which are part of larger wholes, and so forth.

*This concept gets appropriated by Wilber without any attribution.* He substitutes holons for *Sri Aurobindo's planes of consciousness.* He then uses various chapters of *The Life Divine*, especially *The Evolutionary Process—Ascent and Integration*; *Man and the Evolution* and *The Evolution of the Spiritual Man* to develop his famous Twenty Tenets of Holarchical Evolution.

Wilber's first tenet is: 'Reality as a whole is not composed of things or processes but of holons. Composed, that is, of wholes that are simultaneously parts of other wholes, with no upward or downward limit'.[33]

He attributes these ideas to fellow Westerners such as Koestler, whose work was in turn inspired by Indian sources, as we demonstrated earlier. However, in magazine interviews, Wilber acknowledges the Indian sources as if the target readers are familiar with Indian thought. For example, when *Shambhala Sun* magazine (with a largely Buddhist readership) pointed out that his use of holons bears a resemblance to the dharma-s of Buddhist Abhidharma, Wilber says:

> I am a long-time practicing Buddhist, and **many of the key ideas in my approach are Buddhist or Buddhist-inspired.** ... Nagarjuna and Madhyamika; pure Emptiness and primordial Purity is the "central philosophy" of my approach ... . Also Yogachara, Hua Yen, a great deal of Dzogchen and Mahamudra, and yes, **the fundamentals of Abhidharma. The analysis of experience into *dharmas* is quite similar to Whitehead's actual occasions. My presentation of holons was influenced by all of those.**[34]

Even in this instance, he makes sure the attribution to Buddhism gets diluted with references to other traditions – a common ploy to make it seem that he was merely picking up a well-known idea in all sorts of traditions.

Having thus mapped Sri Aurobindo's planes to holons, his other nineteen tenets naturally derive from Sri Aurobindo's writings. In the following pages we compare Sri Aurobindo's writings and Wilber's tenets.[35]

Wilber's third tenet states that new holons with novel qualities emerge in the evolutionary process through the holons already present in nature. For example, molecules emerged from atoms. Molecules gave rise to polymers, from which cells emerged, and so on. Wilber is substituting holons for planes and replicating Sri Aurobindo's assertion of how they came into existence during involution and gradually manifested and emerged on the terrestrial plane; for instance, the emergence of the mind plane from the vital or life planes. The following comparison makes this appropriation undeniable:

**Sri Aurobindo**

Each gradation emerges not only out of its precedent grade but in it, **as Life emerges in Matter** and is largely limited and determined in its self-expression by its material conditions, **as Mind emerges in Life-in-Matter** and is similarly limited and determined in its self-expression by life-conditions and material conditions, **so Spirit too must emerge in a Mind embodied in Life-in-Matter** and must be largely limited and determined by the mental conditions in which it has its roots as well as the life-conditions, the material conditions of its existence here.[36]

**Wilber – Tenet 3**

Holons emerge. Owing to the self-transcendent capacity of holons, **new holons emerge**. First subatomic particles, then atoms, then molecules, then polymers, then cells, and so on. The emergent holons are in some sense novel; they possess properties and qualities that cannot be strictly and totally deduced from their components.[37]

Tenets four and five state that 'holons emerge holarchically', which means that 'each holon transcends but includes its predecessors'. In other words, each bigger holon enfolds and exceeds the smaller ones in increasing complexity and wholeness. For example, cells contain polymers, which contain molecules, which contain atoms, and not vice versa. The source of Wilber's ideas becomes apparent when compared with Sri Aurobindo.

**Sri Aurobindo**

**To each grade in this series** achieved by the evolving Consciousness **belongs its appropriate class of existences,**—one by one there appear material forms and forces, vegetable life, animals and half-animal man, developed human beings, imperfectly evolved or more evolved spiritual beings: but because of the continuity of the evolutionary process there is no rigid separation between them; each new advance or formation takes up what was before. The animal takes up into himself living and inanimate Matter; man takes up both along with the animal existence. There are furrows left by the transitional process or separating demarcations settled by the fixed habit of Nature: but these distinguish one series from another, serve perhaps to prevent a fall back of what has been evolved, they do not cancel or cut the continuity of the evolution. **The evolving Consciousness passes from one grade to another or from one series of steps to another either by an imperceptible process or by some bound or crisis** or, perhaps, **by an intervention from above,**—some descent or ensouling or influence from higher planes of Nature. But, **by whatever means, the Consciousness secretly indwelling in Matter, the occult Inhabitant, is able thus to make its way upward from the lower to the higher gradations, taking up what it was into what it is and preparing to take up both into what it will be.** Thus, having first laid down a basis of material being, material forms, forces, existences in which it seems to be lying inconscient, though in reality, as we know now, always subconsciently at work, it is able to manifest life and living beings, to manifest mind and mental beings in a material world, and must therefore be able to manifest there Supermind also and supramental beings. Thus has come about the present status of the evolution of which man is the now apparent culmination but not the real ultimate summit; **for he is himself a transitional being and stands at the turning-point of the whole movement.** Evolution, being thus continuous, must have at any given moment a past with its fundamental results still in evidence, a present in which the results it is labouring over are in process of becoming, a future in which still unevolved powers and forms of being must appear till there is the full and perfect manifestation.[38]

**Wilber – Tenets 4 and 5**

*Holons emerge holarchically.* That is, as a series of increasing whole/parts. Organisms contain cells but not vice versa; cells contain molecules, but not vice versa; molecules contain atoms but not vice versa.... Each deeper or higher holon embraces its junior predecessors and then *adds* its own new and more encompassing pattern or wholeness.... *Each emergent holon transcends but includes its predecessor(s).* Each newly emergent holon, as we have seen, includes its preceding holons and then adds its own new and defining pattern or form or wholeness.[39] Tenet 6 states that the lower holons set the possibilities of the higher, and the higher make it possible for the lower to manifest. This is yet again a shallow re-statement of Sri Aurobindo's explanation of the relationship between the higher and the lower planes. To substantiate his claim, Wilber credits Ervin László and Rupert Sheldrake as his sources. The following comparison makes Sri Aurobindo's influence clear and also shows that he goes further and explains the role played by the downward 'pressure from some superior plane':

**Sri Aurobindo**

**This ascent**, this successive fixing in higher and higher principles, **does not carry with it the abandonment of the lower grades**, any more than a status of existence in the lower grades means the entire absence of the higher principles. This heals the objection against the evolutionary theory created by these sharp lines of difference; for if the rudiments of the higher are present in the lower creation and the lower characters are taken up into the higher evolved being, that of itself constitutes an indubitable evolutionary process. **What is necessary is a working that brings the lower gradation of being to a point at which the higher can manifest in it**; at that point a pressure from some superior plane where the new power is dominant may assist towards a more or less rapid and decisive **transition by a bound or a series of bounds,—a slow, creeping, imperceptible or even occult action** is followed by a run and an evolutionary saltus across the border. It is in some such way that the transition from the lower to higher grades of consciousness seems to have been made in Nature.[40]

**Wilber – Tenet 6**

*The lower sets the possibilities of the higher; the higher sets the probabilities of the lower.* We saw that as a higher level of creative novelty emerges, it in many ways goes beyond (but includes) the givens of the previous level. However, even though a higher level "goes beyond" a lower level it does not *violate* the laws or the patters of lower level; it cannot be determined by the lower level; but neither can it *ignore* the lower level.[41]

Wilber's seventh tenet of evolutionary principles differentiates between depth and span. Depth is the number of levels between two holons existing in a vertical dimension, while span is the number of holons present at the same level existing in a horizontal dimension. The eighth tenet states that every evolutionary step produces greater depth and lesser span. For example, when molecules emerged from atoms, they had a higher depth than atoms, but atoms had a greater span because there will always be fewer molecules than atoms. Additionally, Wilber states that a holon's consciousness proportionally increases with depth. The following table compares Sri Aurobindo's work with Wilber's.

**Sri Aurobindo**

These gulfs appear deeper, but less wide, as we rise higher in the scale of Nature. If there are rudiments of life-reaction in the metal, as has been recently contended, it may be identical with life-reaction in the plant in its essence, but what might be called the vital-physical difference is so considerable that one seems to us inanimate, the other, though not apparently conscious, might be called a living creature. Between the highest plant life and lowest animal the gulf is visibly deeper, for it is the difference between mind and the entire absence of any apparent or even rudimentary movement of mind: in the one this stuff of mental consciousness is unawakened though there is a life of vital reactions, a suppressed or subconscious or perhaps only submental sense-vibration which seems to be intensely active; in the other, though the life is at first less automatic and secure in the subconscious way of living and in its own new way of overt consciousness imperfectly determined, still mind is awakened,—there is a conscious life, a profound transition has been made. But **the community of the phenomenon of life between plant and animal, however different their organisation, narrows the gulf, even though it does not fill in its profundity. Between the highest animal and the lowest man there is a still deeper though narrower gulf to be crossed, the gulf between sense-mind and the intellect**: for however we may insist on the primitive nature of the savage, we cannot alter the fact that the most primitive human being has above and beyond the sense-mind, emotional vitality and primary practical intelligence which we share with the animals, a human intellect and is capable,—in whatever limits,—of reflection, ideas, conscious invention, religious and ethical thought and feeling, everything fundamental of which man as a race is capable; he has the same kind of intelligence, it differs only in its past instruction and formative training and the degree of its developed capacity, intensity and activity.[42]

**Wilber – Tenets 7 and 8**

The number of levels which a hierarchy comprises determines whether it is "shallow" or "deep," and the number of holons on any given level we shall call its "span".... **Each successive level of evolution produces GREATER depth and LESS span....** The greater the depth of a holon, the greater its degree of consciousness.[43]

Tenets 2a to 2d discuss four fundamental features of holons: self-preservation, self-adaptation, self-transcendence, and self-dissolution.

The following three tables describe how Wilber reformulates three of these characteristics from Sri Aurobindo's ideas.

| **Sri Aurobindo** |
|---|
| Each plane, in spite of its connection with others above and below it, is yet a world in itself, with its own movements, forces, beings, types, forms existing as if for its and their own sake, under its own laws, for its own manifestation without apparent regard for the other members of the great series. Thus, **if we regard the vital or the subtle physical plane, we see great ranges of it, (most of it), existing in themselves, without any relation with the material world and with no movement to affect or influence it, still less to precipitate a corresponding manifestation in the physical formula**. At most we can say that the existence of anything in the vital, subtle physical or any other plane creates a possibility for a corresponding movement of manifestation in the physical world.[44] |

| **Wilber – Tenet 2a** |
|---|
| *Self-preservation.* All holons display some capacity to preserve their individuality, to preserve their own particular wholeness or autonomy.... Holons exist *by virtue* of their interlinking relationship or context, they are *not defined* solely by their context but also by their own individual form, pattern, or structure.... **In short, holons are defined, not by their stuff of which they are made (there is no stuff), not merely by the context in which they love (though they are inseparable from that), but by the relatively autonomous and coherent pattern they display**, and the capacity to preserve that pattern is one characteristic of a holon: the *wholeness* aspect of a holon is displayed in its pattern-preservation.[45] |

**Sri Aurobindo**

An evolutionary process must be by the very terms of the problem to be solved a development, in some first established basic principle of being or substance, of something that that basic principle holds involved in itself or else admits from outside itself and modifies by the admission; for it must necessarily modify by its own law of nature all that enters into it and is not already part of its own nature. This must be so even if it is a creative evolution in the sense of manifesting always new powers of existence that are not native to the first foundation but introduced into it, accepted into an original substance. If, on the contrary, there is already there in involution,—present in the first foundation, but not yet manifested or not yet organised,—the new principle or power of existence that has to be evolved, then, when it appears, it will still have to accept modification by the nature and law of the basic substance: but also it will modify that substance by its own power, its own law of nature. If, further, it is aided by a descent of its own principle already established in its own full force above the field of evolution and pressing down into that field to possess it, then the new power may even establish itself as a dominant element and considerably or radically change the consciousness and action of the world in which it emerges or into which it enters. But its force to modify or change or to revolutionise the law and working of the original substance chosen as the evolutionary matrix will depend upon its own essential potency. It is not likely that it will be able to bring about an entire transformation if it is not itself the original Principle of Existence, if it is only derivative, an instrumental power and not the first puissance.

**Here the evolution takes place in a material universe; the foundation, the original substance, the first established all-conditioning status of things is Matter. Mind and Life are evolved in Matter, but they are limited and modified in their action by the obligation to use its substance for their instrumentation and by their subjection to the law of material Nature even while they modify what they undergo and use.** For they do transform its substance, first into living substance and then into conscious substance; they succeed in changing its inertia, immobility and inconscience into a movement of consciousness, feeling and life. But they do not succeed in transforming it altogether; they cannot make it altogether alive or altogether conscious: life-nature evolving is bound to death; mind evolving is materialised as well as vitalised; it finds itself rooted in inconscience, limited by ignorance; it is moved by uncontrolled life-forces which drive and use it, it is mechanised by the physical forces on which it has to depend for its own self-expression. **This is a sign that neither Mind nor Life is the original creative Power; they, like Matter, are intermediaries, successive and seried instruments of the evolutionary process.** If a material energy is not that original Power, then we must seek for it in something above Mind or Life; there must be a deeper occult Reality which has yet to disclose itself in Nature.[46]

**Wilber – Tenet 2b**

*Self-adaptation.* A holon functions not only as a self-preserving *whole* but also a part of a larger whole, and in its capacity as a *part* it must adapt or accommodate itself to other holons.... The *partness* aspect of a holon is displayed in its capacity to accommodate, to register other holons, to fit into its existing environment.[47]

**Sri Aurobindo**

1. **This movement of evolution, of a progressive self-manifestation of the Spirit in a material universe, has to make its account at every step with the fact of the involution of consciousness and force in the form and activity of material substance.** For it proceeds by an awakening of the involved consciousness and force and its ascent from principle to principle, from grade to grade, from power to power of the secret Spirit, but this is not a free transference to a higher status. The law of action, the force of action of each grade or power in its emergence is determined, not by its own free, full and pure law of nature or vim of energy, but partly by the material

organisation provided for it and partly by its own status, achieved degree, accomplished fact of consciousness which it has been able to impose upon Matter.... **To each grade in this series achieved by the evolving Consciousness belongs its appropriate class of existences,**—one by one there appear material forms and forces, vegetable life, animals and half-animal man, developed human beings, imperfectly evolved or more evolved spiritual beings: but because of the continuity of the evolutionary process there is no rigid separation between them; each new advance or formation takes up what was before. The animal takes up into himself living and inanimate Matter; man takes up both along with the animal existence. There are furrows left by the transitional process or separating demarcations settled by the fixed habit of Nature: but these distinguish one series from another, serve perhaps to prevent a fall back of what has been evolved, they do not cancel or cut the continuity of the evolution. The evolving Consciousness passes from one grade to another or from one series of steps to another either by an imperceptible process or by some bound or crisis or, perhaps, by an intervention from above,—some descent or ensouling or influence from higher planes of Nature. But, by whatever means, the Consciousness secretly indwelling in Matter, the occult Inhabitant, is able thus to make its way upward from the lower to the higher gradations, taking up what it was into what it is and preparing to take up both into what it will be. **Thus, having first laid down a basis of material being, material forms, forces, existences in which it seems to be lying inconscient, though in reality, as we know now, always subconsciently at work, it is able to manifest life and living beings, to manifest mind and mental beings in a material world, and must therefore be able to manifest there Supermind also and supramental beings.**[48]

2. It is throughout evolutionary Nature; Matter could not have become animate if the principle of Life had not been there constituting Matter and emerging as a phenomenon of Life-in-Matter; Life-in-Matter could not have begun to feel, perceive, think, reason, if the principle of Mind had not been there behind life and

substance, constituting it as its field of operation and emergent in the phenomenon of a thinking life and body: so too **spirituality emerging in Mind is the sign of a power which itself has founded and constituted life, mind and body and is now emerging as a spiritual being in a living and thinking body.**[49]

**Wilber – Tenet 2c**

*Self-transcendence....* is a transformation that results in something novel and emergent—different wholes have come together to form a new and a different whole. There is some sort of a creative twist to what has gone before.... "In the self-organization paradigms, *evolution is the result of self-transcendence at all levels.*" In other words, this introduces a *vertical* dimension that cuts at right angles, so to speak, to the horizontal agency and communion. In self-transcendence, agency and communion do not just interact; rather *new forms* of agency and communion emerge through symmetry breaks, through the introduction of new and creative twists in the evolutionary stream. There is not only a *continuity* in evolution, there are important discontinuities as well.[50]

Wilber's tenet 2d states that holons self-dissolve, and there is no parallel to this in Koestler's model. A holon has a tendency for self-assertion but not to disintegrate without any interaction with any other branch of holarchy. This stands in contrast with Indian thought where, for instance, when a person dies, each bodily element merges with a corresponding bigger, natural element, such as breath with vāyu and so on.

Since Wilber is not very clear with his explanation on this, we only consider Sri Aurobindo's original version. Once planes come into existence, they may get modified due to the emergence of newer planes, but they need not always self-disintegrate to go out of existence. In fact, Sri Aurobindo mentions that Nature may, after taking a certain trend, change it and reject the chosen direction of development after some time, especially when the higher support of the spirit, and the sanction of the puruṣa, for whom she makes all these activities, is not given; she then withdraws her creativity and casts aside the forms she made, but there is no self-disintegrating in an ad hoc manner as seen in Wilber's model.

There is a constant correlation between Nature seeking an appropriate form for evolving modes of consciousness, and the sanction of the involution movement from above, supporting this correlation and pointing to the right direction. In Sri Aurobindo's theories, Nature is not mechanical; she experiments in search of the best possible forms for the evolving consciousness and adjusts her work with increasingly precise solutions with the help and support of the puruṣa.

The tenth tenet states that holons do not evolve alone but co-evolve in association with other holons. It is quite apparent that Wilber has derived this idea from Sri Aurobindo's explanation that the higher plane emerges from the lower because (i) it has been involuted in the lower; and (ii) the subsequent higher plane(s), which are involuted but not yet manifested on the terrestrial plane exert(s) a pull on the lower to help it manifest. For example, Life emerged from Matter because a) Life was already involuted in Matter; and b) because the vital plane of Life exerted pressure on Matter to let Life emerge from it. Later, Mind emerges from life as, a) Mind was involuted in Life-in-Matter; and b) because the unmanifest mental plane exerted a pressure on Life to let Mind blossom from it.

In other words, both forces are at work, from below and above: The involuted being is slowly evolving out of the material Inconscient, and the unmanifest being is supporting it from above as the puruṣa, descending from higher levels of consciousness.

**Sri Aurobindo**

If we regard the gradation of worlds or planes as a whole, we see them as a great connected complex movement; the higher precipitate their influences on the lower, the lower react to the higher and develop or manifest in themselves within their own formula something that corresponds to the superior power and its action. **The material world has evolved life in obedience to a pressure from the vital plane, mind in obedience to a pressure from the mental plane. It is now trying to evolve supermind in obedience to a pressure from the supramental plane.** In more detail, particular forces, movements, powers, beings of a higher world can throw themselves on the lower to establish appropriate and corresponding forms which will connect them with the material domain and, as it were, reproduce or project their action here.[51]

**Wilber – Tenet 10**

*Holarchies coevolve.* Holons do not evolve alone, because there are no alone holons (there are only fields within fields within fields. This principle is often referred to as ***coevolution*****, which simply means that the "unit" of evolution is not an isolated holon** (individual molecule or plant or animal) but a holon plus its inseparable environment.[52]

The eleventh tenet simply recapitulates the ancient Indian idea that a human being is a microcosm correlated with the macrocosm, i.e. that s/he has all the planes of cosmic existence within him/her. The human body comprises different kośa-s which represent and relate to the cosmic planes. In Tantra, there are specific points of the body correlated with cosmic energies and intelligences. This correspondence principle is far more profound and widespread than Wilber has been able to capture.

**Sri Aurobindo**

Each thing created here has, supporting it, subtler envelopes or forms of itself which make it subsist and connect it with forces acting from above. Man has, besides his gross physical body, subtler sheaths or bodies by which he lives behind the veil in direct connection with supraphysical planes of consciousness and can be influenced by their powers, movements and beings. **What takes place in life has always behind it pre-existent movements and forms in the occult vital planes; what takes place in mind presupposes pre-existent movements and forms in the occult mental planes.**[53]

**Wilber – Tenet 11**

*The micro is in relational exchange with the macro at all levels of its depth.* This tenet is extremely important, particularly when it comes to holons of greater depth and the types of ecosystems (in the broad sense) that they must co-create and upon which their existence depends.[54]

The twelfth tenet has five sub-tenets describing the nature of the evolutionary process. Wilber defines the evolutionary process as one that has directionality with increasing differentiation/integration, variety, complexity, organization, autonomy, and telos. In other words, there are deeper and wider contexts exerting a pull on limited contexts for a greater resolution. This is almost an identical reproduction of a couple of paragraphs from *The Life Divine*, as the following table elucidates.

**Sri Aurobindo**

Since this is an evolution out of a material Inconscience into spiritual consciousness, an evolutionary self-building of Spirit on a base of Matter, there must be in the process a development of a triple character. An evolution of forms of Matter more and more subtly and intricately organised so as to admit the action of a growing, a more and more complex and subtle and capable organisation of consciousness is the indispensable physical foundation. **An upward evolutionary progress of the consciousness itself from grade to higher grade, an ascent, is the evident spiral line or emerging curve that, on this foundation, the evolution must describe.** A taking up of what has already been evolved into each higher grade as it is reached and a transformation more or less complete so as to admit of a total changed working of the whole being and nature, an integration, must be also part of the process, if the evolution is to be effective [increasing complexity, organization, differentiation/ integration].

The end of this triple process must be a radical change of the action of the Ignorance into an action of Knowledge, of our basis of inconscience into a basis of complete consciousness,—a completeness which exists at present only in what is to us the superconscience. **Each ascent will bring with it a partial change and modification of the old nature taken up and subjected to a new fundamental principle; the inconscience will be turned into a partial consciousness, an ignorance seeking for more and more knowledge and mastery: but at some point there must be an ascent which substitutes the principle of knowledge, of a fundamental true consciousness, the consciousness of the Spirit, for the inconscience and ignorance [increasing telos].** An evolution in the Inconscience is the beginning, an evolution in the Ignorance is the middle, but the end is the liberation of the spirit into its true consciousness and an evolution in the Knowledge. This is the law and method of the process which has hitherto been followed and by all signs is likely to be followed in her future working by evolutionary Nature. **A first involutionary foundation in which originates all that has to evolve, an emergence and action of the involved powers in or upon that foundation in an ascending series, and a culminating emergence of the highest power of all as the agent of a supreme manifestation are the necessary stages of the journey of evolutionary Nature.**[55]

**Wilber – Tenet 12**

***Evolution has directionality.*** This is the famous arrow of evolutionary time first recognized in the biosphere, but now understood, in the sciences of complexity, to be present in all three of the great domains of evolution [physiosphere, biosphere, and noosphere]. **This directionality is usually stated as being one of increasing differentiation, variety, complexity, and organization** [and relative autonomy and *telos*].[56]

Chapter 13

# Wilber-IV: All Quadrants All Levels

Wilber-IV is a crucial and significant phase of Ken Wilber's work, with his trademark All Quadrants All Levels model. The chapter *Reality and Integral Knowledge* in Sri Aurobindo's *The Life Divine* contains the blueprint of the ideas which were borrowed to form the basis of Wilber's AQAL model and we show this in detail.

We first discuss the structures, features, and mechanisms of his AQAL model.

## Comparing Wilber's AQAL Model and Dhārmic Framework

Wilber's stated aim is to do an 'an extensive data search among various types of developmental and evolutionary sequences'.[1] Having collated material from more than two hundred models, Wilber creates his 'All Quadrants All Levels' schema.

Wilber's AQAL model is a layout comprising four quadrants that focuses on Singular and Plural, Subjective and Objective aspects of I, We, It and Its. Wilber calls the four quadrants 'correlative dimensions of the same thing'.

In Sri Aurobindo's model, the subjective and objective views of matter, life, and mind form the primary lens to study puruṣa and prakṛti. These concepts arise out of the metaphysics of the theory itself, whereas in Wilber's work, *they are selected lenses from a random collection without sound explanations.*

Wilber postulates that you cannot have the singular without the collective and the interior without the exterior, but does not explain why. In dhārmic traditions, the yogi assumes the witness perspective to separate and dissociate from prakṛti. This provides the experience from a higher level of consciousness, and the relationship between subjective and objective perspectives becomes clear. Wilber adopts that same dhārmic paradigm of Inside and Outside and Subjective and Objective (similar to Koestler).

Alongside, Wilber selects twelve schools of thought which he considers the most influential in studying consciousness, and takes elements from each: 'My own approach to consciousness studies is based on the assumption that each of these schools has something irreplaceably important to offer, and thus what is required is a general model sophisticated enough to incorporate the essentials of each of them'.[2] He believes that the combination of the four quadrants and the levels they take, along with the twelve disciplines, leads to a near-complete picture of consciousness. The twelve disciplines are:

1. **Cognitive Science,** which looks at consciousness as something that is rooted in the brain and/or mind.
2. **Introspectionism,** which Wilber says 'includes everything from philosophical intentionality to introspective psychology, existentialism and phenomenology'. Introspectionism emphasizes first-hand experience of consciousness against anything from another's experience/knowledge.
3. **Neuropsychology,** which looks at consciousness as anchored in complex neural mechanisms.
4. **Individual psychotherapy,** which looks at treatment of emotional and psychological issues.
5. **Social psychology,** which considers consciousness to be nested in a social and communal system rather than a primary or exclusive implant in an individual.
6. **Clinical psychiatry,** which looks at addressing psychopathological issues, including the use of pharmaceuticals as medicines to treat imbalances.
7. **Developmental psychology,** which 'views consciousness not as a single entity but as a developmentally unfolding process with a substantially different architecture at each of its stages of growth, and thus an understanding of consciousness demands an

investigation of the architecture at each of its levels of unfolding'.[3]

8. **Psychosomatic medicine,** which looks at consciousness interacting with the body as a biological organism. In this method, Wilber includes 'consciousness and miraculous healing, the effects of prayer on remarkable recoveries, light/sound and healing, spontaneous remission, and so on. It also includes any approaches that investigate the effects of intentionality on healing, from art therapy to visualization to psychotherapy and meditation'.[4]
9. **Nonordinary states of consciousness,** which include dreams and psychedelics to understand consciousness through an alternate lens.
10. **Eastern and Contemplative Traditions,** including yoga and meditation look at consciousness as possessing higher levels beyond ordinary perceptions.
11. **Quantum consciousness,** wherein Wilber uses vague meanings of the terms of quantum theory and includes all those ideas which 'view consciousness as being intrinsically capable of interacting with, and altering, the physical world, generally through quantum interactions, both in the human body at the intracellular level (e.g. microtubules), and in the material world at large (psi). This approach also includes the many and various attempts to plug consciousness into the physical world according to various avant-garde physical theories (bootstrapping, hyperspace, strings)'.[5]
12. **Subtle energies,** wherein Wilber includes subtle bio-energies, which link the mind with the body and says, 'For the Great Chain theorists, both East and West, this bioenergy acts as a two-way conveyor belt, transferring the impact of matter to the mind and imposing the intentionality of the mind on matter'.[6]

This choice of twelve schools is entirely arbitrary, and it is especially troubling because they do not share a common cosmology and metaphysics. They share a common quest to understand consciousness but not a common framework. The result is synthetic unity and not integral unity. Wilber admits to being a curator of various theories:

> I examined over two hundred developmental sequences recognized by various branches of human knowledge – ranging from stellar physics to molecular biology, from anthropology to linguistics, from developmental psychology to ethical orientations, from

> cultural hermeneutics to contemplative endeavours — taken from both Eastern and Western disciplines, and including premodern, modern, and postmodern sources (Wilber 1995b, 1996d). I noticed that these various developmental sequences all fell into one of four major classes — the four quadrants — and further, that within those four quadrants there was substantial agreement as to the various stages or levels in each.[7]

This is the approach of a librarian developing a classification system or organizing disparate and independent works. Wilber repeatedly stresses that his models are based on a posteriori conclusions and not any a priori assumptions: 'The holons in each of those four quadrants were not postulated in any sort of a priori or "metaphysical" fashion; they were rather suggested by an a posteriori data search across several hundred disciplines'.[8] This makes his model vulnerable to internal contradictions.

### *Dhārmic methods of obtaining complete knowledge of consciousness*

The yogi first experiences realization (*bhāva*) and then formulates it in *artha* (meaning) and *vāk* (speech) through thought. This is why Vedic texts are replete with references to the yogi as a poet, not merely for symbolic or metaphorical reasons, but because they first experienced consciousness through reception, then tested it by their own spiritual practice, formulated it through mental faculties, and finally projected it as objective experience. Sri Aurobindo advises his disciples to first still the mind and bring silence and quiet to separate the higher intelligence/buddhi.

The scientist's way, on the other hand, begins with empiricism. Both methods have validity in the dhārmic system, and it is a gross misrepresentation to attribute only the contemplative yogic method to India and not the robustly tested method of the scientist as well.

As Wilber builds his quadrant model by picking and choosing from over two hundred approaches, he resolutely avoids metaphysics and relies on a posteriori knowledge as opposed to a priori knowledge. He completely cuts off the yogic way of approaching consciousness. In the absence of metaphysics, he muddles his way through the development of his model:

> The developmental or dimensional analyses all fell into one of these four broad types of sequences, which simply referred to the interior and the exterior of the singular and the collective. This makes a certain amount of intuitive sense; ...some of the simplest distinctions we can make are between singular and plural, inside and outside, ...evolution makes those distinctions as well, because it appears that development occurs in all four of those dimensions, and the four quadrants are a simple and very general summary of those evolutionary developments.[9]

### *Consciousness as nirguṇa and saguṇa Brahman*

The Indian approach to understanding individual and collective consciousness is based on the paradigm that transcends both or treats both as indispensable. One cannot discuss the perspectives of the singular and the collective independent of the integral framework of Absolute Consciousness, which is beyond the attributes of duality and non-duality, i.e. it is nirguṇa Brahman. This Transcendent state contains both unity of all forms and multiplicity of creation, the process of manifestation through evolution, and the resulting individual and collective, both manifesting the same highest consciousness.

Nirguṇa Brahman manifests as saguṇa Brahman with inherently present agency. Similar to the individual having an ego, the collective has its own 'soul' that is integrally unified. The collective is not the synthetic sum of individual parts as in Wilber's model. The collective is a direct manifestation of saguṇa and not an indirect collection of separate individual manifestations in separate egos coming together through social contracts. This integrally connected schema is unique to dhārmic and Sri Aurobindo's models.

### *Key features of AQAL*

By being ambiguous and not clearly indicating to which models he refers from his database of two hundred systems, Wilber creates an issue of non-attribution. Furthermore, there is no agency and causation in his AQAL model that would show the inter-relationships among various components.

Apart from the previously discussed aspects, the other key features of each quadrant are summarized in the following table:

| **Upper Left – Interior Individual (Intentional)** | **Upper Right – Exterior Individual (Behavioral)** |
|---|---|
| • Wilber first considers the right-side quadrants and postulates that every exterior must have an interior. He does a 'data search among the evolutionary trends of interior apprehension', to attribute the following properties in evolving order to this quadrant: prehension, irritability, sensation, perception, impulse, image, symbol, concept, rule, and synthesizing reason.<br>• Wilber cites Whitehead to suggest that prehension can perhaps be extended all the way to atoms, and de Chardin to agree that qualitatively consciousness is a spectrum with gradations. This stands in contrast to Sri Aurobindo, who not only separated the three stages of manifestation of consciousness in terms of Matter, Life, and Mind through clear features, but also maintained that the transition from each stage to the next is a leap.<br>• Wilber cleverly disregards the lack of fundamental agency between his quadrants by saying that 'agency is always agency – in – communion'. As he is trying to synthetically create a model which cannot generate the metaphysics of the dhārmic and Sri Aurobindo's systems, he is forced | • Standard hierarchy represented by evolutionary science includes cells and organisms on the one hand, and atoms and molecules, on the other: 'The Upper Right quadrant is simply a summary of the scientific research on the evolution of individual holons'.<br>• This quadrant best represents Wilber's 'Transcend and Include', where the bigger engulfs the smaller irreversibly and not vice versa due to evolutionary arrow of time. While using even fringe theories under his non-standard school of consciousness, Wilber fails to acknowledge that the arrow of time as a linear flow is a Western construct while Eastern traditions include cyclical models of time.<br>• The holons here represent empirical phenomena and are grasped by the senses and their faculties, and are therefore outward looking.<br>• There is no gradation of consciousness at all in the choice of the holon i.e. an atom is placed at the same level as a cell. The 'depth' that Wilber attributes to the various levels of the same quadrant again has no causality – what produces the higher states of consciousness has no explanation. The question |

| | |
|---|---|
| into a corner where there is no agency *within* the quadrants as well as *between* them. Evolution as a process without Involution, cannot generate causality and hence even agency. | remains, how is the AQAL a complete model that can generate all our present understanding of consciousness? |
| **Lower Left – Interior Collective (Cultural)** | **Lower Right – Exterior Collective (Social)** |
| • This quadrant represents the subjective and collective forms of the individual holons. | • There is no causality, agency or connection between the upper right and the lower right, apart from this quadrant merely representing the collective of individuals, unlike Sri Aurobindo's model. |

### *Deriving AQAL from Sri Aurobindo's model*

Sri Aurobindo postulated an Integral reality in which the transcendental Brahman creates time and space and manifests everything that is visible and invisible in the universe. The lowest and highest manifestations of Brahman are linked through an ascending series of levels. Integral knowledge is the knowledge of the transcendental and cosmic Brahman and everything that mediates in manifestation.

The knowledge of the conscient, inconscient, and superconscient and the physical, infra-physical and supra-physical lie beyond the realm of the sense organs and are the primary informants of knowledge construction for most humans at this stage of phylogenetic evolution. Wilber co-opted Sri Aurobindo's integral knowledge spanning all levels of reality to form the basis of 'all level' in his AQAL integral worldview. This can be seen from the following by Sri Aurobindo:

> An integral spiritual consciousness carries in it a knowledge of all the terms of being; it links the highest to the lowest through all the mediating terms and achieves an indivisible whole. At the highest summit of things it opens to the reality, ineffable because superconscient to all but its own self-awareness, of the Absolute. At the lowest end of our being it perceives the Inconscience from which our evolution begins; but at the same time it is aware of the

> One and the All self-involved in those depths, it unveils the secret Consciousness in the Inconscience. Interpretative, revelatory, moving between these two extremes, its vision discovers the manifestation of the One in the Many, the identity of the Infinite in the disparity of things finite, the presence of the timeless Eternal in eternal Time; it is this seeing that illumines for it the meaning of the universe.[10]

Sri Aurobindo addresses the issue of subjectivity and objectivity in hard sciences and social sciences in the chapter titled *Reality and Integral Knowledge*. He addresses the debate between the Western positivist view that there is a reality irrespective of consciousness (emphasizing the objective to the exclusion of the subjective) and the idealist view that reality is intricately bound to the consciousness that approaches it (privileging the subjective over the objective). He reconciles these comprehensively, contending that the subjective and objective perspectives are two facets of the same reality. They, however, are partial views and need to be understood within an integral worldview. The following are some excerpts of his comprehensive reconciliation:

> There is no such thing as an objective reality independent of consciousness; but there is a truth in objectivity. ... the reality of things resides in something that is within them and is independent of the interpretation our mind gives to them and of the structures it builds upon its observation. These structures constitute the mind's subjective image or figure of the universe, but the universe and its objects are not a mere image or figure. They are in essence creations of consciousness, but of a consciousness that is one with being, whose substance is the substance of Being and whose creations too are of that substance, therefore real. In this view the world cannot be a purely subjective creation of Consciousness.[11]

He further writes:

> The subjective and objective are two necessary sides of the manifested Reality and of equal value, and in the range of the objective itself the supraphysical object of consciousness has as much right to acceptance as the physical objectivity; it cannot be a priori set aside as a subjective delusion or hallucination. Subjectivity

> and objectivity are not independent realities, they depend upon each other; they are the Being, through consciousness, looking at itself as subject on the object and the same Being offering itself to its own consciousness as object to the subject.[12]

Wilber appropriates this idea of subjective and objective being two facets but fails to give a reasoned explanation as Sri Aurobindo does regarding how to accomplish the reconciliation. Instead, he introduces exterior and interior dimensions to make four quadrants into which he puts a host of theories and theorists without resolving the fundamental contradictions between them.

### *Flaws in Wilber's understanding of collective holons*

Unlike Sri Aurobindo, Wilber superficially rejects the idea of a single holarchy from individual holons to social holons because it fails to create ecosystems. The sage had rejected the idea of such a large collective system because its constituents (individual holons) are conscious and semi-conscious individuals. However, Wilber does not identify this crucial point.

Further, Wilber identifies two important differences between individual and social holons. First, 'An individual holon has a dominant monad, a social holon has a dominant mode of discourse'.[13] However, he provides no explanation for this statement.

In contrast, Sri Aurobindo points out that matter begins as a manifestation of Consciousness. Just as the Absolute Consciousness manifests in the individual, the Absolute also manifests in the collective. Multiplicity is the twin face of unity of the ultimate reality.

Sri Aurobindo then shows that at each stage of evolution, from Matter to Life to Mind, there are structures and forces within the collective phenomena manifesting the ultimate reality. The collective society has its own stages of evolution through the pre-rational, rational, and spiritual stages of ascent. Depending on the nature of societies and the pressure of forces at play, societies evolve towards rational first and then spiritual or directly spiritual. The collective society is linked intimately to the individuals; at the same time, it has its own evolution. Wilber, on the other hand, provides no clear reason for the morphology of the social holon.

Wilber says: 'Individuals go through mandatory stages whereas social holons do not'.[14] However, in Sri Aurobindo's model, the collective society inescapably goes through its evolution, for only by doing so does it reach the apex of manifestation. In the absence of such a prerequisite for the evolution of the social holons, it is unclear how the collective (i.e. the 'We' quadrants) relates to spirituality in Wilber's model.

## Further Problems with Wilber's Integral Yoga

1. The claims of each quadrant of AQAL have their own tests, standards, and types of evidence and mechanisms for validity: 'a statement is true if the map matches the territory'.[15] While this is expected in a model based on synthetic unity, it results in a fundamental problem – there is no agency leading from one quadrant to another. The truth claims and their validity may hold in one quadrant while failing in another. Such a lack of coherence and unity does not arise in Sri Aurobindo's model.
2. Wilber addresses only the scientist's mode of gaining knowledge and conflates it with the yogi's approach. The scientist moves from objective experience to an intellectual understanding and then to subjective spiritual experience. In Wilber's language, to test any spiritual experience, one must do the practices and then gain the experience. In dhārmic systems, however, especially under the guidance of a guru, the reverse is equally possible, i.e. first gain the spiritual experience and then formulate it objectively and study its claims.
3. Wilber explains the dichotomies present in Western systems:

   "the Left Hand quadrants all depend upon *interpretation* to some extent", the two Right Hand validity claims (objective truth and functional fit) are grounded in *empirical observation* (and some sort of correspondence theory of truth); whereas the two Left Hand validity claims (subjective truthfulness and intersubjective meaning) require extensive *interpretation or hermeneutics* (and some sort of coherence theory of truth). Why the human knowledge quest has almost always divided into these two broad camps, empirical vs. hermeneutic, positivistic vs. interpretive, scientific vs.

> intuitive, analytic vs. transcendental, Anglo-Saxon and Continental, Right Hand and Left Hand, the correct point being that both are indispensable, and that we should not attempt to go one-handed into that dark strange world known as ourselves.[16]

These dichotomies are absent in Indian systems. He realizes that both poles are important, but merely stating it as a flaw in Western systems does not amount to a solution. In the dhārmic systems, the various forms of yoga (Bhakti, Jñāna, and Karma) have characteristic paths, techniques and methods, and yet, all are bound integrally within Brahman.

4. Having ignored yogic knowledge systems, Wilber further attributes many features of evolution, especially of the upper left quadrant, to theories of consciousness from the twelve schools of thought introduced in his work. In doing so, Wilber commits several grave errors:
   a. On his twelve approaches to knowledge, he says: 'Several of the theories of consciousness that I summarized in the Introduction are predicated on the fact that consciousness evolution seems to show evidence of higher or postformal (or 'post-postconventional') stages of growth. There appear to be, in other words, several higher stages in the Upper Left quadrant'.[17] However, none of his twelve approaches, except the loosely termed 'Eastern and Other Contemplative Tradition', contain any postulates, assumptions, mechanisms or results that lead to evolution beyond the human level. Thus, Wilber attributes to Western knowledge systems claims that they do not make.
   b. Wilber's knowledge of Eastern systems and in particular the work of Sri Aurobindo, should have revealed that it is the sage's Integral Yoga which explicitly sees man as a transitional being, with a 'Superman' as the next stage for man's evolution. Wilber does not even mention, let alone credit the idea to Sri Aurobindo's work while obfuscating and falsely attributing most of it to Western theories.
   c. Wilber writes, 'The school of transpersonal psychology, in particular, has begun to investigate these higher stages. Substantial cross-cultural evidence already suggests that there are at least four broad stages of *postformal consciousness development*

– that is, development that goes beyond but includes the formal operational level: the psychic, the subtle, the causal, and the nondual...*The precise definitions of those four postformal stages need not concern us; interested readers can consult the appropriate authorities* (e.g. Walsh and Vaughan, 1993)'.[18] In the garb of such generic terminology, he attributes quintessential yogic, Vedāntic and other dhārmic concepts to Western schools of psychology without any evidence.

5. He attributes the holarchical view to the Great Chain of Being and says it starts to break down when 'jumping from "I" to "super-I"'. The Great Chain of Being comprises premodern traditions whose central claim Wilber defines as the following: 'reality consists of a great hierarchy of knowing and being which can be summarized as matter to body mind to soul to spirit, and at which any level human beings can operate'. Wilber lumps the dhārmic traditions of Vedānta within the Great Chain of Being, which is a misrepresentation. Neither Sri Aurobindo nor Vedānta subscribe to a model where the collective, or 'super-I' as Wilber calls it, can arise out of his morphology of individual holons into social holons. Such clubbing of ideas under a generic term is shallow and misrepresents the dhārmic traditions.
6. Wilber rebrands dhārmic concepts as 'four higher stages of postformal development', which lead to his 'spectrum of consciousness'. He then adds them to his AQAL framework to claim that this system reproduces the Great Chain of Being from Plotinus to Sri Aurobindo:

> If, with reference to the Upper Left quadrant, **we add these four higher and postformal stages to the standard stages given in Figure 1, we arrive at *the Great Chain of Being*, precisely as traditionally outlined by philosopher-sages from Plotinus to Aurobindo to Asanga to Chih-I to Lady Tsogyal...** ...exact details need not detain us; interested readers can consult other works for a finer discussion (Smith, 1976; Lovejoy, 1964; Wilber *et al.*, 1986). ...the interior dimensions of the human being seem to be composed of a *spectrum of consciousness*, running from sensation to perception to impulse to image to symbol to concept to rule to formal to vision-logic to psychic to subtle to causal to nondual states. In simplified form, this spectrum appears to range from subconscious

> to self-conscious to superconscious; from prepersonal to personal to transpersonal; from instinctual to mental to spiritual; from preformal to formal to postformal; from instinct to ego to God.[19]

This claim is false, and his system cannot include Sri Aurobindo's model because the latter's model is rooted in experience and complex dhārmic metaphysics. Wilber's lack of metaphysics creates fundamental differences between individual and collective holons and a lack of agency amongst the quadrants. Yet he proudly claims, 'And remember, all of this is suggested, not by metaphysical foundations and speculations, but by a rigorous data search on evidence already available and already largely uncontested'.[20]

## Wilber's Four-quadrant Model is Synthetic and not Integral

The AQAL model is a framework comprising four quadrants across which all aspects of individual and collective consciousness are distributed. The lower and upper portions of the left quadrants refer to the collective socio-cultural and individual aspects, respectively. The upper right refers to the externally expressed development of the individual while the lower right quadrant does the same at the collective level. Wilber says he came up with AQAL after going through several Eastern and Western frameworks with the aim of bringing them all into one comprehensive framework.

Wilber does not claim to have discovered this through his personal yoga. He considers it purely a mental exercise of putting disparate ideas together and proudly asserts that he has synthesized it as a clever cocktail by mixing, matching, and comparing multiple Western thinkers' views.

However, at the mental/intellectual level, one cannot discover what transcends it. Hence, all his statements about higher consciousness are mere speculations at best and hubris at worst. One needs to first transcend the mental level through the process of yoga, and *only then* know the higher level as direct experience.

This is a synthetic method that can only produce a synthetic outcome and not an integral one, as discussed in the Introduction. This is a key deficiency: Systems without built-in unity will permanently retain irreconcilable schisms. For instance, Wilber's synthetic mishmash cannot explain agency and causation. In the case of Sri Aurobindo's approach, agency and causation are built into the nature of the cosmos because it is the manifestation of sat-cit-ānanda as the foundation and the intelligence-consciousness involuted into the cosmos.

To understand the following two divisions in AQAL—the inner/outer or subjective/objective division, and the individual/plural division—let us look at Sri Aurobindo's explanations from writings as early as 1927. They show that:

1. The Divine, the Eternal, and the Infinite form is sat-cit-ānanda.
2. From the above, various stages and levels of reality manifest.
3. All agency and causation in the cosmos are the result of this: sat-cit-ānanda is the absolute from which all relative things emerge. The involution-evolution explained in earlier chapters is the process by which manifestation takes place.
4. Therefore, the inner (subjective realm) and outer (objective realm) emerge as manifestations from the same ground.
5. Similarly, the individual and the plural are both manifestations of the same absolute which transcends them.

Points 1, 2, and 3 above are explained at great length in many of Sri Aurobindo's works. The following quotes from his writings give us a summary of his yogic insight on the integral unity of all existence. Only because of this built-in unity can there be a quadrant of inner/outer and individual/plural with causation and agency uniting all quadrants with each other:

> **All begins from the Divine, from the Eternal, from the Infinite, all abides in it alone and by it alone, all ends or culminates in the divine Eternal and Infinite. This is the first postulate indispensable for our spiritual seeking**—for on no other base can we find the highest knowledge and the highest life.... A secret Self is the Alpha and Omega of this manifested existence; it is also the constant term, the omnipresent x into which all things resolve separately or together and which is their sum, their constituting material and their essence. **All here is secretly the Divine, all is the Eternal, all is the Infinite....**

> But this secret truth of things is contradicted by the world's external appearances, it is denied by all the facts placed before us by our mind and senses ... If we go beyond our embodied mind and senses, we break suddenly into something permanent that feels itself to be eternal and infinite, that cannot see itself as anything else and we also cannot conceive of it as anything else, an infinite Self, an eternal Spirit. ... **Every relative supposes an absolute.**[21]

On the other hand, Wilber cannot explain causation and agency in his AQAL model because *he rejects all metaphysics*. He writes that the spiritual traditions of the world have had their

> metaphysics critiqued—'trashed' is probably the better word—by both modernist and postmodernist epistemologies, and there has as yet arisen nothing compelling to take their place.[22]

This is a sweeping dismissal of all metaphysics by merely citing some third-party unnamed 'modernists and postmodernists'. He does not provide any specific refutation of the metaphysics of Indian systems, such as Sāṃkhya and various paths of yoga. His depth of knowledge seems limited to Western metaphysics, which were not developed by the yogic insights of ṛṣi-s but by intellectuals like him. By rejecting those Western metaphysical systems, he arrogantly assumes he has dealt a fatal blow to all metaphysics.

Without going into the specifics of which spiritual traditions he refers to, he states that the aim of his project is the: 'reconstruction of spiritual traditions of the great wisdom traditions but with none of their *metaphysical baggage*'.

This approach has serious repercussions. Without any metaphysical foundation, it lacks integral unity. There is no absolute reality he has been able to reach in his own practices from which he could try to explain all the systems he has curated. At best, he can claim a conceptual unity based on merely intellectualizing playfully and creatively, and this can only lead to synthetic unity.

By way of analogy, if we glue together various parts taken from different plants, it does not mean that any such entity exists as a living plant. It would merely be a construction by us and not something that represents biological reality. A conceptual representation is not necessarily real.

Therefore, *Sri Aurobindo's metaphysics can produce Wilber's four quadrants as an integral whole, but the converse is not true*: Wilber's methodology cannot produce the foundational Vedic tenets.

The following illustration elucidates the differences between the ideas of Sri Aurobindo and Wilber:

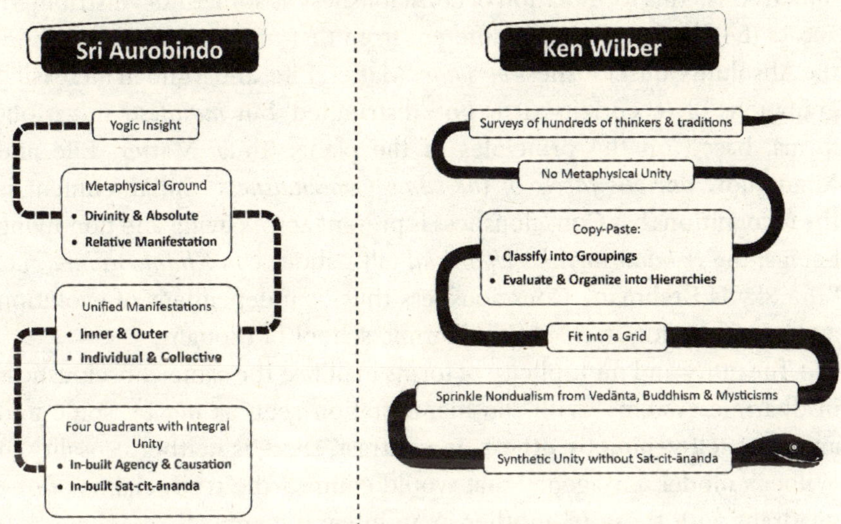


**Figure 5: Differences Between Sri Aurobindo's and Wilber's Models**

## The Problem of Consciousness in Wilber's AQAL Model

Wilber's conception of consciousness is something he pieced together in a synthetic manner from the two hundred sources he studied. In the process of bringing them all into a single organizing principle, he focuses on the commonalities found in these works. He uses broad strokes to convey the impression that two different voices are referring to the same concept, even if he has to force that conclusion by hiding their conflicts.

He also errs on two other major counts: 1) giving the impression that Eastern systems were *only concerned with those paradigms that fit into his upper left quadrant (I/interior)*, which is patently false, as shown in previous chapters; and 2) failing to highlight that the dhārmic framework is complete and total in itself, with unique concepts, and beyond Wilber's AQAL framework. Wilber thus presents a very misleading picture by restricting 'Eastern and Other Wisdom schools', in which dhārmic concepts fall into a single quadrant.

Without using yoga as his method of discovery and by discarding metaphysics, Wilber believes that consciousness 'appears' to be 'distributed across all four quadrants' with all of their various levels and dimensions. This formulation of consciousness as something 'distributed' across the four quadrants is different from that of Sri Aurobindo, where the Absolute Consciousness *pervades* Matter, Life, and Mind in increasing gradations of receptivity; it is not 'distributed' but *manifests* in various forms, based on the principles of the plane. Thus, Matter, Life and Mind show *various facets of the same Consciousness*. Enlightenment is the recognition that Consciousness is present across living and non-living beings; the *Bṛhadāraṇyaka Upaniṣad* talks about *Om Kham Brahma*, i.e. 'The Sky is Brahman'. Consciousness thus, is independent of evolution and manifestation itself in the dhārmic school of thought.

The unity and multiplicity of forms manifest the same consciousness in dhārmic systems, with the manifestation seen as *līla* by some and an act of self-veiling by others. In contrast, there is neither causality in Wilber's model nor agency that would connect the truth claims of one quadrant with those in another in an integral manner.

Further, Wilber remarks that 'Consciousness is not located in the organism. Rather, consciousness is a four-quadrant affair, and it exists, if it exists at all, distributed across all four quadrants, anchored equally in each. Neither consciousness, personality, individual agency, nor psychopathology can be located simply or solely in the individual organism'.[23] This demonstrates that Wilber believes that consciousness cannot be contained entirely in an individual.

In Sri Aurobindo's work, consciousness exists independently and entirely both within the individual (who uses yoga to experience it at its highest gradation) and outside the individual,

> Consciousness is a fundamental thing, the fundamental thing in existence it is the energy, the motion, the movement of consciousness that creates the universe and all that is in it not only

> the macrocosm but the microcosm is nothing but consciousness arranging itself. ...**when consciousness in its movement or rather a certain stress of movement forgets itself in the action it becomes an apparently unconscious energy; when it forgets itself in the form it becomes the electron, the atom, the material object. In reality it is still consciousness that works in the energy and determines the form and the evolution of form. When it wants to liberate itself, slowly, evolutionarily, out of Matter, but still in the form, it emerges as life, as animal, as man and it can go on evolving itself still farther out of its involution and become something more than mere man.**[24]

Wilber believes that physical organs such as the brain, are like containers with consciousness as their content: 'Thus, it is quite true that **consciousness is anchored in the physical brain (as maintained by theories 1, 3, 6, 8). But consciousness is also and equally anchored in interior intentionality (as maintained by theories 2, 4, 7, 10, 11), intentionality that *cannot* be explained in physicalist or empiricist terms nor disclosed by their methods or their validity claims**'.

This stands in stark contrast with the ideas of Sri Aurobindo, who has repeatedly recognized and addressed this particular Western construct:

> Materialism indeed insists that, whatever the extension of consciousness, it is a material phenomenon inseparable from our physical organs and not their utiliser but their result.[25]
>
> Our physical organism no more causes or explains thought and consciousness than the construction of an engine causes or explains the motive-power of steam or electricity. The force is anterior, not the physical instrument.[26]

Consciousness is not the *product* of evolution; rather, evolution, along with its twin process of involution, manifests Absolute Consciousness, which exists independent of the processes themselves. This clear distinction is very important and a huge differentiator between the work of Sri Aurobindo and Wilber. If evolution is the process that creates consciousness as Wilber maintains, one would return to the question which Sri Aurobindo has already resolved in his approach: What is 'that' which evolves?

Wilber's reliance on cutting-edge scientific discoveries to explain this evolution is *a newer restatement of the fundamental starting points of the materialist and the mentalist,* who only believe in that which can be verified externally and rationally explained by the mind. *Though he is clever about hiding it, Wilber is, in effect, a materialist disguised as a spiritualist.*

## The AQAL Model has Modernist-Postmodernist Conflicts

We will show that Wilber's four-quadrant model *is basically an expanded version of the upper right quadrant.* The upper right quadrant represents empiricism, positivism, and realism—different philosophies emerging out of scientific materialism. By Wilber's own admission, scientific materialism was guided by reductionism which reduces the complex nature of phenomena, objects, and reality into simpler or fundamental units or interaction of those units or parts.

His model may seem to be an integration of modernity and postmodernity, but it is actually a replication of modernity, i.e. *a reductionism of quadrants.* Despite heavily critiquing reductionism, Wilber is blind to the fact that in his model, he has attempted an expanded version of exactly what he has critiqued, i.e. reducing the understanding of the epistemological, ontological, and metaphysical underpinnings of our cosmos and existence into an interaction of four quadrants.

The upper right quadrant's methodology is objectivism which has been critiqued from various postmodern angles including cognitive sciences, phenomenology, feminist critical theories and linguistics. The postmodern critiques paradoxically contradict themselves. Their assertions have been criticized as self-referential and their reasoning as self-contradictory.

Postmodernism leads to a complete collapse of what Vedānta calls pairs of opposites (Cartesian dichotomies) like subjective/objective, true/false, subject/object, which correspond to Indian deconstruction of duality, māyā, linguistic discourse, etc. In Vedānta, this deconstruction serves to move the seeker on a yogic quest into the nature of reality. Wilber, on the other hand, incorporates some simplistic contributions of the postmodern critiques into his AQAL model *without resolving the deep tensions between modernism and postmodernism.*

### *Correspondence Theory of Truth in AQAL*

A cornerstone of the upper right quadrant is the 'Correspondence Theory of Truth', which states that the truth or falsity of a statement regarding the nature of reality is determined by how it relates to observable facts. Thomas Kuhn and Paul Feyerabend challenged this theory, maintaining that truth is dependent and contingent upon paradigms and participating individuals. Wilber has ignored these crucial insights, extending instead his version of the correspondence theory of truth to his entire model: His holons of each quadrant have corresponding correlates in the rest of the three quadrants.

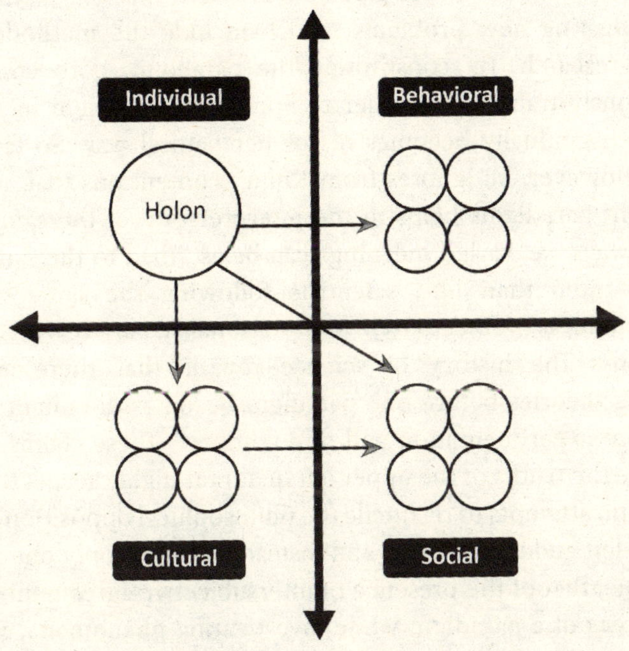


**Figure 6: Wilber's Four Quadrants**

Any integration of the upper right quadrant with the lower left quadrant is fraught with problems until the epistemological and metaphysical opposition between them is resolved. According to Wilber, the upper right quadrant deals with the philosophy of realism, positivism, and empiricism; the lower left deals with issues of intersubjective agreements, for which he names Thomas Kuhn as the representative.[27]

Kuhn challenged the pursuit of science-based on the realist/objectivist/universalist/positivist framework—which defines the upper right—stating that science is primarily dictated by a paradigm that encapsulates within itself unarticulated assumptions that its scientists may be unaware of. For research to take place, the community must agree upon the goals, methodologies, and valid subjects, which constitutes a framework within which the investigation of nature can take place.

The paradigm has two components: a *disciplinary matrix* and *shared exemplars*. The *disciplinary matrix* comprises a certain fundamental set of assumptions that are often unstated and not subject to an empirical test. These assumptions form the basis for testing specific hypotheses. The other component of the paradigm is *shared exemplars*—the models for investigating new problems, which include the methodology for pursuing research. By constituting the paradigm, both components unconsciously train a researcher to approach a problem in a specific way, which gradually becomes his or her natural way. So far, Wilber is right. However, he ignores from Kuhn's contentions that adherence to different paradigms helps in the interpretation of the same data in different ways, i.e. varied meanings can be ascribed to the same data.[28]

More often than not, scientists following the same norms of disinterestedness, objectivity, and rationality arrive at different conclusions. The history of science reveals that there are many competing theories before one paradigm becomes dominant; all have arisen from experimentation and observation.[29] These claims by Kuhn have made the truths of the upper left quadrant highly suspect.[30] Wilber has made no attempts to reconcile the philosophical opposition between the lower left and upper right, and instead has taken only one aspect of the critique, that of the presence of intersubjective agreement between the scientists of a paradigm while investigating phenomena, which he assimilates in his integral model.

We agree with Wilber that extreme relativism and postmodernism lead to a culture of egocentrism, nihilism, narcissism, and ethnocentrism. He has written extensively on this in the journal *One Taste,* explaining that the self-refuting and self-referential nature of postmodern critique destroys its own metaphysical and epistemological foundations. However, because he has not sufficiently incorporated the postmodern critique of modernity, he ends up resurrecting the modernist paradigm. He has failed to achieve his goal of integrating modernism and postmodernism; his model is primarily based on modernist assumptions.

Worse, he replicates the Eurocentric modernist claims. This has absolved him of studying in detail the contributions of the non-Western world or even a nuanced and in-depth intellectual understanding of various spiritual schools of non-Western origin. In three of his four quadrants, he only credits and acknowledges Western contributions. (Even where non-Western contributions could be discussed, such as the Indian influence on the development of postmodernism.) He has simply reproduced the imperialistic discourse on the history of India. He has not critically examined the theories and claims of the European Enlightenment project. Instead of providing comprehensive integral knowledge of the world or humankind, Wilber's integral model is a portal for Western hegemony.

Richard Carlson, author of *Integral Ideology: An Ideological Genealogy of Integral Theory and Practice,* makes a similar observation about Wilber's work, highlighting that he fails to place Sri Aurobindo's work in the context of Indian schools of philosophy while continuing with Eurocentric models. Carlson concludes that Wilber's work is 'by its very nature very hegemonic' because he fails to respect the frameworks of non-Western models. He calls out how Wilber has failed to even acknowledge the vast Indian traditional discourse in which Sri Aurobindo's work is founded.

While highlighting the imperialistic nature of Wilber's project, Carlson writes that the very basis of Wilber's Integral Theory is riddled with bias. It favors Western Europe and North America to identify theorists and attribute to them important ideas, despite Wilber saying he wanted to avoid a racist bias:

> An integral theory which valorizes its own epistemology by denying other traditions, theories, practices their own voice, or by simply reducing them to mere coordinates on a quaternary grid segregates rather than integrates. Any theory which asserts itself ideologically by cannibalizing other traditions and appropriating the voice of alterity as a function of its integral model while discarding the ten thousand nuances, subtleties, traces of culture

> which are essential to indigenous identity, fails at the level of integration itself. These theoretical practices are not integral but imperialist, such discourses do not achieve cultural hybridity but rather cultural hegemony. Such an integral theory is colonialist at its worst and patronizing at its best. How can integral theories be of service to social integration when such integration has historically often occurred through the obliteration of differences of indigenous cultures, which are seen as more primitive (less evolved memes) by colonializing regimes?
>
> The practice of Integral Theory attempts to integrate many disparate cultural theories and practices to obtain a global perspective. Integral Theory itself however, is geographically specific. The overwhelming majority of integral theorists are from North America and Western Europe, and certainly a much higher percentages are male theorists. This in itself is not a reason for condemnation, because in the course of history, philosophy has mostly been a man's game and many philosophical schools have been defined by the particular geographical regions of their origin: a British school, a Continental school, the Frankfurt school. However, one of the chief concerns of critical theory over the past forty or so years are the numerous problems demonstrated with bias rooted in patriarchy or in a specific geographical, cultural, or academic orientation. In the interest of self-disclosure shouldn't integral theory consider a qualifier to a prefix itself as North American or European Integral Theory?[31]

Carlson also brings attention to some claims Wilber made regarding events at the time. Wilber had even interpreted the Iraq war (2003-11) and classified the main players involved based on his reading of their actions.

> We should certainly take Wilber and Beck at their word when they voice abhorrence of racism and colonialism. ... Some of the conclusions they have drawn in times of crisis have been poorly reasoned by referencing a model whose process attractor is a hierarchical ordering of individuals and groups:
>
> ...Placing Tony Blair at the top of an ascending order of world leaders in the run up to the Iraq war,

> ...The cynical dismissal of anti-war demonstrators protesting an illegal unprovoked war as a consequence of the green meme,
>
> ...The christening of Generals Schwartzkopf and Powell as spiral masters in their prosecution of a war which gave tacit approval to the use of the term collateral damage as a way to dehumanize civilian casualties,
>
> ...The claim that George W Bush transcended the lower memetic stages of bipartisan politics,
>
> ...The stereotyping of whole aboriginal and indigenous populations as constituting the lower rungs of the evolutionary ladder...[32]

Carlson further remarks that while Wilber's aim is to order reality in all its multidimensions, what he has essentially done is present a 'monochromatic' hierarchy unwilling to recognize its own ideological blind spots.

Wilber also critiques the anti-foundationalism of Ludwig Wittgenstein and the anti-essentialism of the American philosopher Richard McKay Rorty by showing the self-referential nature of their arguments and revives an essentializing discourse on integralism with as little representation of the non-Western cultures as possible. He critiques the discursive power of Paul-Michel Foucault, the French philosopher, to enforce and polemically argue his case. He argues against Lyotard's anti-universality and anti-metanarrative claims but gives us a primarily universal Western theory of everything. He attacks the anti-hierarchy discourse but ends up championing a highly hierarchical model, despite his claims to the contrary.

Wilber's integral model is a monolithic giant that seeks to quell the liberation potential of postmodern discourse for the oppressed and historically exploited cultures and peoples. Yet, he claims to honour the noble truths and sentiments behind the postmodern discourse, like 'freedom, tolerance, aperspectival embrace, and liberation from unnecessary or unfair conventions'.[33]

He proposes to accomplish such a grand vision on the basis of two concepts: unitas multiplex and universal pluralism. Unitas multiplex refers to having deep universal features along with localized surface features. Given the primacy of his West-leaning model, it turns into what Malhotra has described as Western Universalism – 'The profound assumption is that the shape and direction of world history are leading to a single Western goal – be it salvation or scientific secular progress. All peoples and cultures are forced into the various schemes put forward to bring this about. Indeed, modern laws, regulations, conventions and common practices are formed with this in mind (whether consciously or not)'.[34]

The second principle is that of universal pluralism; however, his model is based on Western Universalism, whereas a superior framework for universal pluralism and mutual respect would be the dhārmic framework. His so-called 'universal' pluralism is an overarching umbrella to sequester and castrate the non-Western world. In the guise of his Integral Theory, he has propagated a reductionist (hence, non-integral) Western worldview.

It would not surprise us if Wilber dismisses our critique as coming from a lower ethnocentric standpoint, as his theory is critiqued from the standpoint of Indian spirituality.

## Wilber Fails to Resolve Postmodern Self-referentiality

Wilber's Integral Psychology relies heavily upon naïve Western realism and scientific materialism, which maintains that there is an objective reality independent of the observer. Postmodernism, however, questions the premise of the rational, unbiased, and value-free pursuit of knowledge given that any observer is necessarily embedded in a social, sociological, historical, political, economic, and paradigmatic context where his or her psychology, cosmological worldview, language, inner states, beliefs, expectations, and previous knowledge of the world impinge on the interpretation and construction of the experience. The universality claimed of the psychological theories, which are Wilber's building blocks, of his AQAL, have been seriously challenged by cross-cultural, cultural, and social-constructivist psychologists around the world. Besides, the various theories Wilber mixes were in mutual tensions that have never been reconciled by their respective proponents. His scheme minimizes these differences by over-simplifying.

He points out the self-referential nature of the postmodern assertions. The *Eye of Spirit* outlines some of the conflicts between objectivism and subjectivism, realism and idealism, hermeneutics and positivism, empiricism and constructivism, etc. He criticizes the self-referential nature of postmodern assertions, seeing them as exclusive truth claims that cannot be independently verified.

Critiquing the social constructivists and how their 'extreme' position leads to self-referentiality, Wilber writes:

> Extreme constructivists claim that there is no such thing as objective truth at all, because our ideas are simply constructed according to various interests—usually power, but also various "isms" and various ideologies (sexism, racism, speciesism, colonialism, etc.). Yet the constructivists themselves claim that their stance is true. And this they cannot do without asserting a theory of truth that is not itself distorted by power or ideology..... They are simply claiming that it is objectively true that there is no objective truth at all.[35]

His following statement on cultural relativism is another example:

> Cultural relativists, extreme pluralists, and multiculturalists are all caught in a similar contradiction: The claim is made that all truths are relative, that there are and can be no universal truths. ... that view itself is claiming to be universally true. It is making a series of strong claims that it insists are true for all cultures (the relative nature of truth, the contextuality of claims, the social relativity of all categories, the historicity of truth, and so on). This view thus claims that there are no universal truths of any sort—except for its own, which are universal and superior in a world where nothing is supposed to be universal or superior at all.[36]

Once paradoxes and contradictions are recognized, such as 'truth is relative', an absolute truth claim about the nature of reality, then the pursuit of knowledge using the mind and rationality reaches a cul-de-sac. In such a situation, a mystical or a spiritual exploration is required. Any knowledge espoused from a rational, intellectual, and mental standpoint about consciousness, reality, truth, and psychology is erroneous.

Nāgārjuna specifically states that any pursuit of knowledge which does not experientially and ontologically transcend dichotomous pairs like subjective/objective, absolute/relative, local/universal, real/non-real and cause/effect, can only result in ignorance or avidyā. These pairs have no meaning beyond their relationship with one another. The solution to the enigma of our existence or the knowledge of the ultimate is gained by the transcendence of all the reified thoughts through a way of 'seeing' and 'being' called prajña.

Similarly, Advaita Vedānta posits that the ordinary cognition of the world comprises dualities and that the Ultimate Reality is beyond all dualities. All entities and concepts in the phenomenal world appear as pairs of opposites, and true knowledge can only be gained when one transcends them.

Wilber chooses to ignore these important dhārmic insights though it is abundantly clear from *The Spectrum of Consciousness* that he is familiar with them. Instead of deepening his writings from a trans-rational and trans-intellectual mode, he attempts a simplistic mental understanding of spirituality within Western psychology. However, this Western psychology from the European Enlightenment is an intellectual activity that cannot perceive reality as a whole and only as divided, classified, compared, and measured. Such knowledge can be synthetic but not integral. Integral knowledge comes only in trans-mental and trans-rational states in which the mind and reason are transcended and are used for dissemination. Sri Aurobindo, commenting on the limitation of the mind on numerous occasions, puts it succinctly:

> Mind in its essence is a consciousness which measures, limits, cuts out forms of things from the indivisible whole and contains them as if each were a separate integer. Even with what exists as obvious parts and fractions, Mind establishes this fiction of its ordinary commerce that they are things with which it can deal separately and not merely as objects of a whole. For, even when it knows that they are not things in themselves, it is obliged to deal with them as if they were things in themselves; otherwise it could not subject them to its own characteristic activity. It is this essential characteristic of Mind which conditions the workings of all its operative powers, whether conception, perception, sensation or the dealings of creative thought. It conceives, perceives, senses things as if rigidly cut out from a background or a mass and employs them as fixed units of the material given to it for creation or possession. All its action and enjoyment deal thus with wholes that form part of a greater whole, and these subordinate wholes again are broken up into parts

> which are also treated as wholes for the particular purposes they serve. Mind may divide, multiply, add, subtract, but it cannot get beyond the limits of this mathematics. If it goes beyond, and tries to conceive the real whole, it loses itself in a foreign element; it falls from its own firm ground into the ocean of the intangible, into the abysms of the infinite where it can neither perceive, conceive, sense nor deal with its subject for creation and enjoyment.[37]

And again:

> Mind is an instrument of analysis and synthesis, but not of essential knowledge. Its function is to cut out something vaguely from the unknown Thing in itself and call this measurement or delimitation of it the whole, and again to analyse the whole into its parts which it regards as separate mental objects. It is only the parts and accidents that the Mind can see definitely and, after its own fashion, know.[38]

Similarly, according to Advaita Vedānta, the mind is not the knower of things but an instrument of knowledge. Just like physical objects can be observed, the mind also can be observed which makes it *an object of knowledge rather than a knower*. Hence, the knowledge of our existence cannot be grasped in its totality by the mind; something else is the knower. That ultimate knower is the Self, which is the self-intelligent, self-aware, self-evident, and self-illumined consciousness.

It is only by purposefully identifying oneself with the consciousness beyond the mind that one finds the truths of one's integral existence, and hence discovers integral psychology. All the things we call our 'real self' are not the self but external aspects of a personality put forth by nature for the play of life. The real self is within, and above all that we usually identify as our self. The identification with the self reveals to us the knowledge of all the mysteries that the universe has concealed from us, including the truth behind the psychology of every human being. Sri Aurobindo comments:

> Since the Self which we come to realise by the path of knowledge is not only the reality which lies behind and supports the states and movements of our psychological being, but also that transcendent and universal Existence which has manifested itself in all the movements of the universal, the knowledge of the Self includes also

> the knowledge of the principles of Being, its fundamental modes and its relations with the principles of the phenomenal universe. **This was what was meant by the Upanishad when it spoke of the Brahman as that which being known all is known. It has to be realised first as the pure principle of existence, afterwards, says the Upanishad, its essential modes become clear to the soul which realises it.** We may ...before realisation, try to analyse by the metaphysical reason and even understand intellectually what Being is and what the world is, but such metaphysical understanding is not the Knowledge. ...we may have the realisation in knowledge and vision, but this is incomplete without realisation in the entire soul-experience and the unity of all our being with that which we realise. **It is the science of Yoga to know and the art of Yoga to be unified with the Highest so that we may live in the Self and act from the supreme poise, becoming one not only in the conscious essence but in the conscious law of our being with the transcendent Divine whom all things and creatures, whether ignorantly or with partial knowledge and experience, seek to express through the lower law of their members.**[39]

## The AQAL Model is Hierarchical

Wilber's modernist and objectivist swing makes his model hierarchical. The planes of consciousness, starting from matter to causal, are arranged in a rigid three-dimensional manner, and all his different lines of growth are arranged in a hierarchical sequence of pre-conventional, conventional, post-conventional, and post-postconventional. This hierarchical cosmology, referred to as holarchical in Wilber's scheme, limits diversity and leans towards absolutism rather than a fine balance between universal and plural.

In Sri Aurobindo's scheme, the planes are not arranged in a three-dimensional hierarchy, and there are countless possibilities of spiritual growth and manifestation without one necessarily being better than the other. Sri Aurobindo's scheme is more like a network model while Wilber's is a hierarchical one.

Wilber's description of the evolutionary stages in social growth is highly linear; for example, archaic is inferior to magic, which is inferior to mythic, and so on. Sri Aurobindo's evolutionary metaphysics, though suggesting a linear teleology in the ultimate sense, does not adopt such a rigid straight-line approach and explains the complexity involved in sociological and individual evolution. Wilber's simplistic linear approach, supported by parroting colonial indology, forces Vedic societies to be at stages such as magical or mythic and be superseded by Europe.

In Sri Aurobindo's scheme, it is only through a conscious spiritual experience of the supramental that the tension between the absolute and the relative can be resolved. This needs to be compared with the way Wilber resolves the problem of absoluteness and relativeness and will be dealt with in significant detail.

Wilber's proclivity towards hierarchal thinking interprets Sri Aurobindo's work in a similar way, enabling him to map the sage's work onto his own. The levels of consciousness described by Sri Aurobindo are not merely theoretical, for they are stages experienced by the sage. While Wilber can bring together under a single umbrella work by Loevinger or Robert Kegan on the matter, doing the same for Sri Aurobindo's work is fundamentally flawed. Nevertheless, Wilber not only brings all of them onto the same platform but increasingly abandons any credit due to Sri Aurobindo and associates the seminal ideas with the Swiss philosopher, Jean Gebser. Wilber's figures and work in *Integral Spirituality* is biased with this misrepresentation.

Wilber's left-brain fixation is the result of his own limited experience of higher states of consciousness. Worse still, this tendency gets magnified as his ideas flow down to other followers who have even less direct experience. The AQAL model is, at best, a mental system for reductionist explanations based on an entity's positioning in the system. Such an approach is not looking for the realization of knowledge but an intellectual classification. As Sri Aurobindo would say about such an approach: 'When everything is explained, nothing is known'.

Along with his quadrant system, Wilber also looks at methods to approaching the quadrants in his Integral Methodological Pluralism. Again, these approaches lack appreciation for Eastern/Indian systems and only use Western references even when they have been initially drawn from Eastern traditions.

We summarize the main issues with Wilber's AQAL and Integral Methodological Pluralism as follows.

| Category | Problem | Consequence | Sri Aurobindo's Solution |
|---|---|---|---|
| Lack of Understanding | Wilber does not distinguish between i) Synthetic Unity metaphysics, which is conjectural; and ii) Integral Unity metaphysics, which is self-realized. | Lack of causality, which cannot be generated by the eight methodologies of IMP. | Deeply rooted in Integral Unity, with dhārmic paradigms including Vedānta, Sāṃkhyā, *Gītā*, and Yoga. |
| | Lack of agency and causality. | What *causes* unity and multiplicity, i.e. the I and We categorization in AQAL? | Sat-cit-ānanda in unmanifest form is unified with every form and has attributes such as unity and multiplicity, one and many, and being and non-being. |
| | Lack of agency and causality. | What causes I/We and It/Its categorization in AQAL? | Sat-cit-ānanda in unmanifest form is unified with every form and attribute; when it manifests as individual/universal, it assumes subjective and objective views. Puruṣa-prakṛti unity is upheld. |
| Eurocentric Bias | None of the eight methodologies of his IMP have any basis in Integral Unity. | Contrary to Wilber's assertions, he cannot regenerate all the experiences he claims to transcend. | |

Chapter 14

# Wilber-V: Integral Post-Metaphysics Compared with Sri Aurobindo's Integral Yoga

Wilber-V is the next stage of Wilber's works. It introduces 'Integral Post-Metaphysics' and includes 1) rejection of metaphysics; and 2) incorporation of the postmodernist dismissal of objective reality in favor of subjective perspectives. This second point leads to the important idea of this phase, i.e. that objective reality does not exist independently but only as structures of human consciousness. Further, Wilber maintains that these structures of consciousness are 'forms that have developed in time, evolution, and history'.[1]

Wilber believes that this phase of his work marks a break from all his earlier material and is apparently without any precedent:

> In any event, those aspects of the following presentation that fall under the rubric of "Integral Post-Metaphysics" all fit within the AQAL matrix, but they reinterpret that matrix in profound ways. ... aspects of my previous writing had at least some historical precedents, much of Integral Post-Metaphysics is without precedents of any sort. Whether or not it has any merit remains to be seen, but it is *abruptly original.* [2]

A closer scrutiny of his claims reveals that all Wilber has done is summarily dismiss Sri Aurobindo's work, deride it as old-school metaphysics, and erase all references to him, while appropriating his model entirely from the sage. He wants to seal his claim as the modern architect of the Integral approach.

Wilber's main thesis is that any spiritual template that does not adapt itself to the present postmodern age deserves no serious study:

> No system (spiritual or otherwise) that does not come to terms with modern Kantian and postmodern Heideggerian thought can hope to survive with any intellectual respectability (agree with them or disagree with them, they have to be addressed) – and that means all spirituality must be post-metaphysical in some sense.[3]

His statement is applicable to religions based on dogma, and 'history-centrism', which Malhotra defines as a 'fixation on specific and often incompatible claims to divine truth revealed in the course of history'.[4] However, dhārmic traditions do not fit into his mold and cannot be dismissed on this basis. Malhotra has made an extensive comparison between the history-centric approach to ultimate truth and the yogic method.

Wilber seeks to 'integrate' spirituality by bringing the role of modern scientific revolutions, revealing once again the tendency to privilege materialism. He claims that modern scientific discoveries can lead to the elimination of 'metaphysical baggage' and writes:

> Second, as Einsteinian physics applied to objects moving slower than the speed of light collapses back into Newtonian physics, so an Integral Post-Metaphysics can generate all the essentials of premodern spiritual and metaphysical systems but without their now-discredited ontological baggage. This, .... is the central contribution of an Integral Post-Metaphysics—it does not itself contain metaphysics, but it can generate metaphysics as one possible AQAL matrix configuration under the limit conditions of premodern cultures.[5]

The problem of metaphysics he wants to confront is a Western one. Sri Aurobindo has repeatedly maintained that Indian spirituality is different from the typical Western understanding of it. When speaking of India, he writes:

> She saw too that man has the power of exceeding himself, of becoming himself more entirely and profoundly than he is, — truths which have only recently begun to be seen in Europe and

> seem even now too great for its common intelligence. She saw the myriad gods beyond man, God beyond the gods, and beyond God his own ineffable eternity; she saw that there were ranges of life beyond our life, ranges of mind beyond our present mind and above these she saw the splendours of the spirit. Then with that calm audacity of her intuition which knew no fear or littleness and shrank from no act whether of spiritual or intellectual, ethical or vital courage, she declared that there was none of these things which man could not attain if he trained his will and knowledge; he could conquer these ranges of mind, become the spirit, become a god, become one with God, become the ineffable Brahman. And with the logical practicality and sense of science and organised method which distinguished her mentality, she set forth immediately to find out the way. Hence from long ages of this insight and practice there was ingrained in her her spirituality, her powerful psychic tendency, her great yearning to grapple with the infinite and possess it, her ineradicable religious sense, her idealism, her Yoga, the constant turn of her art and her philosophy.[6]

In contrast with Wilber's approach, Sri Aurobindo envisioned newer forms of literature, sciences, and philosophies emanating from a society that accords a central place to spirituality while reinventing various external forms. Sri Aurobindo writes:

> Metaphysical thinking will always no doubt be a strong element in her mentality, and it is to be hoped that she will never lose her great, her sovereign powers in that direction; but Indian metaphysics are as far removed from the brilliant or the profound idea-spinning of the French or the German mind as from the broad intellectual generalising on the basis of the facts of physical science which for some time did duty for philosophy in modern Europe. It has always been in its essential parts an intellectual approach to spiritual realisation.[7]

## Sri Aurobindo on Collective Consciousness

While we have so far considered Wilber's dismissal of metaphysics and his model, which considers social and collective aspects of humanity as a patchwork of incompatible theories, it is important to see the contrast in Sri Aurobindo's work.

Most studies of Sri Aurobindo have focused on his Integral Yoga, its philosophy, and metaphysics. However, he was also a prolific writer on matters of cultural, social, and political issues. He has written extensively on the collective evolution of society and humanity. His vision is founded in a source that goes beyond the material and the intellectual and is based on the spiritual.[8] With deep insights into the problems of the present age from the perspective of a yogi, Sri Aurobindo recognized the need for a philosophy that would guide individuals as well as collective humanity toward an integral transformation.

While considering the various principles and methods of social systems, Sri Aurobindo recognized keenly that the lacuna seen in most social theories stems not only from a lack of understanding of man's true reality but also the social aspects of man's life:

> Nothing is more obscure to humanity or less seized by its understanding, whether in the power that moves it or the sense of the aim towards which it moves, than its own communal and collective life. Sociology does not help us, for it only gives us the general story of the past and the external conditions under which communities have survived. History teaches us nothing; it is a confused torrent of events and personalities or a kaleidoscope of changing institutions. We do not seize the real sense of all this change and this continual streaming forward of human life in the channels of Time. What we do seize are current or recurrent phenomena, facile generalisations, partial ideas. We talk of democracy, aristocracy and autocracy, collectivism and individualism, imperialism and nationalism, the State and the commune, capitalism and labour; we advance hasty generalisations and make absolute systems which are positively announced today only to be abandoned perforce tomorrow; we espouse causes and ardent enthusiasms whose triumph turns to an early disillusionment and then forsake them for others, perhaps for those that we have taken so much trouble to destroy. For a whole century mankind thirsts and battles after liberty and earns it with a bitter expense of toil, tears and blood; the century that enjoys without having fought for it turns away as from a puerile illusion

> and is ready to renounce the depreciated gain as the price of some new good. **And all this happens because our whole thought and action with regard to our collective life is shallow and empirical; it does not seek for, it does not base itself on a firm, profound and complete knowledge.** The moral is not the vanity of human life, of its ardours and enthusiasms and of the ideals it pursues, but the necessity of a wiser, larger, more patient search after its true law and aim.[9]

In Wilber's approach, the various disciplines and philosophies used to study the collective are based on empirical ideas and are disconnected from each other because they did not arise from direct integral knowledge. Each approach has a piecemeal analysis of man's existence, with some exclusively focusing on the spiritual and internal matters of the individual and others on the external life of man and society. Sri Aurobindo's work amply demonstrates that he has studied all aspects of Integral Yoga and any analysis that discounts his work in social philosophy for limited focus on his work on individual yoga, constitutes an egregious error of omission. Sri Aurobindo clearly writes that his work in *The Life Divine* and *The Synthesis of Yoga*, his most cited works, relate to

> an individual self-development, and therefore it was necessary to show too how our ideal can work out in the social life of mankind. In The Psychology of Social Development we have indicated how these truths affect the evolution of human society. In The Ideal of Human Unity, we have taken the present trend of mankind towards a closer unification and tried to appreciate its tendencies and show what is wanting to them in order that the real human unity may be achieved.[10]

Author Kishor Gandhi's statement holds immense significance:

> His status amongst the social philosophers of the world should be as high as his status amongst philosophers in general. As he is now widely acknowledged as the greatest philosopher of all ages, so also he should be recognised as the greatest social philosopher of all times. So high an estimate of Sri Aurobindo as a social philosopher may seem to be far exaggerated to some persons, but any lesser

> estimate of him may as well be a mistake of their judgment due to the narrowness of their comprehension.[11]

### *Role of the individual in collective transformation*

Unlike Wilber's approach, which sees the collective as a synthesis of individuals, Sri Aurobindo's approach is steeped in integral unity. Man's individual transformation and unveiling of his true self are not separate from the collective transformation. It is *a necessary condition*:

> The individual is indeed the key of the evolutionary movement; for it is the individual who finds himself, who becomes conscious of the Reality. **The movement of the collectivity is a largely subconscious mass movement; it has to formulate and express itself through the individuals to become conscious:** its general mass consciousness is always less evolved than the consciousness of its most developed individuals, and it progresses in so far as it accepts their impress or develops what they develop. The individual does not owe his ultimate allegiance either to the State which is a machine or to the community which is a part of life and not the whole of life: his allegiance must be to the Truth, the Self, the Spirit, the Divine which is in him and in all; not to subordinate or lose himself in the mass, but to find and express that truth of being in himself and help the community and humanity in its seeking for its own truth and fullness of being must be his real object of existence.[12]

We have seen in previous chapters how sat-cit-ānanda, or Ultimate Reality, manifests itself in multiplicity, with each form and creation representing the same higher consciousness. Ego is a device used for evolutionary purposes to anchor man's interactions with prakṛti and distinguish himself from inconscience. This necessitates the transformation of the individual in order to participate in the transformation of the collective. At the same time, Sri Aurobindo also asserts that one cannot have a spiritual transformation of the kind Integral Yoga speaks without the collective consciousness of man transforming as well. He writes in *The Human Cycle*:

> **The Spirit in humanity discovers, develops, builds its formations first in the individual man:** it is through the progressive and

formative individual that it offers the discovery and the chance of a new self-creation to the mind of the race. For the communal mind holds things subconsciently at first or, if consciously, then in a confused chaotic manner: **it is only through the individual mind that the mass can arrive at a clear knowledge and creation of the thing it held in its subconscient self.** Thinkers, historians, sociologists who belittle the individual and would like to lose him in the mass or think of him chiefly as a cell, an atom, have got hold only of the obscurer side of the truth of Nature's workings in humanity. **It is because man is not like the material formations of Nature or like the animal, because she intends in him a more and more conscious evolution, that individuality is so much developed in him and so absolutely important and indispensable. ...**what comes out in the individual and afterwards moves the mass, must have been there already in the universal Mind and the individual is only an instrument for its manifestation, discovery, development: but he is an indispensable instrument and an instrument not merely of subconscient Nature, not merely of an instinctive urge that moves the mass, but more directly of the Spirit of whom that Nature is itself the instrument and the matrix of his creations. **All great changes ...find their first clear and effective power and their direct shaping force in the mind and spirit of an individual or of a limited number of individuals. The mass follows, but ...in a very imperfect and confused fashion which often or even usually ends in the failure or distortion of the thing created.** ...mankind could have advanced on its way with a victorious rapidity instead of with the lumbering hesitations and soon exhausted rushes that seem to be all of which it has yet been capable.

**...if the spiritual change of which we have been speaking is to be effected, it must unite two conditions which have to be simultaneously satisfied but are most difficult to bring together. There must be the individual and the individuals who are able to see, to develop, to re-create themselves in the image of the Spirit and to communicate both their idea and its power to the mass.** And there must be **at the same time a mass, a society, a communal mind or at the least the constituents of a group-body, the possibility of a group-soul which is capable of receiving and**

**effectively assimilating, ready to follow and effectively arrive, not compelled by its own inherent deficiencies, its defect of preparation to stop on the way or fall back before the decisive change is made.**[13]

*The relationship between the individual and the collective*

Western studies of man's social and political aspects begin with Greek thought and are rooted in rationality. The past few centuries have heralded a scientific outlook, with sociology providing the primary tools to study human society. Its scope is limited to studying social phenomena, but not the deeper cosmology as the basis for societal evolution. The physical and life sciences are separated from philosophy, and scientific knowledge has become the arbiter of the truth of any sociological claim.

Indian approaches to society not only pre-date Western ideas but are also more profound than the mere use of rationality. The *Veda*-s contain the kernels of looking at man as an integral whole, with the various *śāstra*-s providing elaborate insights into the principles, aims, and structures of man's social, economic, political, and cultural activities. In Sāṃkhyā, prakṛti is the world of nature, manifest through phenomena of various forms, forces, functions, and stages. Puruṣa is the ultimate reality that remains unchanged despite imprints of prakṛti. This distinction between the phenomenological aspects of man and his true nature also applies to the collective society.

Sri Aurobindo explains the principles of Integral Yoga applied to humanity and the individual in *The Life Divine*:

> The universe is a manifestation of the Reality, and there is a truth of the universal existence, a Power of cosmic being, an all-self or world-spirit. Humanity is a formation or manifestation of the Reality in the universe, and there is a truth and self of humanity, a human spirit, a destiny of human life. **The community is a formation of the Reality, a manifestation of the spirit of man, and there is a truth, a self, a power of the collective being. The individual is a formation of the Reality, and there is a truth of the individual, an individual self, soul or spirit that expresses itself through the individual mind, life and body and can express**

> **itself too in something that goes beyond mind, life and body, something even that goes beyond humanity.**[14]
>
> **...the primal law and purpose of a society, community or nation is to seek its own self-fulfilment; it strives rightly to find itself, to become aware within itself of the law and power of its own being and to fulfil it as perfectly as possible, to realise all its potentialities, to live its own self-revealing life.** The reason is the same; for **this too is a being, a living power of the eternal Truth, a self-manifestation of the cosmic Spirit**, and it is there to express and fulfil in its own way and to the degree of its capacities the special truth and power and meaning of the cosmic Spirit that is within it.[15]

## *Sri Aurobindo on the collective*

Similar to how the individual is fundamentally a spiritual being experiencing through his mind, life, and body, the collective has a 'group soul'. Sri Aurobindo writes that this group soul is 'more fluid and less organic' than the individual soul and is made up of a complex collection of individuals. These individual members are the cells of the group organism, and their progress contributes to the development of the group.

He writes that the collective takes on the disposition of the individuals it is composed of but is slower to evolve than the individual:

> The initiation of the evolutionary emergence from the Inconscient works out by two forces, a secret cosmic consciousness and an individual consciousness manifest on the surface. The secret cosmic consciousness remains secret and subliminal to the surface individual; it organises itself on the surface by the creation of separate objects and beings. ... While it organises the separate object and the body and mind of the individual being, it creates also collective powers of consciousness which are large subjective formations of cosmic Nature; but it does not provide for them an organised mind and body, it bases them on the group of individuals, develops for them a group mind, a changing yet continuous group body. It follows that only as the individuals become more and more conscious can the group-being also become more and more

> conscious; the growth of the individual is the indispensable means for the inner growth as distinguished from the outer force and expansion of the collective being.[16]

The quote shows that *the inconscient manifests at two levels through subjective formations – the individual and the collective.* The manifestation of the individual leads to the accompanying body and mind and evolutionary journey. For the collective, the inconscient does not provide a body or mind organized as in the individual but develops a group mind as a collective of individuals. Therefore, the more evolved and conscious the individuals are in a society, the more evolved is the collective consciousness.

Thus, the same unmanifest inconscient acts through *both* the manifested individual and the manifested collective.

Similar to the important role played by the ego in an individual's development, Sri Aurobindo writes that the group-soul too, must build up its ego-self and progressively evolve to realize its ultimate goal of unity with Absolute Consciousness. Smaller units of the collective first establish a distinct mind, life, and vital functioning. They enlarge and develop complexity with each growth and transformation, as the units that form the collective are self-conscious individuals themselves. At each stage, the collective depends on the individual and this presents constant challenges of balancing individual interests against the collective in situations where the collective has individuals with differing degrees of self-awareness.

Kishor Gandhi, in his *Social Philosophy of Sri Aurobindo and the New Age,* has studied the various distinctions between Western theories of society and that of Sri Aurobindo. Some of his key comparisons follow.

| | Mainstream Western | Sri Aurobindo |
|---|---|---|
| **Social Contract Theory** (Hobbes, Locke, Rousseau) | Society originated as a result of a deliberate contract between individuals who previously lived in a 'state of nature,' uncontrolled by any social regulations. | 1. Contests the idea that man lived previously in an entirely natural state free from all social regulation, as this is neither supported by history nor by any fundamental principle of his being.<br>2. Without dismissing the entire theory wholesale, he interprets it as a part of man's evolution. |
| **Organic Theory of Society** (Spencer, Bluntschli, Schlaffle, Novicov – Biological) (Plato, Hegel – Psychological) | 1. 'Considers society as a biological organism similar in its structure and functions to an individual organism and subject to similar laws of growth, maturation and decay'.<br>2. 'Maintains that the science of sociology must be based on biology and must be governed by essentially the same principles'.<br>3. Variations include presenting the organic theory from a psychological perspective. | 1. Sri Aurobindo admits to a close parallel between the two but not a complete identification, 'The most important difference is that **the constituents of the physical organism are of the society are self-conscious mental individuals, while those of the individual organism are subconscious biological cells'.**<br>2. Society is considered a subjective being and '...even the physical being of the society is a subjective power, not a mere objective existence'. |

| Mainstream Western | | Sri Aurobindo |
|---|---|---|
| | | 3. Rejects the psychological variant of the theory, 'as the essential reality of the individual is his soul, which is other than his mind as it is other than his body, so also the essential reality of society is its soul which is other than its collective mind as it is other than its collective body'. Sri Aurobindo believes that 'the real determinant of social phenomena is the consciousness of society, which at its deepest is its soul-consciousness'.<br>4. His unique analysis also stands in stark contrast to the proponents of the organic theory as he does not see the relation between the individual and the society as one between part and the whole. This is rooted in the sanātana dhārmic concepts which sees in each part, the whole. |

## *Sri Aurobindo and social evolution*

As seen from the previous table, while presenting his theory, Sri Aurobindo has also considered and critiqued prominent Western social theories. He has provided strong counters while rejecting theories even as he accepts and acknowledges the correct approaches from Western models. His unique work on social and collective models is strongly rooted in Integral Yoga and dhārmic concepts, while highlighting the role of the individual in society and vice versa.

Sri Aurobindo has outlined three sequential stages through which the collective evolves: 1) infrarational; 2) rational; and 3) suprarational/ spiritual.

The first stage is one where man is guided by his impulses, instincts, and vital responses to desires. Sri Aurobindo writes that the needs and responses of this stage are what become 'crystalised in social institutions'.

The second stage is one where man moves beyond the principles of the vital life and lets the intelligent mind be the arbiter of his living. His thoughts, feelings, and actions are guided by the faculties of the mind in this rational stage.

Humanity enters the third stage of the supra-rational, spiritual stage, when human evolution moves beyond the first two – where man will be able to live under the guidance of a divine light, with his thoughts and actions molded in light of divine principles. Sri Aurobindo expands upon the features of each stage further:

> Human society has in its growth to pass through three stages of evolution before it can arrive at the completeness of its possibilities. **The first is a condition in which the forms and activities of the communal existence are those of the spontaneous play of the powers and principles of its life.** All its growth, all its formations, customs, institutions are then a natural organic development, — the motive and constructive power coming mostly from the subconscient principle of the life within it, — expressing, but without deliberate intention, the communal psychology, temperament, vital and physical need, and persisting or altering partly under the pressure of an internal impulse, partly under that of the environment acting on the communal mind and temper. **In this stage the people is not yet intelligently self-conscious**

**in the way of the reason, is not yet a thinking collective being,** and it does not try to govern its whole communal existence by the reasoning will, but lives according to its vital intuitions or their first mental renderings.

...**A second stage of the society is that in which the communal mind becomes more and more intellectually self-conscious,** first in its more cultured minds, then more generally, first broadly, then more and more minutely and in all the parts of its life. It learns to review and deal with its own life, communal ideas, needs, institutions in the light of the developed intelligence and finally by the power of the critical and constructive reason. This is a stage which is full of great possibilities but attended too by serious characteristic dangers. **Its first advantages are those which go always with the increase of a clear and understanding and finally an exact and scientific knowledge and the culminating stage is the strict and armoured efficiency which the critical and constructive, the scientific reason used to the fullest degree offers as its reward and consequence. Another and greater outcome of this stage of social evolution is the emergence of high and luminous ideals which promise to raise man beyond the limits of the vital being,** beyond his first social, economic and political needs and desires and out of their customary moulds and inspire an impulse of bold experiment with the communal life which opens a field of possibility for the realisation of a more and more ideal society. **This application of the scientific mind to life with the strict, well-finished, armoured efficiency which is its normal highest result, this pursuit of great consciously proposed social and political ideals and the progress which is the index of the ground covered in the endeavour, have been, with whatever limits and drawbacks, the distinguishing advantages of the political and social effort of Europe.**

...**It is only by reaching a third stage of the evolution of the collective social as of the individual human being that the ideals first seized and cherished by the thought of man can discover their own real source and character and their true means and conditions of effectuation or the perfect society be anything more than a vision on a shining cloud constantly run after in a circle and constantly deceiving the hope and escaping the**

> **embrace**. That will be when man in the collectivity begins to live more deeply and to govern his collective life neither primarily by the needs, instincts, intuitions welling up out of the vital self, nor secondarily by the constructions of the reasoning mind, but first, foremost and always by the power of unity, sympathy, spontaneous liberty, supple and living order of his discovered greater self and spirit in which the individual and the communal existence have their law of freedom, perfection and oneness.[17]

Sri Aurobindo has written on the various complex and intermediate transitional stages that take place when human societies move from the infrarational to the rational stage. He also mentions that the first stage contains in itself the tendencies of the rational and spiritual stages as well but not to the extent of them being the driving force.

When social development progresses, both tendencies acquire increasing dominance, thus propelling society to a higher stage. He also writes that in some societies, reason follows infra-rational development, and in others, spirituality follows through. While in some societies rationality becomes dominant, it also reaches its limit and is followed by the spiritual stage. When societies undertake this transformation, objectivism, which is a trait of rational societies, increasingly makes way for subjectivism:

> It is the readiness of this common mind which is of the first importance; ...if the condition of society and the principle and rule that govern society are opposed to the spiritual change, even if these belong almost wholly to the vital, to the external, the economic, the mechanical order, as is certainly the way at present with human masses, yet if the common human mind has begun to admit the ideas proper to the higher order that is in the end to be, and the heart of man has begun to be stirred by aspirations born of these ideas, then there is a hope of some advance in the not distant future. ... the first essential sign must be the growth of the subjective idea of life, — the idea of the soul, the inner being, its powers, its possibilities, its growth, its expression and the creation of a true, beautiful and helpful environment for it as the one thing of first and last importance. The signals must be there that are precursors of a subjective age in humanity's thought and social endeavour.[18]

Having clearly explained the various aspects of social evolution, Sri Aurobindo also cautions against false subjectivism. Similar to how the individual can mistake his ego for his true identity, society too can mistake its collective ego for true identity:

> This is what a true subjectivism teaches us, — first, that we are a higher self than our ego or our members, secondly, that we are in our life and being not only ourselves but all others; for there is a secret solidarity which our egoism may kick at and strive against, but from which we cannot escape. It is the old Indian discovery that our real "I" is a Supreme Being which is our true self and which it is our business to discover and consciously become and, secondly, that that Being is one in all, expressed in the individual and in the collectivity, and only by admitting and realising our unity with others can we entirely fulfil our true self-being.[19]

### *Social evolution in dhārmic societies*

India's history provides a prime example of a society that aimed for spiritual development and attained it for several centuries. The *Veda*-s, *Upaniṣad*-s, *śāstra*-s, and various texts provide a richly detailed picture of how society pursued various activities and domains for individual and collective transformations. No activity or arena of man was ignored in India's quest for the Infinite as seen in historical records and literature. India's sciences, arts, architecture, and philosophies are all testament to a vital culture that used each sphere of man's activities to build a robust society and manifesting the spiritual in everyday life.

Throughout his work, Sri Aurobindo highlights that society progresses only as far as its most progressed individuals. With a civilization that has seen countless ṛṣi-s, sages, jñānī-s, and yogi-s, India represents a collective that embodied the best archetype of social evolution.

## Defending Sri Aurobindo Against Ken Wilber's Charges

Since Sri Aurobindo had stated that 'yoga is nothing but practical psychology', *Integral Psychology is Integral Yoga.*

Unfortunately, Wilber claims to have superseded Sri Aurobindo and provides the following explanation:

> Aurobindo's greatest shortcoming is a shortcoming faced by all theorists, namely, the unavailability of the important discoveries made since his time. Aurobindo was most concerned with the transformations of consciousness (Upper Left) and the correlative changes in the material body (Upper Right). Although he had many important insights on the social and political system, he did not seem to grasp the actual interrelations of cultural, social, intentional, and behavioral, nor did his analysis at any point proceed on the level of intersubjectivity (Lower Left) and interobjectivity (Lower Right). He did not...fully assimilate the differentiations of modernity. But the levels and modes that Aurobindo did cover make his formulations indispensable for any truly integral model.[20]

In other words, he patronizingly acknowledges Sri Aurobindo as a useful stepping stone to his own ostensibly superior formulation. The above passage reinforces the continued misrepresentation of Sri Aurobindo as some theorist or other-worldly philosopher who did not have enough information about the concepts, processes, and entities of the physical world. This has been refuted in detail in earlier chapters.

Wilber presupposes that an integral study of social phenomena is possible without an integral change of individual consciousness. He does not see how Sri Aurobindo's Integral Yoga is specifically designed for worldly collective transformation, including lengthy discussions on values, morals, ethics, society, and collective evolution.

Sri Aurobindo's *The Foundations of Indian Culture* explains the differences between East and West and how cultural worldviews affect the consciousness of individuals and societies. The *Human Cycle* and *The Ideal of Human Unity* specifically articulate his social and political philosophy, even anticipating some of the challenges that were to sprout later in the world. He critiqued Marxism's ideas on the influence of the modes of production on human consciousness.

The following passage illustrates that *Sri Aurobindo was aware of the discoveries and theories of all four quadrants: intentional, behavioral, social, and cultural.* According to his approach, rather than relying upon objective methodologies to explain the subjective realms, *we must evolve in the inner instrumentation of knowing to fathom our objective existence.* The foundation should be a platform to harmonize the inner and outer, individual and collective, and subjective and objective. The chapter titled *The Coming of the Subjective Age* from which the following is extracted, explains how the 'Individualistic age of reason' of Europe will eventually be replaced by a 'subjectivist age of intuition' that will transcend and include reason in the post-postmodern world.[21]

> **In Europe and in modern times this [attempt to discover the individual and the world] has taken the form of a clear and potent physical Science**: it has proceeded by the discovery of the laws of the physical universe and the economic and sociological conditions of human life as determined by the physical being of man, his environment, his evolutionary history, his physical and vital, his individual and collective need. ... **it must become apparent that the knowledge of the physical world is not the whole of knowledge; it must appear that man is a mental as well as a physical and vital being and even much more essentially mental than physical or vital.** Even though his psychology is strongly affected and limited by his physical being and environment, it is not at its roots determined by them, but constantly reacts, subtly determines their action, effects even their new-shaping by the force of his psychological demand on life. **His economic state and social institutions are themselves governed by his psychological demand on the possibilities, circumstances, tendencies created by the relation between the mind and soul of humanity and its life and body. ... to find the truth of things and the law of his being in relation to that truth he must go deeper and fathom the subjective secret of himself and things as well as their objective forms and surroundings.**[22]

This is the real power of integrality: It cannot be achieved without realizing the subjective self first and becoming aware of its own power over the forms of nature. Trying to achieve integrality through the outer forms of nature without realizing the unifying power of consciousness may lead, at best, to the creation of some mental theory. Or, there can be worse scenarios, where the ego-sense takes charge and tries to create this integrality by its own means and dogmas. We question if this is exemplified in the case of Wilber's ego trying to create its own integral theory.

In consonance with Sri Aurobindo's vision, The Mother, his spiritual collaborator, later established a new community called Auroville, the City of Dawn, which is functional and thriving today.[23] Her vision incorporated the 'differentiations of modernity' (not specific to the West), and the realms of intentional, behavioral, social, and cultural were duly recognized and given importance.

While speaking about the small percentage of people who are ready to live in such a manner, Wilber cleverly avoids even mentioning Sri Aurobindo's or The Mother's names when referencing such places. But The Mother preceded Wilber by several decades in creating Auroville. She explains the vision of Auroville:

> There should be somewhere on earth a place which no nation could claim as its own, where all human beings of goodwill who have a sincere aspiration could live freely as citizens of the world and obey one single authority, that of the supreme Truth; a place of peace, concord and harmony where all the fighting instincts of man would be used exclusively to conquer the causes of his sufferings and miseries, to surmount his weaknesses and ignorance, to triumph over his limitations and incapacities; a place where the needs of the spirit and the concern for progress would take precedence over the satisfaction of desires and passions, the search for pleasure and material enjoyment.[24]

The *Mother on Auroville* and *Auroville References in Mother's Agenda* give a good overview of her views.[25] She explains how it will differ from socialism, communism, and democracy. Sri Aurobindo and The Mother were not reductionists in explaining consciousness in four separate quadrants. Completely ignoring any reference to them even as he mentions Gebser and a host of other Westerners, Wilber maintains:

> Today we hear a lot about Cultural Creatives and the new and exciting rise of an Integral Culture - a holistic, balanced, inclusive, caring culture that moves beyond the traditional and the modern and into a postmodern transformation. But, in fact, significant psychological evidence indicates that in today's world, less than 2% of the population is at anything that could be called an "integral" wave of awareness (where "integral" means something

> like Gebser's integral-aperspectival, Loevinger's autonomous and integrated stages, Spiral Dynamics' yellow and turquoise memes, Wade's authentic, Arlin's postformal, the centauric self and mature vision-logic, etc.) The same evidence suggests, however, that a very large percentage of the population - close to 25% - is at the immediately preceding wave of development (which is Loevinger's individualistic stage, Spiral Dynamics' green meme, Paul Ray's cultural creatives, Wade's affiliative, Sinnott's relativistic, etc.). ... because most of this population has been at the green-meme wave for several decades, it appears that a large portion - perhaps up to one-third - are ready to move forward to the next wave of expanding consciousness - which means, move forward to a truly integral wave of awareness.
>
> ...that modest 2% of the population that is now integral might soon swell to 5%, 10%, or more. ...as with any evolutionary unfolding, we will especially start to see evidence of this increasingly integral consciousness at the growing tip, or at the leading edge, or in the avantgarde (by whatever appellation) - in academia, the arts, social movements, spirituality, thought leaders.[26]

Further, Wilber traces the West's evolution movement only to Western thinkers claiming, 'Thus we arrive at today: a project of synthesis, an integral age at the leading edge, which is only a few years old'. This is manifestly wrong, for in India, a host of sages have kept this concept alive for several centuries.

## Kosmic Karma and Further Misrepresentation

At times, Wilber uses dhārmic terms after stripping them of their original context. As a typical U-Turner, he retains only the portions he finds useful. The term karma is one such example where Wilber imposes Western interpretations and believes that he has discovered something new.

He explains karma in terms of holons and his quadrants and then shifts to Whitehead for further references despite Whitehead deriving many of his seminal ideas by digesting Buddhism. Wilber writes:

> With a few qualifications, I strongly agree with that general Whiteheadian view of the nature of moment-to-moment existence.

> Whitehead actually discovered the inescapable reason that the Kosmos is holarchical in its very nature: each moment transcends and includes its predecessors, the very definition of holarchy. But we add a crucial item: this is a four-quadrant affair, all the way down—a view we also call quadratic. ...each holon or actual occasion has subjective (I), intersubjective (we), objective (it), and interobjective dimensions (its)—the four quadrants. Whitehead brilliantly described moment-to-moment manifestation in the subjective and (to some degree) intersubjective dimensions. ... the important point is that Whitehead was the first to spot the general features of the microgenetic holarchical nature of moment-to-moment existence, so we are more than glad to be Whiteheadians in this general area.[27]

Wilber then credits the work of Sheldrake, Peirce, Heidegger, and Gebser. Each of them studied Indian systems and appropriated them. Wilber prefers these digested versions rather than the original Indian sources.

He repeatedly ignores Sri Aurobindo's extensive writings on the concepts of karma and rebirth, including their fundamental meanings and roles in different frameworks in *The Life Divine*. Several chapters like *The Philosophy of Rebirth; Rebirth and Other Worlds; and Karma, the Soul and Immortality,* exclusively deal with the concept of karma. He also clearly sets out its role in his Integral Yoga:

> In any survey of the dual character of our consciousness we have first to look at the Ignorance, —for Ignorance trying to turn into Knowledge is our normal status. ...it is necessary to consider some of the essential movements of this partial awareness of self and things which works in us as a mediator between the complete self-knowledge and all-knowledge and the complete Inconscience, and, from that starting-point, find its relation to the greater Consciousness below our surface.
>
> There is a line of thought in which great stress is laid upon the action of memory: it has even been said that Memory is the man, —it is memory that constitutes our personality and holds cemented the foundation of our psychological being; for it links together our experiences and relates them to one and the same individual

> entity. This is an idea which takes its stand on our existence in the succession of Time and accepts process as the key to essential Truth, even when it does not regard the whole of existence as process or as **cause and effect in the development of some kind of self-regulating Energy, as Karma.** But process is merely a utility; it is a habitual adoption of certain effective relations which might in the infinite possibility of things have been arranged otherwise, for the production of effects which might equally have been quite different. **The real truth of things lies not in their process, but behind it, in whatever determines, effects or governs the process; not in effectuation so much as in the Will or Power that effects, and not so much in Will or Power as in the Consciousness of which Will is the dynamic form and in the Being of which Power is the dynamic value.**[28]

Before any of Wilber's Western sources, Sri Aurobindo had lucidly explained the Vedic ideas of karma and moment-to-moment transformation:

> **Man, though a really indivisible stream of Tapas, of conscious energy in Time, capable of acting in the present only by the sum of his past force of working, creating already his future by his past and his present action, yet lives absorbed in the present moment, lives from moment to moment, and is therefore in this superficial action of consciousness ignorant of his future and ignorant of his past except for that small part of it which at any moment he may recall to him by memory.** He does not, however, live in the past; what he recalls is not the past itself, but only the ghost of it, a conceptual shadow of a reality which is now to him dead, non-existent, no longer in being. But all this is an action of the superficial ignorance. **The true consciousness within is not unaware of its past; it holds it there, not necessarily in memory but in being, still active, living, ready with its fruits, and sends it up from time to time in memory or more concretely in result of past action or past causes to the superficial conscious being,—that is indeed the true rationale of what is called Karma.**[29]

Clearly, Wilber chooses not to credit Sri Aurobindo's *The Life Divine.*

Wilber's ideas of Kosmic Habits amount to saying that when a certain number of holons adopt a kosmic pattern, it becomes a habit and is implanted into the fabric. Sri Aurobindo, however, writes that an event of consciousness once experienced, has the potential to be experienced again and can be activated on the surface of the being.

Different methodologies are at play in the different quadrants: 'empiricism and behaviorism primarily engage the Upper-Right quadrant; introspection and phenomenology primarily engage the Upper-Left quadrant; hermeneutics and collaborative inquiry primarily engage the Lower-Left quadrant; the ecological sciences, structural-functionalism, and systems theory primarily engage the Lower-Right quadrant' and become a part of the Integral Operating System (IOS). The importance Wilber attaches to his IOS comes at the cost of other worldviews, for he maintains: 'IOS initiates a self-correcting, self-organizing outreach to all aspects of the universe previously marginalized by worldviews that were too narrow, too shallow, too self-enclosing to serve as more transparent vehicles of Kosmic consciousness'.[30]

## Kosmic Karma and Wilber's Interpretation Using Modern Science

Bringing in terminology from quantum mechanics, Wilber's usage of terms such as 'probability waves' must be considered with reservation. One has seen an increasing propensity to use well-defined scientific terms in a woolly manner in the pursuit of unifying science with spirituality including in the case of Wilber.

Wilber maintains 'Kosmic habits of the universe are simply probability waves for finding a particular type of occurrence in a particular spacetime locale'.[31] One wonders what these particular spacetime locales are? Is he referring to the quadrants? Do they have characteristic features and can they be quantized? Continuing with this hazy equivalence, Wilber makes it seem as though each of these quadrants has their methodologies as the operator.

It must be emphasized that Wilber does not establish any clear equivalence and only sprinkles jargon to give the impression of using modern science. He doesn't do so correctly since he is not a scientist either. While probability space is certainly abstract in physics similar to the space Wilber refers to, it makes predictive results possible; however, Wilber has not made his hypothesis subject to testability. This is a convenient claim of similarity and synthesis with modern science but a refusal to make specific predictions that would be measurable.

He drops names of past luminaries to claim that his model has surpassed the previous giants, when in fact he is using false equivalents:

> For Integral Post-Metaphysics, a "deep pattern" is not an actually existing form or structure but simply a term that represents the probability of finding a particular type of holon in a particular mode of spacetime. A deep pattern, then, is simply a probability wave. The deep features that are characteristic of that probability wave are discovered by doing a reconstructive investigation after the fact of its existence, and not something that we can deduce in a Platonic or Hegelian or Aurobindonian fashion before the fact.[32]

Wilber is careful to ensure that the correlation is only used as an explanatory device and not predictive, as his theories would fail any test. He uses the concept of probability from quantum mechanics to say:

> Some probability waves are so tightly laid down as Kosmic habits that the probability of finding a particular type of holon in that space approaches 100%. This often happens in physical systems (where, as Whitehead pointed out, it was mistaken as pure determinism); but it happens often enough even at higher waves (e.g., the probability of finding certain types of holons at the red probability wave is very high indeed). The deep features of any holon (quark, atom, molecule, meme, etc.) are simply the types of events that are probable within the Kosmic habits already laid down by past creative emergence.[33]

Wilber maintains that a priori, one cannot know the possible outcomes of any event except for shamans and sages. He credits Whitehead:

> ... even the deep patterns of the higher waves of consciousness—that is, higher than green—are now in the process of being formed; not even those patterns are predetermined a priori. ...pioneering shamans, saints, and sages have pushed into these realms and left

> lingering traces of their morphic footprints, but these are yet so few and far between as to be gossamer tracings on the spiritual wind. This "transcend-and-include" relationship, grounded in Whiteheadian prehension, is the basis, on the feeling-side, of the gentle tilt of the Kosmos towards greater and greater complexity and depth, a tilt that by any other name is Eros.[34]

In contrast, the dhārmic model believes that advanced yogi-s are able to access these states, such as the ṛṣi-s of yore.

# Conclusion

In Part 1 of this book, we demonstrated how the Aurobindonian movement, apart from a handful of individuals, failed to rise to counter the Wilberization of their guru's work. Even the institutions founded with the explicit purpose of preserving and developing the sage's work took the easier route of caving to Wilber's takeover.

In Part 2, we have shown the various misinterpretations and misrepresentations that Wilber's work is riddled with. We have systematically shown how each of his phases has captured key ideas from Sri Aurobindo's work and presented them as his while simultaneously claiming to supersede the guru's work and attributing false deficiencies to it.

While this book captures the Wilberization of Sri Aurobindo studies, a larger and deeper problem pervades the study of Indian civilization. The absence of robust schools of thought in post-independent India is a massive failure to protect and further the profound ancient civilizational intellectual property.

A school of thought not only represents unique viewpoints on fundamental questions in philosophy, psychology, and more but also creates the frameworks for engagement with others in the field. It helps preserve and propagate distinct contributions over centuries by creating intellectual lineages. Historically, Bhārata as a civilization created rich *paramparā*-s (lineages) in every field that survived the most brutal attacks. Against this backdrop, it is a matter of great disappointment that we have failed to create resilient schools of thought for intellectual giants like Sri Aurobindo and Swami Vivekananda.

Despite having active communities in Auroville and Pondicherry Ashram and many centres abroad, the colossal works of Sri Aurobindo were mined and discarded with no fair attribution, misinterpreted, and misrepresented. Had an active school of thought existed in these places for the sage's work, it would have been aware of the current research and discourse in the field, recognized what was happening, and defended their guru's work. Instead, some people within the communities were ready to join Wilber as his subordinates and surrender their autonomy. This shows a slavish and colonized mentality.

The same holds for the work of Swami Vivekananda—a giant who triggered many intellectual waves in the West, but his innovative ideas were not pursued in his nation and community. We refer to the absence of a school of thought that would pursue vital research and carry forward original insights. Sri Aurobindo used insights from Swami Vivekananda's work, which was founded in Bhārata's civilizational heritage, and both brought forth their deep realizations to this century. They actively defended Indian traditions and the core corpus from Western distortions and misrepresentations during their times. It is a matter of national shame that we failed to do the same when their work was being cannibalized.

Merely recounting past glory and paying lip service to them amounts to gross negligence of true responsibilities. Our people have been busy promoting themselves as influencers, making documentaries about our heroes, and giving talks at popular events. *What is needed is a home team to continue the serious scholarship and produce original works based on these schools of thought.*

This stands in sharp contrast with Wilber's work. He has constantly attributed ideas to Western sources and established his schools of thought with substantial backing and influence.

The works of our sages continue to hold profound insights that are relevant today. As we encounter newer intellectual weapons in the global kurukṣetra, it becomes all the more important to understand the significance of protecting their work and the larger Indian Knowledge Systems not only from Western digestion but also from internal indolence. Creating and reviving active schools of thought ought to be one of the top priorities. This necessitates not only subject matter expertise in the domain but also active awareness and understanding of non-dharma-based schools of thought to recognize hegemonical forces at play and opportunities for constructive engagement.

Consciousness studies, in particular, is a field at the cusp of dealing with newer challenges and opportunities in the age of Artificial

Intelligence. With several millennia-old systems of philosophical schools and traditions, India has the opportunity to bring its unique perspectives on these deep issues. It is up to us whether we squander the opportunity or reemerge as an authentic and self-confident leader.

# Appendix: Integral Yoga and Transformation

Śakti or prakṛti has two aspects: lower (aparā) and higher (parā). The lower prakṛti operates through her three modes or guṇa-s: sattva, rajas, and tamas. Sattva represents the force of light, truth, harmony, peace, right poise, equilibrium, intelligence, happiness, etc. Rajas denotes the quality of action, energy, domination, possession, creation, will to fight, will to resist, and will to conquer; it is the major driving force of what Sri Aurobindo calls the vital-being in us. The lower part of the vital being usually influences us to act selfishly and is full of dark impulses and desires. However, the higher vital can be a very good conduit for truer emotions and this is the reason why purification of the vital is important in Integral Yoga. Tamas signifies indolence, inertia, unintelligence, sloth, and resistance towards change. All three guṇa-s are present in every action, but the dominance of one or two determines its general character.

When an individual is under the influence of these three guṇa-s of the lower nature, the puruṣa is involved in the play; it is not free and suffers the ups and downs of the lower prakṛti. The first step is to separate the puruṣa from the lower modes of prakṛti by rising into witness consciousness, which is the natural characteristic of the puruṣa. The puruṣa then becomes aware of himself, is not constantly controlled by prakṛti and can watch the movement of her different modes.

Yoga-s, which aim only at liberation, stop here. However, Integral Yoga's objective is not only liberation but transformation. Hence, having attained the witness consciousness, the individual can become open to transformation by the higher prakṛti or Śakti. Besides an immeasurable calm, peace, and quiet experience of the universal and transcendental nature, the being feels the presence of a tremendous force and will that can be used for transformation in a perfect way. Puruṣa is now not bound by the ego-limiting consciousness (ahaṃkāra), the shadow created by the lower prakṛti for his personality, and is not subject to aparā prakṛti, but becomes her master and works in unison with Śakti, which thus becomes the power of the universal puruṣa. In turn, Śakti can then seize upon all the parts of the sādhaka's being - physical, vital, and mental - and transform them with her light and power into divine prototypes.

This life-affirming Integral Yoga requires an uninterrupted flow of Divine energy through our being to carry out the intended work of world-transformation. Consequently, the physical, vital, and mental constitutions of the aspirant need to be purified and transformed. All aspects that are rigid and inflexible need to be made supple.

The mental has the tendency to operate in terms of fixed ideas, opinions, preferences, predilections, habits, and constructions about the nature of truth. These fixities need to be made flexible so that the higher truth can manifest and descend in accordance with the Divine Will.

The vital has the tendency to insist on its own demands, cravings, sensations, pride, desires, passions, arrogance, lust, greed, envy, selfishness, and jealousy—all of these need to be transmuted so that it becomes pure and luminous. Sri Aurobindo distinguishes the lower vital from the higher vital: in contrast to many other systems of yoga where the vital has to be entirely quietened and rejected, he feels the need to purify the lower which becomes the seat of power and strength but without egotism or lower nature.

Similarly, the physical is obstinate and lazy. It needs to be transformed so that the Divine can establish itself with a greater force and ānanda. The spiritual foundation or *ādhāra* within the body must be extremely strong to hold the descent of the higher forces.[1]

This integral transformation of the physical, vital, and mental has to occur through the psychic being: the representative of the Divine present in each individual behind life, mind, and body, and the agent of the true, good, and beautiful.

The first step towards spiritual change is the emergence of the psychic being, which is hidden in the 'cave' of the heart (*hṛidaye guhāyām)*. It is the psychic being that transmigrates from one lifetime to another until it finds its conscious union with the Divine here in Nature. All other components of the individual constitution that are perishable upon death, such as the mental vital, and physical, are transformed and become the immortal representatives of the soul.

The psychic being contains all the possibilities of our human manifestation: it affects our surface being but it is not constituted by it, for it is the ever-pure portion of the Divine in us. When the psychic being is concealed behind the heart and not in control of us, the lower modes of Nature (aparā prakṛti) dominate our psychology. The vital ego and the physical mind, as opposed to the higher mind and purified and psychisized vital, obscure the manifestation of the higher life of peace, love, beauty, delight, etc. However, in proportion to the opening of the psychic being, the Divine Mother or Śakti begins to take control of our life, guiding us towards the intended goal that She thinks best and in accordance with the unique truth of our individual being. She also begins to bring about the psychological and physical purification and transformation.

Correspondingly, all that is ugly, devoid of light, reprehensible, false, erroneous, and evil begins to change into its opposite and disappear from our psychological make-up. The parā prakṛti begins to take control, purifying the thoughts, perceptions, emotions, sensations, actions, and all the movements that assist in a greater manifestation of the Divine. It leads to the emergence of the soul-power in us, and makes us luminous and intense, free from the distortions caused by the turbid vital and mental beings in us. She takes up all our lower instruments and parts and begins to transform them into the light of our supramental nature, for She is the force and the power emanating from the Supermind.

The union with self in Advaita Vedānta brings liberation but does not cause transformation of the outer being. Therefore, in Integral Yoga, it is of capital importance to awaken the psychic being and bring it forward so that it takes control of the outer being and starts its transformation. Since the psychic is involved in the mental, vital, and physical being, its awakening leads these realms to aspire for change in order to become perfect instruments of the Divine.

Bringing the psychic being to the front to take charge of the spiritual practice is the first necessary step towards the other two stages of transformation that Sri Aurobindo espouses as spiritual and supramental. Spiritualization is the second step after psychisization has taken place; it brings a conscious union with the cosmic Divine in both its static and dynamic aspects. The union with the static aspect is the unification with the Brahman, whereas the union with the dynamic aspect connotes a merger with the Divine Mother or the Śakti. Consequently, this brings forth universal knowledge, peace, power, and purity within an individual consciousness. As spiritualization alone does not bring about a total change of the outer nature, psychic transformation is necessary as the first step. The psychic transformation can be brought about by concentration on the heart center, whereas spiritualization can be accomplished by concentrating on the center between the eyebrows and above the head. Sometimes, it is the psychic opening that creates conducive conditions for the spiritual realization; at other times, it is the spiritual realization that helps the psychic to come forward. Whichever way one approaches the practice, giving precedence to one or the other, the awakening of the psychic being cannot be bypassed.

Supramentalization is the process of the complete perfection of body, life, and mind by ascending to the plane of Truth-Consciousness and bringing down its power, will, intuition, and light into the outer being. However, in order to understand the process of supramentalization, we need to understand the Supermind.

Supermind is the plane of gnosis connecting the lower three planes of existence (physical, vital, and mental) and the higher three (Sat, Cit, and Ānanda). This is the plane of unitive consciousness and holds all diversities in itself for their manifestation in planes lower than itself. Supermind is the plane of total knowledge—it knows the right relationships between the eternal absolute and the terrestrial relative, and unlike the mind, which knows by analysis and synthesis and by putting different parts together, it is a plane of direct knowledge.

The Supermind is the possessor of all knowledge, and all mental knowledge contains in itself its latent truth. However, its truth in the mind is obscured and distorted due to the presence of the various aforementioned impurities and also by the mind's own naturally inherent limitations. When an aspirant ascends to the supramental plane, his or her ignorance disappears entirely, culminating in all knowledge—he or she then acquires the capacity to act in divine wisdom, and manifesting the Divine Will. Sri Aurobindo describes the nature of the Supermind as follows:

> The original nature of supermind is the self-conscience and all-conscience of the Infinite, of the universal Spirit and Self in things, organising on the foundation and according to the character of a direct self-knowledge its own wisdom and effective omnipotence for the unfolding and the regulated action of the universe and of all things in the universe. It is, we might say, the gnosis of the Spirit master of its own cosmos, *ātmā, jñātā, īśwaraḥ*. As it knows itself, so too it knows all things—for all are only becomings of itself—directly, totally and from within outward, spontaneously in detail and arrangement, each thing in the truth of itself and its nature and in its relation to all other things. And it knows similarly all action of its energy in antecedent or cause and occasion of manifestation and effect or consequence, all things in infinite and in limited potentiality and in selection of actuality and in their succession of past, present and future.[2]

Deriving its power and existence from the Divine, the Supermind is its organizing principle and power informing all activities in the terrestrial hemisphere, though concealed in its full manifestation by dint of the obscurities inherent in the lower planes of cosmic existence. The physical, vital, and mental, by scaling upwards to regions beyond the mental plane, find their utmost fulfillment in the Supermind. The ascent to the Supermind can be followed by the descent of the Truth-Consciousness, which completes the process of total purification and perfection.

Finally, there is a shift too from concentration on individual realization to collective realization. As opposed to the earlier systems of yoga, which focus on individual liberation, Sri Aurobindo and The Mother spell out a system that concentrates on the liberation and perfection of the human race or collective perfection—a total and complete manifestation of the supramental truth on the earth and in the body, which embraces the entire human condition into its fold. According to Sri Aurobindo, though there had been instances of individual supramental perfection and transformation, never before had the yoga been done for collective supramentalization.

## The Individual and the Transcendent

Brahman, 'the Alpha and the Omega'[3] of existence manifests itself in many forms and activities which the mind grasps even as it is unaware of the former without going through each successive stage. The innumerable forms and activities are themselves the means of self-discovery and the path to the highest consciousness. As Sri Aurobindo writes, 'To fulfill God in life is man's manhood. A divine existence is his objective'.[4] Thus, the individual stands at the core of universal existence, and Life itself consists of three general forms of consciousness – the individual, the universal, and the transcendent (God).

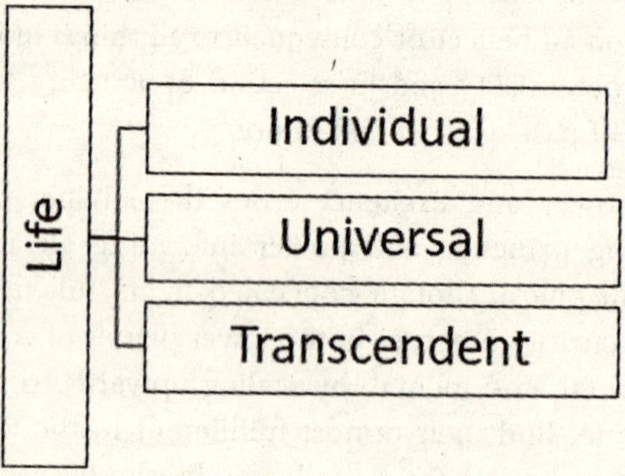


**Figure 7: Three General Forms of Consciousness**

The transcendence and universality are manifested in the individual through the 'transitional device' of the ego. The ego is a necessary, albeit temporary, instrument that enables the expression in numerous forms of the One Brahman. This descent or involution in Man of the Universal takes place on three major planes.

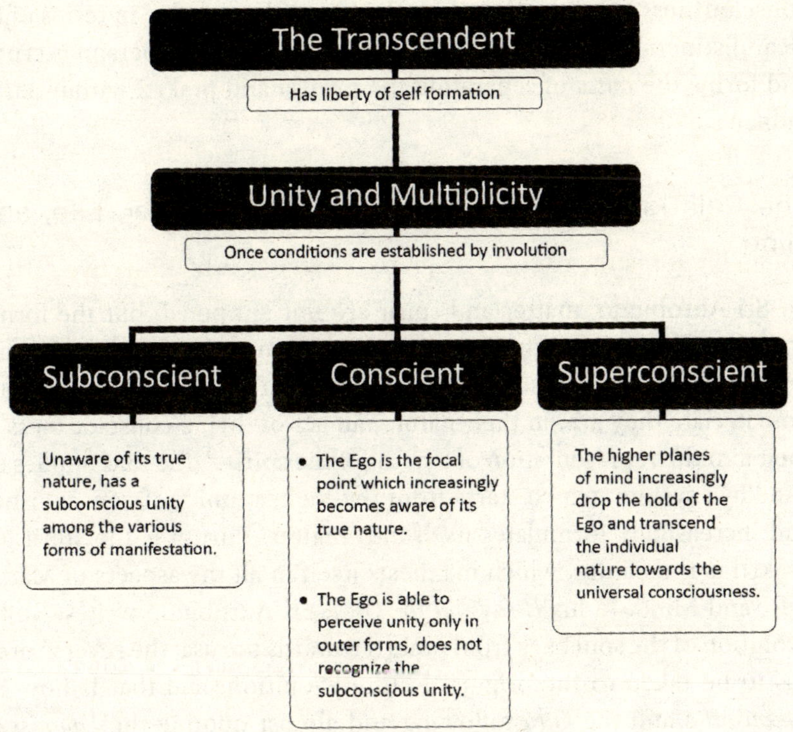


**Figure 8: Manifesting Transcendence**

The Being exists simultaneously as the One and the Multiple, and the same principle finds itself at the heart of every part of the Being. Man is a microcosm of the same principle, and he too holds in his nature multiple gradations of all aspects of prakṛti that comprise the triad of Matter, Life, and Mind. Thus, the Self of Man finds itself in gradations in the form of a physical self, a life self, and a mind self.

The physical self expresses itself through the physical nature, including one's habits, instincts, and functions. The life being expresses itself through an active vital nature that uses sensations, impulses, feelings, desires as well as activities. The mental being uses thoughts and perceptions as its primary expressions. The personality of the man that one usually speaks of comprises these major parts, which act independently as well as influence each other. Integral Yoga, in its goal of transformation, has the seeker first understand these various personalities within himself and turn every part from its human confusion and average consciousness towards the Divine. Ergo, self-knowledge in terms of the clear distinction between the many personalities in the person is crucial and forms the basis of separating the puruṣa and prakṛti within during sādhana.

## The Relationship Between the Self and Matter, Life, and Mind

To Sri Aurobindo, matter and spirit are not antipodal, but the former is the medium to seat the Divine spirit, 'Form and matter can be valid only as shape and substance of manifestation for the incorporeal and immaterial. They are, in their nature, an act of divine consciousness, in their aim the representation of a status of the spirit'.[5] The sage applies the Sāṃkhya system, which starts from the highest unity of consciousness and increasingly formulates itself into matter. Puruṣa is the spirit and prakṛti is the nature, which manifests itself in all the aspects of Matter, Life, and Mind. In his *Essays on the Gita*, Sri Aurobindo writes, 'In the evolution of the soul back from prakṛti towards puruṣa, the reverse order has to be taken to the original Nature-evolution, and that is how the *Upaniṣad*-s and the *Gītā* following and almost quoting the *Upaniṣad*-s state the ascending order of our subjective powers'.[6] Thus, the sage brings together into a single coherent structure both the movements explicitly – the involution that seeded Consciousness into Matter as well as the evolution that progressively transforms and unifies into the same Consciousness.

Prakṛti's guṇa-s form the foundation of Nature in the world from which the five elements – ether, air, fire, water, and earth – evolve. It must be remembered that one must not draw a parallel with the modern scientific elements and confuse the systems. The combination of these five elements creates things as we know and see in the world. Each of these five elements form the essence of the subtle aspects of Matter, i.e. sound, touch, form, taste, and smell. Sri Aurobindo calls this the objective aspect of the cosmic existence.

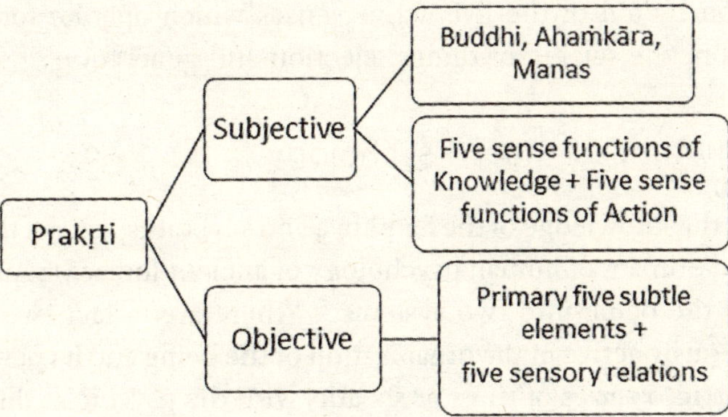


**Figure 9: Prakṛti**

Life is the instrument of the spirit that reveals itself in Matter in its multiple forms and pivots of Consciousness. Sri Aurobindo writes that the 'Brahman is in this world to represent Itself in the values of Life. Life exists in Brahman in order to discover Brahman in itself'.[7] The primary objective of manhood is to realize the ultimate Consciousness in man's life. Life's infinite forms and activities are to be embraced, transformed, and molded into channels for ascent. Sri Aurobindo furthers this as a key tenet of his Integral Yoga, where the sādhaka uses every part of his life – circumstances, forces, impulses, activities – as instruments of transformation.

According to Sri Aurobindo, the subjective aspect of consciousness comprises thirteen principles – buddhi, ahaṁkāra, manas, and its ten sense functions – five of knowledge and five of action. The mind comprises four aspects. The first is buddhi, which is the discerning principle within humans. Ahaṁkāra is the sense of ego, which gives an individual a sense of existence. The buddhi and ahaṁkāra, as sub-planes within the larger plane of mind, are closely and reciprocally intertwined. Sri Aurobindo calls the ahaṁkāra 'the subjective principle in Buddhi'.[8] Manas is the sense faculty of perception. It receives the impulses and touch of outward things (*bāhya sparśa*) and offers reactions to them, in the process forming ideas about the things it interacts with. It receives impulses through the senses of hearing, touch, sight, taste, and smell. These senses themselves 'make the five properties of things their respective objects and specializes certain necessary vital functions of reaction by aid of the five active senses which operate for speech, locomotion, the seizing of things, ejection and generation'.[9]

## The Structure of Inner Psychology

Applying the knowledge of the Sāṃkhya and several aspects of the highly developed domain of human psychology of ancient India, Sri Aurobindo organizes the being into two systems – 'There are in fact two systems simultaneously active in the organisation of the being and its parts;—one is concentric, a series of rings or sheaths with the psychic at the centre; another is vertical, an ascension and descent, like a flight of steps, a series of superimposed planes with the Supermind-Overmind as the crucial nodus of the transition beyond the human into the Divine'.[10]

The concentric system has at its heart the psychic being. We have seen earlier how Sri Aurobindo introduces the term to distinguish it from the Ātman as well as the unborn and eternal Brahman. The psychic is the portion of the Divine in man that is the centre of his evolutionary journey as it grows over every cycle of birth and death. This innermost being is surrounded by the purest form of the three aspects of the master triad Matter-Life-Mind. Thus, the inmost physical, vital, and mental embrace the psychic soul. Together, these two sheaths are also referred to as the subliminal and constitute the puruṣa or the Pure Conscious Being.

The active and instrumental parts of this puruṣa constitute the outer two rings that represent the prakṛti in our being. These are parts of the being that bear the touch of interacting with the universal forces outside the person. The triad of Matter-Life-Mind manifests in the forms of Inner physical, vital, mental and Outer physical, vital and mental. Each of the three physical, vital and mental aspects is not independent but connected and impacts the other through interaction.

The vital mind refers to the being dominated by impulses, instincts, and desires. The physical mind features the characteristics of the matter consciousness such as inertia and mechanical repetitiveness. One feels the corresponding manifestation of these characteristics on the mind in terms of doubts, obsessions and dullness and heaviness. The physical and the vital also interact with each other, resulting in a vital that concerns itself with reactions of desires and impulses for objects in the physical plane.

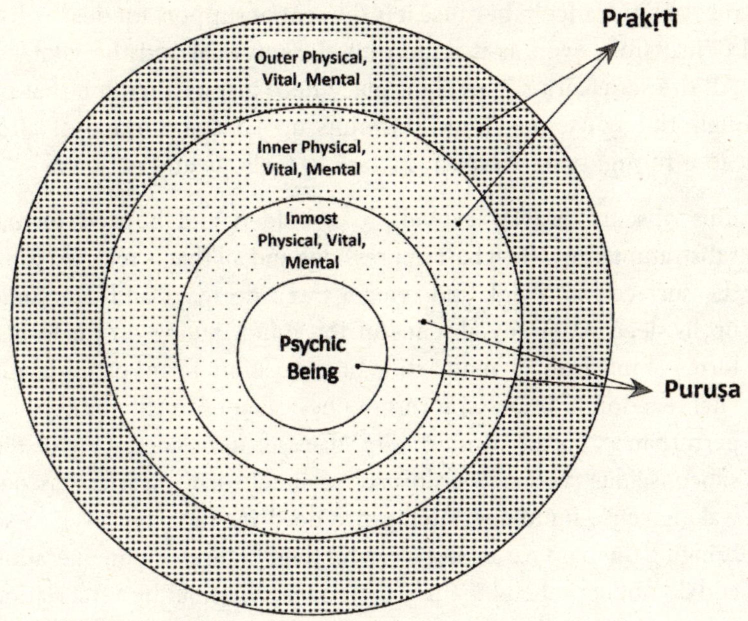


**Figure 10: Organization of the Being**

The second system is one of a series of steps that mark man's ascent from ordinary Consciousness to the ultimate Consciousness. It consists of the ascent of the mind from the physical to the Overmind gnostic or the Supermind.[11]

**The Inconscient:** This is the starting point at which evolution becomes the agency through which Matter begins its ascent toward the Supreme Consciousness. This level has a complete involution of consciousness, what Sri Aurobindo calls 'inverse reproduction of the supreme superconscience'.[12]

**The Subconscient:** This plane lies below the planes of Mind and Life and is 'the process of the Inconscient becoming conscious; it is a support and even a root of our inferior parts of being and their movements. It sustains and reinforces all in us that clings most and refuses to change, our mechanical recurrences of unintelligent thought, our persistent obstinacies of feeling, sensation, impulse, propensity, our uncontrolled fixities of character'.[13] The subconscious exists in both forms – the universal and the individual. Sri Aurobindo calls this plane 'the last fortress of Ignorance'[14] because it is the seat of support for death, disease, and depression, even as it underpins the physical and the vital.

All the saṃskāra-s have their place here just as anything that passes through the conscious mind, coming up to the surface as dreams, repeated thoughts of the past, including feelings and actions:

> This obscure activity extends to a hidden and hooded mental substratum into which past impressions and all that is rejected from the surface mind sink and remain there dormant and can surge up in sleep or in any absence of the mind, taking dream forms, forms of mechanical mind action or suggestion, forms of automatic vital reaction or impulse, forms of physical abnormality or nervous perturbance, forms of morbidity, disease, unbalance. Out of the subconscious we bring ordinarily so much to the surface as our waking sense mind and intelligence need for their purpose; in so bringing them up we are not aware of their nature, origin, operation and do not apprehend them in their own values but by a translation into the values of our waking human sense and intelligence.[15]

The functions which the human has evolved out of but still present in the plant and animal life have their dormant impressions here.

*Transformation*: Since we do not have conscious control over the subconscient, most of the responses it throws up seem involuntary. Sri Aurobindo writes that the way to transform this plane is to rise higher up in the planes and work from above in controlling that which arises in the subconscient, even as he emphasizes that no transformation can be complete without this plane being remolded.

**The Physical:** The physical is predominantly made of prakṛti's tamas, which is also known in the Vedāntic parlance as annamayakośa or the sheath of the matter. This plane gives rise to the human body. The physical plane interacts with the other planes of vital and mind, and hence there is an admixture. The nervous being is the entity that arises when the physical interacts with the vital, and its world comprises desires, impulses, and the pursuit of pleasure in the physical world. This vital physical being is also the seat of most diseases and suffering that arise with any interaction of the physical with outer Nature. There is a physical part in the mind as well, and the mechanical mind, with its nature of being a machine that repeats the same thoughts and feelings in a loop, belongs to this plane. All these aspects of the physical are subject to influences from the subconscient.

*Transformation*: Sri Aurobindo writes that with constant surrender and vigilance, one can transform every part of this plane. The Mother writes about the body, 'In all its cells, there is an intensity of life, of aspiration, of the will to progress which one does not usually even realize'.[16]

**The Vital**: The vital, also called 'the soul of desire' by Sri Aurobindo, is, according to The Mother, 'It is what makes you live, act, move'.[17] The sage describes it as the thing that pursues life for the sake of possession and enjoyment and says, 'This soul of desire is a separative soul of ego and all its instincts are for a separative self-affirmation'. As the vital lies between the mind and the physical, it is able to influence the body as well as the earthly forces and is less spiritually aware than the mind. The Mother writes that the vital has three major sources to fulfill itself. The first is the physical plane that it draws from using sensations. The second is by interacting from its own plane with the universal vital energies. The third is through absorbing inspiration from above and by constantly aspiring for progress.

*Transformation*: Controlling one's desires and sensations and ensuring that the vital increasingly turns towards only the inspiration from above by constantly rejecting the former and aspiring for the latter is the path towards transforming the vital. It is often seen as one of the hardest parts of sādhana.

**The Mind**: The Mind is not the commonly misunderstood term that refers to the entire spectrum of activities that come under the realms of the vital and the physical but, according to The Mother, is the faculty whose role is 'the formation and organization of action'. She emphasizes that 'it is not an instrument of knowledge'[18] instead 'it can use knowledge for action'. The ability to reason is one of the primary functions of the proper mind – also called buddhi – and serves a key role in transforming the vital by controlling the impulses. This role of being a key agency of control goes in tandem with it being an instrument of organization.

The vital mind, seen in the previous section, has tremendous power to undertake activity that creates according to the desires of the vital:

> The vital mind is that part of the vital being which builds, plans, imagines, arranges things and thoughts according to the life-pushes, desires, will to power or possession, will to action, emotions, vital ego reactions of the nature. It must be distinguished from the reasoning will which plans and arranges things according to the dictates of the thinking mind proper, the discriminating reason or according to the mental intuition or a direct insight and judgment. The vital mind uses thought for the service not of reason but of life-push and life-power and when it calls in reasoning it uses that for justifying the dictates of these powers, imposes their dictates on the reason instead of governing by a discriminating will the action of the life-forces.[19]

We have already considered the physical mind earlier, but to reiterate:

> The physical mind is that which is fixed on physical objects and happenings, sees and understands these only, and deals with them according to their own nature, but can with difficulty respond to the higher forces. Left to itself, it is sceptical of the existence of supraphysical things, of which it has no direct experience and to which it can find no clue; even when it has spiritual experiences, it forgets them easily, loses the impression and result and finds it difficult to believe. To enlighten the physical mind by the consciousness of the higher spiritual and supramental planes is one object of this Yoga, just as to enlighten it by the power of the higher vital and higher mental elements of the being is the greatest part of human self-development, civilisation and culture.[20]

**Higher Mind**: This plane marks the beginning of the superconscient and along with the Illumined Mind, Intuition and Overmind, constitute the levels above the ordinary mind from which the higher states of consciousness descend into the lower planes. The essence of this plane is highly spiritual compared to the lower levels even though it exists at the plane of the mind. Thus, it is the seat of the initial spiritual transformation. There is a more consistent awareness of the higher Self, and this stage acts as an intermediary between the highest Truth and the planes below. It conveys the wisdom in a manner that the purified mind can hold, without collapsing, either due to being a poor ādhāra or due to the sheer intensity of the higher Truth.

**Illumined Mind**: This plane of the mind is marked not by the presence of thought but by direct spiritual intelligence and vision. Sri Aurobindo describes the descent of the higher consciousness into this plane as

> a play of lightnings of spiritual truth and power breaks from above into the consciousness and adds to the calm and wide enlightenment and the vast descent of peace which characterise or accompany the action of the larger conceptual-spiritual principle, a fiery ardour of realisation and a rapturous ecstasy of knowledge. A downpour of inwardly visible Light very usually envelops this action; for it must be noted that, contrary to our ordinary conceptions, light is not primarily a material creation and the sense or vision of light accompanying the inner illumination is not merely a subjective visual image or a symbolic phenomenon: light is primarily a spiritual manifestation of the Divine Reality illuminative and creative; material light is a subsequent representation or conversion of it into Matter for the purposes of the material Energy.[21]

The sage explains the difference between the Higher Mind and the Illumined Mind as the following:

> As the Higher Mind brings a greater consciousness into the being through the spiritual idea and its power of truth, so the Illumined Mind brings in a still greater consciousness through a Truth Sight and Truth Light and its seeing and seizing power. It can effect a more powerful and dynamic integration; it illumines the thought-mind with a direct inner vision and inspiration, brings a spiritual sight into the heart and a spiritual light and energy into its feeling and emotion, imparts to the life-force a spiritual urge, a truth inspiration that dynamises the action and exalts the life movements; it infuses into the sense a direct and total power of spiritual sensation so that our vital and physical being can contact and meet concretely, quite as intensely as the mind and emotion can conceive and perceive and feel, the Divine in all things; it throws on the physical mind a transforming light that breaks its limitations, its conservative inertia, replaces its narrow thought-power and its doubts by sight and pours luminosity and consciousness into the very cells of the body. In the transformation by the Higher Mind

> the spiritual sage and thinker would find his total and dynamic fulfilment; in the transformation by the Illumined Mind there would be a similar fulfilment for the seer, the illumined mystic, those in whom the soul lives in vision and in a direct sense and experience: for it is from these higher sources that they receive their light and to rise into that light and live there would be their ascension to their native empire.[22]

One notices the usage of abundant imagery from the *Veda*-s and the *Upaniṣad*-s in Sri Aurobindo's description, even as he highlights that these are not mere comparisons but actual experiences, 'We may compare the action of the Higher Mind to a composed and steady sunshine, the energy of the Illumined Mind beyond it to an outpouring of massive lightnings of flaming sun-stuff'.[23]

**Intuition**: The term intuition here does not refer to the commonly understood idea of knowing without the use of mental faculties such as reasoning; instead Sri Aurobindo refers to the plane closer to the ultimate truth that is able to know about the object through identity with it. This plane does not involve the lower faculties of conception but instead establishes a oneness and hence reveals the concealed knowledge. The sage writes:

> It is when the consciousness of the subject meets with the consciousness in the object, penetrates it and sees, feels or vibrates with the truth of what it contacts, that the intuition leaps out like a spark or lightning-flash from the shock of the meeting; or when the consciousness, even without any such meeting, looks into itself and feels directly and intimately the truth or the truths that are there or so contacts the hidden forces behind appearances, then also there is the outbreak of an intuitive light; or, again, when the consciousness meets the Supreme Reality or the spiritual reality of things and beings and has a contactual union with it, then the spark, the flash or the blaze of intimate truth-perception is lit in its depths.[24]

According to Sri Aurobindo, there are four primary functions of Intuition: 'A power of revelatory truth-seeing, a power of inspiration or truth-hearing, a power of truth-touch or immediate seizing of significance, which is akin to the ordinary nature of its intervention in our mental intelligence, a power of true and automatic discrimination of the orderly and exact relation of truth to truth'.[25] Sri Aurobindo describes the descent of this original intuition with the ascent in consciousness as one that takes place either in periods of brilliant clarity, what he calls a 'play of lightning – flashes' or manifesting constantly in action. This plane is witness to the acts of higher power, and it is by ascending further to the Overmind that intuition can apply the higher knowledge.

**Overmind**: With each ascending step, the plane that one leaves behind is transformed and becomes the vessel for Divine Consciousness. Sri Aurobindo highlights that true union cannot come about when any part still remains hidden from light, for it can then surface and pull down the consciousness to the lower levels. As one leaves behind the influence of the inconscient and the subconscient, one also loses the sway of the individual consciousness, and the Overmind is the first plane that acts as an opening to the universal consciousness in the individual. The precondition to the descent of the Overmind is that the inner being, belonging to the puruṣa, must have become the dominant force of influence and replace the surface mind and its workings.

Writing about the functioning of the Overmind, Sri Aurobindo says:

> When the Overmind descends, the predominance of the centralising ego-sense is entirely subordinated, lost in largeness of being and finally abolished; a wide cosmic perception and feeling of a boundless universal self and movement replaces it: many motions that were formerly egocentric may still continue, but they occur as currents or ripples in the cosmic wideness. Thought, for the most part, no longer seems to originate individually in the body or the person but manifests from above or comes in upon the cosmic mind-waves: all inner individual sight or intelligence of things is now a revelation or illumination of what is not in one's separate self but in the universal knowledge; the feelings, emotions, sensations are similarly felt as waves from the same cosmic immensity breaking upon the subtle and the gross body and responded to in kind by the individual centre of the universality; for the body is only a small support or even less, a point of relation, for the action of a vast cosmic instrumentation.[26]

Intuition has its origin in the plane of the Overmind, and the latter is described as the 'occult link' that is 'the Power that at once connects and divides the supreme Knowledge and the cosmic Ignorance'.[27] As the Overmind is open to universal consciousness, the multiplicity seen in the forms of the universal finds expression in manifesting Godheads for each power. The sage writes:

> All spiritual experiences are taken up and become habitual and normal to the new nature; all essential experiences belonging to the mind, life, body are taken up and spiritualised, transmuted and felt as forms of the consciousness, delight, power of the infinite existence. Intuition, illumined sight and thought enlarge themselves; their substance assumes a greater substantiality, mass, energy, their movement is more comprehensive, global, many-faceted, more wide and potent in its truth-force: the whole nature, knowledge, aesthesis, sympathy, feeling, dynamism become more catholic, all-understanding, all-embracing, cosmic, infinite.
>
> The overmind change is the final consummating movement of the dynamic spiritual transformation; it is the highest possible status-dynamis of the spirit in the spiritual-mind plane. It takes up all that is in the three steps below it and raises their characteristic workings to their highest and largest power, adding to them a universal wideness of consciousness and force, a harmonious concert of knowledge, a more manifold delight of being. But there are certain reasons arising from its own characteristic status and power that prevent it from being the final possibility of the spiritual evolution. It is a power, though the highest power, of the lower hemisphere; although its basis is a cosmic unity, its action is an action of division and interaction, an action taking its stand on the play of the multiplicity.[28]

Sri Aurobindo explains in great detail the nature and purpose of the entire transformation that takes place when the Overmind is opened to the higher power, including the integral nature of the transformation, the manner in which this inner change manifests externally, and so on.

**The Gnostic Being, The Supermind:** The upper edge of the Overmind marks the line of an utter and unequivocal transformation. Up to this point, Sri Aurobindo has spared no principle or its application, no form or its function in explaining the template of the One and the Many, the Individual and the Universal, the Spirit and Consciousness manifesting through the triad of Matter-Life-Mind, the agency of evolution in the upward ascent just as the spirit is involved in the downward descent, the detailed gradations that exist in different levels of consciousness, the ways of transformation as well as the outer manifestations of this change.

As the individual struggle falls behind and man stands in the field of universal consciousness, the gnostic being molds the individual for manifesting the Divine Will in a manner it sees most suitable. Sri Aurobindo calls the gnostic or supramental being the perfect consummation of the spiritual man, with his complete being, including his actions, thoughts, and living, guided and governed by the universal spiritual consciousness. The Supermind is the plane of Truth-Consciousness and is always free from the pull of ignorance, which governs the lower planes.

The trajectory of ascent is free from the influence of all negative forces, and hence, it directly manifests the divine. Even as it participates in evolution to manifest itself to bring down the higher consciousness to the lower planes, it remains free, unbound and unfettered.

Explaining the nature of the passage from the Overmind to the supramental, Sri Aurobindo writes:

> This passage is the stage at which the supermind gnosis can take over the lead of the evolution from the overmind and build the first foundations of its own characteristic manifestation and unveiled activities; it must be marked therefore by a decisive but long-prepared transition from an evolution in the Ignorance to an always progressive evolution in the Knowledge. It will not be a sudden revelation and effectuation of the absolute Supermind and the supramental being as they are in their own plane, the swift apocalypse of a truth-conscious existence ever self-fulfilled and complete in self-knowledge; it will be the phenomenon of the supramental being descending into a world of evolutionary becoming and forming itself there, unfolding the powers of the gnosis within the terrestrial nature.

> [This revelation] can assume the formula of a truth-conscious existence founded in an inherent self-knowledge but at the same time taking up into itself mental nature and nature of life and material body. For the supermind as the truth consciousness of the Infinite has in its dynamic principle the infinite power of a free self-determination. It can hold all knowledge in itself and yet put forward in formulation only what is needed at each stage of an evolution; it formulates whatever is in accordance with the Divine Will in manifestation and the truth of the thing to be manifested. It is by this power that it is able to hold back its knowledge, hide its own character and law of action and manifest overmind and under overmind a world or ignorance in which the being wills on its surface not to know and even puts itself under the control of a pervading Nescience. But in this new stage the veil thus put on will be lifted.[29]

**Sat-cit-ānanda:** Existence-Consciousness-Bliss has been the pinnacle of the Indian conception of the universe as the individual. Sat-cit-ānanda is the eternal force that works through everything in the universe, experiencing delight in existence through its infinite forms, unborn, deathless, timeless, spaceless, the ultimate existence; 'Sat-cit-ānanda is the unity of the many-sidedness of manifested things, the eternal harmony of all their variations and oppositions, the infinite perfection which justifies their limitations and is the goal of their imperfections'.

Since ancient times in India, yoga, especially the jñāna mārga, has sought to obliterate all māya and ignorance of the body, life, and mind by plunging directly into the sat-cit-ānanda. However, in Sri Aurobindo's Integral Yoga, it is essential for the sādhaka to go through each successive plane as the complete, integral transformation of the being is the goal. This complete transformation is what brings down the consciousness into every single aspect of man's body, life, and mind in the world, thus creating a Divine Life on earth.

## Manifesting the Supramental Through Yoga

Sri Aurobindo builds a grand structure, assembling from timeless Indian philosophies the core principles, erecting in great detail on a solid foundation the various rungs of ascending to the highest planes of consciousness to unite with the Truth – rungs that start from the inconscient in which involution of the spirit begins, through the layers of the subconscient, the physical, the vital, the mental as well as the various higher planes before the Supermind. The ultimate synthesis of Matter-Life-Mind finds itself expressed and realized in man's life through yoga. The very principle at the heart of man's purpose and journey as Sri Aurobindo consistently shows, lies in the repeated combining of elements for harmony and complexity as well as each element finding its own specialty, 'only to unite once more in a larger and more puissant synthesis'.[30]

The various forms of this synthesis are also seen in the paths taken to arrive at the union. Yoga, with its well-defined and formulated methods, treads the path of perfect balance – leaving the choice of the way to the sādhaka while at the same time, each path is rigorously conceived and developed. Sri Aurobindo writes thus about yoga: 'The child of immemorial ages, preserved by its vitality and truth into our modern times, it is now emerging from the secret schools and ascetic retreats in which it had taken refuge and is seeking its place in the future sum of living human powers and utilities'.[31]

Emphasizing that all life is indeed yoga, Sri Aurobindo defines yoga itself as 'a methodised effort towards self-perfection by the expression of the secret potentialities latent in the being and—highest condition of victory in that effort—a union of the human individual with the universal and transcendent Existence we see partially expressed in man and in the Cosmos'.[32] Quoting Swami Vivekananda, the sage highlights that through yoga, one achieves in a single lifetime what Nature takes several lives to fulfill.

Traditional schools of Indian Yoga have included Rāja Yoga, Haṭha Yoga as well as the broader paths of Jñāna Yoga, Karma Yoga and Bhakti Yoga. The first two paths reveal the depth and extent to which the Indian has always known and understood man's psychology. Understanding the relationship between matter and the life in terms of the gross body workings and the inner nervous system, the kośa-s, as well as the cakra-s.

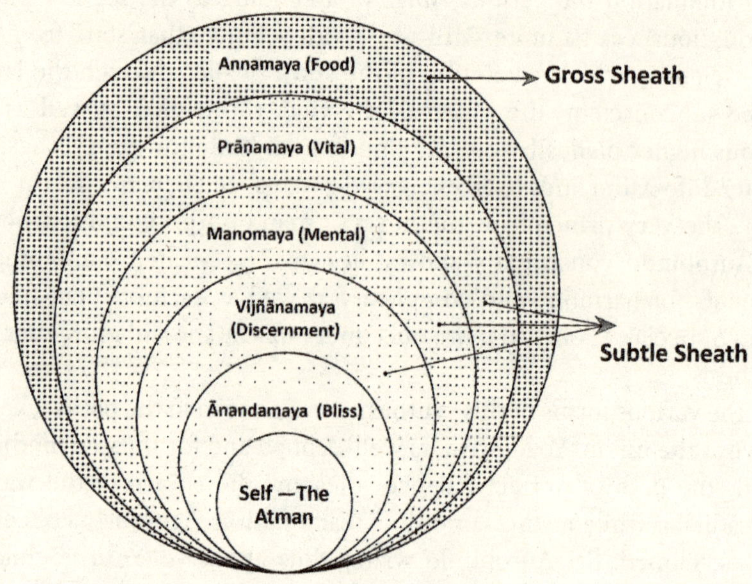


**Figure 11: The Kośa-s**

Haṭha Yoga delves deep into perfecting man's bodily faculties and restoring to each of them the true aim, role, and functioning. Contrary to the purely ascetic ideas the West has of the ancient Indian, Haṭha Yoga, along with the science of Āyurveda, champions divinity in man's body – *śarīram ādhyam khalu dharmasādhanam*. All yogic systems base their methods on the same fundamental principle – there is a life higher than what we perceive at the mental level alone and realizing that truly Divine life on earth is possible. Sri Aurobindo refers to this fundamental principle as the three steps of Nature – 'a bodily life which is the basis of our existence here in the material world, a mental life into which we emerge and by which we raise the bodily to higher uses and enlarge it into greater completeness, and a divine existence which is at once the goal of the other two and returns upon them to liberate them into their highest possibilities',[33] while reiterating the aim – 'Regarding none of them as either beyond our reach or below our nature and the destruction of none of them as essential to the ultimate attainment, we accept this liberation and fulfillment as part at least and a large and important part of the aim of Yoga'.[34]

**Haṭha Yoga**

- Body and Vital are the chief instruments of perfection.
- Āsanas and Prāṇāyāma are the chief agents of change.
- The more ability the body-vital has to hold Prāṇa, the more it establishes universal forces into the individual.

**Rāja Yoga**

- Liberation and perfection of the mental being, control of emotional and sensational life.
- A clear state of mind is established by giving up egoistic pursuits.
- Uses Haṭha yogic methods as well as Kuṇḍalinī śakti.
- Quietens the mind, elevates it through concentration and meditation right upto samādhi.

**Jñāna Yoga**

- Aims at the realization of the Brahman within and without.
- Uses intellectual reflective methods such as vicāra, viveka to distinguish phenomenal being and understand Prakṛti.
- Through right identification with the Self, it proceeds to 'final immergence without return of individual soul in the Supreme.'

**YOGA**

**Bhakti Yoga**

- The Yoga of Devotion uses man's conventional relations but turns the emotions away from the worldly chaos towards the Divine.
- This path purifies the vital of all its egoistic clutches and lets emotions, thoughts become the instrument of ascent.
- In some cases, this path too leads the individual away from world affirmation but Sri Aurobindo places it in its rightful place in Integral Yoga.

**Karma Yoga**

- Gives up all egoistic claim to work and makes of the latter an offering to the Divine
- Recognizes consciously that the Universal energy does all.
- 'The object is the release of the soul from its bondage to appearances and to the reaction of phenomenal activities'.
- Elevates all of man's earthly activities to instruments of freedom, perfection and realization.

**Figure 12: Systems of Yoga**

## The Threefold Life

Recasting all paths of transformation in terms of Matter-Life-Mind, Sri Aurobindo maintains: 'For man, the head of terrestrial Nature, the sole earthly frame in which her full evolution is possible, is a triple birth. He has been given a living frame in which the body is the vessel and life is the dynamic means of a divine manifestation. His activity is centred in a progressive mind which aims at perfecting itself as well as the house in which it dwells and the means of life that it uses, and is capable of awakening by a progressive self-realisation to its own true nature as a form of the spirit. He culminates in what he always really was, the illumined and beatific spirit which is intended at last to irradiate life and mind with its now concealed splendors. Since this is the plan of the divine Energy in humanity, the whole method and aim of our existence must work by the interaction of these three elements in the being'.[35] Each of these three is governed by a characteristic impulse and has meaning as well as purpose.

Even though they have distinct qualities and planes of operation, the three guṇa-s influence each other by combining to create a convoluted system. The distinct character associated with each man refers to this system within him – the play of the three guṇa-s.

Transcending the three guṇa-s is vital for the complete transformation and union with the supreme consciousness. Conquering tamas is inevitable for any ascent along the planes, while mastering rajas is the difficult but highly necessary step as one evolves higher. Sāttvic forces cannot always operate by themselves and need the anchoring of a purified rajas for transformation, thus rising to become *triguṇātīta* – above all the three guṇa-s. Sri Aurobindo writes in *Essays on the Gita*, expanding upon the words of Kṛṣṇa to the karma yogi, Arjuna:

> But man as the individual self, owing to his ignorant self identification with the work and the becoming, as if that were all his soul and not a power of his soul, a power proceeding from it, is bewildered by the ego-sense. He thinks that it is he and others who are doing all; he does not see that Nature is doing all and that he is misrepresenting and disfiguring her works to himself by ignorance and attachment. He is enslaved by the guṇa-s, now hampered in the dull case of tamas, now blown by the strong winds of rajas, now limited by the partial lights of sattwa, not distinguishing himself at all from the nature-mind which alone is thus modified by the guṇa-s. He is therefore mastered by pain and pleasure, happiness and grief, desire and passion, attachment and disgust: he has no freedom.

> He must, to be free, get back from the Nature action to the status of the Akṣara; he will then be *triguṇātīta*, beyond the guṇa-s. Knowing himself as the Akṣara Brahman, the unchanging puruṣa, he will know himself as an immutable impersonal self, the Ātman, tranquilly observing and impartially supporting the action, but himself calm, indifferent, untouched, motionless, pure, one with all beings in their self, not one with Nature and her workings.[36]

## The Methods of Integral Yoga

Sri Aurobindo's epic canvas unifies many fundamental truths from different schools of yoga, and aims for not just the ascent towards sat-cit-ānanda, but the realization of the same in this world itself. To the sādhaka of Integral Yoga, 'All Life is Yoga' remains the foremost teaching.

As we have seen earlier, the psychic is the portion of the Divine in every man that is subject to the evolutionary process. To the Integral yogi, bringing to the forefront the psychic being, enthroning it as the rightful centre of processing the physical, mental, and emotional responses constitutes the first step, while actively letting go of egoistic notions of being the doer of actions and the thinker. This can be done in several ways: by concentrating on the heart centre and aspiring for the psychic being to emerge, by watching oneself and distinguishing the various responses arising from the different planes appropriately and hence controlling egoistic responses, and so on. Simultaneously, Sri Aurobindo urges the Integral sādhaka to follow the triple path of Aspiration-Rejection-Surrender.

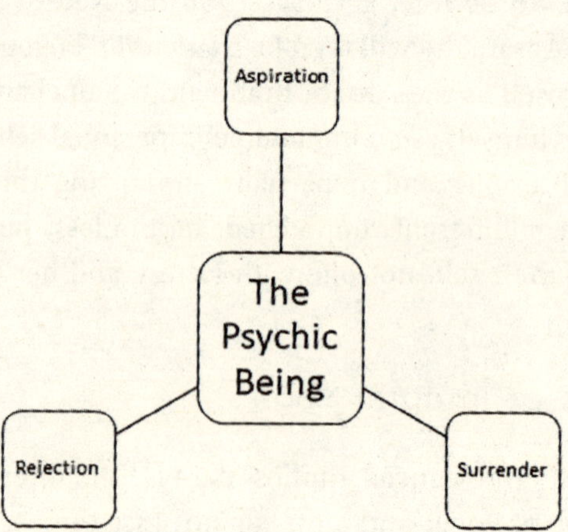


**Figure 13: The Psychic Being**

Sincere aspiration for a higher way of living for Supreme Consciousness founds the very basis of the sādhana. Every action, thought, and will is turned towards the Divine so that all of man's activities become instruments to manifest the consciousness. Rejection involves being mindful of the inner responses in oneself and constantly abandoning the hold of the ego on the vital, and sensational responses to outer and inner impulses. Rejection is the part where the being discriminates against the various chaotic movements within and systematically rejects the reactions of the lower being while letting the psychic being respond. Surrender reiterates the first two steps and offers everything to the Flame within for purification.

Karma Yoga, Jñāna Yoga and Bhakti Yoga too become primary methods of transformation. But unlike the traditional schools, in Integral Yoga, they are always aimed at life-affirming means.

## States of Consciousness

Traditional Indian psychology views consciousness as comprising four states – *jāgrat* (waking state), *swapna* (dream state) and *suśupti* (sleep state). Each of these is present in man with the highest state – *turiya,* the state of supreme being – beyond all these three. Sri Aurobindo has related these states with the planes of consciousness as well.

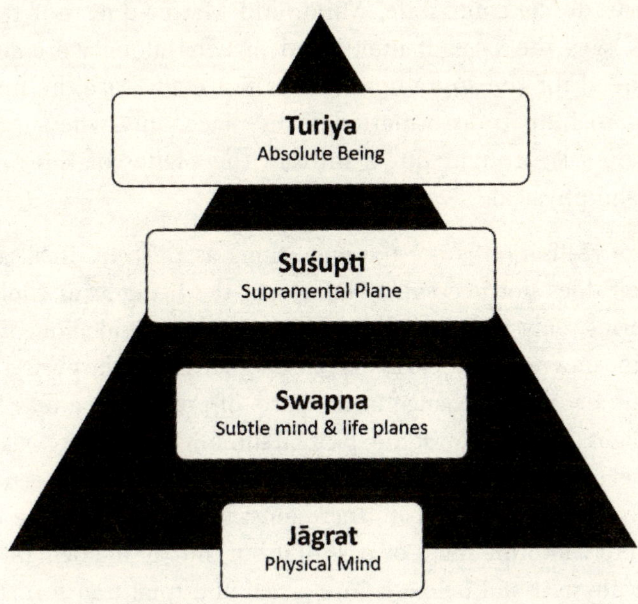


**Figure 14: States of Consciousness**

The waking state or jāgrat is associated with the consciousness of gross matter, where forms are definite and solid while the forces operate at a slower pace. The state of swapna operates on the subtle plane with mental and intuitional faculties working freely when not impacted by the forces of the gross forms. Man's spiritual life belongs to the suśupti state with consciousness freely operating on this plane.

## Transformation

Most schools, such as Advaita Vedānta or Buddhism, place mōkṣa and nirvāṇa as the highest state of attainment, where there is a dissolution of the individual state into an absolute. Liberation or mukti has the role of an 'inner change which is common to all experience of this kind, essential to perfection and is indispensable to spiritual freedom'.[37] The cessation of desire, ego, the three guṇa-s of prakṛti, as well as the dualities of nature, constitutes the characteristic of freedom – mukti. But in Integral Yoga, Sri Aurobindo uses this state not as the ultimate but calls it only a partial realization. The realization of the supreme without any descent into Life, Mind, and Matter does not transform the being, says the sage. If mukti and nirvāṇa alone were sufficient, then the need for the supramental does not even arise, he maintains. According to him, transformation takes place only when the higher consciousness is brought down into all the planes of the mind, the vital and the physical.

> Light of realisation is not the same thing as Descent. Realisation by itself does not necessarily transform the being as a whole; it may bring only an opening or heightening or widening of the consciousness at the top so as to realise something in the puruṣa part without any radical change in the parts of prakṛti. One may have some light of realisation at the spiritual summit of the consciousness but the parts below remain what they were. We have seen any number of instances of that. There must be a descent of the light not merely into the mind or part of it but into all the being down to the physical and below before a real and total transformation can take place. A light in the mind may spiritualise or otherwise change the mind or part of it in one way or another, but it need not change the vital nature; a light in the vital may purify and enlarge the vital movements or else silence and immobilise the vital being, but leave the body and the physical consciousness as it was, or even leave it inert or shake its balance. And the descent of Light is not enough, it must be the descent of the whole higher consciousness, its Peace, Power, Knowledge, Love, Ananda. Moreover, the descent may be enough to liberate, but not to perfect, or it may be enough to make a great change in the inner being, while the outer remains an imperfect instrument, clumsy, sick or unexpressive. Finally, the transformation effected by the sadhana cannot be complete unless it is a supramentalisation of the being. Psychisation is not enough, it is only a beginning; spiritualisation and the descent of the higher consciousness is not enough, it is only a middle term; the ultimate achievement needs the action of the supramental Consciousness and Force. Something less than that may very well be considered enough by the individual, but it is not enough for the earth-consciousness to take the definitive stride forward it must take at one time or another.[38]

The sage further writes, 'By divine realisation is meant the spiritual realisation—the realization of Self, Bhagavan or Brahman on the mental-spiritual plane or else the overmental plane. That is a thing (at any rate the mental-spiritual) which thousands have done. So it is obviously easier to do than the supramental. Also nobody can have the supramental realisation who has not had the spiritual'.[39]

## Perfection of Body

Some yoga-s realize the importance of the human body as a vehicle for spiritual realization but reject it upon spiritual realization because the body brings inertia and obstinacy to realize any spiritual change. Integral Yoga, on the other hand, envisages making it a perfect and fit instrument for divine work, i.e. preparing it so that the Divine Mother's energy can use it in the way She deems fit. The important vital and nervous energies are not to be annulled in pursuit of the Divine but transformed and made fit for a divine instrument. Thus, Sri Aurobindo disagrees with the rejection of the human body once union with the spirit has been achieved. He explains:

> The vital and nervous energies in us are there for a great utility; they too demand the divine realisation of their possibilities in our ultimate fulfillment...It is therefore no integral Yoga that kills these vital energies, forces them into a nerveless quiescence or roots them out as the source of noxious activities. Their purification, not their destruction,—their transformation, control and utilisation is the aim in view with which they have been created and developed in us.[40]

The body needs to be made supple and strong enough to sustain the in-rush of the higher Divine energies without it breaking down under their impact or showing signs of weakness and fatigue in a process of carrying out the Divine Will. For this, the joy that the body takes in different activities does not have to be eliminated; it needs to be brought into the fold of spiritual life so that it is given a spiritual hue for the progressive manifestation of the Divine in all its expressions.

His idea of a complete transformation of the body differs from that of the materialist who sees the functioning of the body due to chemicals composed of atoms and molecules, and all the cognitive processes and psychological states are a by-product of the presence of the various chemicals, where matter is the cause of our consciousness. However, for Sri Aurobindo, it is the spirit that causes and sustains the body. In our mortal state of existence, the ātma is involved in the body and therefore, completely identifies with it. As the spiritual evolution proceeds, the ātma in an individual frame begins to realize that it is not the body, thereby becoming cognizant of the occult powers of the invisible realms. These occult powers have a tremendous capacity to transform all that is gross and animal in us into their divine prototype. The transformation, resulting from the perfection that he is alluding to, is fairly radical in that it is based on the promise of taking the human body to the next level of human evolution. He contended that the perfection of the body would even lead to changes in certain bodily organs and that the body would develop powers of communication that it does not normally possess. Sri Aurobindo described that the difference between a human being and a supramental being would be of the same measure as that between an ape and a human. He explains:

> The new type, the divine body, must continue the already developed evolutionary form; there must be a continuation from the type Nature has all along been developing, a continuity from the human to the divine body, no breaking away to something unrecognisable but a high sequel to what has already been achieved and in part perfected. The human body has in it parts and instruments that have been sufficiently evolved to serve the divine life; these have to survive in their form, though they must be still further perfected, their limitations of range and use removed, their liability to defect and malady and impairment eliminated, their capacities of cognition and dynamic action carried beyond the present limits. New powers have to be acquired by the body which our present humanity could not hope to realise, could not even dream of or could only imagine.[41]

## Perfection of Mind

Some yoga-s discard the mind and its primary functions of logic and reasoning once its purpose has been achieved, for their aim is not to make the mind perfect in order for the Divine Mother to use it for the evolution of life on earth. This is understandable because their objective is union with the static self as Vedānta conceptualizes or releases into nirvāṇa as Buddhism seeks. They consider the mind as an impediment in attaining the spiritual objective, and therefore, the emphasis is on purification (as in the case of Rāja Yoga) and dis-identification (as in the case of Jñāna Yoga). Sri Aurobindo agrees that the mind cannot take us into the spiritual realms and that it is an instrument of ignorance, but he states that when the descent of the dynamic Divine Force occurs, a supple and flexible mind can become its powerful instrument. Therefore, for a complete and world-affirming Divine life, the perfection of the human mind is of crucial importance:

> Mind comes to be regarded as an unworthy deformation and a supreme obstacle, the source of an illusory universe, a negation of the Truth and itself to be denied and all its works and results annulled if we desire the final liberation. But this is a half-truth which errs by regarding only the actual limitations of Mind and ignores its divine intention. The ultimate knowledge is that which perceives and accepts God in the universe as well as beyond the universe; the integral Yoga is that which, having found the Transcendent, can return upon the universe and possess it, retaining the power freely to descend as well as ascend the great stair of existence. For if the eternal Wisdom exists at all, the faculty of Mind also must have some high use and destiny. That use must depend on its place in the ascent and in the return and that destiny must be a fulfilment and transfiguration, not a rooting out or an annulling.[42]

Drawing from the traditional Vedāntic knowledge, Sri Aurobindo incorporates in his system the four-fold classification of the mind or the antaḥkaraṇa: citta or the basic mental consciousness, manas or the sense mind, buddhi or the intelligence, and ahaṁkāra or the ego-sense. Since the mind evolves out of matter and life, it is colored and contaminated with their presence, thus creating impediments in the higher spiritual evolution of the human being. Mind, however, is also the link between the higher and the lower planes of human existence; therefore, it also has traces of light and power which can assist in spiritual evolution. Purification is the process by which it is able to get rid of its contaminations (discussed below) and consequently is able to accentuate the spiritual light and power that it already has—the two processes being complementary.

Citta, the basic mental consciousness, is largely subconscient. It fundamentally has two modes of operation: passive and active. In the passive mode, it registers and processes all the information that the active conscious mind does not, forming a subconscious memory. This subconscious memory formed due to the abovementioned process as well as from the experiences gained in past lives, when coming into the active mode, forms bodily and psychological habits or the *citta-vṛtti*. The citta-vṛtti, because of its subconscious nature, is very difficult to get rid of. However, it can be done away with by making the subconscious conscious, a process very similar to psychoanalysis, by illuminating it through the use of conscious will, and by circulating universal prāṇa energy, which can be done by practicing *prāṇāyāma*, the process central to the philosophy and the practice of Rāja Yoga. This is the process of purification; however, when it is made subservient to force, and the will of the Divine Śakti, its perfection, and transfiguration can be integral and complete.

Manas, the sense mind, is dependent on the sense organs for knowledge and on the organs of the body for action. The sense mind is involved in citta and is the progenitor of what we usually call senses: sight, hearing, smell, etc. However, manas also has a subtle aspect to it, which is connected to the plane of the universal mind and is capable of communicating with other levels of mental consciousness without the use of the sense organs. When its association with the sense organs is loosened, correspondingly its subjection to the vital, pranic energy decreases. Consequently, the hold of the desire-soul on an individual reduces, leading to purification in the mental consciousness.

Buddhi, roughly translated as the intelligence and the will of the conscious being, is a plane of consciousness that is the link between the higher planes of existence beyond the mind and the lower two—the planes of matter (*anna*) and life (*prāṇa*). Also, among the three sub-planes within the antaḥkaraṇa or the mind, it is the highest sub-plane. Therefore, it has the inherent potential of leading an individual to the realms beyond thought and reason as well as of purifying citta and manas. Since it is in touch with the higher realms beyond the mind, it also has the characteristic of passionately pursuing knowledge and desiring to discover the ultimate truths of human existence.

Buddhi centers itself and its mental action around the ego-idea, the ahaṁkāra. Since the Vedāntic spiritual reality suggests that one is not the mind, life, and body but a spiritual consciousness, the buddhi needs to be liberated from the clutches of ahaṁkāra, citta, and manas so that it can disinterestedly pursue the fundamental truths of one's existence and get into regions beyond the mental, into the farther regions of the Supermind.

Though the right principle of this life-plane is to enjoy, possess, and live for the sake of the Divine, in its deformed manifestation it creates a desire-soul in humans that ubiquitously invades all the different aspects of the antaḥkaraṇa creating insatiable hunger, lust, wants, desires, and different pairs of affective opposites such as likes and dislikes, love and hate, etc. The mind, which otherwise is a free and powerful instrument that humans possess, thereafter, instead of controlling life and body, comes under their control. The proper principle of the psychic prāṇa is to manifest the will, but it gets deformed in the lower states of human consciousness and manifests as self-centered desire. Hence, the purification process involves getting rid of the desire-principle so that the psychic prāṇa not only becomes a perfect vehicle for manifesting the Divine Will but also liberates and purifies the antaḥkaraṇa, making buddhi available for illuminating the citta and the manas as well as for the pursuit of the realms beyond the mind. The psychic prāna then, instead of controlling the human mind, comes under its control. Finally, the buddhi needs to understand its own limitation as an instrument for knowing spiritual realities, for it can only know them piecemeal: It is an instrument for knowing realities in parts but not as a whole. Once it comes to realize that the spiritual realities are primarily trans-mental, its final emancipation and purification is accomplished: a journey culminating in a union with the Truth-mind or Supermind, its perfection is attained.

# Selected Bibliography


Apte, Vasudeo Mahadeo. 1960. *Brahma Sutra Sankara Bhashya* Bombay: Popular Book Depot.

Auroville. 1981. *Mother's References in Agenda.* Auroville, India: Auroville Press.

Bohac Clarke, Veronika, ed. 2018. *Integral Theory and Transdisciplinary Action Research in Education.* IGI Global.

Brilliant, Larry. 2016. *Sometimes Brilliant: The Impossible Adventure of a Spiritual Seeker and Visionary Physician Who Helped Conquer the Worst Disease in History.* HarperCollins.

Capra, Fritjof. 1988. *Uncommon Wisdom: Conversations with Remarkable People.* Simon and Schuster.

Carlson, Richard. 2008. 'Integral Ideology: An Ideological Genealogy of Integral Theory and Practice'. Integral World. Accessed March 31, 2024. http://www.integralworld.net/carlson.html

Chaudhuri, Haridas. 1951. *The Prophet of Life Divine.* Calcutta, India: Sri Aurobindo Pathamandir.

Chaudhuri, Haridas, and Frederic Spiegelberg. Eds. 1960. *The Integral Philosophy of Sri Aurobindo.* London: George Allen and Unwin Ltd.

Chaudhuri, Haridas. 1977. *The Evolution of Integral Consciousness.* Wheaton, IL: Theosophical Publishing House.

Cortright, Brant. 1997. *Psychotherapy and Spirit.* State University of New York Press.

Coward, Harold. 1990. *Derrida and Indian Philosophy.* Albany: State University of New York Press.

Dalal, Ardeshir. S. 2001. *A Greater Psychology: An Introduction to the Psychological Thought of Sri Aurobindo.* New York: Jeremy Tarcher/Putnam.

Durant, Will. 1954. *The Story of Civilization Part 1: Our Oriental Heritage.* New York: Simon and Schuster.

Edwards, Mark. 2003. 'A Brief History of Holons'. Integral World. http://www.integralworld.net/edwards13.html

Ellwood, Robert S. 1996. 'Religion and Modernization in Postmodern Perspective' in *East-West Encounters in Philosophy and Religion*, eds Smart, Ninian, and B. Srinivasa Murthy, 53-71. Long Beach, CA: Long Beach Publications.

Esbjörn-Hargens, Sean, and Michael E. Zimmerman. 2011. *Integral Ecology: Uniting Multiple Perspectives on the Natural World.* Shambhala Publications.

Fanon, Frantz. 1963. *The Wretched of the Earth.* New York: Grove Press.

Gandhi, Kishor. 2008. *Social Philosophy of Sri Aurobindo and the New Age* (1965 1st ed). Pondicherry: Sri Aurobindo Society.

Gaskin, Ina May. 1975. *Spiritual Midwifery*. Summertown, Tennessee: Book Publishing Company.

Gebser, Jean. 1985. *The Ever-Present Origin* Athens, OH: Ohio University Press.

Godin, Christian. 2000. 'The Notion of Totality in Indian Thought'. *Diogenes* 48, no. 189: 58-67.

Hemsell, Rod. 2006. 'Ken Wilber and Sri Aurobindo: A Critical Perspective'. Integral World. Accessed March 31, 2024. http://www.integralworld.net/hemsell.html

Huntington, C.W. 1989. *The Emptiness of Emptiness: An Introduction to Early Indian Mādhyamika*. Honolulu, HI: University of Hawaii Press.

Huntington, Samuel. 1997. *The Clash of Civilizations and the Remaking of the World Order*. New York: Touchstone.

Joo, Swami Lakshman. 2007. *Vijnana Bhairava: The Practice of Centering Awareness*. Varanasi: Indica Books.

Kannan, K. S. 2021. 'Western Indology on Rasa: A Pūrvapakṣa'. *Reclaiming Sanskrit Studies: Book 4*. Infinity Foundation India.

Kazlev, Alan. 2006. *Historical and Comparative use of 'Integral'*. Integral World. https://www.integralworld.net/kazlev1.html

Kineman, John Jay. 2017. 'A causal framework for integrating contemporary and Vedic holism'. *Progress in Biophysics and Molecular Biology* 131: 402-423.

Koestler, Arthur. 1945. *The Yogi and the Commissar*. New York: The Macmillan Company.

Koestler, Arthur. 1949. *Insight and Outlook*. London: Macmillan and Co.

Koestler, Arthur. 1959. *The Sleepwalkers*. New York: The Macmillan Company.

Koestler, Arthur. 1960. *The Lotus and the Robot*. London: Hutchinson and Co.

Koestler, Arthur. 1964. *The Act of Creation*. New York: The Macmillan Company.

Koestler, Arthur. 1967. *The Ghost in the Machine*. New York: The Macmillan Company.

Kohlberg, Lawrence. 1981. *Essays on Moral Development*. Vol. 1: The Philosophy of Moral Development. San Francisco: Harper & Row.

Kuhn, Thomas. S. 1970. *The Structure of Scientific Revolutions* (2nd ed.). Chicago: University of Chicago Press.

Laszlo, Ervin. 2007. Science and the Akashic Field: An Integral Theory of Everything (2nd ed.). Inner Traditions.

Lovejoy, Arthur. 1971. *The Great Chain of Being: A Study of the History of an Idea*. Harvard University Press.

Lyotard, Jean Francois. 1979. *The Postmodern Condition: A Report on Knowledge*. Manchester University Press.

Maitra, Susil Kumar. 1956. *Fundamental Questions of Indian Metaphysics and Logic*. Calcutta: Chuckervertty Chatterjee & Co.

Malhotra, Rajiv. 2013a. *Being Different: An Indian Challenge to Western Universalism*. HarperCollins.

Malhotra, Rajiv. 2013b. 'Vivekananda's Ideas and the Two Revolutions in Western

Thought', in *Vivekananda as the Turning Point: The Rise of a New Spitiual Wave*, ed. Swami Shuddhidananda, 559-583. Kolkata: Advaita Ashram.

Malhotra, Rajiv. 2013c. 'Author's Response: The Question of Dhārmic Coherence' in International Journal of Hindu Studies 16, 3: 369-408.

Malhotra, Rajiv and Satyanarayana Das Babaji. 2020. *Sanskrit Non Translatables: The Importance of Sanskritizing English.* Amaryllis.

McDermott, Robert (ed). 1987. *The Essential Aurobindo.* MA: Lindisfarne Books.

McGuigan, Richard J., and Nancy Popp. 2016. *Integral Conflict: The New Science of Conflict.* State University of New York Press.

Mohrhoff, Ulrich J. 2008. 'Evolution of Consciousness According to ean Gebser'. *AntiMatters 2*, no 3.

Moore, Walter J. 1989. *Schrodinger: Life and Thought.* Cambridge University Press.

Mysterium.com. 'The American Academy of Asian Studies'. Accessed March 31, 2024. http://www.mysterium.com/aaas.html

Nicholson, Sarah E., and Vanessa D. Fisher, eds. 2014. *Integral Voices on Sex, Gender, and Sexuality: Critical Inquiries.* State University of New York Press.

Nirodbaran. 1983. *Nirodbaran's Correspondence with Sri Aurobindo* (Vols. 1-2). Pondicherry, India.

Olson, Carol. 2002. *Indian Philosophers and Postmodern Thinkers.* Oxford University Press.

Parks, George A., G. Alan Marlatt, Sarah W. Bowen, Tiara M. Dillworth, Katie Witkiewitz, M. Larimer, and L. Meijer. 2003. 'The University of Washington Vipassana Meditation Research Project at the North Rehabilitation Facility'. *American Jails* 17, no. 3: 13-17.

Radhakrishnan, Sarvepalli. 1953. *The Principal Upanishads.* London: Allen and Unwin.

Reynolds, B. 2004. *Embracing Reality: The Integral Vision of Ken Wilber.* New York: Jeremy P. Tarcher/Penguin.

Rowan, John & Daniels, Michael & Fontana, David & Malcolm,. 2009. *A dialogue on Ken Wilber's contribution to transpersonal psychology.* Transpersonal Psychology Review. 13.

Salmon, Don. 2008. 'Integral Psychology beyond Wilber-V Inviting Open-Minded Skepticism of the Materialist View'. Integral World. Accessed March 31, 2024. http://www.integralworld.net/salmon2.html

Schammel, Michael. 2009. *Koestler — The Literary and Political Odyssey of a Twentieth-Century Skeptic.* Random House.

Schrodinger Erwin. 1961. *Meine Weltansicht.* Wien: Paul Zsolnay.

Schrodinger, Erwin. 2012. *What is Life?: The Physical Aspect of the Living Cell with Mind and Matter and Autobiographical Sketches.* Cambridge University Press.

Sen, Indra. 1986. *Integral Pyschology: The Psychological System of Sri Aurobindo.* Sri Aurobindo Ashram.

Smith, Andrew. 2006. *The Intersubjective Meditator: A Critical Look at Ken Wilber's Integral Spirituality.* Integral World. https://www.integralworld.net/smith21.html

Smuts, Jan, C. 1926. *Evolution and Holism.* New York: The Macmillan Company.

Sri Aurobindo. 1972a. *The Life Divine: Sri Aurobindo Birth Centenary Library* (Vols. 18-19). Pondicherry, India: Sri Aurobindo Ashram.

Sri Aurobindo. 1972b. *Letters on Yoga: Sri Aurobindo Birth Centenary Library* (Vols. 22-24). Pondicherry, India: Sri Aurobindo Ashram.

Sri Aurobindo. 1972c. *Sri Aurobindo Birth Centenary Library: Vol. 25. On Himself.* Pondicherry, India: Sri Aurobindo Ashram.

Sri Aurobindo. 1972d. *Arya's Fourth Year, in The Hour of God and Other Writings, Sri Aurobindo Birth Centenary Library* (Vol. 17). Pondicherry, India: Sri Aurobindo Ashram.

Sri Aurobindo. 1997a. *Essays on the Gita: Vol. 19, The Complete Works of Sri Aurobindo.* Pondicherry, India: Sri Aurobindo Ashram.

Sri Aurobindo. 1997b. *Essays Divine and Human: Vol. 12, The Complete Works of Sri Aurobindo*. Pondicherry, India: Sri Aurobindo Ashram.

Sri Aurobindo. 1997c. *The Human Cycle, The Ideal of Human Unity, War and Self-Determination: Vol. 25, The Complete Works of Sri Aurobindo*. Pondicherry, India: Sri Aurobindo Ashram.

Sri Aurobindo. 1997d. *Renaissance in India and Other Essays on Indian Culture: Vol. 20, The Complete Works of Sri Aurobindo*. Pondicherry, India: Sri Aurobindo Ashram.

Sri Aurobindo. 1997e. *The Human Unity: Vol. 25, The Complete Works of Sri Aurobindo.* Pondicherry, India: Sri Aurobindo Ashram.

Sri Aurobindo. 1997f. *Karmayogin: Vol. 8, The Complete Works of Sri Aurobindo.* Pondicherry, India: Sri Aurobindo Ashram.

Sri Aurobindo. 1998a. *The Complete Works of Sri Aurobindo: Vol. 12. Essays Divine and Human.* Pondicherry, India: Sri Aurobindo Ashram.

Sri Aurobindo. 1998b. *The Complete Works of Sri Aurobindo: Vol. 20. The Renaissance in India.* Pondicherry, India: Sri Aurobindo Ashram.

Sri Aurobindo. 1998c. *The Complete Works of Sri Aurobindo: The Synthesis of Yoga* (Vols. 23-24). Pondicherry, India: Sri Aurobindo Ashram.

Sri Aurobindo. 1998d. *The Complete Works of Sri Aurobindo: Vol. 25. The Human Cycle.* Pondicherry, India: Sri Aurobindo Ashram.

Sri Aurobindo. 1999. *The Synthesis of Yoga: Vols. 23-24, The Complete Works of Sri Aurobindo*. Pondicherry, India: Sri Aurobindo Ashram.

Sri Aurobindo. 2001a. *Record of Yoga, Vols. 10-11, The Complete Works of Sri Aurobindo.* Pondicherry, India: Sri Aurobindo Ashram.

Sri Aurobindo. 2001b. Kena and Other Upanishads, *Vol. 18, The Complete Works of Sri Aurobindo*. Pondicherry, India: Sri Aurobindo Ashram.

Sri Aurobindo. 2003. *Early Cultural Writings, Vol. 1, The Complete Works of Sri Aurobindo.* Pondicherry, India: Sri Aurobindo Ashram.

Sri Aurobindo. 2005a. *The Life Divine: Vols. 21- 22, The Complete Works of Sri Aurobindo.* Pondicherry, India: Sri Aurobindo Ashram.

Sri Aurobindo. 2005b. *Letters on Yoga, Sri Aurobindo Birth Centenary Library Vols. 22-24.* Pondicherry, India: Sri Aurobindo Ashram.

Sri Aurobindo. 2012. *Letters on Yoga – I: Vol. 28, The Complete Works of Sri Aurobindo.* Pondicherry, India: Sri Aurobindo Ashram.

Sri Aurobindo. 2013. *Letters on Yoga – II: Vol. 29, The Complete Works of Sri Aurobindo.* Pondicherry, India: Sri Aurobindo Ashram.

Sri Aurobindo. 2014a. *Letters on Yoga – III: Vol. 30, The Complete Works of Sri Aurobindo.* Pondicherry, India: Sri Aurobindo Ashram.

Sri Aurobindo. 2014b. *Letters on Yoga – IV: Vol. 31, The Complete Works of Sri Aurobindo.* Pondicherry, India: Sri Aurobindo Ashram.

Sri Aurobindo Ashram. 1999. *The Mother on Auroville.* Pondicherry, India. Sri Aurobindo Ashram.

Stace, Walter Terence. 1961. *Mysticism and Philosophy*. London: Macmillan and Co.

Swami Satprakashananda. 1977. *The Universe, God, and God-realization: From the Viewpoint of Vedanta.* St. Louis, MO: Vedanta Society of St. Louis.

Swami Vivekananda. 1896. *Vedanta Philosophy: Lectures on 'The Cosmos'*. New York: Harjes and Wright.

Swami Vivekananda. 1901. *The Vedanta Philosophy*. New York: The Vedanta Society.

Swami Vivekananda. 1908. *Raja Yoga or Conquering the Internal Nature.* Calcutta: Udbodhan Office.

Swami Vivekananda. 1955. *Jnana-Yoga*. Calcutta: Advaita Ashrama.

Swami Vivekananda. 1959. 'The Cosmos and The Self'. In *The Complete Works of Swami Vivekananda,* 5. Calcutta: Advaita Ashrama.

Swami Vivekananda. 1970. *The Complete Works of Swami Vivekananda* (Vol. 2). Calcutta, India: Advaita Ashrama.

The Mother. 1999. *The Mother on Auroville*. Copyright Sri Aurobindo Ashram Trust. Pondicherry, India: Madanlal Himatsingka on behalf of Vak Trust.

The Mother. 2003a. *Knowledge of the Scientist and the Yogi* in *Questions and Answers 1929-1931: Collected Works of The Mother*. Pondicherry, India: Sri Aurobindo Ashram.

The Mother. 2003b. *Vol. 6: Questions and Answers (1954)*. Sri Aurobindo Ashram.

The Mother. 2004. *Vol. 8: Questions and Answers (1956)*. Sri Aurobindo Ashram.

van Vrekhem, Georges. 2000. *The Mother: The Story of Her Life*. HarperCollins.

Whicher, Ian. 'Countering World-Negation: The World Affirming and Integrative Dimension of Classical Yoga'. Presented at the Global Renaissance: Indic Contributions Colloquium, 2002. https://www.infinityfoundation.com/indic_colloq/papers/paper_whicher2.pdf

Whicher, Ian, and David Carpenter, eds. 2003. *Yoga: The Indian Tradition*. RoutledgeCurzon.

White, John. 1986. 'The Einstein of Consciousness'. *Yoga Journal*, no. 69 (July/August): 84-85.

White, John. 1999. Foreword to *The Collected Works of Ken Wilber* (Vol. 1) by Ken Wilber, 33-7. Boston, MA: Shambhala.

Wilber, Ken. 1975. 'Psychologia perennis: The Spectrum of Consciousness'. *Journal of Transpersonal Psychology* 7, no. 2: 105-132.

Wilber, Ken. 1997a. *The Eye of Spirit: An Integral Vision for a World Gone Slightly Mad.* Boston, MA: Shambhala.

Wilber, Ken. 1997b. 'An Integral Theory of Consciousness'. *Journal of Consciousness Studies* 4, no. 1: 71-92.

Wilber, Ken. 1980. *The Atman Project: A Transpersonal View of Human Development*. Quest Books.

Wilber, Ken. 1981. *Up from Eden: A Transpersonal View of Human Evolution*. Anchor Press.

Wilber, Ken. 1982. *The Holographic Paradigm and Other Paradoxes*. Boston, MA: Shambhala.

Wilber, Ken. 1983. *Eye to Eye: The Quest for the New Paradigm*. Random House.

Wilber, Ken. 1995. *Sex, Ecology, Spirituality*. Boston, MA: Shambhala.

Wilber, Ken. 1996. *A Brief History of Everything* (2nd ed. 2001). Boston, MA: Shambhala.

Wilber, Ken. 1996b. *The Atman Project* (Second edition). Wheaton Illinois: Quest Books.

Wilber, Ken. 1999. *The Collected Works of Ken Wilber* (Vol. 1). Boston, MA: Shambhala.

Wilber, Ken. 2000a. *Integral Psychology: Consciousness, Spirit, Psychology, Therapy*. Boston, MA: Shambhala.

Wilber, Ken. 2000b. *One Taste: Daily Reflections on Integral Spirituality*. Boston, MA: Shambhala.

Wilber, Ken. 2000c. *A Brief History of Everything*. Boston, MA: Shambhala.

Wilber, Ken. 2000d. *The Collected Works of Ken Wilber, Vol. 8*. Boston, MA: Shambhala

Wilber, Ken. 2000f. *The Collected Works of Ken Wilber, Vol. 6*. Boston, MA: Shambhala

Wilber, Ken. 2006. *Integral Spirituality: A Startling New Role for Religion in the Modern and Postmodern World*. Integral Books.

Wilber, Ken. 2018. *Integral Buddhism: And the Future of Spirituality*. Shambhala.

Wilber, Ken. 2021. *Vol. 2, Kosmos Trilogy* (Unpublished). Integrales Forum. https://www.integralesforum.org/attachments/Excerpt_A-_Kosmos_II.pdf

Wilber, Ken. 2000a. *Integral Psychology: Consciousness, Spirit, Psychology, Therapy*. Boston, MA: Shambhala.

Wilber, Ken. 2000b. *One Taste: Daily Reflections on Integral Spirituality*. Boston, MA: Shambhala.

Wilber, Ken. 2000c. *A Brief History of Everything*. Boston, MA: Shambhala.

Wilber, Ken. 2000d. *The Collected Works of Ken Wilber, Vol. 8*. Boston, MA: Shambhala

Wilber, Ken. 2006. *Integral Spirituality: A Startling New Role for Religion in the Modern and Postmodern World*. Integral Books.

Wilber, Ken. 2018. *Integral Buddhism: And the Future of Spirituality*. Shambhala.

Wilber, Ken. 2021. *Vol. 2, Kosmos Trilogy* (Unpublished). Integrales Forum. https://www.integralesforum.org/attachments/Excerpt_A-_Kosmos_II.pdf

Wilber, K. *Sex, Karma, Creativity* (Unpublished) *Vol. 2, Kosmos Trilogy* https://integralarchive.wordpress.com/ken-wilber/kosmos-trilogy/

Wilber, Ken, Jack Engler, and Daniel P. Brown. 1986. *Transformations of Consciousness: Conventional and Contemplative Perspectives on Development*. Boston, MA: Shanmbhala.

Young, Robert. 2004. *White Mythologies*. New York/ London: Routledge.

# Notes

## INTRODUCTION

1 Auroville. 'Auroville: The City of Dawn'. Accessed 31 March 2024. https://auroville.org
2 (Malhotra 2013a, 106)
3 (Malhotra 2013a, 116)
4 Some of the material in this section, including the diagram, draws from work published by Infinity Foundation, *Sanskrit Non-Translatables*.
5 For instance, Jung went to stages 2 and 3 but he was open about his debt to India. After him, his successors, i.e. present Jungians, erased these Indic sources and have sometimes denigrated the Indic sources as inferior in various ways. T.S. Eliot was very Hindu for a period when he composed his most famous poems, including *The Waste Land.* But today, this Indic influence is never mentioned in literature courses on Eliot.

## CHAPTER 1: THE IMPORTANCE OF CHALLENGING WILBERISM

1 (White 1986, 84)
2 Kosmos, Journal for Global Transformation. 'Ken Wilber'. Accessed 31 March 2024. https://www.kosmosjournal.org/contributor/ken-wilber
3 Integral Life. 'Who is Ken Wilber?' Accessed 31 March 2024. https://integrallife.com/who-is-ken-wilber
4 Ubiquity University. 'Chancellor'. Accessed 31 March 2024. https://www.ubiquityuniversity.org/chancellor
5 Ubiquity University, course: 'The Dance of Shiva: A Pilgrimage to South India with Andrew Harvey'. Accessed 31 March 2024. https://www.ubiquityuniversity.org/courses/the-dance-of-shiva-a-pilgrimage-to-south-india-with-andrew-harvey-july-28-31-2021
6 (Wilber 1980, 76)
7 (Sri Aurobindo 2005a, 730-753)
8 (Wilber 1997a, 238)
9 (Wilber 1983, 13)
10 (Wilber 1997a, 303)
11 (Wilber 1980, 3)

## CHAPTER 2: LOBBYING THE AUROBINDONIANS

1 Email dated May 2000
2 Integral Institute. 'History'. Accessed 31 March 2024. https://integralinstitute.org/history.htm
3 Email dated 29 May 2000
4 Email dated 31 May 2000
5 Collaboration.org. 'Transcript of the talk and discussion with Rajiv Malhotra : 24th JUNE, 2000'. Accessed 31 March 2024. https://www.collaboration.org/Auroville/malhotra_interview.htm
6 Email dated 20 August 2000

## CHAPTER 3: AN INITIAL HOME TEAM EMERGES

1 Email dated 31 May 2000
2 Email dated 31 May 2000
3 Email dated 1 June 2000
4 Email dated 1 June, 2000
5 The Educational Council on Indic Traditions. 'Guest Book'. Accessed 31 March 2024. https://infinityfoundationecit.com/guest-book
6 Ibid
7 (The Mother 2003a, 162)
8 Email dated 23 May 2000
9 Email dated 23 May 2000
10 Email dated 22 June 2002
11 Indian Psychology Institute. 'Third International Conference on Integral Psychology: 30 May 30-1 June 2003'. Accessed 31 March 2024. https://ipi.org.in/events/ip3.php
12 Email dated 5 August 2000

## CHAPTER 4: RECLAIMING INTEGRAL PSYCHOLOGY

1 Email dated 30 May 2000
2 He wrote: '[The conference] objective is specifically to elucidate and work out the psychological elements of Sri Aurobindo's work. What I see as our main task at this stage is to bring out the solid theoretical underpinning for consciousness studies that Sri Aurobindo developed on the basis of the Indian tradition, and his work on the next step of the evolution'.
3 Email dated 25 August 2000
4 (Sen 1986)
5 4-7 January 2001. See: Sri Aurobindo Centre for Consciousness Studies. 'Consciousness and its Transformation'. Accessed 3 February 2003. http://www.saccs.org.in/TEXTS/IP2/IP2-Contents.html
6 Email dated 15 January 2001, 'Dear Rajiv, the IP conference is over and it was, I think, more successful than anyone had thought possible. Many participants

were personally deeply touched by the spiritual atmosphere and there was a lively intellectual exchange between people from Auroville, Ashram, Indian and Western universities. I hope to send you a formal report in a couple of days. Herewith already are my deeply felt gratitude for your assistance to Don, Jan, Kundan and Brant. All four made valuable contributions... .'

7 Email dated 5 February 2001

8 See: (Sri Aurobindo 2003)

9 (Sri Aurobindo 1997d, 125)

10 For more on this, see: (The transformative potential of Integral Yoga has spread the Aurobindonian movement worldwide, Kannan 2021)

11 (Sri Aurobindo 2003, 451)

12 (Malhotra & Babaji 2020, 161)

13 (Sri Aurobindo 1997d, 126)

14 (Whicher 2002)

15 (Whicher and Carpenter 2003, 59)

16 (Whicher and Carpenter 2003, 60)

17 (Whicher and Carpenter 2003, 61)

18 (Brilliant 2016, 86)

19 Seva Foundation. 'Philosophy: Compassion in Action'. Accessed 27 October 2007. http://www.seva.org/site/PageServer?pagename=about_philosophy

20 Good News India. 'Tihar Jail is a Good Model for Prisons in India'. Accessed 25 August 2008. http://www.goodnewsindia.com/Pages/content/transitions/tihar.html

21 (Parks et al. 2003)

22 In the 1970s, birth was also reclaimed as a spiritual rather than a medical event, largely through the work of Ina May Gaskin, wife of hippie spiritual teacher Stephen Gaskin. Her book, *Spiritual Midwifery*, was first published in 1975. Although she doesn't say much about any Indic influences, she put rows of Buddhas on the book cover. (Gaskin 1975).

23 Email dated 12 June 2002

24 Harvard's Samuel Huntington writes in *The Clash of Civilizations* that in 1750, India had 25% of the world's manufacturing output while Europe and America combined had less than 18% (Huntington 1997, 86).

25 Will Durant summarizes the details to be discussed in this section, in his book *Our Oriental Heritage* on page 459: 'The Mohammedan Conquest of India is probably the bloodiest story in history. It is a discouraging tale, for its evident moral is that civilization is a precarious thing, whose delicate complex of order and liberty, culture and peace may at any time be overthrown by barbarians invading from without or multiplying within. The Hindus had failed to organize their forces for the protection of their frontiers and their capitals, their wealth and their freedom, from the hordes of Scythians, Huns, Afghans and Turks hovering about India's boundaries and waiting for national weakness to let them in. For four hundred years (600-1000 A.D.) India invited conquest; and at last it came.. The bitter lesson that may be drawn from this tragedy is that eternal vigilance is the price of civilization.

A nation must love peace, but keep its powder dry'.

26 India's influence on works of Emerson, Thoreau, Whitman, Browning, Eliot, Isherwood, Hesse, Ginsburg, Kerouac, diPrima, among others were to be studied. Indic ideas have shaped modern psychology, cognitive sciences and the emerging worldview, including its influence on thinkers such as Schrödinger, Jung, de Chardin, Wilber, etc. India was a heavy influence on the development of European and Asian languages and linguistics.

## CHAPTER 5: THE DEBATE BECOMES GLOBAL

1 Email exchange in August 2000
2 Email dated 23 August 2000.
3 Email dated 23 August 2000.
4 Email dated 23 August 2000.
5 Email dated 15 August, 2000
6 Email dated 23 August 2000.
7 Email dated 8 November, 2000 by David Brookman
8 Email dated 23 May 2000 by Julian
9 Email dated 15 August 2000
10 Email dated 22 August 2000
11 Email dated 22 August 2000
12 Email dated 26 August 2000
13 Email dated 6 August 2000
14 Email dated 29 August 2000
15 Email dated 06 August 2000.
16 Email dated 31 August 2000
17 Email dated 1 September 2000
18 Email dated 10 August 2000.

## CHAPTER 6: BETRAYAL BY THE CALIFORNIA INSTITUTE OF INTEGRAL STUDIES

1 (Mysterium.com 2024)
2 (Mysterium.com 2024)
3 Mysterium.com. 'From the American Academy of Asian Studies to the California Institute of Integral Studies'. Accessed 31 March 2024. http://www.mysterium.com/aaas-ciis.html
4 (Mysterium.com 2024)
5 (Chaudhuri 1977, 135-6)
6 Chatterji, Angana P. 'Biographical Sketch'. Accessed 31 March 2024. https://www.anganachatterji.net/wp
7 Scofield, Be. 26 December 2108. 'How a Cult Infiltrated the California Institute of Integral Studies'. https://www.gurumag.com/how-a-cult-infiltrated-the-california-institute-of-integral-studies

8 Schmidt, Peter. 12 January 2012. 'Questions of Undue Influence Unseat 2 Professors'. https://www.chronicle.com/article/questions-of-undue-influence-unseat-2-professors
9 Email dated 22 April 2002
10 Email dated 24 April 2002
11 Email dated 24 April 2002
12 Dawn.com. 2 June 2002. '*DAWN* – Letters'. https://www.dawn.com/news/1063185
13 Draft shared with Kundan on 3 June 2002
14 Email dated 13 July 2002
15 Email dated 9 September 2002
16 Email dated 15 July 2002
17 Email dated 5 September 2002
18 Email dated 8 September 2002
19 Email dated 5 September 2002
20 Email dated 17 July 2002
21 Email dated 21 July 2004
22 Email dated 21 July 2004
23 Email dated 22 July 2004
24 Springer, Richard. 14 December 2011. 'CIIS Fires Two Professors after Student Complaints'. India West. https://web.archive.org/web/20120108004549/http://www.indiawest.com/news/1981-ciis-fires-two-professors-after-student-complaints.html

## CHAPTER 7: PREDATOR PROJECT TO HIJACK SRI AUROBINDO'S WORK

1 (Wilber 1975, 115)
2 (Wilber 1975, 129-30)
3 See: AgileDC. 24 October 2016. 'Integral Agile: Deliver More Effectively Using This Powerful Lens and Awareness'. https://confengine.com/agiledc-2016/proposal/2865/integral-agile-deliver-more-effectively-using-this-powerful-lens-and-awareness; Aqal Integral Investing. 'You canot not invest'. Accessed 31 March 2024. https://aqalgroup.com
4 See: (Esbjörn-Hargens & Zimmerman 2011, xv)
5 See: (Bohac 2018)
6 See: (McGuigan & Popp 2016); (Micholson & Fisher 2014)
7 (Wilber 2018)
8 (Wilber 2021, 25)

## CHAPTER 8: WILBER-I: THE MINING EXPEDITION BEGINS

1 (White 1999, 33)
2 (Wilber 1975, 129)
3 (Wilber 1999, 138)

4 (Wilber 1999, 327)
5 (Schrodinger 1961); (Moore 1989, 170-3)
6 (Moore 1989, 173)
7 Wilber, 1982, 217-8)
8 The Postscript (pp. 60) in 'A dialogue on Ken Wilber's contribution to transpersonal psychology' (2007) involving John Rowan, Michael Daniels, David Fontana & Malcolm Walley, has John Rowan clearly stating that he checked with Wilber if he independently came up with the system and he replied in the affirmative.
9 (Wilber 1999, xi)
10 https://en.wikipedia.org/wiki/Perennial_philosophy.
11 Colombo, John Robert. 2010, June 16. '"THE PERENNIAL PHILOSOPHY" revisited'. Gurdjieff's teaching: for scholars and practitioners. http://gurdjieffbooks.wordpress.com/category/the-perennial-philosophy-revisited
12 'Consciousness and Force are the twin essential aspects of the pure Power of existence; Knowledge and Will must therefore be the form which that Power takes in creating a world of relations in the extension of Time and Space. This Knowledge and this Will must be one, infinite, all-embracing, all-possessing, all-forming, holding eternally in itself that which it casts into movement and form. The supermind then is Being moving out into a determinative self-knowledge which perceives certain truths of itself and wills to realise them in a temporal and spatial extension of its own timeless and spaceless existence. Whatever is in its own **being**, takes form as self-knowledge, as Truth-Consciousness, as Real-Idea, and, that self-knowledge being also self-force, fulfils or realises itself inevitably in Time and Space'. (Sri Aurobindo 2005a, 154)
13 (Sri Aurobindo 1972b, 258)
14 (Sri Aurobindo 1998c, 129)
15 (Sri Aurobindo 1972b, 63)
16 (Sri Aurobindo 1972b, 65)
17 'The highest spirituality indeed moves in a free and wide air far above that lower stage of seeking which is governed by religious form and dogma; it does not easily bear their limitations and, even when it admits, it transcends them; it lives in an experience which to the formal religious mind is unintelligible. But man does not arrive immediately at that highest inner elevation and, if it were demanded from him at once, he would never arrive there. At first he needs lower supports and stages of ascent; he asks for some scaffolding of dogma, worship, image, sign, form, symbol, some indulgence and permission of mixed half-natural motive on which he can stand while he builds up in him the temple of the spirit. Only when the temple is completed, can the supports be removed, the scaffolding disappear. The religious culture which now goes by the name of Hinduism not only fulfilled this purpose, but, unlike certain credal religions, it knew its purpose. It gave itself no name, because it set itself no sectarian limits; it claimed no universal adhesion, asserted no sole infallible dogma, set up no single narrow path or gate of salvation; it was less a creed or cult than a continuously enlarging tradition of the Godward

endeavour of the human spirit. An immense many-sided many-staged provision for a spiritual self-building and self-finding, it had some right to speak of itself by the only name it knew, the eternal religion, sanatana-dharma. It is only if we have a just and right appreciation of this sense and spirit of Indian religion that we can come to an understanding of the true sense and spirit of Indian culture'. (Sri Aurobindo 1997d, 179)

18 This superior look is a result of apprehensive approach to knowledge by reason, which is mainly verbal and values everything in terms of space as material objects, objectively existing, there is no need for it in the subjective comprehension and experience.

19 Note #30 in (Wilber 2000d, 62)

20 He repeatedly elaborates the important distinction between different realizations, speaking of nirvana as the fundamental spiritual realization, but not as the only one or the final goal in the spiritual journey, as illustrated by the following excerpts:
'Nirvana in my liberated consciousness turned out to be the beginning of my realisation, a first step towards the complete thing, not the sole true attainment possible or even a culminating finale'. (Sri Aurobindo 1972b, 50)
'I don't base the gospel of the transformation of Nature on an impossibility of taking a static release [in pure undifferentiated consciousness] as final—the static release is necessary, but I don't consider that to take it as final is the object of coming into world-existence. I hold that the static release is only a beginning, a first step in the Divine'. (Sri Aurobindo 1972b, 57)
'For this yoga...the experience of Nirvana can only be a stage or passage to the complete realisation. I have said also that there are many doors by which one can pass into the realisation of the Absolute (Parabrahman), and Nirvana is one of them, but by no means the only one'. (Sri Aurobindo 1972b, 59)

21 (Malhotra 2013c, 385-389)

22 (Sri Aurobindo 1998c, 43-44)

23 (Wilber 1980, 3)

24 (Wilber 1997a, 303)

25 (Chaudhuri 1951)

26 (Wilber 2021, 243)

27 Alan Kazlev (2006) writes: 'In my edition of Sex, Ecology, Spirituality (coll. Works vol.6, 2nd ed. 2000), on p.637 (end of note 8) Wilber quotes from *The Life Divine*, giving the book and chapter number, but not the page number; and on p. 792 (references) he mentions both in the *Collected Works Centenary Edition.* Just out of curiosity, I googled a text string from the Aurobindo quote in question. Here is the passage from an Aurobindonian website http://www.miraura.org/lit/sa/ld/ld2-26b.html, which includes Selections from the Sri Aurobindo Birth Centenary Library - from Volume 18 and 19, *The Life Divine:*
"The spiritual evolution obeys the logic of a successive unfolding; it can take a new decisive main step only when the previous main step has been sufficiently conquered: even if certain minor stages can be swallowed up or leaped over by a

rapid and brusque ascension, the consciousness has to turn back to assure itself that the ground passed over is securely annexed to the new condition. It is true that the conquest of the Spirit supposes the execution in one life or a few lives of a process that in the ordinary course of Nature would involve a slow and uncertain procedure of centuries or even of millenniums: but this is a question of the speed with which the steps are traversed; a greater or concentrated speed does not eliminate the steps themselves or the necessity of their successive surmounting".

'This is a different edition to mine; I have *The Life Divine* in a single volume (10th ed. 1977, Pondicherry). But I found the above quoted passage on p. 931-2 of my edition; it is word for word the same.

'Now, Google also found the same text string in Ken Wilber Online; at two urls: http://wilber.shambhala.com/html/books/psych_model/psych_model3.cfm/ and http://wilber.shambhala.com/html/books/ontast_wastco.cfm/ Both give the same text, which is also in my edition of Sex, Ecology, Spirituality.

"'The spiritual evolution obeys the logic of a successive unfolding; it can take a new decisive main step only when the previous main step has been sufficiently conquered: even if certain minor stages can be swallowed up or leaped over by a rapid and brusque ascension, the consciousness has to turn back to assure itself that the ground passed over is securely annexed to the new condition; a greater or concentrated speed [which is indeed possible] does not eliminate the steps themselves or the necessity of their successive surmounting" (Aurobindo, *The Life Divine*, II, 26).

'Note that Wilber cuts out an entire sentence (after 'new condition' and before 'a greater or concentrated speed', and adds some of his own material (in square brackets). However, unlike the quote in *The Atman Project*, Wilber does not here indicate with ellipses (...) that he has removed a section of material. While this may indicate carelessness, another explanation is that this text of the version is not from the original *Collected Works*. All this helps explain why Wilber doesn't understand Aurobindo at all; he simply hasn't read the original material'.

28 (Wilber 2000a, 84)

29 (Sri Aurobindo 2005a, 240)

30 (Sri Aurobindo 2005a, 241)

31 (Sri Aurobindo 2005a, 244)

32 'This calls for the appearance not only of isolated evolved individuals acting in the unevolved mass, but of many gnostic individuals forming a new kind of beings and a new common life superior to the present individual and common existence. A collective life of this kind must obviously constitute itself on the same principle as the life of the gnostic individual. In our present human common physical life-fact and all that arises from it, community of interests, a common civilisation and culture, a common social law, an aggregate mentality, an economic association, the ideals, emotions, endeavours of the collective ego with the strand of individual ties and connections running through the whole and helping to keep it together. Or, where there is a difference in these things, opposition, conflict, a practical

accommodation or an organised compromise is enforced by the necessity of living together; there is erected a natural or a constructed order. This would not be the gnostic divine way of collective living; for there what would bind and hold all together would be, not the fact of life creating a sufficiently united social consciousness, but a common consciousness consolidating a common life. All will be united by the evolution of the Truth-consciousness in them; in the changed way of being which this consciousness would bring about in them, they will feel themselves to be embodiments of a single self, souls of a single Reality; illumined and motived by a fundamental unity of knowledge, actuated by a fundamental unified will and feeling, a life expressing the spiritual Truth would find through them its own natural forms of becoming. An order there would be, for truth of oneness creates its own order: a law or laws of living there might be, but these would be self-determined; they would be an expression of the truth of a spiritually united being and the truth of a spiritually united life. The whole formation of the common existence would be a self-building of the spiritual forces that must work themselves out spontaneously in such a life: these forces would be received inwardly by the inner being and expressed or self-expressed in a native harmony of idea and action and purpose. An increasing mechanisation, a standardisation, a fixing of all into a common mould in order to ensure harmony is the mental method, but that would not be the law of this living. There would be a considerable free diversity between different gnostic communities; each would create its own body of the life of the spirit: there would be, too, a considerable free diversity in the self-expression of the individuals of a single community. But this free diversity would not be a chaos or create any discord; for a diversity of one Truth of knowledge and one Truth of life would be a correlation and not an opposition. In a gnostic consciousness, there would be no ego-insistence on personal idea and no push or clamour of personal will and interest: there would be instead the unifying sense of a common Truth in many forms, a common self in many consciousnesses and bodies; there would be a universality and plasticity which saw and expressed the One in many figures of itself and worked out oneness in all diversities as the inherent law of the Truth-consciousness and its truth of nature. A single Consciousness-Force, of which all would be aware and see themselves as its instruments, would act through all and harmonise their action together. The gnostic being would feel a single consonant Force of supernature acting in all: he would accept its formation in himself and obey or use the knowledge and power it gave him for the divine work, but he would be under no urge or compulsion to set the power and knowledge in him against the power and knowledge of others or affirm himself as an ego striving against other egos'. (Sri Aurobindo 2005a, 1068-1070)

33 (Wilber 1999, 55)

34 See *Īśopaniṣad* 9-11

## CHAPTER 9: WILBER-II: APPROPRIATING SRI AUROBINDO'S THEORY OF EVOLUTION

1 (Malhotra 2013b)

2 See: (Swami Vivekananda 1970, 207-8). Also, 'Sankocha and Vikasha mean shrinking and expanding. The whole universe, as it were, shrinks, and then it expands again. To use the more accepted words of modern science, they are involved and evolved. You hear about evolution, how all forms grow from lower ones, slowly growing up and up. This is very true, but each evolution presupposes an involution.... Only the manifestation varies, being involved and evolved. So this cycle is the evolution out of the involution of the previous cycle, and this cycle will again be involved, getting finer and finer, and out of that will come the next cycle. The whole universe is going on in this fashion. Thus we find that there is no creation in the sense that something is created out of nothing. To use a better word, there is manifestation, and God is the manifester of the universe. The universe, as it were, is being breathed out of Him, and again it shrinks into Him, and again He throws it out. A most beautiful simile is given in the Vedas —"That eternal One breathes out this universe and breathes it in". (Swami Vivekananda 1970, 427)
'Inside of it all, behind all this vast mass of what we call life, of millions of forms and shapes, millions upon millions of varieties, beginning from the lowest atom to the highest spiritualised man, we find existing a certain unity. Every day we find that the wall that was thought to be dividing one thing and another is being broken down, and all matter is coming to be recognised by modern science as one substance, manifesting in different ways and in various forms; the one life that runs through all like a continuous chain, of which all these various forms represent the links, link after link, extending almost infinitely, but of the same one chain. This is what is called evolution. It is an old, old idea, as old as human society, only it is getting fresher and fresher as human knowledge is progressing. There is one thing more, which the ancients perceived, but which in modern times is not yet so clearly perceived, and that is involution.... The ancient philosophers of India .... [held that] every evolution presupposes an involution. Nothing can be evolved which is not already there... Evolution does not come out of zero; then, where does it come from? From previous involution. The child is the man involved, and the man is the child evolved. The seed is the tree involved, and the tree is the seed evolved. All the possibilities of life are in the germ. The problem becomes a little clearer. Add to it the first idea of continuation of life. From the lowest protoplasm to the most perfect human being there is really but one life. Just as in one life we have so many various phases of expression, the protoplasm developing into the baby, the child, the young man, the old man, so, from that protoplasm up to the most perfect man we get one continuous life, one chain. This is evolution, but we have seen that each evolution presupposes an involution. The whole of this life which slowly manifests itself evolves itself from the protoplasm to the perfected human being — the Incarnation of God on earth — the whole of this series is

but one life, and the whole of this manifestation must have been involved in that very protoplasm. This whole life, this very God on earth, was involved in it and slowly came out, manifesting itself slowly, slowly, slowly. The highest expression must have been there in the germ state in minute form; therefore this one force, this whole chain, is the involution of that cosmic life which is everywhere. It is this one mass of intelligence which, from the protoplasm up to the most perfected man, is slowly and slowly uncoiling itself. Not that it grows. Take off all ideas of growth from your mind. With the idea of growth is associated something coming from outside, something extraneous, which would give the lie to the truth that the Infinite which lies latent in every life is independent of all external conditions. It can never grow; It was always there, and only manifests Itself'. (Swami Vivekananda 1970, 227-228)

3 (Swami Vivekananda 1901, 9-10). Also see the passage from the lecture, '*The Cosmos: The Macrocosm*', delivered in New York on 19 January 1896:

'The mountain comes from the sand, and goes back to the sand; the river comes out of vapour, and goes back to vapour; plant life comes from the seed, and goes back to the seed; human life comes out of human germs, and goes back to human germs. The universe with its stars and planets has come out of a nebulous state and must go back to it. What do we learn from this? That the manifested or the grosser state is the effect, and the finer state the cause. Thousands of years ago, it was demonstrated by Kapila, the great father of all philosophy, that destruction means going back to the cause'. (Swami Vivekananda 1896, 5)

A week later, Swami Vivekananda delivered a sequel to the previous lecture in which he makes the following remarks on involution-evolution:

'Applying the law we found in the case of the macrocosm, that each involution presupposes an evolution, and each evolution an involution, what is instinct therefore? Involved reason. So all that which we call instinct in men or animals must therefore be involved degenerated voluntary actions, and voluntary actions are impossible without experience. Experience started that knowledge, and that knowledge is there. This fear of death, this going into the water, and all involuntary actions in the human being which have become instinctive, are the results of past experiences, now become extinct'. (Swami Vivekananda 1896, 19-20)

4 (Swami Vivekananda 1955, 27-8)

5 (Swami Vivekananda 1955, 183)

6 (Swami Vivekananda 1959, 255)

7 (Sri Aurobindo 1972b, 44)

8 (Sri Aurobindo 1972a, 3-4)

9 (Wilber 1980, xvii)

10 Interestingly, Jantsch was influenced by Ervin László's work. However, we show in separate writings that László was himself very much a student of many Hindu and Buddhist teachers, among them Swami Muktananda, a prominent international exponent of Kāśmīrī Śaivism. But this influence has been buried by Western writers. (See László 2007)

11 Wilber's explanations and ideas on involution-evolution from Wilber-II stage onwards are significantly different from the ones held at Wilber-I stage. In *The Spectrum of Consciousness,* he does use the terms involution-evolution but they do not mean anywhere close to how he describes them here onwards. In fact, evolution is involution and vice versa in *The Spectrum of Consciousness*. Further, there is no allusion of any connection whatsoever to materialistic evolution with either spiritual involution or spiritual evolution. At best, one can say that Wilber-I shows similarities with Sri Aurobindo on matters of involution-evolution that are very rudimentary in nature.
12 (Wilber 1980, 60)
13 (Sri Aurobindo 2005a, 275)
14 (Wilber 1996a, 313)
15 (Reynolds 2004, 9)
16 (Sri Aurobindo 1972a, 253-8)
17 (Wilber 1980, 1-2)
18 See (Sri Aurobindo 2005a, Chapter XXVI); also pp. 332 of the same
19 (Sri Aurobindo 1972a, 39-40)
20 (Wilber 1980, 4)
21 (Sri Aurobindo 2014b, 112)
22 (Wilber 1980, 3)
23 (Sri Aurobindo 2005a, 923)
24 (Sri Aurobindo 2014b, 118)
25 (Sri Aurobindo 1997b, 169)
26 (Sri Aurobindo 2014b, 404)
27 (Sri Aurobindo 2014b, 404)
28 (Sri Aurobindo 1997b, 167)
29 (Sri Aurobindo 2014a, 30)
30 (Sri Aurobindo 2014a, 97)
31 (Sri Aurobindo 1972a, 702-3)
32 (Wilber 1997a, 238)
33 (Wilber 1980, 48)
34 (Sri Aurobindo 2014a, 338)
35 (Sri Aurobindo 2014a, 338)
36 (Sri Aurobindo 2014a, 38)
37 (Sri Aurobindo 2014a, 490)
38 (Sri Aurobindo 2001a)
39 He writes many detailed accounts in his diaries, such as: 'Joy of the spirit in the Ekam which expresses itself (the basis of shuddhananda, chidananda & sadananda together making kaivalyananda) is as yet obscure & involved in the lower anandas. Since yesterday, the ahaituka kamananda & today the sahaituka tivrananda are manifesting. Yesterday also the discomfort of heat & cold and pain were again exiled, though not entirely. Experiments made with the body show that below a certain intensity all pain now gives ananda of bhoga at the time of the feeling of pain, & pain beyond

that degree brings it after the immediate acuteness has passed. Sometimes sahaituka raudrananda results. As I write ahaituka tivrananda, raudrananda & vaidyutananda (negative) are recommencing; also vishayananda sahaituka and ahaituka, begun yesterday, are becoming more definite. The bhoga of all these forms is already established. The greatest difficulty is found in the pro-longed contact of intense heat with a sensitive part of the body, eg. the heated stone of the floor under the midday sun. The intensity of the heat to the sensation can be increased, lessened or inhibited by Will; the prolonged contact tends to remove the element of suffering unless the Will is made to increase or maintain it, or unless the stream of Will (chit-shakti) is kept tamasic suffering weakly the con- tact instead of meeting it. This daurbalyam has been created in order to bring about certain forms of intense ananda, chiefly viparita. It is possible, as is now clearly seen, to render it a great element of strong positive (not viparita) ananda, but in that case the daurbalyam must be merely a form of balam, in other words, it must be supported by dhairyam and anandadharanashakti'. (Sri Aurobindo 2001a, 47-8)

40 (Wilber 1983, 13)

41 (Reynolds 2004, 30)

42 Quoted in (Reynolds, 2004, 29)

43 (Sri Aurobindo 1972a, 44-5)

44 (Sri Aurobindo 1972a, 65-6)

45 (Sri Aurobindo 1972a, 239)

46 (Wilber 1980, 7)

47 (Sri Aurobindo 1972a, 256)

48 (Wilber 1980, 22-3)

49 (Sri Aurobindo 1972a, 257)

50 (Wilber 1980, 41)

51 (Sri Aurobindo 1972a, 550)

52 (Wilber 1996b, 98). Italics in original

53 (Wilber 1980, 100-1)

54 (Sri Aurobindo 1972b, 354-5)

55 (Wilber 1980, 101)

56 (Sri Aurobindo 1972a, 736)

57 (Wilber 1980, 106-7); It is interesting that Wilber took the term unconscious, which means something different than inconscient in Sri Aurobindo's terminology. Unconscious implies the absence of consciousness, whereas inconscient means involved consciousness. Subconscious means the level where consciousness is submerged.

58 (Sri Aurobindo 2012, 221)

59 (Wilber 1980, 112-3)

60 (McDermott 1987, 56)

61 (McDermott 1987, 60)

62 (McDermott 1987, 61)

63 (Sri Aurobindo 1972b, 1616-7)

64 (Wilber 1980, 127-8)
65 (McDermott 1987, 64-5)
66 (Wilber 1981, 9-10)
67 (Wilber 1981, 10-11)
68 Cited in (McDermott 1987, 64-5)
69 (Wilber 1981, xix)
70 Symbolic age is when human beings express their knowledge of the known and the unknown through symbols. Symbolic age gives rise to a human society which is governed by firm but not rigid temperament and psychic type. Where Symbolic is primarily religious and spiritual, the Typal is predominantly psychological and ethical. The psychological, ethical, economic, and physical are subordinated to religious and spiritual principles in Symbolic age whereas religious and spiritual are subordinated to psychological and ethical principles in Typal age. The Conventional stage of the society comes when the external expressions of the spiritual and psychological gains precedence over the inner—metaphorically put, in the Conventional age, clothes and jewelry becomes more important than the individual. Individualist age is the period when the hiatus between the truth and the convention becomes so wide that men of intellect using their reason and thought begin to tear down the rigid ways of the Conventional.
71 (Wilber 1981, 341), italics in original
72 (Sri Aurobindo 1998d, 255-7)
73 (Wilber 1981, 346-7)
74 (Sri Aurobindo 1972b, 27)
75 (Sri Aurobindo 1972b, 27-8)
76 (Wilber 1981, 330)
77 (Wilber 1981, 317). J. White's edited book, *Kundalini, Evolution, and Enlightenment* is also mentioned. Since it is an edited book, we cannot for sure attribute the original use of involution to White.
78 'I am not alone in this overall view. Sri Aurobindo, India's greatest modern sage, has written extensively on just this view point—Brahman getting lost in involution and then evolving back—from matter to prana to mind to overmind to Supermind and Atman, and he sees it occurring cosmologically as well as psychologically. Aurobindo, of course, is one of the few geniuses and full mystics (East or West) who also had the opportunity and willingness to study the anthropological and paleontological records compiled so carefully by modern science, and he found those records to be not only compatible with his view but supportive of it. Aurobindo is joined in his view by many other modern Indian giants, Radhakrishnan, Chaudhuri, Gopi Krishna, etc.' (Wilber 1981, 330-1)
79 Schelling, as per Wilber, described involution as the centrifugal movement of the spirit away from its center, and evolution as the centripetal movement towards the center. Creation, thus, is the Fall as a centrifugal movement. However, Schelling was a well-known Sanskrit scholar who openly referenced Vedic *śāstra*-s in his writings.

80 (Wilber 1981, 332)

81 Wilber seemed to misunderstand the two stages of creation (involutions) presented by Sri Aurobindo and The Mother. The first involution was the Fall of the first emanations, laying ground for the future manifestations. The second involution was of the descent of the Divine into the Fallen Self of the first involution and the beginning of evolution out of material inconscience.

82 (Sri Aurobindo 1998d, 6)

83 (Sri Aurobindo 1998b, 80-1)

84 (Wilber 1997a, 303)

85 (Hemsell 2006)

## CHAPTER 10: WILBER-III: APPROPRIATING LINES OF DEVELOPMENT AND PSYCHIC BEING

1 (Wilber 1997a, 338)

2 (Wilber 1997a, 234)

3 (Wilber 1997a, 227)

4 (Wilber, Engler, and Brown 1986, 140-1)

5 (Sri Aurobindo 2003, 450)

6 (Sri Aurobindo 1997d, 260)

7 (Wilber 1997a, 213), italics in original

8 (Wilber 1997a, 222)

9 J.S. Mill is well known as the champion of Universal Liberalism and human rights of the nineteenth century, while he worked for the East India Company all his adult life. He theorized that Indians were like children and needed to be supervised by Whites in their own best interests. Hence, the White Man's Burden to colonize them.

10 (Wilber 1997a, 216)

11 (Sri Aurobindo 1998c, 73)

12 (Sri Aurobindo 1998c, 73-4)

13 (Sri Aurobindo 1998c, 74)

14 (Sri Aurobindo 1998c, 74)

15 (Sri Aurobindo 1998c, 142-4)

16 Wilber does not seem to adequately understand that all real changes in different 'development lines' of activities take place through changes in consciousness. To try to understand the higher changes in accordance with mental idea is not enough, it will only modify them in their old and outer form. It is like trying to explain to the monkey the beauty of Beethoven's symphonies. So, without trying to change one's own consciousness to speak about those changes theoretically and, especially without learning and humble attitude and reference to those who did this profound work within their own consciousness, is a vain and arrogant idea.

17 (Sri Aurobindo 2005a, 892)

18 (Sri Aurobindo 1998c, 619-20)

19 (Sri Aurobindo 1998c, 617)
20 (Sri Aurobindo 1972b, 50)
21 (Sri Aurobindo 1998c, 620)
22 Sri Aurobindo has used Supramental interchangeably with Supermind.
23 (Sri Aurobindo 1998c, 799)
24 (Sri Aurobindo 2005b, 17)
25 Wilber's new definition of spirituality is 'that line of development in which the subject holds its ultimate concern...[And] the line of ultimate concern will itself unfold through the same general expanding sphere of consciousness, from preconventional concern (egocentric) to conventional concern (sociocentric) to postconventional concern (worldcentric), to post-postconventional concern (bodhisattvic)'. (Wilber 1997a, 221)
26 (Sri Aurobindo 1999, 140)
27 According to Sri Aurobindo there are twelve major qualities of parā prakṛti expressed through psychic being: sincerity, humility, gratitude, perseverance, aspiration, receptivity, progress, courage, goodness, generosity, equality and peace.
28 (Sri Aurobindo 1972b, 258)
29 (Sri Aurobindo 1972b, 251)
30 (Wilber 1997a, 140)
31 (Wilber 1997a, 141)
32 (Wilber 1997a, 141-2)
33 (Sri Aurobindo 1972a, 711)
34 (Sri Aurobindo 1972b, 258)
35 (Wilber 1997a, 340), footnote #16
36 (Wilber 2000a, 276)
37 (Wilber 2000a, 268)
38 (Cortright 1997, 73)
39 (Wilber 1999, 268)
40 'By the very nature of the principal Yogic schools, each covering in its operations a part of the complex human integer and attempting to bring out its highest possibilities, it will appear that a synthesis of all of them largely conceived and applied might well result in an integral Yoga. But they are so disparate in their tendencies, so highly specialised and elaborated in their forms, so long confirmed in the mutual opposition of their ideas and methods that we do not easily find how we can arrive at their right union. An undiscriminating combination in block would not be a synthesis, but a confusion. Nor would a successive practice of each of them in turn be easy in the short span of our human life and with our limited energies, to say nothing of the waste of labour implied in so cumbrous a process.... The synthesis we propose cannot, then, be arrived at either by combination in mass or by successive practice. It must therefore be effected by neglecting the forms and outsides of the Yogic disciplines and seizing rather on some central principle common to all which will include and utilise in the right place and proportion their particular principles, and on some central dynamic force which is the common

secret of their divergent methods and capable therefore of organising a natural selection and combination of their varied energies and different utilities. This was the aim which we set before ourselves at first when we entered upon our comparative examination of the methods of Nature and the methods of Yoga and we now return to it with the possibility of hazarding some definite solution'. (Sri Aurobindo, 1998, 41-2)

41 (Wilber 1999, 206-9)

42 (Wilber 1999, 113)

43 (Sri Aurobindo 1972a, 647)

44 (Sri Aurobindo 1972a, 649)

45 Sri Aurobindo writes: 'The supraphysical is as real as the physical; to know it is part of a complete knowledge. The knowledge of the supraphysical has been associated with mysticism and occultism, and occultism has been banned as a superstition and a fantastic error. But the occult is a part of existence; a true occultism means no more than a research into supraphysical realities and an unveiling of the hidden laws of being and Nature, of all that is not obvious on the surface. It attempts the discovery of the secret laws of mind and mental energy, the secret laws of life and life-energy, the secret laws of the subtle-physical and its energies,—all that Nature has not put into visible operation on the surface'. (Sri Aurobindo,1972a, 651).

46 (Sri Aurobindo 1972a, 647-8)

47 (Sri Aurobindo 1972a, 652-3)

48 (Sri Aurobindo 2005, 675)

49 (Sri Aurobindo 1997b, 180-1)

50 (Sri Aurobindo 1997b, 181)

51 (Sri Aurobindo 1997e, 57-8)

52 (Sri Aurobindo 1997e, 60)

53 Wilber: 'While an integral or truly comprehensive paradigm will draw freely on the eye of flesh and the eye of mind, it must also draw significantly on the eye of contemplation. This means that a new and integral paradigm—if such is ever to exist—would be in the extremely favorable position of being able to use and integrate all three eyes—gross, subtle, and causal.... By and large, empiric-analytic science belongs to the eye of flesh, phenomenological philosophy and psychology to the eye of mind, and religion/meditation to the eye of contemplation. Thus a new and integral paradigm would ideally and ultimately be a synthesis and integration of empiricism, rationalism, and transcendentalism'. (Wilber 1996a, 7)

54 For instance, Wilber feels that if the eye of contemplation tries to explain the realm of gross matter, which is accessed by the eye of flesh, ignorance instead of knowledge results. There will be a similar result if there is confusion between the functions of the eyes of flesh and reason.

55 (Wilber 1997a, 65)

56 (Swami Vivekananda 1908, 4-5)

## CHAPTER 11: WILBER-IV: PREMODERN-POSTMODERN AND APPROPRIATION OF IMMANENCE-TRANSCENDENCE

1 See (Malhotra 2013) for a deeper understanding of this especially pp. 67-8, 236, 314 and 317.

2 (Lyotard 1979)

3 For further discussion comparing modernism and postmodernism, see (Ellwood 1996).

4 (Wilber 2000a, 163 onwards)

5 (Huntington 1989, 121)

6 The concept of śūnya, when approached psychologically, implies the absence of kinetic activities of consciousness, where it is perceived in its pure state. However, when it is approached philosophically or rather rationally, in the Western sense, then it is perceived as emptiness.

7 (Coward 1990)

8 (Coward 1990, 36-7)

9 (Wilber 2000b, 329)

10 (Wilber 1997a, 32)

11 Both Lovejoy and Smith developed their ideas through their long association with Vedānta. Smith's association is well-documented as a student of Swami Satprakashananda, founder and head of Vedanta Society of St. Louis. Lovejoy was a student of William James whose ideas of perennialism were developed in association with Swami Vivekananda. Lovejoy's book, *The Great Chain of Being: The Study of the History of an Idea*, explains the thoughts of Platonists, Plotinus, Pseudo Dionysius, Augustine and Thomas Aquinas among many others, using Vedāntic ideas. Koestler was heavily influenced by India and traveled there. The following description of the Great Chain on a website devoted to Wilber credits Aldous Huxley and Huston Smith as the developers of this idea, without a hint that both scholars acknowledged their debt to Indic traditions with great respect. The culmination of this idea is credited to German Idealism, whose own debt to the Indic influences of that era's German thought remains ignored. Meanwhile, Indian spiritual traditions get marginalized as 'monism' and are seen to lack this notion, until much later when the Theosophists are credited with bringing it to India. Here is how the Wilber camp today explains the history of this idea: 'Although the Great Chain of Being represents a central element of what Aldous Huxley (following Leibnitz) called the *Perennial Philosophy* and Huston Smith the *Primordial Tradition*, it is probably not as universal as is sometimes claimed. This concept is found in sophisticated form in Middle and Neoplatonism and Gnosticism in the late Classical World. From Neoplatonism it spread to Christianity and the Islamic world, and it was also assimilated into Kabbalah. In India it plays a big part in Kashmir Shaivism and other traditions, although it is never as widespread as it is in the West, due to a preponderance of Monism. In Taoism it appears in only undeveloped form. In the philosophical and naturalistic West it reaches a

culmination in the 18th through to early 19th century continental philosophers (especially evolutionary schools of German Idealism and Nature Philosophy), and was never as strongly developed in the East. In the late 19th and 20th century it was revived by Theosophy and Hermeticism (Theon, Golden Dawn, etc.), and in India in the teachings of Sri Aurobindo. Theosophical versions are influential in aspects of the New Age movement'. See: Kheper.net. 'Interpreting the Chain of Being: From Esoteric Great Chain of Being to Postmodern Great Nest of Being'. Accessed 29 June 2004. http://www.kheper.net/topics/Wilber/Great_Nest_of_Being.html

12 (Wilber 2000a, 54-5)

13 (Wilber 2000a, 68)

14 (Wilber 2000a, 68)

15 (Wilber 2000a, 68)

16 (Wilber 2000a, 68)

17 (Wilber 2000a, 64-5)

18 (Wilber 2000a, 69)

19 In *The Human Cycle*, Sri Aurobindo speaks about the Individualist Age as the creation of the Western civilization, which started from the Italian Renaissance and combined the knowledge by the Greeks and the ardent aspiration for the Divine by Christianity. It led eventually to the Classical Western Philosophy, French Revolution and Industrial Revolution in the West, introducing democracy and equality among men as its result. It is perhaps this great achievement of the Western civilization that has made its mind superior and aggressive in its approach to other civilizations. According to Sri Aurobindo, the future stage of human civilization is coming with the Subjective age, which cannot be arrived at by the Western approach alone without Indian spiritual heritage. The West has exhausted its spiritual resources and does not have anything more to offer or to draw from. India, on the other hand, has a great spiritual knowledge of the *Veda*-s, *Upanisad*-s, *Gītā* and Tantra. These resources will be used in the next stage of the spiritual development of mankind, which makes India indispensable for the future Subjective age of humanity.

Drawing from the spiritual knowledge of India, the Western mind tries to animate its own body of knowledge, making it alive and spiritual by finding anything that could resemble the spiritual experience in its own tradition, enlarging it with the fresh and luminous perception of Indian knowledge. In other words, it wants to survive by adopting the spiritual approaches of Indian traditions, which it does not have, and thus to preserve its dominating position which it gained in creating the Individualist age. Wilber is no exception in this case.

20 (Sri Aurobindo 1997d, 15)

21 He continues: 'What a fine monument of political and administrative genius is the Śukra-Niti, to take one example only, and what a mirror of the practical organisation of a great civilised people! Indian art was not always solely hieratic,—it seemed so only because it is in the temples and cave cathedrals that its greatest work survived; as the old literature testifies, as we see from the Rajput and Mogul paintings, it was devoted as much to the court and the city and to cultural ideas and the life of

the people as to the temple and monastery and their motives. Indian education of women as well as of men was more rich and comprehensive and many-sided than any system of education before modern times. The documents which prove these things are now available to anyone who cares to study. It is time that this parrot talk about the unpractical, metaphysical, quietistic, anti-vital character of Indian civilisation should cease and give place to a true and understanding estimate'. (Sri Aurobindo 1998b, 125-6)

22 He continues: 'Not only was India in the first rank in mathematics, astronomy, chemistry, medicine, surgery, all the branches of physical knowledge which were practiced in ancient times, but she was, along with the Greeks, the teacher of the Arabs from whom Europe recovered the lost habit of scientific enquiry and got the basis from which modern science started. In many directions India had the priority of discovery, —to take only two striking examples among a multitude, the decimal notation in mathematics or the perception that the earth is a moving body in astronomy, —calā pṛthvī sthirā bhāti, the earth moves and only appears to be still, said the Indian astronomer many centuries before Galileo. This great development would hardly have been possible in a nation whose thinkers and men of learning were led by its metaphysical tendencies to turn away from the study of nature. A remarkable feature of the Indian mind was a close attention to the things of life, a disposition to observe minutely its salient facts, to systematise and to found in each department of it a science, Shastra, well-founded scheme and rule. That is at least a good beginning of the scientific tendency and not the sign of a culture capable only of unsubstantial metaphysics'. (Sri Aurobindo 1998b, 123-4)

23 (Wilber 2006, 219)

24 (Smith 2006); bold emphasis ours

25 (Smith 2006)

26 In the Vedic tradition we also find similar concern, the dispute between the ṛṣi-s Yājñavalkya and Vaiśampāyana, where Yājñavalkya protested against the first introduction of the Brahmanic commentaries into the Saṃhitā text of *Yajurveda* by Vaiśampāyana. Their disagreement led to the split of the *Yajurveda* into two different *śākha*-s: *Kṛṣṇa* and *Śukla Yajurveda.*

27 (Sri Aurobindo 1997c, 12)

28 (Sri Aurobindo 1998b, 388)

29 He continues: 'This subjection of the sovereign power to the Dharma was not an ideal theory inoperative in practice; for the rule of the socio-religious law actively conditioned the whole life of the people and was therefore a living reality, and it had in the political field very large practical consequences. It meant first that the king had not the power of direct legislation and was limited to the issue of administrative decrees that had to be in consonance with the religious, social, political, economic constitution of the community,—and even here there were other powers than that of the king who shared with him the right of promulgating and seeing to the execution of administrative decrees independently issued,—neither could he disregard in the general tenor and character and the effective result of

his administration the express or tacit will of the people'. (Sri Aurobindo 1998b, 391-392)

30 (Wilber 2000a, 64-65)

31 (Wilber 2000a, 143-4)

32 (Ibid)

33 (Sri Aurobindo 1998a, 275-7)

34 (Wilber 2000a, 75-7)

35 (Wilber 2000a, 68)

36 (Wilber 2000a, 144)

37 Sri Aurobindo's Theory of Evolution is based on the Vedic vision of the transformation of our nature by the powers of higher consciousness, which is taking place gradually in time. It was an integral vision of reality, where Nature was seen as the Power, Śakti, of the Lord, the enterprise of the spirit. However, in the post-Vedic period it was replaced by the ideal of liberation from Nature rather than its transformation. The idea of evolution of consciousness is still found in some Tantric schools, but it is rather rare. The reason for this shift in a major trend of Indian tradition from liberation of Nature in time (evolutionary view) to liberation from Nature (static view) is given by Sri Aurobindo, explaining that humanity was not ready for such a difficult endeavor of transformation, therefore the split took place where one part, the Chaldean tradition became predominantly focused on the preservation of working in Nature and built up the Western civilization as we know it, and the other concentrated more on the spirit, the Advaitic tradition, Buddhism and Jainism, etc. However, the time has come to reestablish the Vedic Integral Vision of reality in the light of which other great systems of Integral Knowledge: *Upaniṣad*-s, *Gītā* and Tantra find their rightful and meaningful place.

38 (Wilber 2000a, 56). This view is introduced by Jean Gebser in 1940s in his *The Ever-Present Origin*. The mental structure of consciousness is very destructive and critical to all other structures that came before it: mythical and magic. Integral Structure will be the next step, which through transparency will make them efficient contributors to the Integral Knowledge.

39 We perceive that in the Indian ascetic ideal the great Vedāntic formula, 'One without a second', has not been read sufficiently in the light of that other formula equally imperative, 'All this is the Brahman'. The passionate aspiration of man upward to the Divine has not been sufficiently related to the descending movement of the Divine leaning downward to embrace eternally Its manifestation. Its meaning in Matter has not been so well understood as Its truth in the Spirit. The reality which the sannyasin seeks has been grasped in its full height, but not, as by the ancient Vedāntins, in its full extent and comprehensiveness. But in our completer affirmation we must not minimize the part of the pure spiritual impulse. As we have seen how greatly materialism has served the ends of the Divine, so we must acknowledge the still greater service rendered by asceticism to life. We shall preserve the truths of material science and its real utilities in the final harmony,

even if many or even if all of its existing forms have to be broken or left aside. (Sri Aurobindo 1972a, 24)

40 (Sri Aurobindo 1972a, 25-6)
41 See Chapter 14 of (Wilber 1996a)
42 See Chapter 17 of (Wilber 1996a)
43 (Lovejoy 1971, 256)
44 (Sri Aurobindo 1998c, 81-2)
45 (Sri Aurobindo 1997d, 239-40)
46 (Sri Aurobindo 2013, 429-30)
47 (Sri Aurobindo 1999, 610)
48 (Sri Aurobindo 1972c, 86-7)
49 (Sri Aurobindo 1998a, 319)
50 (Sri Aurobindo 1998a, 323)
51 (Sri Aurobindo 1998a, 333-4)
52 (Sri Aurobindo 1972b, 1608-9)

## CHAPTER 12: THE INDIAN INFLUENCES ON ARTHUR KOESTLER'S HOLONS AND THEIR IMPACT ON WILBER-IV

1 The earliest reference to India in Koestler's works, according to Michael Schammel's biography of Arthur Koestler: *Koestler–The Literary and Political Odyssey of a Twentieth-Century Skeptic* (2009) is in 1925, when Koestler first tried his hand at being a journalist at the young age of twenty in Vienna to write about literature and politics. Schammel writes:
'He brought Akzin a draft of his first article, destined for the Zionist Wiener Morgenzeltung (Vienna Morning Gazette), which was published in August 1925—a wide-ranging survey of recent developments in India and the Far East entitled "World Balkanization," signed not with Arthur's name but with his initial, Ka'. (Schammel 2009, 52)
2 (Koestler 1945, 3-4 )
3 (Koestler 1945, 24)
4 (Koestler 1945, 244)
5 (Koestler 1945, 246)
6 'Members of such very early, preanimistic types of society may be described as living in a state of original self-transcendence of consciousness. Their experience of mystic participation is so strong and immediate that it is directly lived in dance and rite, and not yet symbolized in myth, spirit, and ancestor worship. Hence the paucity of myths in these early societies whose mentality seems to correspond, to the presymbolic, unverbalized level of intelligence. Levy-Bruhl calls them preanimistic, because they do not yet recognize individual spirits or souls animating people and things, only one all-pervading universal force which acts through individual people and things: a homogeneous, ubiquitous substance or energy variously named "mana" by the Melanesians, "'wakanda" or "'orenda" by different West Indian tribes,

and which reaches its sublimest formulation in the Hindu Atman, the "undivided ocean of light". This cosmic consciousness stands in inverse ratio to consciousness of the ego:

'At the time when souls and spirits are not yet individualized, the individual consciousness of every member of the group is and remains strictly attuned to the collective consciousness – It does not distinctly break away from it; it does not even contradict itself in uniting with it; that which dominates it is the uninterrupted feeling of participation. Only later, when the human individual becomes clearly conscious of himself as an individual, when he explicitly differentiates himself from the group of which he feels himself a member, do beings and objects "outside himself also appear to him as provided with individual minds or spirits during this life and after death"'. (Koestler 1949, 175-176).

'The evolution of cosmic consciousness from these primitive forms of symbiosis between the universe and the not yet completely differentiated self, towards the voluntary transcendence of the self (emerging at the other end of the tunnel as it were) in the meditative techniques of Brahmanism, Buddhism, and so forth, reflects the working of the integrative tendency at various levels of mental development. The stability and inner equilibrium of the great Eastern civilizations of the past seem to have been mainly due to this particular form of integration. The contrast between the facilitation of cosmic self-transcendence in Eastern civilizations and its thwarting in contemporary Western society will be touched upon later'. (Koestler 1949, 176)

7 (Koestler 1949, 207)

8 'One of the most relevant comparisons from our point of view is that of the relative facilitation of the development of the Integrative and self-assertive tendencies in ancient Eastern and contemporary Western civilizations. **Had China or India produced a science of analytical psychology, the self-transcending emotions would head their list, as the trinity hunger-rage-fear stands out in Western psychology**. The Oriental psychologist would probably even deny the latter the title of "major" or "true" emotions and dismiss them as illusions, garish colours in the veil of Maya, just as the Western psychologists suspect the self-transcending emotions as partaking of hysteria and morbidity. The beginning and end of Eastern philosophy is the striving towards cosmic integration through the annihilation of the self and its absorption into the Atman, the All-One. The long centuries of stability, the continuity of tradition, the self-sufficiency of the great Eastern empires based on quietist philosophies Taoism, Brahmanism, Buddhism—would not have been possible if the self-transcending emotions were not basic in human nature. Contemplation, nonattachment, passivity, contempt of the body and its needs, the three silences, the cycles of rebirth and metempsychosis were realities as elementary in the lives of millions during millennia, as competition, domination, individualism, sex-asserting activities are for us. Even their only approved activity, the acquisition of merit, aimed at the liberation of the self from the bondage of re-birth and thus stood directly in the service of self-transcendence. For Western man, on the other

hand, all "good works" still serve the self-assertive purpose of individual rewards in afterlife; and even his prayers are primarily petitionary rather than contemplative. 'To sneer at these Eastern aspirations means to negate the tendencies and values of the greater part of the human specie throughout the greater part of its recorded history. To admire them blindly and recommend their unconditional imitation as a cure of all Western diseases means a failure to recognize the price which the Orient paid for its excessive indulgence in the oceanic feeling and its corresponding neglect of the self-asserting tendencies. The result of this development was that the integrative tendencies could only experience themselves on the cosmic, not on the social level. The thwarting of competitive striving, the denial of attention to the bodily self, the extinction of the will to power produced the familiar phenomena of Oriental squalor and disease, of intellectual stagnation, and social resignation by acceptance of caste. Epidemics, starvation, and puerperal sepsis, absolute rule and fatalistic submission, are some of the results of the thwarting of the self-assertive drives, just as many of the evils of Western civilization result from, the reverse process'. (Koestler 1949, 218)

9 Refer to (Capra 1988, 43)

10 (Koestler 1959, 53)

11 'The aim of certain mystic practices—such as Hatha Yoga—is to permeate the self with awareness of itself by gaining voluntary control over visceral processes and isolated muscles. It would seem that this focussing of consciousness on the self, the inward core of the contracting spiral, is the direct opposite of the self-transcending aspirations of other schools of mysticism—the expansion of consciousness in an unfolding spiral, and its final dissolution in the 'oceanic feeling'. In fact, however, the Yogi's effort to gain conscious mastery of the body is considered as merely a detour towards attaining 'pure consciousness'—that is, 'consciousness without object or content other than consciousness itself'. Thus turned upon itself, pure consciousness is supposed to penetrate the Real Self—which, unlike the transient self, is part and parcel of the Atman, the universal spirit.[1] Both methods, therefore, each with a long historical ancestry, share the same ultimate aim situated at the point where opposites meet; after all, as the bright little boy said, 'the infinite is where tilings happen which don't*'. (Koestler 1964, 634)

'It is even stranger that the same Sanskrit root matr split, by mitosis, as it were, into maya—the Oriental's web of illusions, and metron, metre, the Occidental's yardstick to measure the world'. (Koestler 1964, 642)

12 Michael Schammel's biography of Arthur Koestler: *Koestler–The Literary and Political Odyssey of a Twentieth-Century Skeptic* is regarded as amongst the most authoritative works on the man. We learn that Koestler's visit to India was sponsored by Congress for Cultural Freedom, an anti-communist outfit, that hoped to use Koestler's lectures to strengthen their own motives. We also see the high regard Koestler had for Vinobha Bhave and the Kanchi Kāma Koti Mahāperiyar as against his known disdain for M.K Gandhi. See: (Schammel 2009, 442)

13 (Schammel 2009, 636)

14 'The Upanishads, and to a perhaps slightly less extent the Gita, are of course the great fountainheads of Hindu mysticism. If our thesis of the universal solidarity of mysticism in general, and in particular of the experience of the dissolution of individuality, is valid, we shall expect to find in those ancient Indian documents expressions of this loss of personal identity. The expectation is not disappointed. Thus in the Brihadaranayaka Upanishad one finds the following:
'As a lump of salt thrown into water melts away ... even so, O Maitreyi, the individual soul, dissolved, is the Eternal—pure consciousness, infinite, transcendent. Individuality arises by the identification of the Self, through ignorance, with the elements; and with the disappearance of consciousness of the many, in divine illumination, it disappears.
'The middle part of this passage, which gives an explanation of how individuality arises, is not descriptive of experience, but is the intrusion of a metaphysical doctrine borrowed from the Samkhya system of philosophy. It can therefore be ignored for our purposes. The rest of the passage is a more or less straightforward description of the same kind of experience of the dissolution of personal identity in the introvertive type of mystical consciousness which we have found elsewhere'. (Stace 1961, 118)

15 'We should also call to mind Koestler's statement that "the I ceases to exist because it has established communication with or been dissolved in the universal pool," and yet that this experience brings "the peace which passeth all understanding." .....We must conclude that there are two possible alternative views of the nature of the future life—if we choose to assume that there is a future life. There is the Western view that it means the persistence of separate individualities. Tom is to remain Tom, Dick Dick, and Harry Harry. But we have found that the Indian view of the absorption of the separate individual in the life of the Universal Consciousness, or in nirvana, while yet not suffering annihilation, is a real though paradoxical alternative. Hence the question now to be asked is which view the evidence of the mystical consciousness tends to support. And I do not see how it is possible to avoid the conclusion that the Indian view is more in accord with mysticism'. (Stace 1961, 314)

16 (Stace 1961, 120)

17 (Koestler 1967, 45)

18 (Koestler 1967, Appendix I.1.) Emphasis in bold ours

19 (Bohm 1983, 15)

20 (Koestler 1967, 343)

21 (Koestler 1967, 61)

22 (Schrodinger 2012, 130)

23 (Kineman 2017, 403)

24 (Godin 2000, 66)

25 (Koestler 1960, 151)

26 (Apte 1960, 213)

27 (Maitra 1956, 74)

28 (Sri Aurobindo 2001b, 132)
29 (Radhakrishnan 1953, 201)
30 (Radhakrishnan 1953, 205)
31 (Edwards 2003)
32 (Sri Aurobindo 1972b, 253)
33 (Wilber 2000c, 18)
34 (Wilber 2000b, 327)
35 Since the tenets are numbered from 1-12 and that tenets 2 and 12 actually have respectively 4 and 5 tenets numbered from 2a to 2d and 12a to 12e, critics have pointed that the tenets do not add up to twenty but nineteen. Wilber, however, adds (see Wilber 1995, 35-78) that he does not consider tenets 7 and 9 as tenets but 'simple word definitions', and that the three additions he has made throughout the book are three tenets, which takes the total number to twenty. We will therefore not cover tenet 9 but will cover the three additions, one of which is being taken into account in this section.
36 (Sri Aurobindo 1972a, 851-2)
37 (Wilber 1995, 46)
38 (Sri Aurobindo 1972[a], 706-7)
39 (Wilber 1995, 49)
40 (Sri Aurobindo 1972a, 711)
41 (Wilber 1995, 54)
42 (Sri Aurobindo 1972a, 708-9)
43 (Wilber 2000f, 64-5)
44 (Sri Aurobindo 1972b, 253). Sri Aurobindo is very precise in his definitions. He states that independence of anything in the physical world is determined by corresponding formations on the vital and subtle physical planes. That is why things have their autonomy and do not change easily, for the change is to come from the vital, mental and supramental planes.
45 (Wilber 1995, 40-41). Wilber is just stating the phenomenon without explaining it.
46 (Sri Aurobindo 1972a, 703-5)
47 (Wilber 1995, 41)
48 (Sri Aurobindo 1972a, 706-7)
49 (Sri Aurobindo 1972a, 853)
50 (Wilber 1995, 43)
51 (Sri Aurobindo 1972b, 253-4)
52 (Wilber 1995, 63)
53 (Sri Aurobindo 1972b, 254)
54 (Wilber 1995, 66)
55 (Sri Aurobindo 1972a, 702-3)
56 (Wilber 1995, 67)

## CHAPTER 13: WILBER-IV: ALL QUADRANTS ALL LEVELS

1 (Wilber 1997b)
2 (Wilber 1997b, 71)
3 (Wilber 1997b, 72)
4 (Wilber 1997b, 72)
5 (Wilber 1997b, 72)
6 (Wilber 1997b, 73)
7 (Wilber 1997b, 73)
8 (Wilber 1997b, 75)
9 (Wilber 1997b, 75)
10 (Sri Aurobindo 1972a, 634)
11 (Sri Aurobindo 1972a, 645)
12 (Sri Aurobindo 1972a, 647-8)
13 Wilber, Ken. 16 March 2016. 'A Miracle Called "We"'. Integral Life. Accessed 31 March 2024. https://integrallife.com/miracle-called-we
14 (Wilber 1997b)
15 (Ibid)
16 (Ibid)
17 (Ibid)
18 (Ibid)
19 (Ibid)
20 (Wilber 1997b, 9)
21 (Sri Aurobindo 1997b, 179)
22 (Wilber 2006, 33)
23 (Wilber 1997b)
24 (Sri Aurobindo 2005a, 236-7)
25 (Sri Aurobindo 2005a, 92)
26 (Sri Aurobindo 2005a, 236-7)
27 (Wilber 1997a, 10)
28 Illustrating how the same entity can be interpreted in different ways under the influence of different paradigms or theories, Thomas Kuhn writes: 'An investigator who hoped to learn something about what scientists took the atomic theory to be asked a distinguished physicist and an eminent chemist whether a single atom of helium was or was not a molecule. Both answered without hesitation, but their answers were not the same. For the chemist the atom of helium was a molecule because it behaved like one with respect to the kinetic theory of gases. For the physicist, on the other hand, the helium atom was not a molecule because it displayed no molecular spectrum. Presumably both men were talking about the same particle but they were viewing it through their own research training and practice'. (Kuhn 1970, 50-1)
29 Comments Kuhn: 'Early developmental stages of most sciences have been characterized by continual competition between a number of distinct views of

nature, each partially derived from, and all roughly compatible with, the dictates of scientific observation and method. What differentiated these various schools was not one or another failure of method—they were all "scientific"—but what we shall come to call their incommensurable ways of seeing the world and of practicing science in it'. (Kuhn 1970, 4)

30 The aforementioned brief description of Kuhn's thesis should suffice to explain and contextualize the self-referential and self-refuting character of his arguments. Paradigms guide research in terms of observation and interpretation of data. By extension it can be said that he has culled out data from the body of the history of science to support his theory that paradigms guide research. In other words, the data was collected with the theory—paradigm guides research—already in his mind. As soon as we recognize this, Kuhn's arguments become circular. A paradoxical situation emerges: Kuhn's arguments are true and false at the same time. True because there is evidence to support his claim, and false because he contradicts himself by inviting his arguments on himself, thus becoming self-refuting. Secondly, Kuhn has cited evidence to show that facts and data have no meaning in themselves; they acquire meaning when interpreted against a theory or framework. There is an implicit circularity and paradox here too. By force of Kuhn's arguments, it can be argued that the evidence he has used to demonstrate the truth of his arguments is meaningful only against his contention that evidence has no meaning in the absence of a framework. Evidence lends support to his theory whereas a similar kind of contradiction as described above, and the fact of being oblivious to his own subjectivity, while attributing the crucial role of the scientist's subjectivity in guiding research, renders Kuhn's theory problematic. If the evidences of the other scientists are not sacrosanct, it can as well be said that Kuhn's are not either.

31 (Carlson 2008)

32 (Ibid 2008)

33 (Wilber 2000b, 288)

34 (Malhotra 2013a, 309).

35 (Wilber 1997a, 25)

36 (Wilber 1997a, 27-8)

37 (Sri Aurobindo 1972a, 162-3)

38 (Sri Aurobindo 1972a, 127)

39 (Sri Aurobindo 1998c, 374-5)

## CHAPTER 14:WILBER-V: INTEGRAL POST-METAPHYSICS COMPARED WITH SRI AUROBINDO'S INTEGRAL YOGA

1 (Wilber 2006, 234)

2 (Wilber 2021, 2)

3 (Ibid)

4 (Malhotra 2013a, 6). For more, see 'Embodied Knowing versus History-centrism'.

5 (Wilber 2021, 2)

6 (Sri Aurobindo 1997d, 7)

7 'Though in later times it led too much away from life, yet that was not its original character whether in its early Vedantic intuitional forms or in those later developments of it, such as the Gītā, which belong to the period of its most vigorous intellectual originality and creation. Buddhism itself, the philosophy which first really threw doubt on the value of life, did so only in its intellectual tendency; in its dynamic parts, by its ethical system and spiritual method, it gave a new set of values, a severe vigour, yet a gentler idealism to human living and was therefore powerfully creative both in the arts which interpret life and in society and politics. To realise intimately truth of spirit and to quicken and to remould life by it is the native tendency of the Indian mind, and to that it must always return in all its periods of health, greatness and vigour. All great movements of life in India have begun with a new spiritual thought and usually a new religious activity. What more striking and significant fact can there be than this that even the new European influence, which was an influence intellectual, rationalistic, so often antireligious and which drew so much of its idealism from the increasingly cosmopolitan, mundane and secularist thought of the eighteenth and nineteenth centuries, precipitated in India from the very first an attempt at religious reformation and led actually to the creation of new religions?' (Sri Aurobindo 1997d, 24)

8 'We say to humanity: "The time has come when you must take the great step and rise out of a material existence into the higher, deeper and wider life towards which humanity moves. The problems which have troubled mankind can only be solved by conquering the kingdom within, not by harnessing the forces of Nature to the service of comfort and luxury, but by mastering the forces of the intellect and the spirit, by vindicating the freedom of man within as well as without and by conquering from within external Nature. For that work the resurgence of Asia is necessary, therefore Asia rises. For that work the freedom and greatness of India are essential, therefore she claims her destined freedom and greatness, and it is to the interest of all humanity, not excluding England, that she should wholly establish her claim"'. (Sri Aurobindo 1997f, 26)

9 (Sri Aurobindo 1997c, 279); Emphasis added

10 (Sri Aurobindo 1972d, 402)

11 (Gandhi 2008, 13)

12 (Sri Aurobindo 2005a, 1087)

13 (Sri Aurobindo 1997c, 246)

14 (Sri Aurobindo 2005a, 1086-7)

15 (Sri Aurobindo 1997c, 35)

16 (Sri Aurobindo 2005a, 720)

17 (Sri Aurobindo 1997d, 398–400)

18 (Sri Aurobindo 1997c, 248)

19 (Sri Aurobindo 1997c, 47-8)

20 (Wilber 2000a, 84); Wilber explains his terms as follows: 'In my definitions, "social" refers to the Lower-Right quadrant (the inter-objective dimension, including forms

of the techno-economic base, social systems, institutions, and physical structures), and "cultural" refers to the Lower-Left quadrant (the intersubjective dimension, including collective worldviews, ethics, values, and meaning)'. (Wilber 2000a, 145)

21 Post-postmodern age is our term; Sri Aurobindo, in our opinion, calls it the 'Subjective Age'. The postmodern Western world is challenging the foundations of the modernist world view, and it is seeing the limitations of reason and analytical thought but it does not primarily have the wider vision of collectively taking a trans-rational and trans-mental leap into inquiring into the nature of Reality.

22 (Sri Aurobindo 1998d, 28-9)

23 (van Vrekhem 2000, 163)

24 He continues: 'In this place, children would be able to grow and develop integrally without losing contact with their soul. Education would be given, not with a view to passing examinations and getting certificates and posts, but for enriching the existing faculties and bringing forth new ones. In this place titles and positions would be supplanted by opportunities to serve and organise. The needs of the body will be provided for equally in the case of each and every one. In the general organisation intellectual, moral and spiritual superiority will find expression not in the enhancement of the pleasures and powers of life but in the increase of duties and responsibilities. Artistic beauty in all forms, painting, sculpture, music, literature, will be available equally to all, the opportunity to share in the joys they bring being limited solely by each one's capacities and not by social or financial position. For in this ideal place money would be no more the sovereign lord. Individual merit will have a greater importance than the value due to material wealth and social position. Work would not be there as the means of gaining one's livelihood, it would be the means whereby to express oneself, develop one's capacities and possibilities, while doing at the same time service to the whole group, which on its side would provide for each one's subsistence and for the field of his work. In brief, where the relations among human beings, usually based almost exclusively upon competition and strife, would be replaced by relations of emulation for doing better, for collaboration, relations of real brotherhood'. (The Mother 1999, 6-7)

25 (The Mother 1999)

26 (Wilber 2021, 4)

27 (Wilber 2021, 10)

28 (Sri Aurobindo 2005a, 519)

29 (Sri Aurobindo 2005a, 606)

30 (Wilber 2021, 19)

31 (Wilber 2021, 16)

32 (Wilber 2021, 24)

33 (Wilber 2021, 25)

34 (Wilber 2021, 25)

## APPENDIX: INTEGRAL YOGA AND TRANSFORMATION

1 (Sri Aurobindo 1998c, 76-8)
2 (Sri Aurobindo 1998c, 799)
3 (Sri Aurobindo 2005a, 38)
4 (Sri Aurobindo 2005a, 41)
5 (Sri Aurobindo 2005a, 41)
6 (Sri Aurobindo 1997a, 98)
7 (Sri Aurobindo 1997a, 98)
8 (Sri Aurobindo 1997a, 73)
9 (Sri Aurobindo 1997a, 73)
10 (Sri Aurobindo 2012, 84)
11 See The Incarnate Word. 'Overmind Gradation To Mind Overmind Gnosis'. Accessed 31 March 2024. https://incarnateword.in/compilations/the-hierarchy-of-minds-the-mind-levels/overmind-gradation-to-mind-overmind-gnosis
12 (Sri Aurobindo 2005a, 570)
13 (Sri Aurobindo 2005a, 763)
14 (Sri Aurobindo 2012, 226)
15 (Sri Aurobindo 2005a, 762)
16 (The Mother 2004, 140)
17 (The Mother 2004, 140)
18 (The Mother 2004, 189)
19 (Sri Aurobindo 2012, 190)
20 (Sri Aurobindo 2012, 202)
21 (Sri Aurobindo 2005a, 979)
22 (Sri Aurobindo 2005a, 981)
23 (Sri Aurobindo 2005a, 292)
24 (Sri Aurobindo 2005a, 981)
25 (Sri Aurobindo 2005a, 984)
26 (Sri Aurobindo 2005a, 985)
27 (Sri Aurobindo 2005a, 292)
28 (Sri Aurobindo 2005a, 986)
29 (Sri Aurobindo 2005a, 1002)
30 (Sri Aurobindo 1999, 5)
31 (Sri Aurobindo 1999, 5)
32 (Sri Aurobindo 1999, 6)
33 (Sri Aurobindo 1999, 19)
34 (Sri Aurobindo 1999, 19)
35 (Sri Aurobindo 1999, 20)
36 (Sri Aurobindo 1997, 231)
37 (Sri Aurobindo 1999, 674)
38 (Sri Aurobindo 2013, 399)
39 (Sri Aurobindo 2013, 413)

40 (Sri Aurobindo 1998c, 11-12)

41 Much that can now only be known, worked out or created by the use of invented tools and machinery might be achieved by the new body in its own power or by the inhabitant spirit through its own direct spiritual force. The body itself might acquire new means and ranges of communication with other bodies, new processes of acquiring knowledge, a new aesthesis, new potencies of manipulation of itself and objects. It might not be impossible for it to possess or disclose means native to its own constitution, substance or natural instrumentation for making the far near and annulling distance, cognizing what is now beyond the body's cognisance, acting where action is now out of its reach or its domain, developing subtleties and plasticities which could not be permitted under present conditions to the needed fixity of a material frame. These and other numerous potentialities might appear and the body becomes an instrument immeasurably superior to what we can now imagine as possible. There could be an evolution from a first apprehending Truth-Consciousness to the utmost heights of the ascending ranges of Supermind and it may pass the borders of the Supermind proper itself where it begins to shadow out, develop, delineate expressive forms of life touched by a supreme pure existence, consciousness and bliss which constitute the worlds of a highest truth of existence, dynamism of tapas, glory and sweetness of bliss, the absolute essence and pitch of the all-creating Ananda. The transformation of the physical being might follow this incessant line of progression and the Divine body reflects or reproduces here in a Divine life on the earth something of this highest greatness and glory of the self-manifesting Spirit. (Sri Aurobindo 1972c, 556-7)

42 (Sri Aurobindo 1998c, 18-19)

# Acknowledgments

At the outset, we extend our deepest thanks to Dr Karan Singh, statesman, philosopher, and philanthropist for blessing the book with his endorsement.

The authors wish to acknowledge and thank the following people for their incredible efforts and contributions to this book. A few established and senior Aurobindonians provided moral support and encouragement in the early years of this project, most notably Deepti in Auroville and Anand Reddy in Pondicherry, as well as Vladimir. The team at Infinity Foundation India has been an enormous source of support. Sanjana Roy Choudhury has been a fine editor and true friend, providing her expertise and insights while reviewing the book with great attention to detail. Subhodeep Mukhopadhyay led the creation of the extensive Bibliography and Notes, paying meticulous attention to detail. Rajkumar Thorat created the elegant diagrams, and we appreciate his quick and enthusiastic response to our requests. Peali Dutta Gupta captured the essence of our idea for the cover with excellent fidelity, and we are thankful for her creative involvement.

Finally, we express our heartfelt gratitude to Shri G.D. Sharma, principal secretary to Dr Karan Singh, for his help in getting the front cover endorsement.

# Acknowledgements

[illegible]

[illegible]

[illegible]

# Index